KEYS TO THE KITCHEN

AIDA MOLLENKAMP'S
KEYS
TO THE
KITCHEN

THE ESSENTIAL REFERENCE
FOR BECOMING A MORE ACCOMPLISHED, ADVENTUROUS COOK

305 RECIPES   **40** FUNDAMENTAL TECHNIQUES   **300** PHOTOGRAPHS & ILLUSTRATIONS

PHOTOGRAPHS BY ALEX FARNUM
ILLUSTRATIONS BY ALYSON THOMAS

CHRONICLE BOOKS
SAN FRANCISCO

Library of Congress Cataloging-in-Publication Data
Mollenkamp, Aida.

Aida's modern kitchen manual : a complete reference
with 130 recipes / Photography by Alex Farnum.
    pages cm
ISBN 978-1-4521-0129-3
1. Cooking. I. Title.

TX651.M575 2012
641.5--dc23

2012002642

Manufactured in China

Design by Alice Chau
Typesetting by Helen Lee

Food styling by Lillian Kang
Prop styling by Christine Wolheim

Nestlé is a registered trademark of Société des Produits Nestlé S.A.

10 9 8 7 6 5 4 3 2

Chronicle Books LLC
680 Second Street
San Francisco, California 94107
www.chroniclebooks.com

"Everything in moderation . . . including moderation."

—Julia Child

CONTENTS

PART 3: THE RECIPES

PART 4: THE RIFF

PREFACE

Too few of us were taught how to cook and, as a result, there's now a lost generation of cooks. Basic kitchen skills that were once commonplace have been replaced by frozen conveniences and take-out orders, making the act of cooking and the kitchen daunting. This book aims to change that.

Consider this a guide to conquering your kitchen written by someone whose full-time job is to answer how and why. It's filled with answers to the questions I'm most frequently asked, as well as those you may have not yet thought to ask.

When it comes to food, I've learned it tastes better when it's prepared by hand and made with whole ingredients, which is why I'm so insistent that everyone should know their way around the kitchen. The amazing thing about cooking is that while it is extremely artistic and creative, it can also be explained through science and inquiry. This mixture of art and science is what first drew me to the kitchen and I immediately felt I had met my destiny. For over a decade now I've been cooking, the last few years of which have been spent as a modern-day home economist, minus the kitschy apron and the beehive.

I work in a food laboratory. Not the kind that comes up with numbered dyes or unpronounceable ingredients, but the kind that develops reliable recipes. That began when I worked at CHOW, where I ran a test kitchen and food team. On a daily basis, we determined the proper timing, measurements, and ingredients required to produce the best possible result. In the process I've tested and tasted my way through thousands of recipes.

Since then, I've been working tirelessly online, on television, and now in book form to share my experiences and discoveries with you. All this with the aim of encouraging people to get their hands dirty in the kitchen and learn a bit about what we're eating and where it comes from.

The recipes in this book are modern and memorable yet approachable and reliable. They're based on a solid technique that, once mastered, is like a good jazz song, begging to be riffed upon. As you build your cooking confidence, I encourage you to underline, dog-ear, splatter, or otherwise use these pages, as that's what this book is intended to be: a tireless resource.

INTRODUCTION

There's a Chinese proverb that states "Give a man a fish, and you feed him for a day. Teach a man to fish, and you feed him for a lifetime." That's what this book is—a self-help resource for the kitchen. While most cookbooks are a silo of recipes, this book is a holistic resource, covering everything you need to know to conquer your kitchen. That said, before you even get to the recipes, there is a wealth of info from tips on how to shop to how to store food and what to buy.

Now that you know what to expect from this book, I'm going to tell you what I need from you: I need you to care.

First, have fun and be ready for some adventures. Allow the fundamental kitchen knowledge to stick with you, and it will, in turn, free your creativity.

Second, don't be lazy. Not to say that you are, but it's up to you to get engaged and foster curiosity about food.

Before you start cooking, do yourself a favor: read the pointers to make sure your kitchen's doing more for you than you for it. Then really get to know this book, as it will prepare you for cooking success. Once you get the basics down you can cook up a storm and, before you know it, you'll be successfully pulling off dinner parties and date nights. Whether you've never stepped foot in your kitchen or you practically sleep there, this book will become an essential reference because it's chockful of all sorts of cooking wisdom.

This isn't about becoming pretentious about food, but rather the opposite. The minute you take the time to learn these basics, you'll waste less food, you'll get more for every food dollar you spend, and you'll become a healthier, more accomplished, and more adventurous cook.

If cooking were a math formula, it would look something like this:

QUALITY INGREDIENTS
+
KITCHEN SKILLS
+
TECHNIQUE
+
COOKING METHOD
=

GOOD FOOD

Not to get too analytical, but I showed you that formula because it's the basis for this book. Specifically, this book is broken down as follows:

PART

THE SET-UP

This section is about what to do at the store, before you ever enter your kitchen; the focus is on quality ingredients. You'll learn where to shop, how to shop, and what to shop for, for both ingredients and equipment.

PART 2

THE HOW-TO

Just like it sounds, this section is all about honing your technique, but it extends beyond knife handling to cover everything from prepping through cooking. It covers the best tips and methods for storing food and equipment, the must-know cooking skills, and a review of the various cooking methods out there.

PART 3

THE RECIPES

Here they are. The recipes—118 of them to be precise—reflecting a variety of ingredients, cuisines, and techniques. They're various levels of difficulty but are all rooted in my West Coast style wherein fresh, seasonal ingredients are combined in a modern way.

PART

THE RIFF

This is where you go from following recipes to cooking from the hip. There are techniques to help you think outside the box when it comes to cooking and coming up with menus. To get your creativity cranking, there are over 100 additional cooking ideas including how to reinvent last night's leftovers.

Whether you're a curious beginner or intermediate cook, this book will help you conquer your kitchen. And then your cooking can become adventurous, creative, and fun.

PART 1
THE SET-UP

Good cooking is based on a solid foundation. That's usually in reference to technique, but it really should be broadened. You wouldn't drive a car without the keys, so you shouldn't cook without first having the keys to the kitchen. This is the vital info on how to shop, how to chop, and what to use, so you'll be all set when you finally turn on the stove.

Know What to Buy

Buy good food and it'll reward you with good flavor—even when you're still working on becoming a good cook yourself. Aside from the leisurely sunny afternoon where I get to personally choose every item, I absolutely hate shopping. But, after years of going to stores of all shapes and sizes multiple times a week, I've got tips to make shopping more efficient and less painful.

BECOMING A RESPONSIBLE COOK

The minute you buy food, you're voting with your food dollars, so, use that vote wisely and responsibly. Here are the lessons I've adopted over the past few years in an effort to become a more conscientious cook.

Know Where Your Food Comes From This may seem obvious: I mean, steak comes from cows, right? But do you know its backstory? Eating grass-fed beef isn't important just because it tastes better but also because it's better for the animal. Remember, you're eating whatever an animal ate during its lifetime, so, ask questions, because if it ate junk, then you are, too.

Eat Lower on the Food Chain The higher on the food chain you eat, the more calories required to make that food (i.e. it has a bigger carbon footprint), so by eating lower on the food chain, you're leaving less of a dent in things.

Make It a Meatless Monday It's your choice to eat meat or not, but, if you do eat it, consider eating it less often. To help get you started, I've put together a whole chapter of meatless recipes—see Meatless Mains, page 240.

Shop Responsibly You've heard the terms thrown around: local, seasonal, and sustainable. What they translate to is better-quality food for you, more support for your local economy, and less strain on the environment.

Store It Right There's no point in buying good food if you end up ruining it through poor storage habits at home. Read up on this (see Tips for Storing Leftovers, page 422) and your food will have a longer shelf life, with less waste.

Waste Not (Use It All) Most of the food we eat—especially the produce—can be used in its entirety, so there are a lot of tips in this book (see The Riff, page 380) about how to make the most of what you have.

Unplug, as Possible Energy gets used whenever unused appliances remain plugged in, so after you grind your coffee or finish mixing those cookies, unplug.

Clean with Green Not only for the environment, but also for your own health, opt for eco-friendly cleaning products. There are a lot of brands out there these days that do as good if not a better job than the traditional house cleaners. Check out ideas on all-natural cleaning solutions later in the book (see The Aftermath, page 418).

Compost and Recycle If your neighborhood doesn't have a community compost and recycling program, make yourself heard and ask for one. Or, if you have the time and space, set up your own compost; it takes getting used to, but the payoff is black gold dirt that makes the most amazing fertilizer.

Know Your Indulgences Everyone has a guilty pleasure, so acknowledge it instead of trying to repress it. Extreme locavorism is beneficial for the environment but it can make you nutty if you're hankering for foods from far away such as coffee or chocolate.

Be Grateful Not to get too spiritual, but be present when you're cooking and eating and you'll be more satisfied. Too often people are just satiating hunger instead of really eating—don't be one of those people.

WHERE TO SHOP

Where you shop is just as important as what you're shopping for. Anytime you get shoes and produce under the same roof, you're sacrificing a lot more than just quality. Compared to the rest of the world, we spend an extremely small amount on our food and the price we pay is mediocre quality. So, if you can, support shops where there's a true meat and fish (if not also, cheese) counter. In addition to the environmental advantages, it will allow you to leverage the employees' knowledge to fill your basket with the top in quality and taste.

Seek Out Specialty Stores Make a concerted effort to stop by the specialty stores in your area. Not only are you supporting a local business, but you get the chance to discover new products. In recent years, there has been a resurgence of artisan producers, including small-scale bakeries, pastry shops, cheese shops, butcher shops, and the like. Check them out, as you're likely to be rewarded with some high-quality food options and more personal service.

Explore Ethnic Options Ethnic and international markets sell specialty items from all over the world and are an ideal place to find ingredients you may not have seen before.

Frequent Your Farmers' Markets Farmers' markets have multiplied like rabbits in the past few years and almost every nook and cranny has one. Try to go often for super-fresh (just-picked!) produce and you can also pat yourself on the back for supporting your local economy.

Consider a Co-Op The focus of co-ops (a.k.a. cooperatives)—collectively owned grocery stores—is selling natural, local foods. They can be rigid about their beliefs but they have their hearts in the right place so they're worth checking out.

Show Your Community Support If you're ready for a challenge, consider joining a CSA (community supported agriculture) program. Through websites like Local Harvest (www.localharvest.org/csa) you can opt to buy a share of a farm's bounty, which is delivered to you on a regular basis, and really push yourself to go seasonal. Produce CSAs have taken off but there are also meat CSAs popping up where you can readily get locally raised meat. The boon and bane of a CSA is that you're at the will of the farm and what they've reaped that week. So, you can either look at it as a glass half empty or half full of cooking opportunity.

HOW TO SHOP

Chew on this: you're shopping in order to buy what you need to use what you have. Now, I know that's not the case every time you shop, but thinking this way will allow you to get the most out of the food you already have lying around.

Check Your Fridge Do a scan of what's in your fridge so you have a mental note of what's on hand. Tons of mustard? Maybe it's time to make a honey-mustard roast chicken. No condiments at all? Well your cooking may be missing out on a fun punch of flavor that a dash of soy or spoonful of mustard could add.

Make a Shopping List Shopping lists are the stuff of Type A shoppers—or are they? Most stores stock the perishable foods on the outer perimeter and the packaged foods in the center, so, if you organize your list by how you walk around the store, it'll go much faster.

But Be Flexible Not everything you want or need will always be available, so be flexible, think outside the box, and check out Substitutions, page 120 for ideas on how to make what you have work. Would that dish you're shopping for be tastier with tomatillos instead of tomatoes? There's only one way to find out.

And Be Adventurous Try to buy at least one new and different product or ingredient each time you shop. Sure, there's a chance you won't like it, but the majority of the time you'll discover something you wouldn't otherwise have tried or even known about.

Go for What's in Season (and, If Possible, Local) There's a litany of political, ethical, and environmental reasons why eating seasonal and local is a good choice. But there's also a big cooking advantage: in-season produce means you're buying it at its prime so it'll taste better and likely be more affordable.

PLAN OF ATTACK

Here are pointers for how to take on the store with success:

Your Fridge is an Ice Cream Cone My high school French teacher always told us we needed to build our language skills off a solid base (the cone) or it would leak and we'd end up with a mess. Shopping for your kitchen follows the same principle. By no means do you have to eat only Greek food for the rest of your life, but it makes way more sense to buy olives if you already have feta than to reach for a jar of hoisin sauce.

Don't Shop Hungry The hungrier you get, the more likely you are to grab the cheese puffs and make a run for it. Fine, if that's your thing, but it may be a bit challenging to make it the main ingredient for dinner.

Ugly Isn't Gross Rotting, moldy, mushy food is really not okay but that doesn't mean food has to be pretty either. There has been a bias toward perfect-looking food and it has made all the less-than-perfect food a little self-conscious. Food that's heirloom or organic may have a very particular look or a few odd patchy bits on its surface, but take a note from the romance ballad and love it just the way it is.

Make Friends Even if you shop at a humungous supermarket, get chatty with the produce guy. He'd much rather talk to you than that melon he just set on the shelf, and, well, that's his job. Also, if you don't see something in the market or you don't like what you see, say something.

Buy "Undone" Recently, I came across a head of garlic that had the top lopped off so the cloves were exposed, wrapped in plastic, and put on the shelf for sale. And you know what? It was over ten times more expensive than a whole head of garlic.

Anytime you see something prepped and packaged know that you're paying a premium. And often one, if not all, of the following have occurred: it's been adulterated with preservatives, you're paying for the labor that went into it when you could do it yourself, or the produce isn't as fresh because it's been pressed up against plastic wrap.

Buy Larger Cuts Continuing with the principle of "undone," meat, poultry, or fish that has been skinned, boned, or whatever is going to cost more than if you buy it whole and un-prepped. Sometimes you don't have the time or patience, so go ahead and pay the premium. But, generally, save your pennies and step up to the challenge of learning how to skin, bone, or trim the meat yourself.

Buy in Bulk You pay less when you buy from the bulk bins and they generally have a higher turnover than some dusty package of grain from the back of some random shelf. If you bring your own container to fill, give yourself a hug, as you're also being green!

LABEL LINGO

Consider this section a cipher to the grocery store that will help you make smarter, more informed purchases. As much as labels reveal, they also highlight how much is unregulated and still unclear, so also be sure to ask where your food comes from.

NATURAL The USDA allows livestock to be labeled "natural" when it has been raised without artificial colors, flavors, ingredients, or preservatives and has been minimally processed. Keep in mind this does not take into account the environment in which the animal was raised or if it was fed additives.

NATURALLY RAISED The USDA allows animals to be labeled "naturally raised" when they have been raised without hormones, antibiotics, or animal by-products.

ARTISANAL A product or service is considered artisanal when traditional techniques are used in its preparation or execution. It is also often implicit, but not mandated, that artisanal products be made by hand and in small batches.

BIODYNAMIC This holistic agricultural method advocates farming that is respectful of the environment's natural harmony via sustainable practices like crop rotation and composting. There is an independent, third-party certification required to earn a biodynamic label.

CAGE-FREE As the name implies, this indicates that poultry has been raised outside of cages. However, it doesn't specify if the animal was raised in contained quarters or with access to the outdoors. The better label to look for is "pastured" or "pasture-raised."

CONVENTIONAL The least regulated, most widespread agricultural practice in the industry, conventional farming allows the use of pesticides, GMOs (genetically modified organisms), fertilizers, antibiotics, hormones, and other unsustainable commercial farming practices.

DRY-AGED An aging process where meat is stored in a controlled cold and dry room for up to a month in order to intensify flavor and tenderness. It is an expensive process so it's usually reserved for the more prized cuts of meat.

FREE-RANGE Meat labeled "free-range" has been allowed access to the outdoors for some time every day. The USDA regulates this term only for poultry and, specifically, only birds raised for consumption and not egg-laying hens.

GMOS One of the biggest debates in the food world centers on GMOs (genetically modified organisms) as people vehemently support or oppose the practice. Food is genetically modified when the genetic makeup is somehow altered so that the inherent traits are altered. Currently, the most common GMO crops are corn, soy, and canola. GMOs are allowed in conventional farming but not in organic farming.

GRAIN-FED Most animals that are factory farmed or in CAFOs (concentrated animal feeding organizations) are grain-fed, which is very hard on the digestive system for ruminants such as cows.

GRASS-FED The USDA allows animals (cattle, bison, sheep, and goats) to be labeled "grass-fed" when they are raised on a diet of pasture and stored grasses. An animal can be grass-fed if it is pasture-raised for its whole life, or up until the last few months of its life when it is moved to a feedlot. The best choice is animals that are grass-finished or pasture-finished, as it means they spent their whole life at pasture.

HEIRLOOM These are crops that come from traditional varieties developed and preserved by farmers through the process of seed saving.

HERITAGE A term that refers to livestock and crops from historic and often endangered breeds as a means to save animals from extinction and preserve genetic diversity. There is no regulation on heritage production standards though the majority of heritage farmers engage in sustainable farming practices.

HORMONE-FREE Defined by the USDA only for meat and poultry, this designation means that the animal must not have received any growth hormones during the course of its lifetime.

HUMANELY TREATED This implies that the animals were treated with compassion and allowed to live according to their natural behavior.

IRRADIATED Irradiated food (usually meat and eggs) is treated with high levels of radiation in order to kill off bacteria. It is used to make food safer yet most irradiation does not combat agricultural diseases and is too often used as a safeguard against any unsanitary production or slaughter conditions.

LOCAL Commonly used to refer to food grown within a 100-mile radius of where it's being sold. This is beneficial to you as a consumer as the food will be fresher and better for the environment because it didn't have to travel as far to get to you.

ORGANIC The opposite of food produced by conventional farming, food labeled organic has been grown or raised without synthetic fertilizers, chemicals, pesticides, or sewage sludge and cannot be genetically modified or irradiated. Any food product (except fish) labeled organic must be certified as such by an official USDA accredited certifier.

SUSTAINABLE This implies that the manner in which produce is grown or animal reared is done in a way that can be repeated and replicated without consequences to the environment.

Mastering the Store: Section by Section

This is the lowdown on what to buy, what not to buy in each section of your typical grocery story. Read this through before your next trip to the market to increase your food knowledge and buying power.

WHAT NOT TO BUY

Jarred Minced Garlic Who knows how long ago that stuff was cut up? And, once it's chopped, it starts to lose flavor and build up off gasses, which alone should be enough to turn you off.

Pre-Grated Cheese The minute cheese is grated or shredded, it starts to lose its flavor. If you have a lot of cheese to grate or shred, the disc attachment on your food processor will make quick work of it.

Prepped Vegetables Same story as with garlic: when veggies are cut ahead of time, all that happens is they lose flavor and quality. It takes a few minutes more to prep them yourself, but it makes for better-tasting food.

Jarred Tomato Sauce This stuff tends to have a ton of sugar so is best avoided—especially seeing as you can make your own (Basic Tomato Sauce, page 116) in just a few minutes' time.

Iodized Table Salt Kosher salt is preferable as it's easier to measure and has a cleaner flavor than iodized salt. The recipes in this book call for kosher salt, but, if you can't find it, opt for sea salt instead. Here are equivalents:

1 tablespoon kosher salt = 1 teaspoon table salt

1 tablespoon kosher salt = 1½ teaspoons sea salt

Ground Black Pepper The oils in pepper (which lend the flavor) are very volatile and dissipate very quickly, which is why pre-ground pepper is pretty much flavorless. Instead, buy whole peppercorns and grind them as needed.

Dried Herbs Aside from bay leaf, which is almost impossible to find fresh, I cannot think of one place where dried herbs would be better in a dish than fresh herbs. Yes, they're dehydrated and therefore have more intense flavors, but they don't have the same purity of flavor and tend to go stale quickly, so I believe fresh is better.

Boneless, Skinless Chicken A lot of people buy this cut so I've included a few recipes in the book for it. But you'll notice that each recipe has something in it that adds a lot of flavor (prosciutto and goat cheese, for example) because this cut can dry out very quickly. Make an effort to cook with skin-on cuts and you'll have better flavor.

Fake Maple Syrup It's fake. It's not real. Don't buy it.

Or Anything Fake, for That Matter Actually, avoid anything that's a fake substitute for the real thing (like margarine, imitation vanilla, mayonnaise), as it is worse for your health than the real thing.

Things with Ingredients You Can't Pronounce How would you know what you're putting in your body if you can't even pronounce the ingredients it's made from?

WHERE EVERYBODY KNOWS YOUR NAME

The single most important tip for becoming a stellar grocery store shopper is to work the *Cheers* effect (shop so everybody knows your name). By losing your anonymity, you'll establish valuable relationships with store employees who will clue you in on what's fresh, turn you on to a new ingredient, or even get you cooking something you never thought you'd like. Armed with this info, your next meal will already be that much better because now you've got the good goods. Nice moves!

PORK, BEEF, AND LAMB

These are the qualities, listed in order of most to least important, you want to look for when buying meat.

Grades The USDA grades for beef, lamb, and pork indicate quality. Prime, Choice, and Select are the three top grades and the most available consumer grades for beef and lamb. Pork is graded by ratio of lean to fat, with one being the top quality.

Fat for Flavor Fat brings more flavor to the final dish. For steaks, you want a fine marbling throughout. For roasts and other cuts, there should be fat on the outside.

Good Color Red meat is called that for a reason so look for meat that is blood red, while pork should be light pink and consistent in color. See something gray? Walk away, that's just gross.

Buy from a Butcher Buy meat from a butcher counter, as you'll get a lot of useful information, perhaps even a few recipe ideas, along with your meat.

No Excess Liquid in Packages If you buy packaged meat, tip it to one side and make sure there isn't liquid pooling up, an indicator that the meat was previously frozen and has been sitting around a while. That is most likely not blood (which is removed during slaughter) but water resulting from the chilling process or from defrosting.

Fresh-Smelling Hopefully it's obvious that nasty smelling meat means, well, that the meat is nasty. The meat you buy should smell pleasant. Red meat should have a slight whiff of iodine while pork and chicken should smell a tad sweet.

Bone-In versus Boneless Opt for the bone-in whenever you have a choice as the meat will cook faster, the bones act as a natural roasting rack, and the end result will be more flavorful.

Where It's From and How to Cook It The least exercised parts of the animal result in the most tender meat (loin and ribs), whereas the most exercised areas make for the least tender meat (for example, chuck and round). In general, the cheaper the cut, the less tender it will be. Tender cuts can hold up to faster, dry-heat cooking (searing, roasting, grilling) while less tender cuts should be cooked in a slow, low heat, moist manner (braising or stewing).

Pork has been bred to be super lean so opt for a heritage pig if you have a choice; it'll have more of the right kind of fat and more flavor.

PORK

---

1 / BOSTON SHOULDER

Boston Butt
BRAISE, STEW

Blade Roast
BRAISE, STEW

2 / PICNIC SHOULDER

Hock
(smoked or fresh)
BRAISE, STEW

Picnic
(smoked or fresh)
BRAISE, STEW

Link Sausage
PANFRY

Ground Pork
PANFRY, STEW, BRAISE

---

3 / LOIN

   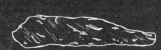

Sirloin
ROAST, BRAISE

Canadian Bacon
PANFRY

Boneless Loin Roast
ROAST, BRAISE

Bone-In Center Loin
ROAST

Pork Tenderloin
GRILL, PAN-ROAST, ROAST, PANFRY

Loin Chop
GRILL, PAN-ROAST,
ROAST, PANFRY

Rib Chop
GRILL, PAN-ROAST,
ROAST, PANFRY

Blade Chop
GRILL, BRAISE

Back Ribs
SMOKE, BARBECUE,
BRAISE

Country-Style Ribs
SMOKE, BARBECUE, BRAISE

---

4 / SIDE

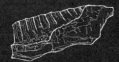

Spareribs
SMOKE, BARBECUE, BRAISE, OVEN ROAST—MOIST

Bacon
BRAISE, PANFRY

Pork Belly
BRAISE

5 / LEG

Cured Ham
BAKE

Fresh Ham
BAKE, BRAISE

BEEF

1 / SHOULDER/CHUCK

Chuck Pot Roasts
BRAISE, STEW

Blade Roast
BRAISE, STEW

Shoulder Pot Roast
BRAISE, SLOW-ROAST

Chuck Steak (Blade Steak)
BROIL, GRILL, PAN-BROIL

Stew Meat
STEW, BRAISE

Ground Meat
GRILL, PANFRY, STEW

Flat Iron Steak
BRAISE

2 / SHANK/BRISKET

Whole Brisket
BRAISE, SLOW-ROAST, STEW

Flat Brisket
BRAISE, SLOW-ROAST, STEW

Shank
BRAISE, STEW

3 / RIB

Rib Roast
ROAST

Rib Steak, bone-in
BROIL, GRILL, PAN-ROAST

Rib-Eye Steak, boneless
BROIL, GRILL, PAN-ROAST

Spareribs
BROIL, GRILL, BRAISE

4 / SHORT LOIN

 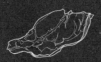   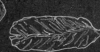

T-Bone
BROIL, GRILL

Club/ Delmonico Steak
BROIL, GRILL

Porterhouse
BROIL, GRILL

Tenderloin
BROIL, GRILL, ROAST

Shell Roast
ROAST

Strip Steak
BROIL, GRILL, PAN-ROAST

Hanger Steak
MARINATE & BROIL, GRILL

5 / SIRLOIN

Tri-Tip
GRILL, ROAST

Sirloin Steak
BROIL, GRILL,
PAN-BROIL

Ground Meat
GRILL, PANFRY, STEW

6 / PLATE

Skirt Steak
MARINATE & BROIL,
GRILL, PAN-BROIL

Short Ribs
BRAISE, STEW

Stew Meat
BRAISE, STEW

7 / FLANK

Ground Meat
GRILL, PANFRY, STEW

Flank Steak
MARINATE & BROIL,
GRILL, PAN-BROIL

8 / ROUND

Round Steak
TARTAR, ROAST

**Rump Roast/
Bottom Round**
POT ROAST

Ground Meat
GRILL, PANFRY, STEW

LAMB

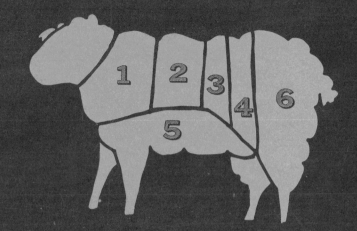

1 / SHOULDER

Blade Chop
MARINATE & BRAISE, STEW

Arm Chop
BRAISE, STEW

Shoulder Roast
ROAST

2 / RIB

Rack of Lamb
ROAST

Rib Chop
PAN-FRY, BROIL, GRILL

Rib Roast
ROAST

3 / LOIN

Loin Chop
GRILL

Loin Roast
ROAST

4 / SIRLOIN

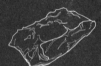

Sirloin Roast
ROAST

Sirloin Chop
ROAST

5 / BREAST

Breast
BRAISE

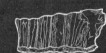

Spareribs
BRAISE

Riblets
BRAISE

6 / LEG

Whole Leg Roast
BRAISE, ROAST

Shank Roast
BRAISE

Boned Leg
BRAISE, ROAST

POULTRY

Often dismissed as boring, poultry, specifically chicken, will reward with much more flavor if you buy good-quality meat. Keep the following in mind when shopping for poultry:

No Excess Liquid in Packages If you buy packaged poultry, tip it to one side and make sure there isn't liquid pooling up, an indicator that the meat was previously frozen and has been sitting around a while. That is most likely not blood (which is removed during slaughter) but water resulting from the chilling process or from defrosting.

Fresh-Smelling Hopefully it's obvious that nasty smelling poultry means, well, the meat is nasty. The poultry you buy should smell a tad sweet.

Go for Good Looks For poultry, you can tell the bird's diet based on the color of its skin. You want to buy a chicken with yellow or cream-colored skin that is smooth and free of any bruising or damage. Don't be deterred, however, by darkening around the bones (both before and after cooking). This is common in young chickens whose bones have not completely calcified thus allowing pigment from the bone marrow to seep in.

Air-Chilled "Tastes like Chicken" If you come across a chicken labeled "air-chilled," buy it immediately. Chickens that are air-chilled after slaughter have, like dry-aged beef, much more flavor (and genuine chicken flavor) than the standard supermarket chicken.

POULTRY

THE CASE FOR THE WHOLE BIRD

Pigs get all the praise for being an animal that you can eat from nose to tail, but you can pretty much eat all the chicken too. Check this out to see what I mean:

Wings
Use for appetizers, for stews, or for flavoring stocks.

White Meat
Go for white meat that's been cooked on the bone and with skin on as it's much moister than boneless, skinless chicken.

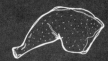

Dark Meat
Given the choice, I'll always choose dark over white meat because it has much more flavor; a difference is very apparent when the meat is roasted or braised.

Neck
Not only great for flavoring stock (along with the giblets and carcass), but a key in making gravy. Roast it alongside the bird for even deeper flavor.

Giblets
Everything but the liver can be added to stock. The liver should instead be panfried (preferably, with onions, herbs, and sweet wine).

Oysters
Along the backbone of the chicken, just behind the thigh, is an extremely tender and flavorful piece of meat known as the oyster (which it resembles in size and shape).

Carcass
Use it in a classic stock recipe (see page 180) or roast the carcass for a more flavorful, dark chicken stock.

SIZES

The age of a bird will determine its tenderness. Chicken is sold by the following age-based classifications.

Squab Chicken (Poussin) Not to be confused with the other squab out there (domesticated pigeon), squab chickens are very young (just a few weeks old), very small birds (around 1½ lb/.68 kg) that are best roasted or grilled.

Cornish Hen This is actually a hybrid of two chicken breeds (Cornish and White Rock chickens) and is a very small bird 1½ to 2 lb/.68 to .91 kg. They are best when broiled or roasted.

Broiler-Fryer Weighing 3 to 4 lb/1.4 to 1.8 kg and just a few months old, it is best broiled.

Roaster The most versatile whole bird out there, it's a few months old and weighs anywhere from 3 to 7 lb/1.4 to 3.2 kg. This is considered the most flavorful chicken because it has a higher fat content but is not tough.

Stewing Hen The oldest bird and largest bird on the market, usually 12 to 18 months old and 3 to 6 lb/1.4 to 2.7 kg. While this bird has a lot of flavor, it isn't very tender and is best suited to long-stewed recipe like coq au vin (see Coriander Chicken, Cilantro, and Chard Stew, page 270).

Capon Not a hen but a castrated rooster, this bird is usually slaughtered around 10 months old and weighs 4 to 8 lb/1.8 to 3.6 kg.

THE OTHER BIRDS

Though chicken is the most ubiquitous poultry, it's important to remember there's a whole family of birds out there. Depending on where you live, you may have access to a variety of poultry and fowl such as duck, goose, guinea fowl, pheasant, and turkey. While turkeys, ducks, and geese undergo mandatory inspection by the USDA, the quality grading is voluntary. As with chicken, no hormones are permitted for these birds.

Guinea fowl is a less common bird but is worth seeking out for its distinct gamey flavor. It has dark meat that tends to be a bit dry but works well when prepared as you would a whole chicken.

Pheasant is harder to find and usually has to be special ordered. They are leaner and drier than other birds, so they should be cooked in a moist environment or with added fat (the perfect use for a bacon wrap).

I don't cover recipes for these birds in this book but I encourage you to get to know them once you're comfortable in the kitchen.

HERITAGE BIRDS

When it comes to fowl, the label "heritage" is most frequently used in reference to turkeys. In order to be designated as such, the bird must have: the ability to reproduce naturally, the ability to live a long life span, and the ability to grow slowly and thus fully develop before being slaughtered.

Squab Chicken
1½ lb
.68 kg

Cornish Hen
1½–2 lb
.68–.91 kg

Broiler-Fryer
3–4 lb
1.4–1.8 kg

Roaster
3–7 lb
1.4–3.2 kg

Stewing Hen
3–6 lb
1.4–2.7 kg

Capon
4–8 lb
1.8–3.6 kg

FISHING OUT THE BEST SEAFOOD

It's not pleasant, but the reality is that seafood is in low supply after decades of irresponsible fishing practices. Fortunately, there are a lot of options that are both good for the environment and taste fabulous. Check out sites like Seafood Watch (see Resources, page 431) to stay current on sustainable options. For all seafood, here's what to look for at the market.

Ocean Smell Seafood should smell clean with a slightly sweet, mineral scent. If it smells like funky fish it probably is, but if it smells like the ocean, you've found a keeper.

Shiny, not Slimy Like mold, sliminess is usually a sign of deterioration, so choose fish that are vibrantly shiny and damp.

Clear Eyes, Clean Scales, and Bright Gills

For whole fish, look for eyes that are clear and not sunken, and gills that are a bright, rich, red color. Also, if scales are present, they should be clean and not falling off.

Fresh or Frozen? Unless you live close to the fishing source, the freshest fish is usually frozen because it's processed as it is caught. So, all told, buying frozen can result in fresher fish. All fish should be stored in the coldest part of the refrigerator, tightly wrapped and used within 2 days of purchase.

Closed, Responsive Shells Some shellfish need to be sold alive. To be sure they're still with us, tap on their shells—they should close up. If they don't, discard them along with any guys with chipped or cracked shells.

FISH TYPES AND HOW TO COOK THEM

When you know the flavor and texture of the fish you're cooking, you'll know how to prepare it and which fish to substitute if you're in a fix.

Lean, Flaky Texture

FISH: cod, John Dory, flounder, halibut, mullet, perch, pike, sand dabs, sole, turbot

HOW TO COOK: baked, broiled, fried, grilled, panfried, poached

Lean, Firm Texture

FISH: blue marlin, cobia, grouper, lingcod, mahi-mahi, marlin, monkfish, pompano, sea bass, shark, skate, striped bass, swordfish, tilapia, toothfish (a.k.a. Chilean sea bass)

HOW TO COOK: baked, broiled, fried, grilled (in a basket so it holds together) poached, roasted, sautéed, steamed

Fatty, Flaky Texture

FISH: barramundi, black cod, butterfish, herring, mackerel, sablefish, salmon, sardines, smelt, trout

HOW TO COOK: baked, broiled, fried, grilled, poached, smoked

Fatty, Firm Texture

FISH: anchovies, basa, catfish, skipjack, sturgeon, tuna

HOW TO COOK: baked, fried, poached, smoked

FISH

THE CASE FOR THE WHOLE FISH

Roasting a whole fish is not only impressive but also results in loads of hidden treasures. Here are a few of the ways you can use almost every bit of the fish, from head to tail.

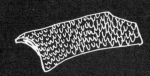

Skin

Panfry for a snack or a salmon-skin salad.

Head, Cheek, and Collar

The heads of larger fish have lots of meat that make a delectable addition to fish soup. If you deep-fry a whole fish, you can eat the whole head, except the eyeballs. Cheeks are a hidden treasure of deliciousness in the larger species of fish, so take the time to fish them out (they are just in front of the gills). The fish collar (the cut behind the head where the fin is attached) of larger fish, such as yellowtail, bass, and salmon, is tasty marinated, grilled or broiled, and served with a squeeze of lemon.

Fillets and Steaks

Serve these as the centerpiece to your meal (See Harissa-Marinated Cod with Braised Chickpeas, page 322).

Belly Meat

Bury in salt to make salted fish (like salt cod) or, for fattier fish like salmon and tuna, use to make fish jerky.

Bones

Use for fish stock although some adventurous eaters deep-fry the bones of smaller fish (such as smelt) and eat them as a snack.

UNDERSTANDING FARMED AND WILD

If you're a seafood eater, it's important to stay informed about fishing practices. With the advent of technology we've become extremely good at fishing but through unsustainable practices, it's estimated that we've decimated the ocean's supplies of fish by nearly 90 percent. It's imperative that we all understand the practices that can make wild fishing more sustainable.

Here are the pros and cons for each method. In the end, the seafood you buy will be largely a species-by-species decision, so get educated as to what's out there. Refer to Resources (page 431) for more information.

FARMED (A.K.A. AQUACULTURE)

Seafood has largely become unsustainable. Seafood farming, or aquaculture, has been explored more and more in recent years as an alternative to wild-caught seafood. However, it is a species-by-species decision.

ADVANTAGE: Raised in a sustainable manner and levels are managed without depleting the natural supplies.

DISADVANTAGES: Some farmed seafood is raised on feed that has carcinogenic ingredients. Historically, the methods for raising some farmed fish can have negative impacts on the environment, they further ruin natural habitats, and can spread disease, among other issues. While we haven't found all the solutions, there are many efforts being made to develop aquaculture that promotes sustainable practices while simultaneously resulting in delicious food.

WILD

It's easy to forget but sea creatures are wildlife—they're one of the last foods that we hunt to eat. Historically, there have been many unsustainable practices in wild fisheries such as illegal fish, overfishing, and damage to the natural habitat. Fortunately, there are more conscientious efforts being made to manage fisheries in a sustainable way.

ADVANTAGE: Fish live in their natural habitat.

DISADVANTAGES: Overfishing is a pressing issue as many fish are caught at unsustainable rates. Increased pollution levels in lakes, oceans, and rivers also negatively impact fish in the wild. Wild salmon, cod, and tuna are in devastatingly low supply.

SHELLFISH

There are two main types of shellfish: crustaceans, such as crab, crayfish, lobster, prawns, and shrimp; and mollusks, such as abalone, clams, mussels, octopus, oysters, scallops, and squid. Buying, storing, and preparing of shellfish is a bit different from other fish, so here are a few things to keep in mind.

Crustaceans

This group of shellfish are distinguished by their elongated, jointed bodies. Shrimp is the most popular of the bunch so I have included a few recipes in the book for them, including Shrimp Simmered in Garlicky Beer Sauce, page 333.

WHAT TO BUY: If buying fresh, they should have a sweet, ocean smell (no hints of ammonia, a sign they are going bad). If buying frozen, buy IQF (individually quick frozen) shrimp in the shell as they'll be better quality when defrosted.

HOW TO STORE: If frozen, keep frozen until ready to use, then thaw in a sealed bag under cold running water. Store fresh or thawed frozen shrimp in an open container covered with a paper towel, or heavy-duty plastic bag, and nest on a bed of ice in a large bowl in the refrigerator and change the ice as it melts. Use within a day of thawing, if frozen, or of purchase, if fresh.

HOW TO COOK: steam, stew, broil, grill, poach, sauté, stir-fry

Mollusks

The three most common mollusks—mussels, clams, and oysters—are sold alive so you need to take special precautions when buying, storing, and cooking them. Other mollusks, such as octopus, scallops, and squid, are usually sold prepared (and, in the case of scallops, without the shell).

WHAT TO BUY: Shells should be closed or close immediately when gently tapped. Buy more than you'll need as you'll inevitably lose a few in the process.

HOW TO STORE: Place in an open container or bag and nest on a bed of ice in a large bowl. Cover with a damp paper towel, changing the ice as it melts. Use within a day of purchase.

HOW TO COOK: broil, fry, grill, steam

DAIRY AND EGGS

When it comes to dairy, I steer clear of cooking with nonfat products—they're full of stabilizers that will negatively affect a dish's texture. It's totally understandable if you're looking to save a few calories in your breakfast cereal or morning coffee, but don't do it with baking or the results will be compromised. Use whole milk in all the baking recipes in this book that call for milk for the best texture and flavor. I use whole plain (whole or lowfat milk, unflavored) yogurt in all cooking for the same reason. Keep it on hand for a quick appetizer or recipes like Indian "Burritos" with Curried Cauliflower, page 254, or Peach Melba Cream Popsicles, page 377.

To shop the dairy section, here's what you should know.

HOW TO BUY EGGS

Buy Them Fresh Whenever possible, I buy eggs at farmers' markets because they're fresher. Try it once and the superior quality and taste should be convincing enough.

Terminology For information about egg terms, check out Label Lingo (page 21).

Color Means Nothing The color of an egg shell indicates nothing more than the breed of hen that laid the egg. So ignore any marketing about shell colors and focus instead on how the hens were treated and what they ate.

Size Matters Most baking recipes call for large eggs, so be sure you're buying (and using) the right size. If the eggs are for cooking savory food (not baking) then buy any size or variety (such as duck or goose eggs) that you want.

NO GROWTH HORMONE

Unless the milk you drink and other dairy products you consume specifically say they are rBST- or rBGH-free or organic, they could contain recombinant bovine growth hormone, a genetically engineered version of E. coli bacteria. Not only does this food additive have health consequences for you and the animal, but it may also upset your stomach, so search out products that are labelled rBGH- or rBST-free or "from cows not treated with rBST."

CHEESE

This is the chameleon of the food world, with countless versions, but it all comes down to the same basic process. So, no matter how overwhelming the cheese counter gets, remember: it's just milk thickened until it separates into the whey, the liquid that gets discarded or used in another manner, and curds, the solids that get pressed, formed, or otherwise tweaked to become cheese.

CHEESE HANDLING

Before we get into types of cheese, let's talk overall cheese handling tips. While each variety has its quirks, there are some universal truths, so keep these in mind no matter what kind of cheese you're dealing with:

- Aged cheese gets more pungent, drier, and more crumbly the older it gets, and as a result, aged cheese will last a lot longer than fresher cheese.
- Semisoft and semi-firm cheeses are the best choice for melting because other cheeses may become rubbery when cooked.
- Store cheese wrapped in its original packaging or wrapped in wax paper in the cheese drawer or a cold part of the refrigerator (usually the bottom of the back shelf). If the cheese is particularly pungent, wrap it in a resealable plastic bag or container. Never place cheese near onions or garlic, which could impart an off flavor to the cheese.
- Before serving (especially for a cheese board), let the cheese come to room temperature for at least 20 minutes.

No matter which style of cheese you buy, avoid any with dry, cracked bits, mold (unless it's a blue cheese), or hint of ammonia smell.

Shop at markets that have a high turnover and store their cheeses properly, so the cheese you buy isn't overripe from sitting in the case too long. Whenever possible, choose cheese cut to order from the wheel over one that is prepackaged.

CHEESE TYPES

There are a ton of ways you could breakdown cheese—by type of milk used, by age, by country—but I think it simplest to think of them based on their production method and their texture.

Non-Cheeses

PROCESSED (IMITATION) CHEESE

Before we discuss cheese types, I'd like to emphasize that processed/imitation cheese is not actual cheese. I'm sure that sounds serious, but keep it in mind because those products don't have the same flavor or texture as the real deal.

BY-PRODUCTS OR WHEY CHEESE

Some things we think of as traditional cheese are actually by-products of the cheese-making process. The best-known example is ricotta, which is historically made from the whey (remember earlier I told you how those get separated from the curds during the cheese-making process?). However, there are a lot of modern versions of this ricotta that are made by mixing together whey with whole milk. So, while it's one of my favorite snacks and I like to cook with it (see Roasted Squash Pasta with Sage Brown Butter, page 223), it's not technically cheese (a good factoid to keep in mind for *Trivial Pursuit* games).

FRESH

PASTA FILATA

SOFT

BLUE

SEMI-FIRM

SEMISOFT

FIRM/HARD

BY PRODUCTION METHOD

FRESH OR UNRIPENED

These fresh cheeses are made by letting milk thicken until it separates into curds and whey and then pressing the curds into the desired shape.

TYPES: CREAM CHEESE, FARMER'S CHEESE, AND COTTAGE CHEESE.

Soft-Ripened or Surface-Ripened

These cheeses are usually neither cooked nor pressed but are exposed to bacteria that helps ripen the cheese from the outside in until spreadable and creamy. The texture of a soft-ripened cheese ranges from soft to semisoft.

Ripened Cheeses

Cheeses are ripened when the curds are drained and then cured or treated in some way, such as cooking or soaking, and then aged until the desired consistency. The texture of ripened cheeses varies from semisoft to semifirm, and hard (aged).

ALL SOFT-RIPENED AND RIPENED CHEESE CAN BE FURTHER CLASSIFIED BY TEXTURE.

SOFT

These cheeses are soft enough that they can be spread on crackers and are not usually cooked. Buy cheese with a soft, creamy texture with no signs of the cheese interior (pâté) bulging out of the rind (a sign of overripe cheese).

COMMON USES: Sliced or Spread

TYPES: BRIE, CAMEMBERT, CRESCENZA, EPOISSES, PONT L'EVEQUE, REBLOCHON

SEMISOFT

These cheeses may or may not be cooked but they will be pressed only until they are sliceable yet still soft.

COMMON USES: Melted, Shredded, or Sliced

TYPES: GOUDA, HALOUMI, HAVARTI, JACK, PORT SALUT, TALLEGIO

SEMI-FIRM

These ripened cheeses are shaped and pressed then aged until firm but not enough to be crumbly. Buy cheese that is an even color and has a consistent texture with no signs of drying out.

COMMON USES: Shredded, Sliced, or Melted

TYPES: ASIAGO, CHEDDAR, COMTÉ, EDAM, FONTINA, GRUYÈRE, JARLSBERG, MANCHEGO, RACLETTE

FIRM/HARD

These are cheeses that have been shaped, pressed, and aged for a long period of time (usually at least 18 months). The cheese should be even color throughout without any cracking (a sign it's drying out).

COMMON USES: Grated, Shaved, Sliced, or Shredded

TYPES: DRY JACK, GRANA PADANO, MIMOLETTE, PARMIGIANO-REGGIANO, PECORINO

SPECIALTY CHEESES

These cheeses are made by a different production method and can be a semisoft or semi-firm texture.

PASTA FILATA

These are cheeses where the curds are worked through kneading until they reach the desired texture.

COMMON USES: Melted, Shredded, or Sliced

TYPES: MOZZARELLA, PROVOLONE

BLUE

These are semisoft to semi-firm cheeses that are treated (via inoculation or spray) with penicillin mold, resulting in veins of blue-gray mold. Some cheeses have mold spores injected before aging whereas others have spores mixed into the curds. The cheese should be distinct in flavor but never salty, bitter, or strong.

COMMON USES: Crumbled, Sliced, or Melted

TYPES: CAMBOZOLA, GORGONZOLA, MAYTAG, ROQUEFORT, STILTON

PICKING PRIME PRODUCE

Of all the sections of the store, the produce department tends to have the most pitfalls. That's probably because of all the food a store carries, produce tends to be the most delicate, and also because our produce travels far (often out of season) in order to get to us so it's no longer at its best. Here are pointers to look for in order to pick the best produce.

Weight Matters As a general rule, look for fruit and produce that is relatively heavy for its size—an indicator that it is ripe.

Free from Bruising Bruised, overly soft food is one step closer to rotting, so check what you pick up carefully before putting it in your bag or cart. Also, avoid any produce with cracked skin, as it will introduce bacteria into the produce.

Not Necessarily Picture-Perfect This is especially important when buying organic produce. The rind of a fruit may have grown with a bumpy patch on it, but so long as it's not soft or bruised, it will still be good.

Local and Seasonal Buying local and seasonal is especially important for produce because the flavor quickly deteriorates when it travels.

Know the Clean Ones If you don't want to buy organic, then know which produce has the least and most amounts of pesticide residue.

LEAST PESTICIDES
BUY THESE

ASPARAGUS	MANGO
AVOCADOS	ONION
BROCCOLI	PAPAYA
CABBAGE	PEAS
CANTALOUPE	PINEAPPLE
CORN	SWEET POTATOES
EGGPLANT	TOMATOES
GRAPEFRUIT	WATERMELONS
KIWI	

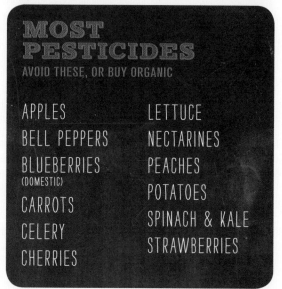

MOST PESTICIDES
AVOID THESE, OR BUY ORGANIC

APPLES	LETTUCE
BELL PEPPERS	NECTARINES
BLUEBERRIES (DOMESTIC)	PEACHES
CARROTS	POTATOES
CELERY	SPINACH & KALE
CHERRIES	STRAWBERRIES

SEASONALITY CHART

Exact seasonality varies slightly depending on where you live, but generally, these are the ingredients in season during different parts of the year.

WINTER

CABBAGE

CHICORIES

CITRUS

HARD-SKINNED WINTER SQUASH (SUCH AS ACORN, BUTTERNUT, DELICATA, AND SPAGHETTI)

MUSHROOMS

ONIONS

TROPICAL FRUIT

WINTER MELONS

SPRING

ARTICHOKES

ASPARAGUS

CARROTS

FENNEL

FIDDLEHEAD FERNS

GREEN GARLIC

HERBS

KOHLRABI

NETTLES

NEW POTATOES

PEAS

PEA SPROUTS

RAMPS

RHUBARB

STRAWBERRIES

SUMMER

BERRIES

CHERRIES

CORN

CUCUMBER

EGGPLANT

PEPPERS

STONE FRUIT (FRUIT WITH A PIT)

SUMMER MELONS

SUMMER SQUASH (SQUASH WITH SOFT SKIN)

TOMATOES

FALL

APPLES

CARDOONS

FIGS

GRAPES

MUSHROOMS

PEARS

PERSIMMONS

POMEGRANATES

QUINCE

WINTER SQUASH

HERBS TO EXPLORE

A dish can be taken to new heights by adding herbs, and the flavor of a recipe can be altered depending on which herbs you add, so be sure to play with herbs in your cooking. Herbs are broken into two categories based on type of stem: those with a tender stem that are grass-like and those that have rough leaves and a woody stem.

WOODY HERBS

These herbs have hardy leaves, wood-like stems, and a more robust flavor. Because they're hardier than the tender herbs, they can be added at either the start or the end of cooking, however you generally shouldn't eat them raw.

ROSEMARY

WHAT: Resin- and menthol-flavored herb with leaves like pine needles.

USE: With garlic, olives, Italian food, roasts, breads, potatoes.

BAY

WHAT: Leaves from a tree usually from California or Turkey, bay leaves are commonly found dry.

USE: Flavor for stocks, stews, soups, braises, stuffing, and other slow-cooked meals.

THYME

WHAT: Key to French cuisine, thyme has a very perfumed scent.

USE: In many cuisines from Caribbean to French for pasta, soups, stews, and roasts, with carrots and leeks.

OREGANO

WHAT: Cornerstone of Greek cuisine, it has a very pungent aroma.

USE: In Greek, Italian, as well as pan-Mediterranean cooking for sauces or with meats.

SAGE

WHAT: Somewhat bitter and musty with a slight mint flavor.

USE: With poultry, pork, stuffing, in breads, and in pastas.

MARJORAM

WHAT: Can be eaten raw—think of it as oregano light.

USE: Carrots, pork, fish, pasta dishes, stews, southern French cuisine.

ROSEMARY

BAY

THYME

OREGANO

SAGE

MARJORAM

With delicate leaves and stems, these herbs can be used in their entirety and eaten raw. Always add them at the end of cooking unless specified in the recipe because they'll lose their flavor if cooked too long. Use the stems for flavoring broths or to add extra flavor to sauces.

MINT

WHAT: An aromatic herb with grassy, menthol notes, it is used in both savory and sweet dishes.

USE: With fruit, cocktails, as garnish, pesto, in salads.

BASIL

WHAT: An aromatic herb with notes of anise, cinnamon, lemon, and pepper that is related to mint.

USE: A favorite in many cuisines especially European and Asian. Try torn in salads or pesto (page 218).

CILANTRO

WHAT: Known as coriander in many countries (and grown from coriander seeds), cilantro has a distinct grassy flavor that turns some people off. It's common to confuse parsley with cilantro so be sure to double check when you're at the store. Parsley leaves are drier with a jagged edge, while cilantro's are more delicate and rounded.

USE: In Asian, Caribbean, and Latin cuisines for salsas, pestos, and marinades.

PARSLEY

WHAT: Possibly the most ubiquitous herb ever in a pantry, it has a very bright, grassy flavor. The two most common forms are the curly-leaf and the flat leaf (a.k.a. Italian) parsley. I use the flat-leaf variety exclusively because it is easier to cut and has a cleaner flavor. It's common to confuse parsley with cilantro so be sure to double check when you're at the store. Parsley leaves are drier with a jagged edge, while cilantro's are more delicate and rounded.

USE: In pasta, soup, vegetables, salads, mushrooms.

CHERVIL

WHAT: Hard to find but one to look for, chervil has a flavor that's a cross between parsley and tarragon.

USE: Amazing with potatoes and also in cream-based dishes such as pastas, or in sauces (for example, replacing the tarragon in Tarragon-Cream Chicken, page 288.

DILL

WHAT: A distinctly flavored herb that's reminiscent of fennel.

USE: Popular in American and Scandinavian cuisines and is often used with salmon, in soups, in salads, and with mustard.

TARRAGON

WHAT: An herb with an anise flavor.

USE: With fish, chicken, or cream, on potatoes and tomatoes.

CHIVES

WHAT: Related to onions and leeks, chives have a sharp note.

USE: Garnish for eggs, soups, salads, and potatoes.

MINT

BASIL

THAI BASIL

CILANTRO

PARSLEY

CHERVIL

DILL

TARRAGON

CHIVES

PANTRY POINTERS

The aisles and aisles of pantry goods are easily the most boring section of the whole store. But those aisles are stocked with all the elements that play supporting roles in cooking such as condiments that boost flavor, staples that add heft, and spices that add, well, a hint of spice.

Get to Know the Bulk Bins As long as you shop somewhere with high turnover, bulk bins are a gold mine. They're usually filled with nutritionally dense foods like legumes and whole grains. They are cheaper, and, without packaging, you don't have as much waste. I like them because you can experiment with new foods with less risk.

Transfer to Airtight Containers Don't store bulk items in the plastic bags provided by the market as they'll deteriorate faster and clutter your pantry. If your store will permit it, you might want to shop with your own containers (such as glass jars, mesh bags, or resealable plastic bags) for bulk purchases to further reduce waste.

Store in Freezer If Used Infrequently

If you don't use your grains or flours that often, store them in an airtight container in the refrigerator or freezer. Doing so will extend their shelf life significantly, to about 6 months total.

Canned and Bottled When buying canned and bottled foods, check their expiration dates. Just because they can last up to 2 years doesn't mean that you should buy them at the end of their life span. Be wary of goods with high amounts of sodium and other preservatives. Aside from canned tuna, tomatoes, tomato paste, coconut milk, and the occasional can of beans, limit canned goods for bare pantry moments.

When it comes to bottled goods, the main thing to consider is the age and storage conditions. Avoid any bottled ingredients whose top is in any way bulging, is dusty, or that has been stored in bright light (a faded label is a clue). All bad, people, all bad.

SPICES TO KNOW

Whole spices keep better than ground and have a much stronger flavor. No matter which you buy, do so from a place with a good amount of turnover so that the spices are as fresh as possible.

ALLSPICE

WHAT: Called allspice because its scent is reminiscent of clove, cinnamon, and nutmeg, it's commonly used in Caribbean and South American cooking.

COMMON FORM: whole berries and ground

USE: In baking and marinades.

ANISE SEED

WHAT: A small seed with a tail, this green-brown seed has a distinct licorice flavor. The flavor is more assertive and savory than fennel seed and it is largely used in Southeast Asian cuisines. It's best known as the main flavoring for anise-based liqueurs.

COMMON FORM: whole seeds

USE: In alcohol, pastries, or savory dishes.

CARAWAY SEED

WHAT: This aromatic seed is related to parsley but with a nutty, anise flavor. It tastes more like fennel than anything else.

COMMON FORM: whole seeds

USE: Widely used in Eastern European cooking, use it in dressings, soups, stews, or with breads and cheese.

CARDAMOM

WHAT: Both pods and black seeds have a strong perfume of citrus and a eucalyptus flavor. The pods should be removed after cooking, although the seeds are edible if ground and mixed into a dish.

COMMON FORM: whole pods or ground

USE: In Middle Eastern and Indian food for stews, pilafs, desserts, and other sweets.

CAYENNE

WHAT: This is made by grinding dried chiles from South America.

COMMON FORM: ground

USE: In Creole cuisine, gumbos, stews, and chilis.

CINNAMON

WHAT: The bark of a tropical tree, it has a distinct musky flavor.

COMMON FORM: whole sticks and ground

USE: In sweet or savory dishes from tomato sauces and braises to pies.

CLOVES

WHAT: A very strong, pungent spice, cloves are the dried unopened buds of the myrtle flower.

COMMON FORM: whole and ground

USE: In African, Middle Eastern, and Caribbean foods, in sweets, and hams.

CORIANDER

WHAT: A citrusy, orange, nutty spice that's sweeter than cilantro leaves.

COMMON FORM: whole seeds and ground

USE: In soups, stews, or sautés.

CUMIN

WHAT: Small brown highly aromatic seeds whose taste you either love or hate.

COMMON FORM: whole seeds and ground

USE: A signature spice in Latin American, Indian, and Middle Eastern cuisines in breads, stews, and chili.

FENNEL SEED

WHAT: Small and green with an anise flavor.

COMMON FORM: whole seeds

USE: With pork, poultry, or in cookies.

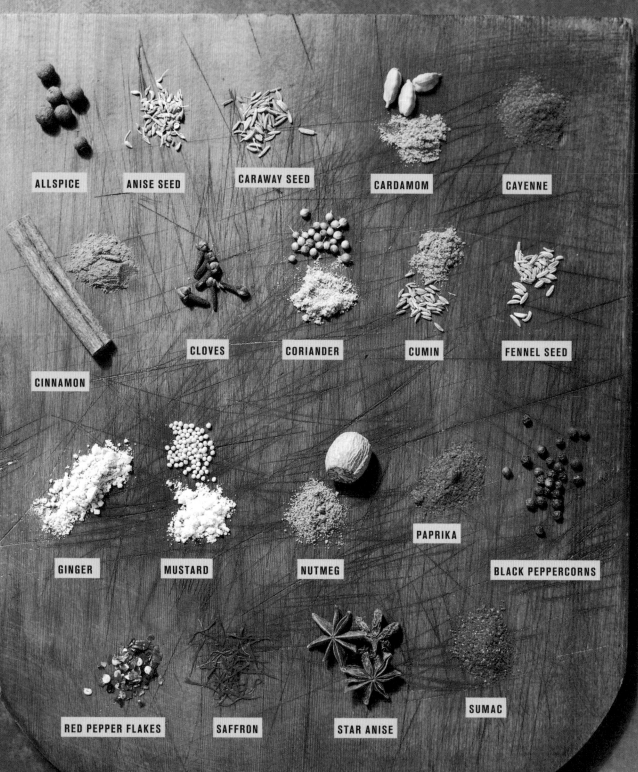

ALLSPICE

ANISE SEED

CARAWAY SEED

CARDAMOM

CAYENNE

CINNAMON

CLOVES

CORIANDER

CUMIN

FENNEL SEED

GINGER

MUSTARD

NUTMEG

PAPRIKA

BLACK PEPPERCORNS

RED PEPPER FLAKES

SAFFRON

STAR ANISE

SUMAC

CHILE POWDER

WHAT: Not to be confused with a ground chili blend, a pure chile powder is ground from one type of chile, such as ancho or chipotle, with no other seasonings added. Chile powder's flavor and heat vary according to the chile used to make it.

COMMON FORM: ground

USE: In chilis, sauces, and Latin American foods.

GROUND GINGER

WHAT: Made from dried ginger with a sweet, spicy taste, this is common to Indian, North African, and Carribean food.

COMMON FORM: ground

USE: In baked goods, spice blends, and curries.

MUSTARD

WHAT: Small round seeds that are yellow, brown, or black.

COMMON FORM: whole and ground

USE: In pickles, chutneys, or sautéed foods.

NUTMEG

WHAT: Warm, sweet spice flavor.

COMMON FORM: whole and ground

USE: Very versatile with everything from French to Caribbean food and from cream to potatoes.

PAPRIKA

WHAT: Dried sweet peppers are ground to a red powder; available as mild, bittersweet, or smoked.

COMMON FORM: ground

USE: In Spanish food, it's key. Try in red pepper sauce, with roasted potatoes, or on grilled meats.

BLACK PEPPERCORNS

WHAT: The counterpart to salt in most recipes, black pepper adds a pungent spiciness to dishes. It is essential that you buy whole peppercorns and use a grinder as they have volatile oils that dissipate quickly if pepper is stored in ground form.

COMMON FORM: whole seeds

USE: As an all-purpose seasoning.

RED PEPPER FLAKES

WHAT: Also called crushed red pepper, this is the crushed seeds and flesh of dried chiles.

COMMON FORM: crushed flakes

USE: Add to sauces, stews, and sautés.

SAFFRON

WHAT: A dried stamen of a flower, it's the most expensive spice in the world. Always buy in whole threads as it stays fresher longer. Beware—there are many imposters out there.

COMMON FORM: whole and ground

USE: In Middle Eastern foods, paella, risottos, marinades, ice cream, and custards.

STAR ANISE

WHAT: A large star-shaped seed pod with a very sweet, aromatic anise flavor.

COMMON FORM: whole pods

USE: In stocks, stews, and braises for a musky, anise note.

SUMAC

WHAT: From the berry of a bush, it has a fruity and tart flavor slightly reminiscent of raspberries.

COMMON FORM: ground (often preseasoned so go easy on the salt until you've added the sumac)

USE: Mostly used in Middle Eastern cuisines, its distinct berry flavor is beautiful with roast chicken and fish, or as a dip with olive oil.

Store It Right

Buying good-quality food is key but all that effort is for naught if you don't store it properly. An embarrassingly huge amount of the food we buy ends up unused and in the trash, so being more diligent about how we store food can go a long way.

GENERAL KNOWLEDGE

There are some overarching themes when it comes to food storage, so be sure to keep these things in mind.

Store Food How You Bought It Notice how the food you're buying is kept at the market and store it the same way at home. Most everyone I know wants to store tomatoes in the fridge, and that kills their texture.

First in, First Out Keep in mind what's been in the fridge the longest and be sure to use that first. You don't need to be militant about it if you want to use the spinach you just bought with the pears from last week, but just paying attention to the age of things will help you reduce waste—a lot.

Label It A simple way to keep track of what went in when is to label everything. These days there's freezer tape and waterproof markers that will keep labels on and legible even in the cold and moist environment of the fridge.

KITCHEN LAYOUT

Organize your kitchen for maximum efficiency.

Unless you're one of the lucky few that gets to design a kitchen from scratch, you're inevitably going to have a kitchen that has a few layout hiccups.

As for deciding where to store what, start with the stove and move away from it. You want knives, pots, pans, cooking utensils, salt, pepper, and towels within reach of the stove. Everything else goes farther away in decreasing order of use and need. So you can imagine that my crystallized ginger is nowhere near my stove while my sharpening steel is right next to it.

Create a triangle by positioning a cutting board between your sink and your stove so you can easily maneuver around. Also, create

stations—dedicated work areas—around the kitchen appliances so that things are close by when you need them. For example, I have a coffee station surrounding my grinder. I keep all my beans, filters, and teakettle nearby, and I have a baking area for leaveners, baking spices, and sweeteners in the cabinet above my stand mixer.

From there, do what works for you. If you have the ceiling and wall space, consider pot racks and magnetic knife strips, otherwise you may need an in-drawer knife block or space in lower cabinets to stack heavy pots.

Take care of yourself if you're going to be in the kitchen a long time. I wear kitchen clogs and have fatigue mats on the floor and they both make a world of difference when I log long kitchen hours. You can find both online (see Resources, page 431) or at your local restaurant supply store.

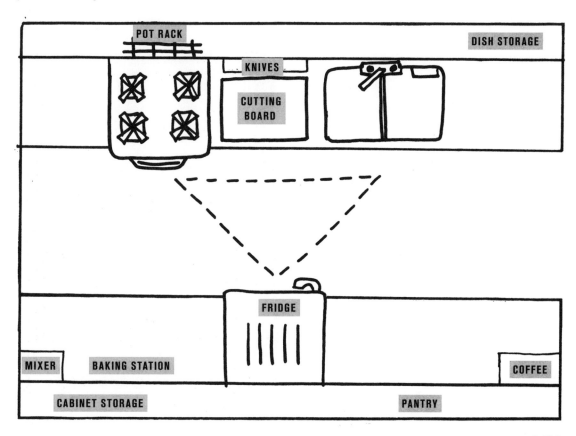

REFRIGERATOR

You know what it's for, but do you know how best to stock it?

Get a refrigerator thermometer to make sure it stays properly cold (35°F to 41°F/2°C to 5°C). They're cheap and pay for themselves by ensuring your food is kept at safe temperatures.

WHAT'S IN THE REFRIGERATOR

Butter Keep butter wrapped airtight in the butter drawer and use within 1 month (or store in the freezer if you don't use it that often or to always be ready to make biscuits, page 170).

Cheese Wrap in cheese paper, doubled-up parchment paper, or even cheesecloth, and store in its own drawer.

Eggs Store in the carton on the back of the bottom shelf of the fridge, where it's coldest.

Herbs Store fresh herbs wrapped in damp paper towels in the vegetable drawer so they stay fresh. Alternatively, store them as you would flowers, with their stems in containers filled with water, but place a plastic bag over the leaves to keep them humidified.

Meat and Poultry Wrap in butcher paper (ask the butcher to do so) or waxed or parchment paper placed in a plastic bag or nested in a container. Store in the coldest part of the fridge—the back of the bottom shelf—to keep from contaminating other food.

Shellfish and Fish Store on a bed of ice in a perforated tray or container nested in another container to catch any melting ice. Cover the whole tray with a damp paper towel or wet kitchen towel.

Fruit and Produce Remove produce from any plastic bags and wrap in damp paper towels or reusable mesh bags and store in the humidified drawers.

Mushrooms Store in paper bags on a refrigerator shelf until ready to use.

WHAT'S NOT IN THE REFRIGERATOR

Garlic, Tomatoes, Onions, and Potatoes

Their texture and taste is completely compromised by fridge storage. Store them at cool room temperature.

FREEZER

Too often, the freezer is where good food goes bad. Here are ways to maintain the quality of your frozen food.

Use a freezer thermometer to check that the freezer compartment is at proper temperature (0°F/-18°C)

FREEZER ETIQUETTE

Label Well To help jog your memory down the road, label the food with the date, name, and the weight or quantity (especially helpful for meats and seafood).

Freeze Flat Try to freeze things flat so that they're stackable. For example, I put homemade stock in freezer bags and store them stacked.

Use Stackable Containers Keep smaller frozen items in stackable containers for easy retrieval.

Keep It Pretty Full It may seem counterintuitive but a full (not packed) freezer runs more efficiently and keeps things colder.

Save Space Leave space for a tray or rimmed baking sheet. That way if you need to quickly cool something (like a piecrust on a particularly hot day) or freeze something before storing it (like berries), well, you can.

WHAT'S IN THE FREEZER

The freezer rarely gets used to its full potential. Look at it not only as a place to store leftovers but also as a place to extend the shelf life of pantry items (like butter and flour and grains), a place to store last season's produce (like frozen berries and peas), and as a storage place for cooking ingredients (such as homemade stock or piecrust).

HOW TO FREEZE

Knowing how best to freeze your food will allow it to stay in top shape once it's frozen.

Put cooled (never hot) food in the freezer.

For most ingredients and foods, squeeze out air in the containers to avoid freezer burn.

With watery ingredients, place in a container that leaves room for expansion (about 2 in/5 cm of space between the food and the lid).

For items that you want individually frozen (berries, etc.), first place on a rimmed baking sheet and freeze until frozen solid. Then place in a resealable plastic bag or an airtight container and freeze.

Bacon and Other Cured Pork Store wrapped tightly in plastic.

Bones Freeze bones to use for stock later on.

Butter Freeze butter to use in pastries such as shortcakes and biscuits.

Cooked Beans Cover with water or cooking liquid and freeze.

Dough Get in the habit of keeping pie, pizza, and cookie dough in the freezer. To use it, just defrost and proceed with the recipe.

Fresh Ginger Peel, cut into gratable chunks, and freeze to use whenever you need grated ginger.

Frozen Fruits and Vegetables See How to Freeze Vegetables and Fruits, page 55, for DIY.

Herbs Store as compound butters, pesto, or in ice trays covered with water.

Homemade Stocks Store homemade stock in the freezer in usable portions (such as pint or half-pint portions since most recipes call for a few cups at a time).

Leftovers Divide food, such as lasagna, individual pieces of meat, or soup into portion sizes and freeze in a freezer- and ovensafe container so you can pull it out and quickly warm it up when you're in need of a quick meal. Braises, soups, and stews are great contenders for freezing.

Nuts If you don't use nuts often, you can freeze them for up to 6 months.

Perishable Oils All oils are pretty perishable but nuts and squash oils are particularly so.

Puff Pastry Keep some high-quality, all-butter puff pastry on hand for crusts and recipes such as the Caramelized Fennel Tarte Tatin (page 54).

Tomato Paste So often you buy a can of tomato paste and only use part of it. When this happens, portion out the remainder in tablespoon-size portions and store it in the freezer so that it is easier to use in the future.

Tomato Sauce Place this in a resealable plastic container leaving room for expansion, and freeze.

Vegetable Scraps Store vegetable peels and scraps, such as onions, leeks, carrots, celery, garlic, and herbs to flavor a broth or stock.

WHAT'S NOT IN THE FREEZER

There's something about the freezer that makes people tend to throw almost everything into it. Unfortunately, not everything freezes well, so here are some of the main things I'd suggest keeping far away from your freezer.

Dairy Products Milk, cream, cheese, and yogurt can be frozen but they separate when defrosted, so freeze only as a last resort.

Coffee It loses all its character in the freezer and takes on some off flavors as well, so don't do it.

Stuff with Freezer Burn Ditch it.

Unidentified Frozen Objects Don't know what it is? Ditch it and label better next time.

HOW TO FREEZE VEGETABLES AND FRUITS

If you find yourself with an excess of raw produce, and have cooked up your fill, go ahead and freeze the extra amounts. It should be said that freezing produce is not a way to get rid of past-its-prime produce. If they're on the verge, freeze them. But if they're slimy, mushy, or otherwise compromised, compost it.

Once you've prepped the produce, spread it out on a rimmed baking sheet and freeze until solidly frozen. Once frozen, transfer to an airtight container labeled as to the contents and date it went into the freezer.

VEGETABLE/FRUIT	PREP	USE
BANANAS (RIPE)	Peel, cut or chop if desired, and freeze.	Banana bread, muffins, smoothies, ice cream
BERRIES	Hull (strawberries), clean, and dry well.	For baking, smoothies, ice cream, parfaits
BROCCOLI/CAULIFLOWER	Cut into small florets and blanch (see page 83) briefly (2 minutes).	Pastas, quiches, soups, stir-fries
CHERRIES	Wash and dry (pit if desired).	For baking, sauces, smoothies, ice cream
CORN	Husk and blanch whole (about 3 minutes), then cut off kernels.	Substitute for fresh corn except in no-cook preparations
GREEN BEANS, SNAP, AND SNOW PEAS	Trim ends, string, and blanch (see page 83) just until bright (about 1 minute).	Substitute for fresh beans and peas except in no-cook preparations
TENDER HERBS (BASIL, CHIVES, CILANTRO, MINT, AND PARSLEY)	Clean and dry well. Place whole sprigs or whole leaves in an airtight container. Alternatively, puree herbs and freeze in ice cube trays.	Any cooked recipe where you'd normally use fresh herbs
SHELLING PEAS (ENGLISH PEAS)	Shell and blanch (see page 83) until bright green (about 1 minute).	Substitute for fresh peas except in no-cook preparations
SPINACH AND OTHER COOKING GREENS	Wash, trim, and blanch (see page 83) 1 minute.	Lasagna, soups, and recipes calling for wilted greens
TOMATOES	Peel by blanching (see page 83) then cut into quarters and seed.	Sauces, soups, and casseroles
STONE FRUIT	Peel (not necessary for apricots), halve, and pit.	For baking, smoothies, ice cream, parfaits

PANTRY ORGANIZATION

Like the freezer, the pantry can quickly get out of control with bags of this stacked on bottles of that. Here are a few tips for keeping it under control.

Perfect Conditions Keep your dry storage items in a cool, dark area (like a pantry or dark shelf) so that they stay fresher longer.

Date It to Remember For things you don't use often, put the purchase date on the outside of the can so you know how long it's been hanging around.

Maximize Your Space If, like me, you don't have nearly enough space in your kitchen, remove things from their original packaging and put them into stackable, airtight containers to maximize the space you have.

Container Cooking If you're someone who is a cooking purist and makes something Thai one night and Italian the next, consider storing all ingredients of a similar ethnicity in a tray or basket so they're easy to access.

Or Cook Creatively But if you're trying to get out of your cooking comfort zone, consider organizing everything by type of dry good (like legumes, spices, canned goods). That way if you're out of sticky rice, you might be inspired to try the dish with the couscous that you do have.

OILS

A few key pointers will significantly extend the life of your cooking oils; here are the most important ones.

Keep It Dark and Cool Fats will go rancid if exposed to light and heat.

WHICH OIL TO USE WHEN

There's nearly an aisle's worth of oil at most grocery stores so it helps to know what to use when so that you can navigate all the options.

OLIVE OIL This is one of the healthiest and most diverse oils available. You could prepare 99 percent of your food with just this oil, as it's used for everything from cooking to dressing. Turn to pure olive oil for times when you want the health of olive oil but don't want the flavor; it is a lower grade than extra-virgin so make sure you get the best in its class. Use extra-virgin olive oil when you want a distinct olive oil flavor to shine through, and reserve the most expensive ones for finishing a dish.

Note: Don't use olive oil for frying and searing as it has a low smoke point and will break down.

NEUTRAL OIL This family of oils are all-purpose because of their neutral flavor and high smoke-points. The most common neutral oils are canola, peanut, and grapeseed oils, all of which can be used interchangeably in recipes.

NUT AND SQUASH OILS The most common of these types of oils are walnut, hazelnut, and pumpkin seed oil. Use these as finishing oils but know they tend to go rancid very quickly. Buy roasted nut and squash oils when available as they'll last longer. Also, store them in the freezer as you most likely won't use them as often as other oils.

ALTERNATIVE OILS Coconut oil got a bad rap back in the day because it is one of the only non-animal fats that is saturated fat. As of late, many have become fans of virgin coconut oil because it is considered to have a vanilla-like flavor, it works as a good butter substitute for vegan recipes, and is claimed by some to be a *good* fat when consumed in moderation. Use it as you would butter. Also gaining in popularity is argan oil from North Africa. It has a distinct nutty flavor and works anywhere you'd use olive oil.

Be Anti–Clear Glass If you buy oils in clear glass jars, either be sure to store them in a dark corner of the kitchen or transfer them to dark glass jars so they aren't overexposed to light, which would cause them to go rancid quickly.

Small Jars for Finishing Oils I keep oils I use to finish dishes (top-quality olive and nut oils) near the stove in smaller, dark glass jars. Be sure they're far enough from the heat that they don't degrade over time from proximity to high temperatures.

VINEGAR

When a dish needs some help, a hit of vinegar is the answer as it heightens flavors and adds brightness. You can substitute citrus—lemon and lime—for vinegar; you can also use orange for a delicate sweetness.

HIGHEST TO LOWEST ACIDITY

Vinegars vary in acidity levels so it's helpful to know how the different types compare. Pretty much all wine vinegars are interchangeable, but let your taste buds guide with the other vinegars. Here they are listed in order of strongest to mildest:

Distilled White Vinegar Very pungent, this is best used for cleaning (see page 419).

Balsamic Vinegar Caramelly and dark, a mid-grade balsamic is great to have on hand for cooking. I reserve a more expensive, aged one for finishing dishes.

Sherry Vinegar A staple in Spanish cooking, this potent wine vinegar can be used as a more assertive twist on red wine vinegar.

Wine Vinegar Available white or red, these are mostly used in European cuisines.

Cider Vinegar A mild, fruity apple-based vinegar commonly used in barbecue—from marinades to mops to sauces to slaws.

Rice Vinegar Very mild and common in Asian cuisine.

SPICES AND DRIED HERBS

Proper storage of your spices and dried herbs will significantly increase their shelf life and their quality of flavor. Here are a few things to keep in mind.

Keep Them in a Dry, Dark Place Whether you store spices and dried herbs in a drawer, on a shelf, or on a rack, label and date them so it's easy to tell what is what.

Clean out your seasonings periodically as most spices go bad after 6 months.

SALT SELECTION

There are a lot of salts out there so it's important to know how they differ. The main thing to keep in mind is that a salt is more or less salty depending on the size of its crystals. So a teaspoon of one type of salt may be more salty than an equal amount of a different type of salt. For example, you cannot equally substitute table or sea salt (more salty) for kosher salt (less salty) in a recipe. Generally, the substitution is 1 teaspoon table salt equals 1 tablespoon kosher salt, so if some of my recipes seem salty to you, it may be because you're using the wrong salt.

Kosher Salt There are two types of kosher salt on the market: coarse and regular. The coarse type is great for using in salt crusts but is too coarse for seasoning. The regular kosher salt is my go-to salt when I cook beause the large flakes are easier to see and it has a clean, consistent taste. I use Diamond Crystal kosher salt in almost all of my cooking.

Sea Salt Pricier than kosher salt, with a smaller grain, sea salt varies in flavor depending on where it was harvested. If you can't find kosher salt, use sea salt, but keep in mind it is saltier, so use this equivalent: 1 tablespoon kosher salt = 1½ teaspoon sea salt.

Table Salt The most widely available type of salt, I steer away from it because it usually has additives and is iodized, which gives it a slightly bitter flavor.

Specialty Salts There are many kinds of specialty salts out there now, so be adventurous and try them out. Keep in mind that these salts are largely finishing salts and are to be used for garnishing.

SHELF LIFE

BUTTER	2 WEEKS IN FRIDGE
	1 MONTH IN FREEZER
CANNED ITEMS	2 YEARS
CEREALS, GRAINS, AND PASTA	6 MONTHS
FROZEN FOOD (FRUIT, VEGETABLES, AND NUTS)	6 MONTHS
FROZEN LEFTOVERS (COOKED)	1 MONTH
FROZEN MEATS (UNCOOKED)	3 MONTHS
OILS	6 MONTHS AT ROOM TEMPERATURE
	12 MONTHS IN THE REFRIGERATOR OR FREEZER
SPICES AND DRIED HERBS (WHOLE, LEAVES, AND GROUND)	6 MONTHS ONCE OPENED

THE FULLY STOCKED PANTRY

Now that you know what to buy, here is your shopping list, the basic pantry and the baker's pantry, the must-haves and the nice-to-haves.

BASIC PANTRY

These are the items you'll want to have on hand in order to be fully equipped for cooking. For most of the recipes in this book, you'll want the "Need" items while the "Nice" items are things you can work up to over time.

Canned and Bottled Foods

NEED: canned tomatoes, tomato paste, reduced-sodium chicken and vegetable broths, canned chipotles en adobo, coconut milk, nut butter

NICE: canned beans, but only for emergencies: cannellini, kidney, chickpeas (garbanzo beans); oil-packed chunk tuna; oil-packed sardines; oil-packed sun-dried tomatoes; roasted red peppers

Condiments

NEED: Dijon mustard, low-sodium soy sauce or Worcestershire sauce, hot sauce

NICE: capers, anchovies, pickles, hot pickled peppers, chili-garlic sauce, hoisin sauce, miso, curry paste, fish sauce

Dry Storage

NEED: onions, garlic, shallots, potatoes, winter (hard-skin) squash

NOTE: Onions, garlic, and shallots do best when stored in a cool, dark area, but don't store them with potatoes or their texture will be negatively affected.

STORE IT RIGHT

Grains and Legumes

NEED: assorted dried beans (garbanzo, cannellini, and black beans are a good start), rice, pasta, whole-wheat couscous, quinoa, old-fashioned oats

NICE: regular and quick-cooking barley, cracked bulgur, dried lentils, farro or spelt, polenta, dried split peas

Nuts, Seeds, and Dried Fruit

NICE: Shelled, unsalted nuts (especially walnuts, pecans, almonds, and cashews)

Seeds (especially sesame seeds, pumpkin seeds, and flax seeds)

Dried fruit (especially apricots, dates, cranberries, raisins, currants, or cherries)

All-natural peanut, almond, or cashew butter

Oils

NEED: pure olive oil, neutral oil (such as canola, grapeseed, or peanut)

NICE: nut oils, toasted sesame oil, extra-virgin olive oil (for finishing)

Seasonings

NEED: kosher salt, black peppercorns, dried bay leaves, red pepper flakes, ground cinnamon, vanilla extract

NICE: sea salt or other finishing salt, ground cumin, cayenne pepper, pure chile powder, ground mustard, ground coriander, ground allspice, ground ginger, ground nutmeg

SPICE MIXTURES: five-spice, curry powder, chili powder, ras el hanout

Vinegars

NEED: white, cider, red wine, balsamic, rice

NICE: aged balsamic, sherry

Avid bakers have their pantries stocked at all times with these essentials so they can start to bake whenever the urge hits.

- Flours: unbleached all-purpose, unbleached white whole-wheat flour, unbleached whole-wheat flour, and unbleached whole-wheat pastry flour (store whole-wheat flours in the refrigerator or freezer)
- Baking powder
- Baking soda
- Active dry yeast
- Cornstarch
- Light brown sugar
- Granulated sugar
- Honey or agave nectar
- Molasses
- Nonstick baking spray

Of course, not all of us have the time, money, space, or desire to have the perfect pantry. If you plan on cooking at all, I'd recommend you at least have these items on hand as a bare-bones pantry.

- Salt
- Whole black peppercorns (use a peppermill to fresh grind as needed)
- Oil or other cooking fat
- Vinegar or other acid
- One sweetener (sugar, honey, agave nectar, maple syrup)
- Something with umami (soy, Worcestershire, miso)
- Something cured (capers, pickles, or anchovies)

Equip Yourself

Using second-rate equipment can challenge even the best chef. But arm yourself with the good stuff and you'll be making like an Iron Chef before you've even turned on the gas.

WHERE TO SHOP

When it comes to equipment, look for tools that are durable and hardworking. To fulfill these requirements, I usually buy equipment designed for commercial kitchens or vintage tools, as they tend to be built to last.

Restaurant Supply Restaurant supply stores are key, as they have utilitarian equipment that's seriously affordable. I may still go to higher-end cookware stores when I'm feeling indulgent, but I don't dare buy unless I've first checked a restaurant supply and online sources.

Antique Shops and Flea Markets For someone like me who's into antiques, this is an easy trip. But even if you're not, consider going a few times a year just to check it out. Who knows? If you find yourself with a vintage food mill, you may be inspired to mill and not mash your potatoes.

Online Shopping for equipment online lets you comparison shop and also provides access to sources for unique, hard-to-find items that would otherwise be all but impossible to locate. Check out Resources, page 431.

The Gist With well-developed kitchen skills you can work in pretty much any environment with any equipment. But until you're there (or to make it easy even if you are there), get yourself a few good-quality tools and you'll be set.

KNIVES

These guys are the workhorses of the kitchen, so, if you're going to splurge on equipment, have it be your knives. With a small investment up front and proper care, the reward is knives that are less dangerous, easier to use, and longer-lasting.

GETTING TO KNOW A KNIFE

Understanding how a knife's made will help you choose the right one. Here's the knife jargon you need to know to get you going.

Blade I trust you know what a blade is. The key here is that a sharp blade will hold its edge, put up with wear and tear, and ultimately make things easier for you in the kitchen.

Handle There are various types of handles but look for one that feels comfortable in your hand.

Bolster This is the thick metal piece between the handle and the blade of the knife that both protects your hand from the blade and helps balance the knife.

Tang The continuation of the blade that runs through the handle. A knife can have no tang, a half tang, or a full tang (meaning it passes all the way through the handle), which is considered to be the top quality because it makes for a well-balanced knife. Some tangs are concealed, so a knife may have one even if you can't see it—a salesperson can tell you more when you buy knives.

HOW IT'S MADE

Knives are either stamped or hand-forged; and many believe that the handmade knives are of higher-quality.

WHAT IT'S MADE FROM

High-Carbon Steel The upside is that this material is easy to sharpen and is usually more flexible. The downside is that it will rust with time, so be sure to keep it clean and dry.

High-Carbon Stainless Steel Stain- and rust-proof, this is a terrific option for a long-term investment knife. It isn't quite as sharp as a high-carbon steel, but it's easier to maintain.

Ceramic This is a newer style of knife and has the advantage of being lightweight and very sharp.

Aluminum If you're into hand-me-downs and antiques, you should be aware that some older knives can be made of aluminum and will react with some ingredients.

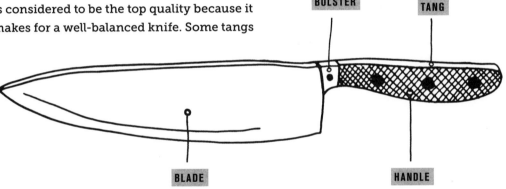

BOLSTER TANG

BLADE HANDLE

POTS AND PANS

You don't need many pots and pans but you do need good ones. If the material is substandard or too thin, the cookware will warp and get hot spots that will burn your food no matter what you do. Whatever material you choose, get a pan that is ovenproof so that you can take it from the stovetop to the oven as is often required in recipes that call for pan-roasting, broiling, or braising. Nonstick is the exception, as very few nonstick pans can withstand high oven temperatures.

Aluminum The most economical and lightweight of metals for cooking, aluminum will work if you buy good-quality ware (check out restaurant supply stores). Be aware that aluminum does react with some ingredients like eggs, tomatoes, and artichokes, so use pans made of other materials when you cook them. Aluminum is your best bet for really large pots such as a stockpot because its lighter weight makes it easy to handle and carry. There is also anodized aluminum, which is treated with an electrochemical process to give it the advantage of being almost nonstick and less reactive than regular aluminum. It's costlier than regular aluminum but worth the investment.

Cast Iron As it holds heat like no other, a cast-iron pan is often used for searing and for stovetop-to-oven recipes such as pan-roasted meat. It is widely available and very affordable but also quite heavy, so you'll get a workout when you use it. A disadvantage to cast iron is that you're cooking on a dark surface so it can be tough to judge the doneness of ingredients. Also, acidic ingredients like tomatoes may take on a metallic flavor in a cast-iron pan.

Copper No other metal in the kitchen is as good a conductor of heat. However, it isn't naturally nonstick, is very expensive, and can tarnish easily, so it requires impeccable care. Older copper pots may be lined with tin, which wears out relatively quickly and must be professionally reapplied, whereas most new pots are manufactured with a permanent stainless steel lining. Don't use pots that are unlined as copper reacts with a lot of ingredients.

Enamelware This is actually cast iron or steel that is coated in enamel and is most often used for Dutch ovens. Not only is enamel attractive but it is also nonreactive, a good heat conductor, and easier to clean than uncoated cast iron. This gives you the heat and reliability of cast iron without worrying about the food reacting with the cast iron itself. Clean only with nonabrasive utensils so the enamel doesn't scratch or chip.

Stainless Steel A superstar of cooking materials, stainless steel is strong, easy to clean, nonreactive, and very durable, but it doesn't conduct heat as well as other metals. If you're only buying one type of pan, this is a good bet.

Clad These pans are made by sandwiching different metals for optimum performance. The most common combination is to sandwich aluminum or copper between stainless steel, which offers the former's superior heat conductivity and the latter's durability.

Nonstick This is the material of choice for cooking delicate ingredients like eggs. It is not a good option though when you want food to develop a crust or when you're going for fond (browned bits on the pan) to deglaze for a sauce. Be sure to buy high-quality nonstick pans that have a nontoxic coating as some cheaper pans have coatings that can be hazardous to your health.

TOOL KITS

Now that you know what to look for in general when buying knives and cookware, here's the equipment you actually need to stock a kitchen. I'm a believer that less is more in the kitchen so this list covers only what you'll use the most.

THE BASIC KITCHEN

If you stock your kitchen with this list, you'll be able to cook most of the savory recipes in the book.

Chef's Knife Arguably the most essential piece of equipment in a kitchen, the chef's knife is extremely versatile. Most have blades that are 6 to 12 in/15 to 30.5 cm in length. Get one that you can comfortably hold and maneuver because you, not the knife, should be in control. If you're into baking, you might want to consider buying a second, cheaper knife for chopping nuts and chocolate and a sharper one for more refined chopping and mincing.

Paring Knife This is a small, but mighty knife, typically with a 4-in/10-cm blade. A paring knife is good for detail work such as deveining shrimp (see page 106), seeding chiles (see page 80), or thinly slicing garlic. I have paring knives in a variety of sizes and styles (some with serrated blades or blades made of ceramic or steel), but start with a stainless steel knife and you'll be set.

Serrated Knife
Also known as a bread knife, at least one serrated knife is needed for slicing squishy items like bread and tomatoes.

Pepper Grinder I've preached about the power of freshly ground pepper so many times that just writing about it makes me blue in the fingers. But seriously, you need to freshly grind your pepper; otherwise, you're pretty much just putting black flecks of tastelessness on your food.

Measuring Cups (Liquid and Dry)

Like the black pepper thing, I'm adamant that you use the right cup for the right tool. There are cups for liquid measure (the glass or plastic carafes with spouts) and others for dry (the metal or plastic ones) and—especially for baked goods and casseroles—you need to use the right one for the right job.

Measuring Spoons Your goal is to be an observant-enough cook so you can eventually tell how much a teaspoon of salt is just by looking. But until you're there (and always when you're baking), use measuring spoons to figure it out.

Dutch Oven Also known as a French oven or *cocotte*, an enameled cast-iron saucepan like this is key for dishes that require a slow simmer, like Real-Deal Pancetta and Pork Ragù, page 226, or a braise. The most versatile size is round, 5 to 6 qt/4.7 to 5.7 L in volume, and at least 4 in/10 cm high. Almost all cast-iron Dutch ovens are enameled so that they don't react with any acidic ingredients, but some are made of stainless steel or cladded metals, also nonreactive.

Nonstick Frying Pans: 6 in/15 cm and 10 or 12 in/25 or 30.5 cm

Frying pans have short sides and a wide base designed to minimize liquid and maximize color (think Caramelized Onions, page 116). Make sure the nonstick coating is top quality and nontoxic (heaven forbid it nicks), and always buy heavy-bottomed pans with ovenproof handles. Nonstick pans with crappy, toxic coatings and handles that aren't ovenproof can't handle oven temperatures. The small size is for single portions and for omelets. The bigger size is for most any other dish you'll make.

Stainless Steel Frying Pan with Lid: 10 or 12 in/25 or 30.5 cm

This is the pan I'll call for when you're going to need to give something a good sear, so don't be chintzy. Again make sure it has a thick bottom and an ovenproof handle. If you buy a 10-in/25-cm nonstick frying pan, then buy this one 12 in/30.5 cm, and vice versa.

Heavy-Bottomed Saucepans: 1 and 2 qt/960 ml and 2 L

With high sides relative to the pan base, this is what you turn to when you want to meld flavors and retain moisture (think sauces and soups). A heavy bottom will heat more evenly even with heavy use.

Large Pot with Lid: 6 qt/6 L

Anytime you're dealing with a large amount of liquid (for stock or soup), turn to this pot. Look for something that is light enough for you to pick up without throwing out your back but not so thin that everything burns.

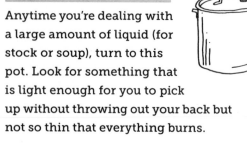

Can Opener

Try to go without it and you'll know exactly why you need it.

Thermometers
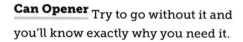
Most over- and under-cooked foods can be avoided by using thermometers—they're a worthwhile investment.

INSTANT-READ: You can never have too many of these—just make sure they're properly calibrated (see page 71). These thermometers are not meant to leave in throughout cooking. To use, insert it in the middle of the food you're measuring, avoiding any bone, wait for the reading, then remove.

OVEN: Most ovens are off by 50 degrees, either too hot or cold. An oven thermometer will tell you if the heat and temperature setting match.

FREEZER AND FRIDGE: To know that you're keeping your food at safe temperatures.

U-Shaped Peeler
Also called a speed peeler because its shape helps you get through loads of veggies faster than you would with the traditional straight peeler.

Fine-Mesh Sieve
For straining sauces, soups, and anything else that ends up a bit lumpy.

Colander
For draining bigger things from blanched vegetables to pasta.

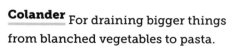

Rimmed Baking Sheets: 12 by 16 in/30.5 by 40 cm

I use these for everything from baking cookies to roasting vegetables and have one nonstick set and another that's uncoated heavy-gauge metal. It's really important that you buy heavy-gauge pans; lighter pans can warp from heat and slingshot food across your oven.

Three Cutting Boards Plastic cutting boards are cheaper but they'll wear away your knife's edge faster, while wooden boards are costlier and bulkier but are antimicrobial. No matter what style you choose, buy three (raw meat, raw poultry, and vegetables and cheese) so you don't risk contaminating other food. Also, buy a large one with a moat for carving roast meats or working with food like corn that may fly around as you cut it.

Three Nonreactive Bowls

Buy small, medium, and large nesting bowls that are nonreactive so you can use them for anything from melting chocolate (see page 93) to storing soup.

Small Prep Bowls Have a set of prep bowls around and they'll make organizing the prep work for a recipe much more orderly. If you buy bowls that are also attractive, you can use them for serving things at happy hour or cocktail party gatherings.

Heatproof Spoon Have at least one heatproof wooden or metal spoon around for stirring. If you get more than one, make sure one of them is slotted so that you can use it for picking up foods that need to drain.

Flat-Edged Wooden or Heat-Resistant Spatula The flat edge lets you scrape up the browned bits on the bottom of a pan, and heat-resistant, well, that's probably obvious.

Ladle Use it for serving up soups, stews, and other liquids, of course.

Whisk These days you can find all shapes and sizes of whisks, but, at the most basic, you'll need a big balloon whisk for whipping cream or egg whites and a small whisk for jobs where you want to mix things efficiently but don't need to add a ton of air (like mixing flours or custard).

Parchment Paper Use it for wrapping cheeses, lining baking sheets for easy cleanup, or lining baking pans so baked goods release without a hitch.

Pastry Brush I have one for savory foods and another for sweet foods because you don't want your caramel sauce to taste like barbecue sauce—or do you? Look for brushes made with natural bristles because they're more delicate, tend to hold more liquid, and are less likely to warp or melt (an issue with nylon brushes).

Aluminum Foil Look for recycled aluminum foil as it works just as well as the original stuff and is better for the environment.

Large Resealable Plastic Bags I'm talking the gallon-sized ones here. You can use resealable containers rather than plastic bags (or plastic wrap) in most cases. However, heavy-duty gallon-sized plastic bags are simply unequaled for marinating large pieces of meat.

Ruler or Measuring Tape Ideal for measuring the length of kitchen string, or double-checking that you did indeed roll the piecrust to the correct thickness.

Waterproof Pen or Marker and Tape Use it for labeling everything and anything with all pertinent information.

Box Grater and Microplane (Rasp-Style) Grater The box grater is good for shredding large amounts of cheese or vegetables (though you could also use the grating attachment on your food processor) while the handheld fine rasp-style graters are best used for finishing dishes.

Salad Spinner Not just for salad greens, use this for herbs or anytime you need to get a vegetable really clean and dry before using it.

NICE TO HAVE

Boning Knife The rigid blade and shape of this knife make it the best choice for removing bones from meat.

Cleaver Buying whole pieces of meat is more economical but will require you to get friendly with your cleaver. The key to using a cleaver is to keep it sharp and let the weight of the knife lead your hand rather than the other way around.

Fillet Knife Just as the name implies, this knife has a flexible blade so that it can easily fillet fish (see "Seafood" in Fundamental Prep Techniques, page 90). I also use mine to slice cured meats and smoked salmon.

Slicing or Carving Knife Some call it a carving knife, others a slicing knife, but no matter what you call it, you should consider getting one if you plan on doing Norman Rockwell-esque dinner parties that require large roasts, hams, and birds to be sliced.

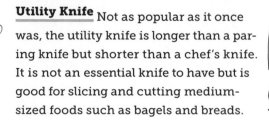

Utility Knife Not as popular as it once was, the utility knife is longer than a paring knife but shorter than a chef's knife. It is not an essential knife to have but is good for slicing and cutting medium-sized foods such as bagels and breads.

Fish Spatula This one is key if you're going to cook up delicate, flaky fish and you don't want it to fall apart on you.

Tongs They make it easier to turn and serve food. Just be sure you handle food gently when using tongs and don't pierce it.

Deep-Fry (Candy) Thermometer Anytime you're deep frying or making candy, make sure you have one of these on hand.

Coffee Maker Notice I don't say machine because I'm not talking about some multi-thousand-dollar espresso maker. Instead, invest in a good-quality maker that produces the kind of coffee you like, be it espresso, French press, or drip. This not only keeps you going when you're cooking but also is useful for recipes that call for coffee, like the Coffee-Molasses marinade (page 413).

Food Processor It can chop, puree, and blend and make things like pestos and doughs more doable. In my kitchen, I have a larger one for bigger chopping work and a small one for things like pestos. Most food processors come with a variety of blades so be sure to keep them on hand. I use the grating disc all the time for shredding cheese, or vegetables for recipes such as carrot cake (see page 365).

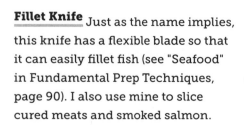

Grill Pan Even if you have an outdoor grill, you might want to invest in a grill pan for times when it's too cold or too much of a hassle to light the grill.

Straight-Sided Sauté Pan

Not a frying pan (though frying pans are often mislabeled as sauté pans), a sauté pan has higher sides than a frying pan (a.k.a. skillet), which keep some of the moisture in the food during cooking. This pan is a perfect option for one-dish stovetop meals like braised fish and Tarragon-Cream Chicken with Fresh Peas (page 288).

Blender Use one to make quick work of smoothing soups, sauces, and the like. If you're mostly going to blend things cooked in pots (like soups), you might want a stick (a.k.a. immersion) blender. Otherwise, go for the carafe blender and be sure to get one that's versatile.

Mandoline This hand-operated slicer has a reputation of being dangerous, but if you buy a good one, keep it sharp, and use it cautiously, it will reward you by making quick work of slicing.

Electric Mixer versus Stand Mixer

If you have the money, invest in a stand mixer because a well-crafted one will last a very long time. They also have an advantage over handheld portable mixers as they are more powerful and free your hands while you bake, with a variety of uses from whipping cream to making

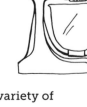

ice cream and pasta (with attachment items). If you can't afford a stand mixer, a quality handheld mixer will work just as well. However, using one for the recipes in this book may take a bit longer than specified in the recipe because I often use a stand mixer.

Specialty Small Appliances

You don't need specialty appliances like waffle makers, ice cream makers, or pasta machines, but they're worthwhile investments if you think you'll be making those foods with any regularity. I'm by no means a Luddite but I've found that with a lot of kitchen equipment, the more bells and whistles, the less it's worth. Think about it—a French press pretty much always results in a better cup of coffee than a drip coffee maker.

Plastic Wrap I try to use plastic wrap as rarely as possible as most of the time I can just use a resealable container or aluminum foil, but I keep it around for the odd job.

THE BAKER'S KITCHEN

I'm listing this separately because people tend to be drawn toward or far away from baking. If you are into it, consider adding the following equipment to your kitchen in addition to the things listed in The Basic Kitchen (page 63) and Nice to Have (page 66).

Scale A scale is helpful for all sorts of cooking but is essential for serious baking. Use it not only to measure out ingredients but also for making sure you have equally divided batters or doughs.

Chopping Knife I keep a cheaper chef's knife around for blade-dulling work common to pastry, such as chopping nuts or chocolate. That way I can hack away at things without worrying about destroying the blade for more refined work. However, even though it's cheap, I still take care of it as I would a standard chef's knife.

Bench Scraper (Bench Knife)

Classically used for handling and scraping up dough, I use it for anything from cutting soft cheese, leveling a cup of flour, carrying veggies from the cutting board to the stovetop, or for smashing garlic cloves.

Baking Dishes You'll want at least a square baking dish that is 9 by 9 in/23 by 23 cm and another that is 13 by 9 in/ 33 by 23 cm. I like using glass dishes because I can see the crust or underside of whatever dish I'm cooking.

Cake Pans Invest in a few round cake pans that measure 8 or 9 in/ 20 or 23 cm in diameter to start and make sure you label them so you use the right pan for the recipe.

Springform Pan Used most frequently for cheesecake, this pan has two parts—a base and a removable, spring-loaded ring for the sides—so that you can "unmold" pastries and cut them without damaging them. Look for a springform that will hold its seal really well while things bake so that you don't have dessert leaking all over your oven.

Pie Plate Go for a glass pie plate as it conducts heat well and it allows you to see how the crust is baking up.

Tube Pan If you plan on making angel food cake, you'll need this two-piece pan (it has a removable bottom for easier unmolding of the cake). The Bundt pan is a fluted one-piece variation on the tube pan.

Loaf Pans: 9 by 5 in/23 by 13 cm and 8 by 4 in/20 by 10 cm Pay special attention to dimensions of the loaf pan called for in a recipe; using the wrong size will result in different cooking times.

Muffin Tins Look for muffin tins that are heavy enough to conduct heat well and won't warp while baking. They're useful for more than just muffins and cupcakes. In fact, use them for nearly any recipe that calls for a ramekin or for recipes where you want to portion out individual sizes for baking, such as Baked Eggs (page 116), Frittatas (page 117), and quiches.

Straight French Rolling Pin

A pin without handles, this style allows you more maneuverability than the traditional rolling pin.

Wire Racks

If you're baking a lot, wire cooling racks can be really helpful for anything from cookies to cakes to breads. If you're tight on space get numerous small racks or look for stackable racks. In a bind, use the racks from your oven or your toaster oven.

Tart Pan

This pan is necessary only if you're planning to make tarts. I usually get my tart pans from antique shops that sell vintage cookware as they're often well made and more affordable than new pans.

Pastry Brush

If you've stocked The Basic Kitchen (page 63), then you already have one of these. However, if you're going to bake a fair amount, consider getting one that's only used for pastry work such as dusting excess flour off doughs, making caramels, brushing melted butter on doughs, greasing pans, and painting chocolate coatings on desserts.

Baking Weights

Use these ceramic weights anytime you need to bake an unfilled pastry crust so as to prevent it from puffing up. In a bind, you can use dried beans or rice, although don't use them afterwards for eating as their texture will be compromised.

Biscuit Cutters

The straight sides and sharp edges of biscuit cutters make for clean, precise cuts that will give your baked goods more height and better flakiness. In a bind, you can use anything to cut biscuits and shortcakes from a clean can to a small glass, but it'll cost you in the height of the final product.

DESERT ISLAND KITCHEN

This is the list if you can't afford a whole kitchen's worth of equipment, or want to know what to take to a vacation rental.

- Aluminum foil
- 1 baking dish
- 1 rimmed baking sheet
- 1 large saucepan
- 1 large stainless steel ovenproof pan
- 3 bowls
- Can opener
- Chef's knife
- Cutting board
- Measuring spoons
- Measuring cups (dry and liquid)
- Pepper grinder
- Sieve
- U-shaped peeler (though you could do most peeling with a spoon or paring knife)
- Tablespoon
- Thermometer
- Wooden spoon

MAINTENANCE

You can buy the best equipment out there, but if you don't take care of it, it's pointless. Here are some basic maintenance pointers so your equipment goes the extra mile.

KNIVES

Keep Them Clean Hand-wash your knives with hot, soapy water after each use and dry well.

Store Properly Keep knives so the blades are protected and stay shaped with a knife block, a magnetic knife strip, or in a protective sleeve.

Hone It Every time you go to use a knife, use your honing steel first. To hone the blade, place your knife blade at a 20-degree angle to the steel and swipe it back and forth a few times, for about 15 seconds.

Leave It to the Pros Send your knives to a professional knife sharpener every 6 to 12 months so they can be reshaped and sharpened. (You can also give professional sharpeners any other blades—such as food processor blades or kitchen shears that need sharpening.)

Don't . . .

- ever run your knives through the dishwasher.
- leave your knives wet.
- store your knives in a drawer.
- throw your knives in the sink and walk away—you're asking for an injury.

POTS AND PANS

Treat your pans well and they'll last a very long time. Try to avoid dinging them (a problem with lightweight metals) as that will cause hot spots that create uneven heat in the pan.

Follow manufacturer's information when cleaning more high-maintenance materials such as copper, aluminum, and enamelware.

As a general rule, I don't put my pans in the dishwasher. Even if the manufacturer says it's okay to do so, a run in the dishwasher usually strips off the patina (nonstick coating) that you build up on a pan over time.

Store your pans close to your stove and in a place you can get to easily (and without throwing out your back). If you have very limited kitchen space, then nest your pans in cabinets. Just be sure to place a paper towel in between each pan so that they don't nick the pan below them (especially crucial for seasoned cast-iron and nonstick pans).

For information on how to remove tarnish from copper, check out pages 419–420.

For pointers on how to scour off burnt-on food, check out page 420.

For advice on cleaning cast iron, check out page 420.

CUTTING BOARDS AND OTHER WOODEN TOOLS

To sanitize your cutting boards, (especially important if they were used for raw meat), clean them with a sanitizing solution of 1 tablespoon chlorine-free liquid bleach to 1 gl/3.8 L water.

Periodically, you need to oil a wooden cutting board (and other tools) with mineral oil to keep it in good shape. When the board is new, oil it daily for the first week, weekly for the next month, and then monthly for the life of the board.

Never put your wooden kitchen tools in the dishwasher or they'll warp. Instead hand-wash them in warm soapy water and clean with a rinse of one part vinegar and one part water. Dry well.

CALIBRATE FOR ACCURATE COOKING

Periodically, you'll need to calibrate your oven and your thermometers to make sure everything's working. Your oven should be calibrated by a technician to ensure it's done correctly; however, you can easily calibrate your thermometers by doing the following: Have your thermometer and a set of pliers handy. Bring a small pan of water to a boil. Dip the thermometer into the water and adjust it by tweaking the bolt and the base of the gauge with the pliers until it accurately records boiling water at 212°F/100°C.

PART 2

THE HOW-TO

You want to put the bulk of your effort here. Mastering the skills in this part of the book will allow you to become a confident cook who can truly cook from the hip.

That said, I've gone into depth about kitchen skills, techniques, and methods so you can eventually work without a recipe. But, until you get there, use this section as a cooking school cheat sheet. It has everything from techniques you need to know to how to solve common cooking pitfalls. After that, head on to Parts 3 (page 122) and 4 (page 380) to try your hand at the recipes.

B.C. (Before Cooking)

The B.C. (Before Cooking) period, when people tend to lack awareness in their cooking, often leads to loads of frustration. Skim this section so that you're prepped to cook once the urge hits.

The kitchen can quickly become a dangerous place so use common sense and be careful.

SANITATION

Avoid Cross-Contamination Keep surfaces that are regularly used scrupulously clean, particularly after working with raw eggs and poultry. In general, designate areas for raw food preparation (be it dirty vegetables or raw meat) so cleanup is more manageable.

Dodge the Danger Zone Keep your food out of the danger zone (40°F to 140°F/5°C to 60°C) at all costs as bacteria thrives at these temperatures. It will likely be in this range when served, but your goal is to get it hotter or colder than that range within two hours of serving it.

CAYGO (Clean As You Go) Clean as you go and keep things tidy (use prep bowls while you're cutting ingredients, keep a compost bowl for scraps) to avoid cross-contamination and to lessen the cleanup later.

Sanitize Sponges Periodially take your sponges for a spin (about 30 seconds) in the microwave or dishwasher. Or, if you're a tea drinker, sanitize sponges by soaking with extra boiling water from the teakettle.

For leftover-specific food safety information, check out Tips for Storing Leftovers, page 422.

KNIFE SAFETY

Sharp blades incite fear in beginner cooks, but, with a few tips, you'll be confident and far less likely to injure yourself.

Sharper Knives Are Safer It sounds contradictory but the sharper the knife, the less pressure you exert and the less likely you are to hurt yourself.

Hold It Right Hold the handle with your middle, ring, and pinkie fingers and then rest your index finger against one side of the blade (curl back your finger) and place thumb on opposite side. Choke up on the knife by pinching the spine of the knife where it meets the handle between your thumb and forefinger and wrap the rest of your hand around the handle. It will take getting used to but will pay you back with better knife control.

Keep It Curled Anytime you're cutting, be sure you curl back the fingertips of the hand that is holding the food being cut. Doing so will protect you that much more should a dreaded slipup occur.

Point It Down Always walk around with the knife by your side with the tip of the knife pointed down—no exceptions.

Slow and Steady Unless you were born with mad knife skills, start out slow and steady. It may not look very exciting but soon enough you'll be comfortable and agile enough to keep up with the best out there.

Anchor the Cutting Board All of that knife handling is for naught if you're cutting board rests on a slippery surface. Before you start cutting, always anchor the cutting board by placing it on a clean, damp towel.

PERSONAL SANITATION

Most of this is likely stuff you'd already do, but I've got to mention it just to be sure.

Wash Hands I should hope you're already doing this on a regular basis, but are you doing it right? You need to lather with soap for at least 20 seconds and then wash with very hot water.

Closed Shoes, Hair Back, and No Loose Clothing To protect your feet from heat and sharp objects, because no one wants hair in their food, and because loose clothing might cause you to knock something over.

FIRST AID FOR THE KITCHEN

GREASE SPILLS When cooking oil has been spilled in the kitchen, cover it completely with a generous amount of flour. The flour should fully cover the spill, and be enough to soak up the oil. Do not immediately begin trying to clean up the spilled cooking oil but allow the flour to soak it up for several minutes before continuing. Sweep up the oil-flour mixture and discard then clean the floor with a vinegar solution (page 421) to cut through the grease.

BURNS Avoid burns by taking extra care when putting food in hot fat, and using a folded dry towel or pot holder whenever dealing with something hot. If you burn yourself, run the spot under cold water, rub with an ice cube, then apply a burn cream.

CUTS Put pressure on the cut with clean towels to stop bleeding. Then clean, disinfect, and bandage. If it's really bad, seek medical attention.

FIRES Have an all-purpose extinguisher on hand. In general, try to put out a fire if it's small. If you're going to fight it, the key is to deny oxygen and fuel by turning off the gas or other source of heat.

If grease starts burning, quickly slide a lid over the pan to cover it completely and cut off the oxygen supply. Turn off the heat.

For small grease or electrical fires, smother the flames with baking soda and turn off the heat.

RECIPE ASSUMPTIONS

When I write my recipes, I make a few assumptions about how you'll use them. Read this section through so that we're communicating as clearly as possible.

Read the Recipe If you're not using a recipe, then you can skip this step. But, if you are, please do all us recipe authors a favor and read it all the way through before starting to cook. This one step will let you become familiar with the technique, and flag any ingredient you may be missing.

General Ingredients Information For the recipes in this book, the following are the default forms for these basic ingredients unless otherwise specified.

- All produce is ripe
- All produce is medium size
- All dairy is full fat
- Butter is unsalted
- Eggs are large
- Salt is kosher (I test with Diamond Crystal brand)
- I use pure (not extra-virgin) olive oil for cooking
- I use canola, grapeseed, or peanut oil for vegetable oil (but it can be swapped with corn or vegetable oil, as needed)

Equipment

- Timing for all recipes in the book is based on gas ovens and stoves (although tested on both gas and electric)
- Oven rack is in the middle position unless otherwise noted
- I use a stand mixer unless otherwise noted
- I use a carafe (not stick) blender

Measurement Check out Measuring Properly (page 82), for tips on how to do it properly, but here is a brief summary.

- I use the dip-and-sweep method for measuring flour
- Brown sugar is always packed into cup or spoon measures
- When measuring citrus zest, do not pack it or you'll end up with too much. Just lightly fill the measuring device.

Modifiers Matter As is standard, if the prep verb is before the listed food—½ cup finely chopped parsley—it is finely chopped and then measured.

Look for "Meanwhiles" I use "meanwhile" a lot in recipe instructions. These are times when one part of the recipe doesn't require your attention and you can focus on the next step of the recipe in order to get ahead.

Hands-on Time This is the amount of time you'll need to be actively cooking or working on the recipe.

Total Time This is the start-to-finish time required to make the recipe; however, this doesn't include the time needed to measure out ingredients or otherwise prep them as indicated in the ingredient list, so always allocate a few extra minutes for that.

AT THE STOVE

Mise en Place (MEP) Watch any cooking show for any period of time and you'll eventually hear this term. Mise en place (pronounced *meez ahn plass*) means to have everything prepped and in its place before you start cooking. A recipe ingredients list is like a code and all those actions contained in the list (for example, "1 carrot, minced") are keys from the author as to what you need to do before you start cooking.

TAYGO Taste (and season) as you go. Remember that when a dish has to cook down for a while, the flavors and salt will get concentrated so don't go overboard at the start.

Don't Change Too Much Recipes are written to be followed, though not everyone follows them to the letter. If you need to or want to make substitutions, check out Substitutions (page 120). Also, only change a few things at a time because too many changes (especially in baking) may produce a negative result.

Try a Little When you're trying to adjust the flavor of a dish, take into account flavor balance (see Striking Balance, page 390). and only alter a small portion at a time so you don't botch a whole batch of soup with one wrong move.

Use Your Senses Eating relies on all your senses so it makes sense that cooking would too. While cooking, judge the dish with all your senses and over time, you'll be able to hear when something's boiling and smell when something's done, even if you're not right next to the stove.

Keep Notes With the advent of electronic media, a lot of us have ditched the concept of note taking on a recipe. Well, I give you full permission to note take, dog ear, or otherwise break in this book so you add as much to it as it does for you.

Take Your Time There's definitely no scientific explanation, but when you rush through cooking, the results tend to be lackluster. So, take your time and your food will benefit from it.

HOW TO USE A KNIFE

Think of the chef's knife as a multiuse tool and work with it that way. The tip is best for refined slicing of small items, the middle for more rigorous chopping, and the heel for smashing garlic or getting through bones. If you're going to spend money on your knives, it should definitely be on the chef's knife as this is one of the pieces of kitchen equipment you'll reach for daily.

How to Hold a Knife Hold the handle near the blade, grasping it between your thumb and forefinger (see page 75).

How to Slice Use your other hand to hold the food to be cut, and curl your fingers under so that you knuckles form a protective barrier. Rock the knife in a fluid movement from tip to heel and move the fingers of your other hand back with each cut to expose the next portion of food to be cut.

Basic Knife Cuts It's as simple as this: cut your food into uniform pieces and it will cook more evenly. These are the knife cuts you'll use the most in the kitchen.

MINCED
⅛-in/3-mm
pieces

FINELY CHOPPED
⅛- to ¼-in/
3- to 6-mm
pieces

ROUGHLY CHOPPED
½- to ¾-in/
12-mm to 2-cm
pieces

MEDIUM DICE
½-in sq/
12-mm sq
pieces

LARGE DICE
¾-in sq/
2-cm sq
pieces

CUT INTO CHUNKS
Cut into pieces, size
indicated in recipe.

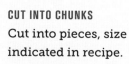

SLICED Food is cut into thin, flat pieces, size indicated in recipe.

CUT ON THE BIAS Food is cut on an angle.

CHIFFONADE Food is stacked, rolled, then sliced into thin strips.

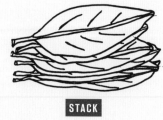
STACK

ROLL

SLICE

PREPPING COMMON FOODS

Here are some pointers for preparing the most common ingredients you'll come across when cooking.

PEELING

Peeling Beets If using beets raw, trim root end and peel with a regular peeler. If peeling cooked beets, run them under running water and rub the skin until it comes off.

Peeling Fresh Ginger Use a teaspoon to scrape off the skin of ginger.

Peeling Root Vegetables You don't need to peel root vegetables if they are going to cook for a long time as most of them have skin that is edible. However, remove skin with a peeler or paring knife if eating raw.

> **USING LEMON WATER** Here's a nerdy term for you: acidulated water. It's water to which an acid (such as lemon juice or vinegar) is added. It is used to help prevent peeled vegetables (such as fennel, apples, or pears) from browning.

Peeling Tomatoes and Stone Fruit Mark an X on the bottom of the fruit with a knife and then plunge into boiling water. Blanch very briefly (about 30 seconds) then plunge into an ice water bath. Drain and peel.

Roasting and Peeling Peppers and Chiles

The best way to do this is to char them over an open flame or on a baking sheet under a broiler until charred, blistered, and collapsed. Place the charred pepper in a bowl, cover with plastic wrap, and let sit at least 5 minutes. Remove plastic and peel off the blistered skin. If it is hard to remove, hold the vegetable under running water and rub off the skin with your fingers.

Peeling a Pineapple or Melon

Use a serrated knife to trim off the ends of the pineapple. Stand it upright and, using a downward sawing motion, remove the skin.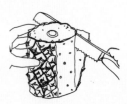

Peeling Kiwi Trim off kiwi ends, then slip a small spoon between the skin and the fruit. Turn the kiwi so that you're using the spoon to peel off the skin then push the flesh out of the skin.

> **POTATOES IN WATER** You can prep potatoes for mashing or roasting well ahead of time by cutting them and storing in water. If making mashed potatoes, just transfer soaking water and potatoes to a pot and turn on the heat, as the starch in the water will make for a better mash. If making roasted or fried potatoes, soak in acidulated water (water with vinegar) for better crispness. (Make sure they are impeccably dry before roasting.)

STEMMING AND SEEDING

Stripping Tender Herbs While some recipes call for a whole bunch of herbs or just a sprig (single stem) or two, others need just the leaves. This is how to remove the leaves: for tender herbs (where the stalk is soft, see page 44), hold the bunch of herbs by the stem and shave off the leaves with a sharp knife. If you only need a few, pick them off one at a time.

Stripping Woody Herbs For herbs with a woody stem (see page 42), do the following: pinch the top of the stem with one hand and, with your other hand, run the thumb and index finger down the length of the stem against the direction of the leaf growth.

Stemming Cooking Greens To remove the stems from large spinach leaves or other cooking greens, hold the stem in one hand, lightly pinch the leaves in your other hand then slide your hand down the stem to pull off the green leaves. Chop the stems and use in recipes as you would onion.

Seeding a Chile For a chile that you will halve, first halve it lengthwise, then use a small spoon to scoop out the white ribs and seeds. For a larger chile that you plan to use whole, trim off the stem end, then insert a grapefruit spoon or apple corer in the chile and rotate to trim off all of the ribs and seeds. Take precaution to avoid touching the seeds of the chile (you may want to wear gloves) because they contain a lot of heat.

Pitting an Avocado Cut the avocado in half lengthwise around the pit and twist the halves in opposite directions to separate. Put the half with the pit on a cutting board and carefully tap the blade of a knife into the pit. Twist and lift the knife to remove the pit.

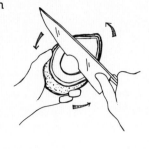

CUTTING

Chopping a (Hard) Winter Squash This can get dangerous so take precaution. Pierce the squash all over with the tip of a knife and then microwave for 30 seconds to 2 minutes or put in an oven while heating for 2 to 5 minutes until it cuts easily. Make sure your cutting board is well anchored by resting it on a damp kitchen towel, then place a dry kitchen towel on the cutting board and use a serrated knife to gently saw through the outer skin.

Peeling and Dicing an Onion Something you'll master quickly as you'll do it often when cooking. To peel, trim off both ends of the onion then slice the onion in half stem to root end and peel back the outer skin. To dice, place one onion half, cut-side down and root end away from you, on a cutting board. Slice downward (but not through the root) at parallel intervals. Hold the root of the onion and do the same thing parallel to the board toward the root end. Now, go perpendicular to the cuts and slice so that the onion falls apart into small pieces. Add the root piece to your frozen vegetable scraps or to a soup to flavor it.

Coring Cabbage or Fennel Quarter the cabbage or fennel through the core. Notch out the core in each piece and discard.

Trimming Cauliflower or Broccoli Pull off any greens, then turn upside down on a cutting board. Use a paring knife to cut around the core to remove florets.

Cutting Round Vegetables If you need to cut the vegetable into even size (like a medium dice), cut off the odd bits and square off the vegetable, then cut as desired. If you just need the vegetable chopped, you can halve it and then place it cut-side down on the cutting board and cut until you reach the desired size.

Catching Runaway Corn Kernels Shuck the corn and then do one of two things: line a baking dish with a towel, stand the cob upright, then saw off kernels with a serrated knife. Or, place a paper towel in the center tube of a Bundt pan (pan is right-side up), stand the shucked corn cob upright, with the tip of cob placed in the open tube of the pan. Holding the cob steady, with a serrated knife carefully saw downward to slice off the kernels, which will fall in the pan.

Cutting Ripe Tomatoes Use a serrated knife and be gentle.

Trimming Leeks and Green Onions Trim off the root end of the leek or green onion. Pull off any wilted pieces, cut off the green part then trim off any extra green bits (some recipes may tell you to leave the light green parts as well as the white). Prepare as needed.

HOW TO CLEAN FOOD

Here are a few tips on cleaning the most common ingredients you'll come across in the kitchen.

Cleaning Clams and Mussels Scrub under running water with a stiff-bristled brush to remove any grime. Soak in water with a few tablespoons of cornmeal and a pinch of salt for at least 30 minutes so they flush themselves out.

Cleaning Berries and Cherries Soak briefly in water just before using and gently pat very dry.

Fruit without Peels (Such as Apples, Stone Fruit, and Pears) Wash in warm water and scrub briefly.

Cleaning Leeks

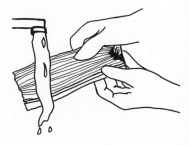

Halve trimmed leeks (see above) lengthwise. Hold each half under running water, pulling back the layers to wash away any grit.

Cleaning Mushrooms Contrary to common belief, mushrooms can and should be washed. As with everything, it's best to wash them just before using them. To do so, plunge them into a bowl of cold water and swirl around. Remove to paper towels and pat dry. Some larger mushrooms, such as portobellos, have "gills" under their caps. Use a teaspoon to scoop them out before cooking or they will turn your dish a dark color.

Cleaning Herbs and Greens Fill a large bowl with cold water and plunge in the leaves. Gently stir then let sit a few minutes. Carefully scoop them up and transfer to a salad spinner. As needed, re-soak the herbs or greens until they are clean and free of dirt. Spin gently in the salad spinner to dry. Remove from spinner and pat dry with a paper towel, as needed (this is especially key for salad greens where you want the dressing to adhere).

MEASURING PROPERLY

If you remember nothing else, remember that there are tools for measuring liquids and tools for measuring dry ingredients and that using the right one will make the difference in the outcome of your final recipe (especially with baked goods). These are the measuring techniques to use for each type.

Dry Ingredients Use measuring cups intended for dry ingredients and measuring spoons. The best technique (and the method used in this book) is the "dip and sweep" method. Just as the name suggests, you dip the measuring cup into the ingredient to be measured and then sweep away any excess with a straight-edged utensil like a spatula or knife.

Sticky Ingredients For sticky ingredients like honey, use a liquid measuring cup or a measuring spoon and coat either with vegetable oil or cooking spray before filling and it will be much easier to empty out.

Liquid Ingredients Use a spouted glass or plastic measuring cup for liquid ingredients. To get an accurate measure, fill the cup on a flat surface then drop down to read it at eye level.

Kitchen Scale You won't need a scale for the majority of the recipes in this book. However, if you plan on baking a lot or if you're concerned about precise portion size, it's a worthwhile investment.

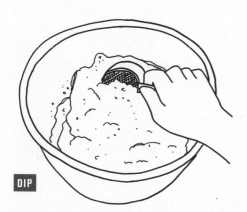

DIP

SWEEP

VOLUME EQUIVALENTS

3 TEASPOONS	1 TABLESPOON
4 TABLESPOONS	¼ CUP
2 CUPS	1 PINT
2 PINTS	1 QUART
4 QUARTS	1 GALLON

COOKING AND BAKING METHODS

From a purely technical point of view, cooking is when heat is applied to food and there is a change in its structure. The definition is a bit literal, but it does help understand what the heck cooking is. Almost every recipe in this book is based on one of the following common cooking methods (unless it is marinated or doesn't require cooking), so it's helpful to understand these methods and what each means.

BAKE To bake is to cook food in the dry heat of an oven at a temperature usually below 400°F/200°C. Sweets, breads, and desserts are most commonly baked.

BLANCH To blanch is to briefly cook food in boiling water then plunge it into cold water to "shock" or stop the cooking. Use this method to loosen skins, to set the color of a food, or to partially cook a food (technically known as parboiling) so as to decrease overall cooking time.

BOIL A liquid is at a boil when bubbles break the surface (212°F/100°C for water). Most food is never boiled (aside from pasta, for blanching, or briefly for stews, soups, and sauces) as boiling can quickly deteriorate texture and flavor.

BRAISE For braising, food is first browned in a bit of fat and then simmered (on the stovetop or in the oven) covered or partially covered with a small amount of liquid, then topped with a cover, and simmered until the food is very tender and soft. It is commonly used for cooking cuts of meat such as brisket or shoulder that would otherwise be tough.

BROIL To broil is to cook food within a few inches of a very hot (over 500°F/260°C) heat source. It is commonly used to finish a dish (for example, a frittata (page 117), to brown a topping (like shepherd's pie) or to char vegetables (as in a tomatillo salsa, page 324).

FRY Frying means to cook food in hot fat (usually between 275°F/135°C and 425°F/220°C). It is shallow-fried or panfried when using a small amount of fat (about 1 in/2.5 cm or less), and deep-fried when the food is completely submerged in the fat.

GRILL Food is grilled when cooked over a direct heat source, usually heated by wood or charcoal. Not to be confused with barbecue where food is covered and cooked low and slow over wood or coals.

POACH Poaching means to cook food gently in simmering liquid; it is important that the liquid is at a simmer but never boils. The most common poached foods are eggs, fish, and chicken.

ROAST To cook food, uncovered, in an oven, with the food often elevated (a turkey on a rack, for example) so that it has good air circulation. The goal is to get a brown exterior and a moist interior and is best for vegetables, tender meat, poultry, and seafood. Roasting usually occurs at a temperature above 375°F/190°C.

SAUTÉ To sauté is to cook food over medium to high heat in a small amount of fat. Sautéing and panfrying are similar cooking methods, although sautéing generally uses less fat than panfrying.

SIMMER To cook food gently at a point where the liquid is moving and small bubbles break the surface. A good way to understand the difference between a simmer and a boil is that, at a simmer, the liquid is just giggling, whereas it is outright laughing—bubbles break the surface—when it is at a boil.

STEAM Steaming means to place food in a basket, rack, or insert and cook it above a few inches of simmering water, covered. It is commonly used for cooking vegetables and seafood. Nutritionally, it is a better method than boiling or poaching, as it allows the food to retain more of its nutrients.

STEW This method is similar to braising except that more liquid is used. To stew, the food is just barely covered in liquid and is then simmered slowly in a covered or partially covered pot.

MICROWAVE I've put this last because it's my least favorite way to cook. In fact, I haven't had a microwave for years because anything you'd need it for can be accomplished between a toaster, an oven, and a stovetop.

TEMPERATURES

COOKING TEMPERATURES

No matter how good a cook you become, you should take the temperature of cooked meats before serving. The USDA sometimes recommends high temperatures that compromise quality or texture of the finished dish, but I'm including them here so you are aware of what is recommended (especially important for children or those whose immune systems might be compromised).

WATER BOILS
212°F / 100°C

REHEATED LEFTOVERS
165°F / 74°C

FOOD DANGER ZONE
42°F-140°F / 5.5°C-60°C

IDEAL REFRIGERATOR TEMPERATURE
38°F / 3.3°C

FREEZING
32°F / 0°C

BEEF & LAMB

Rare
115°F-120°F
46°C-49°C

Medium-rare
125°F-130°F
52°C-54°C
USDA 145°F / 63°C

Medium-well
150°F
65.5°C

Ground
160°F
71°C

PORK

Medium
138°F-142°F
59°C-61°C
USDA 160°F / 71°c

Well-done
160°F
71°C
USDA 170°F / 77°c

Ground
160°F
71°C

CHICKEN
160°F-165°F
71°C-74°C

FISH
135°F
57°C

BREAD
190°F
88°C

CUSTARD
180°F
82°C

KNOW WHEN IT'S DONE

Taking a food's temperature is always the best way to know when it's done, but it's not the only way. Here are some other tests for doneness.

STEAKS

Until you can tell visually, use your thermometer but work toward being able to tell without one. Look at the surface of the meat and get to know the firmness as it cooks. For medium-rare steaks, there will be droplets of blood on surface. To test firmness, many people use the following trick:

Rare When you touch your index finger to the tip of your thumb, the fleshy area of your palm below the thumb is what rare meat feels like.

Medium-Rare Touch your middle finger to the tip of your thumb. The fleshy area on your palm below the thumb is what medium-rare feels like.

Medium Press the tip of your ring finger and your thumb together. The fleshy area on your palm below the thumb is what medium feels like.

Medium-Well Press the tip of your pinkie finger and your thumb together. The fleshy area on your palm below the thumb is what medium-well feels like.

BRAISED MEATS

The meat is meltingly tender and pulls apart with a fork.

CHICKEN

The juices run clear and the joints move easily.

SEAFOOD

Stick the tip of a skewer into the middle of the fish and hold it there for 8 seconds. Press the skewer to your bottom lip. If it's hot, it's done.

The edges of a fish fillet or the tail of the fish will flake. (Don't wait for the middle of the fillet to flake or it will be overdone.)

The flesh is the same color all the way through (with the exception of tuna and salmon, which should be cooked like steaks).

On whole fish, the eyes will be totally white.

VEGETABLES

They should be knife-tender or, in some case, fork-tender.

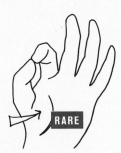

RARE

MEDIUM-RARE

MEDIUM

MEDIUM-WELL

TIPS AND TRICKS

These are the hard-earned tips I've learned over the years that help make my time in the kitchen a bit easier.

Getting More Juice from Citrus Roll a lemon, lime, orange, or grapefruit on a flat surface a few times before juicing.

Removing Pomegranate Arils The arils (like the seeds) of a pomegranate can be stubborn. To help release them, slice the fruit in half and then holding one half in your hand, cut-side down over a bowl, knock the back of the fruit with a wooden spoon.

Refreshing Vegetables When you've got wilted vegetables (limp carrots or floppy greens), soak them in a bowl of ice water for a few minutes. Do this anytime you want to offer veggies with a dip, as they'll look perkier when you set them out.

Making Bitter Greens Less Bitter Again ice water is the key here. If you soak bitter greens in a few changes of ice water, it will significantly cut down on the bitterness. If you are cooking them, add a little sweetener to the dish and it will cut down on bitterness.

Making Raw Onions Less Sharp Soak cut-up onions in vinegar for a few minutes before using to cut the sharpness. If they're for a salad, soak them in the same vinegar as in the dressing. If you don't want any vinegary flavor, sprinkle the onions with salt, let them sit a few minutes, then rinse off the salt.

Making Cucumber Less Bitter Most of the bitterness is in the skin and seeds of a cucumber, so simply peel it and scoop out the seeds. Also, as with raw onions, a sprinkling of salt will also help. Salting also concentrates flavor, so it's a good move if you're making a dish where cucumber is the centerpiece (see Cold Cucumber Raita Soup, page 197).

Loosening Peel from Garlic Cloves You have some options, depending on how you'll use the cloves.

If you need to peel a whole head of garlic, this technique works quickly: Place a head of garlic on a cutting board and smash with your hand to break into cloves. Sweep the cloves into a bowl and cover with a second bowl of the same size. Hold the bowl tightly and shake about 5 to 10 seconds, until all the cloves are peeled.

If you need them whole and they are going to be cooked, you can pour boiling water over them and let them soak for 15 to 20 seconds, and the skins will be easier to remove. (This method also works well for pearl onions, though you need to soak them for a few minutes.)

If you are going to chop or mince individual cloves, the easiest thing to do is to, with one hand in a fist, quickly and carefully tap the garlic clove with a pan or a flat side of a knife blade (with the blade facing away from you) to loosen the skin without totally smashing it (unless you need it smashed, in which case, go for it).

Quickly Mincing Garlic, Ginger, or Onions

For soups and other cooked dishes where you need minced garlic, ginger, or onion, just grate it on the small holes of a rasp grater and proceed. Just be sure to gather and include any grating juice as it has a lot of flavor, easy to do if you grate over a dish or sheet of waxed paper.

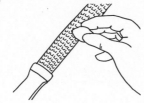

Quickly Peeling Carrots and Parsnips

Hold the vegetable in one hand and, with a peeler, quickly move up and down the vegetable without lifting the peeler off the vegetable.

Husking Corn

Either pull back the husk and remove or, for a quantity of cobs, trim off the ends with a serrated knife and just peel off the husk.

Removing Corn Silk

Rub shucked corn with a damp kitchen towel to pull off any excess corn silk.

Easily Coring Pears and Apples

Halve fruit lengthwise then insert a melon baller or teaspoon in the core and rotate once to pop out the core.

Quickly Coring a Bell Pepper

Trim off the bottom of the pepper. Slice around the stem so as to make a little hat on the top. Push that hat through the bottom of the pepper and it will take the core and seeds with it.

Easily Seeding a Cucumber or Zucchini

Halve the vegetable then use a teaspoon to scrape out the seeds.

Juicing a Lemon without a Juicer

Halve the lemon then pierce a cut side a few times with a fork. To juice, insert the tines of the fork into the cut side and twist.

Cutting an Onion Without Crying

Some people swear by wearing goggles, but I find that younger onions are the key. Also, it helps to put the onion in the refrigerator for up to 20 minutes before cutting it. (Just don't store the onion in the refrigerator, as it will compromise the flavor and texture.)

Grating Cheese

All cheese is easier to grate when cold. To grate, use a food processor fitted with the fine grating disk, or use the fine teeth on a handheld box grater. For soft cheese, use the large holes on the box grater. If your soft cheese is particularly hard to grate, you can dab some oil or put cooking spray on the teeth of the grater so the pieces will slip off easier.

Reconstituting Dried Mushrooms or Chiles

Put the mushrooms or chiles in a bowl. Pour just enough simmering liquid (water, broth, sweet wine, or juice) over the mushrooms or chiles to cover and let sit until the veggies are very soft and pliable. Use the soaking liquid in the recipe for added mushroom or chile flavor.

Preventing Chile Burn on Hands

Either use gloves or put a dab of vegetable oil on the part of your hand that will touch the chile.

Getting Rid of Chile Burn

Whether you've ingested chiles or their fire is on your skin, a glass of milk for the former or soak in yogurt for the latter is the key to soothing the burn.

Zesting Citrus without Bitterness

When zesting citrus, only zest the fruit once or twice in the same area. You don't want to get any of the white pith layer just under the colored peel as it is bitter.

Cracking a Raw Egg Tap the egg on a flat hard surface and try to do it in one tap, so as to limit the risk of the eggshell getting in your food.

Separating an Egg There are other methods, but this one is the safest so long as your hands are clean. Have two bowls ready and crack the egg. Place your hand, palm-side up, over a bowl and drop the egg into your cupped hand. Let the egg white pass through your hand while containing the yolk. Alternatively, if you have a lot of eggs to work through, crack them all into a bowl. Then, using your clean hands, transfer the whites and yolks into two different bowls. This method ensures you don't get egg yolk in your egg whites, which would prohibit you from getting the whites to mount well.

Peeling a Hardboiled Egg Drain the cooked eggs and return them to the pan. Cover the pan and shake it to crack the shell. Dunk in an ice water bath for a few minutes, then peel.

Bringing Eggs to Room Temp Quickly

Place eggs in a bowl of warm water and you can use them in 5 to 10 minutes.

Testing a Salad Dressing To make sure a salad dressing is properly seasoned, first dip one leaf of the salad greens in the dressing and taste. If it is too sour, add some sugar, if too sweet, some salt. If it is too watery, add more oil, mustard, or roasted garlic. If it is too thick, add some vinegar or water.

Dressing a Salad It seems simple, but often salads are overdressed. To do it properly, evenly drizzle less dressing than you think you need (just a few spoonfuls) over clean, dry greens, then toss with splayed fingers

(spread wide as if you're combing them through your hair) until each green is just coated. You do not want the dressing dripping off the leaves. If in doubt, pass the vinaigrette on the side.

DO AHEAD: Put the vinaigrette in the base of a serving bowl, then the serving utensils, and then the greens. Toss just before serving.

Makeshift Roasting Rack

ALUMINUM FOIL: Twist pieces of aluminum foil into a cord and fold them into figure-eight shapes. Place the foil shapes in a roasting pan and set the meat on top of the foil.

VEGETABLES OR BREAD: Create a bed of cut vegetables (such as the Balsamic Caramel Chicken with Roasted Eggplant, page 264) or with large cubes of bread. Do this with a roast chicken as the vegetable and bread get basted by the juices and can be served on the side.

Safely Filling a Bain Marie Recipes for delicate baked goods may call for baking them in a bain marie (water bath) so as to protect eggs from curdling. But carrying a filled tray of boiling water to the oven can be dangerous. Instead, nest the baking dish in a larger pan (like a roasting pan), place it in the oven, and then pour boiling water into the large pan with a teakettle, which reduces the risk of spilling hot water all over the kitchen.

Makeshift Pot Lid If you don't have the proper size lid for a specific pot, substitute a frying pan, baking sheet, or lid from another pot—just be careful as it may drip condensation or you could accidentally knock it off the pot.

Getting Rid of Smelly Hands Rub your hands with lemon juice or vinegar (beware of any nicks in your hands!), rub your hands on something made of stainless steel, or do both.

Blending Hot Liquids Fill a blender two-thirds full with liquid, cover with the lid and remove the plug from the center, then place a clean kitchen towel (that you don't mind getting dirty) over the top of the blender. Hold the towel down with one hand and turn on the blender to its lowest setting. Increase the speed of the blender until the liquid is smooth and creamy.

Checking a Brine Solution Uncooked whole eggs (still in shell) will float to the surface when the liquid mixture is at the right ratio for brining.

Weighting Down a Brine Fill a resealable plastic bag with water. Rest it over the brine to keep the food in the brine fully submerged in the liquid.

Slicing Meat Thinly Frozen meat is easier to slice. To help slice meat very thinly (as for Cheat Sheet Beef Pho, page 183), first freeze it briefly (15 to 30 minutes).

> **CUTTING MEAT AGAINST THE GRAIN** Check out the meat and you'll notice that, similar to wood, it has a grain. Always slice at a 90-degree angle, perpendicular, to the grain.

Softening Butter Quickly Either cut the butter into small cubes and let them sit at room temperature until your finger leaves a mark in the surface when lightly pressed (but it's not starting to melt) or, if you need it really quickly, cut the butter into cubes and work it with a spatula or beat it with a rolling pin until very spreadable.

Portioning Out Cookies Quickly Use an ice cream scoop with a sweep to easily scoop cookie dough or batters for muffins or cupcakes. Using a scoop also affords portion control so everything bakes at the same rate and looks more professional because all are the same size.

Cutting Sticky Foods Coat the blade of the knife with a dab of vegetable oil or nonstick cooking spray.

Sifting without a Sieve Use a whisk or fork and run it through the dry ingredients to aerate them and break up any lumps.

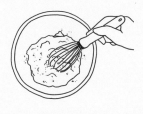

Windowpane Test for Yeasted Dough To test if the dough is ready, grab a piece of dough between your thumbs and forefingers and draw fingers apart to pull the dough into a 2-in/5-cm square (a "windowpane"). If the dough stretches without breaking, you're good to go. Otherwise, keep mixing.

Rising to the Right Height A good rise will result in a great bread. To keep tabs on the dough, put it in a clear, straight-sided container and mark its initial height with a piece of tape. Then follow the recipe instructions and let it rise to the necessary height.

Fundamental Prep Techniques

These techniques are the building blocks of cooking—the not-so-glamorous but very useful things you need to know how to do to cook well.

BLOOMING WHOLE SPICES

This helps bring out a spice's flavor. To do so, heat some oil over medium heat until it's hot but not smoking. Add spices and cook briefly until very fragrant but not browned. Remove from heat and proceed with the recipe.

TOASTING AND GRINDING WHOLE SPICES

In an ideal world, you would always have time to toast and grind your spices. Since that's not realistic, do this when you want extra oomph from the spices. To toast, spread the spices in a single layer in a pan and cook over medium heat. Swirl the pan and only cook until you begin to smell their aroma. Transfer to a plate to cool then grind in a spice grinder or pound and grind with a mortar and pestle.

BLANCHING VEGETABLES

Almost any vegetable can be blanched though the most common ones are greens, beans, and root vegetables (such as potatoes before grilling).

Fill a bowl halfway with water and ice to make an ice water bath, and set aside. Bring water to a boil and add enough salt to make it taste like saltwater. Add the vegetable and cook until bright in color and just knife-tender (al dente), or, in the case of greens, brightly colored and wilted. Immediately, drain and dunk the vegetables in the ice water bath. Let chill in the ice bath until it warms to room temperature. Drain well to remove excess water.

TIP: Blanch substantial vegetables like green beans and broccoli up to 1 day in advance of serving and refrigerate wrapped in paper towels in a resealable plastic bag.

PEELING FAVA BEANS

Fill a bowl halfway with water and ice to make an ice water bath, and set aside. Bring a large pot of heavily salted water to a boil. Shell the fava beans. When the water is boiling, drop the beans into the pot and boil for 1 to 2 minutes. Transfer the beans to the ice water bath and let sit until cool; drain. Remove the fava skins by splitting open the skin and squeezing out the bean.

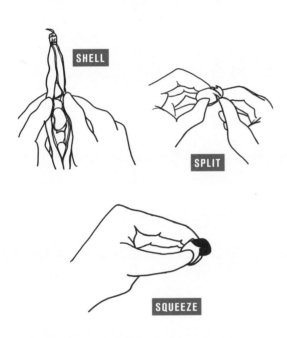

SHELL

SPLIT

SQUEEZE

MAKING VINAIGRETTE: WHISK AND JAR METHODS

WHISK METHOD: Combine 1 part vinegar with a pinch of salt in a large nonreactive bowl and whisk to evenly combine. Slowly whisk in 3 to 4 parts oil until completely combined; taste and season with salt and freshly ground pepper.

JAR METHOD: Combine 1 part vinegar with 3 to 4 parts oil in a jar, close top, and shake until well combined; taste and season with salt and freshly ground pepper.

TIP: Add a spoonful of roasted garlic, an egg yolk, mustard, or anchovy paste to the vinegar to make the emulsification of the dressing more stable.

BREAD

BREAD CRUMBS

FRESH: Remove the crusts from day-old bread (or bread that is just beginning to dry out). Process in a food processor fitted with the metal blade until crumbs are of the desired size.

DRIED: Heat crustless bread on a baking sheet in a 250°F/120°C/gas ½ oven until it is dry and golden but not browned. Process in a food processor until the crumbs are of the desired size.

BREADING FOODS

To coat, set up plates of breading ingredients (such as flour, beaten eggs, and bread crumbs). Hold the dry food in one hand and dredge in the seasoned flour; shake off any excess. With your other (clean) hand, dip the food into the eggs, let excess drip off, then roll in the bread crumbs, pressing to adhere as necessary.

EGGS

WHIPPING EGG WHITES

Place egg whites in the bowl of a stand mixer fitted with the whisk attachment and beat on medium speed until soft peaks form, about 2 minutes. Increase speed to high and beat until the whites are glossy, cling to the whisk when it is lifted out of the whites, and are droopy (slightly bent like an eagle's beak), about 3 minutes more.

TIP: Make sure the bowl and whisk you use for the egg whites are impeccably clean, as any fat or oils will prevent the whites from holding air.

Don't over-whisk the whites or they'll deflate while baking. Whisk whites until they cling to the whisk when pulled out of the whites.

Older eggs whip up more easily and consistently than fresher eggs.

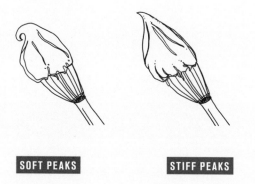

SOFT PEAKS   STIFF PEAKS

MAKING MAYONNAISE

BY HAND: Place 1 egg yolk, 1 teaspoon Dijon mustard, 1 teaspoon freshly squeezed lemon juice, and a pinch of salt in a nonreactive bowl and whisk until smooth. Whisking constantly, add oil in a thin stream until completely incorporated and mayo is thick (when the whisk is lifted, the mayo should hang off the whisk, but not fall off). Taste and add a few drops of vinegar or lemon juice, whisking until the mayonnaise is slightly whiter in color and the flavor is brighter and more pronounced. Taste and add more salt and pepper, as desired.

BY FOOD PROCESSOR: Combine 1 egg yolk, 1 teaspoon Dijon mustard, 1 teaspoon freshly squeezed lemon juice, and a pinch of salt in a food processor fitted with the metal blade and pulse until smooth. With the processor running, slowly add oil in a thin stream until completely combined. Add a few drops of vinegar or lemon juice, pulsing until the mayonnaise is slightly whiter in color and the flavor is brighter and more pronounced. Taste and add more salt and pepper, as desired.

BAKING

MELTING CHOCOLATE

Make a water bath (a.k.a. bain marie) by nesting a heat-resistant bowl over a saucepan of simmering water, but don't let the water boil or touch the bottom of the bowl. Place the chocolate in the bowl and cook, stirring frequently, until evenly melted.

WHIPPING CREAM

Combine all ingredients (cream and flavorings, if any) in the bowl of a stand mixer fitted with the whisk attachment and whip on low speed until smooth, about 30 seconds. Increase the speed to high and beat until stiff peaks form, about 2 minutes.

TIP: For success with whipped cream, make sure the cream is chilled and the bowl and beaters are clean, as fat will prevent the cream from holding air.

CLARIFYING BUTTER

Cut the butter into small cubes then place in a medium frying pan over medium heat. Swirl the pan a few times so it cooks evenly, and cook until the butter melts and white milk solids separate out. Remove from the heat and pour into a spouted glass container. Let cool until the milk solids have totally settled on the bottom of the glass. Pour off the liquid butter into an airtight container and discard the milk solids (the white stuff). Store, refrigerated, in an airtight container up to 1 month.

BROWNING BUTTER

Cut the butter into small cubes then place in a medium frying pan over medium heat. Swirl the pan occasionally so it cooks evenly and cook until the butter melts and white milk solids turn a nut brown. Immediately remove from the heat and pour into a heat-proof bowl until ready to use. Store, refrigerated, in an airtight container up to 1 month.

FLAVOR: This technique is used for making biscuits (see pages 170–172). For a savory flavor, when the butter starts foaming, you can add some woody herbs (rosemary, thyme, oregano, marjoram, or sage) for a simple brown butter sauce. Add capers and red pepper flakes for a pungent sauce. Add a squeeze of lemon juice and serve over fish.

PREPARING A SOUFFLÉ DISH

Thoroughly brush the inside of the soufflé dish or ramekin with melted butter then dust with an ingredient used in the recipes (flour, bread crumbs, cocoa powder, grated cheese, or sugar), to help give the soufflé lift.

PREPARING A BAKING PAN

Grease the pan liberally with a coating of shortening, softened butter, melted butter, or cooking spray. If the recipe calls for a floured pan, add a spoonful of flour then tilt and turn the pan so that all the inside surfaces of the pan get coated. Turn it over and tap gently to rid of any excess flour.

PREPARING A FLUTED BUNDT PAN

Brush on melted butter, then coat with flour if called for in the recipe.

CUTTING A CAKE IN HALF HORIZONTALLY

Use this technique to create a multi-layered cake with filling. Use a ruler to measure the height of your cake and then use toothpicks to demarcate the halfway point in about three or four places around the sides of the cake. Using a serrated knife, slice all the way through the cake, guided by the toothpicks.

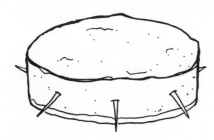

TRIMMING A DOMED CAKE

Use a serrated knife to trim the top of the cake so it is flat. Alternatively, if the dome isn't that bad and you're making a layered cake, you can flip the cake so the flat side is up and the domed side is in toward the filling.

CREAMING BUTTER

When a recipe calls for creaming butter—beating butter and sugar—it is essential to continue until the butter is airy and lightened in color, anywhere from 3 to 5 minutes.

CUTTING IN FAT

When a recipe, such as a pie dough says to cut in the flour, this is how you do it: add the butter in small pieces to the flour mixture, toss to coat in flour, then rub into the flour with your fingers until the mixture forms pea-sized pieces (some big chunks should remain) and comes together in fist-sized clumps when squeezed, about 1 minute.

ROLLING PIE DOUGH INTO A ROUND

Lightly flour a clean, even work surface with a few pinches of flour and coat a rolling pin with a small amount of flour. Place the chilled dough on the work surface. Start in the center and roll away from you (toward twelve if it were a clock). Continue to roll in every one of the following "clock" directions (three, six, nine, then twelve again), occasionally flipping and re-flouring the dough as needed to ensure it doesn't stick. Roll dough into a circle, approximately ⅛ in/3 mm thick.

TRANSFERRING PIZZA DOUGH

On a clean, lightly floured surface, using a lightly floured rolling pin, roll the pizza dough on parchment paper into a 9-in/23-cm round or oval. Use the parchment to transfer the dough onto the baking sheet.

TRANSFER PASTRY TO A PIE PLATE

Roll up the pastry around the rolling pin, carry to the pie plate, and unroll it into the plate.

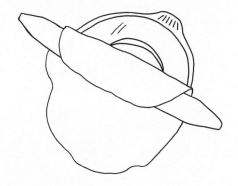

LINING A PIE PLATE

Transfer the dough to a pie plate and trim the edges so there is a ½-in/12-mm overhang. Use the excess dough to press the crust into the pie plate. Fold the crust overhang back on itself and press, as desired, into a decorative edge.

FROSTING A CAKE

To frost, place a cake layer on an inverted cake pan. Brush away any stray crumbs and spread about one-third of the frosting over the top of the layer. Stack the second layer, and evenly spread another one-third of the frosting over the top. Before frosting the sides, place the cake on a serving platter and tuck a few strips of parchment or waxed paper under the sides of the cake to keep the serving platter clean. Apply a thin layer of frosting (a.k.a. the crumb coat) to the sides of the cake; don't fuss over looks at this point as this is just a base coat. Refrigerate until the frosting is just set, 10 to 15 minutes. Remove from the refrigerator and spread the remaining frosting over the top and sides of the cake as evenly as possible.

MEAT

TRIMMING MEAT

Remove fat by slicing under it with a sharp boning knife, then pull off the fat with your hands. Do your best to remove excess fat but not to tear or nick the meat. Keep in mind you want to leave enough fat to allow the meat to baste itself while it cooks.

USE: Look over every roast or large piece of meat before you cook it and remove any excessive amounts of fat.

TRIMMING SILVER SKIN

Pull off the silver skin (membrane) from the meat by angling the knife against the membrane and pulling it back and up.

USE: Remove silver skin from cuts of meat such as tenderloin so that they don't end up misshapen or tough.

CRISPING BACON

If you're just cooking a few pieces, lay them in a large frying pan or cast-iron skillet and cook over medium heat until browned to your liking. If you are going to serve it crumbled, you can chill the bacon in the freezer (see page 53), then cut up as desired. If you're making bacon for a big group, cook it in a 375°F/190°C/gas 5 oven, turning occasionally, until crisp. Remove the bacon to a paper towel–lined plate to drain off excess fat.

FLAVOR: You can baste the bacon with honey or maple syrup before cooking to give it a sweet note. Add pepper flakes or cracked black pepper to the honey or maple syrup for a kick.

TYING A ROAST

WITH A BUTCHER LOOP: Cut a piece of kitchen string that is at least twice as long as the meat **1**. Tie a single loop around one end of the meat and knot to secure **2**. Wrap the remaining string around your hand once to form a loop so that the loose end passes underneath the tied end **3**. Slip this loop over the meat and adjust so that it is a few inches away from the first loop **4** (you should now have two loops securing the meat **5**). Continue this process until you've evenly secured the meat **6**. Thread extra string under the roast and back to the starting point of the string **7** **8** **9**. Tie the loose end of the string to the starting point and trim excess string **10**.

SHORTCUT WAY: If you don't want to do this or your meat is misshapen, you can just cut several lengths of kitchen string and tie every few inches down the length of the roast until it is secure.

USE: This is essential anytime you are cooking a piece of odd-shaped meat (like boneless leg of lamb, beef or pork tenderloin, or boneless roast) or anytime you have stuffed a piece of meat (see Walnut Pesto–Stuffed Leg of Lamb, page 314) so that it cooks more evenly.

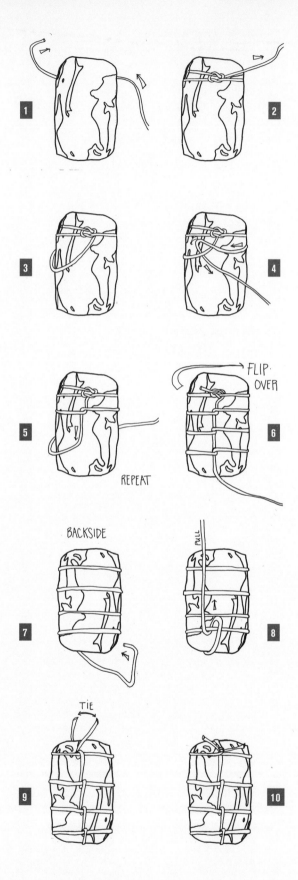

CHICKEN

PREPARING A CHICKEN FOR ROASTING

For the most basic way to prepare a chicken for roasting, see page 98.

BUTTERFLYING (SPATCHCOCKING) A CHICKEN

To butterfly the chicken, remove the backbone with a pair of sharp poultry shears or kitchen scissors and discard it. Press down in the center of the breast to flatten it. If it's not totally flat, flip the chicken skin-side down, and score the cartilage on the back of the breastbone. Flip the chicken skin-side up, and press down until the chicken is completely flat.

USE: Allows you to cook a whole bird faster since it is flattened out and has a larger surface area. Use in roasting or grilling recipes.

TRUSSING A TURKEY FOR ROASTING

With the bird breast-up and the tail of the bird toward you, center a piece of kitchen string around the back of the thighs then cross over joints and tighten to bring together. Wrap around end of legs and tie to secure closed.

USE: Allows a bird to cook more evenly, which is important with turkeys and other large birds.

CUTTING A CHICKEN INTO EIGHT PIECES

See page 100.

USE: Allows you to butcher a whole chicken yourself thus saving you money and increasing your knife skills.

CARVING A CHICKEN

Cut the chicken where the leg meets the breast.

Bend back the whole leg and push up on the joint to pull the leg piece away from the carcass.

Cut through the joint to remove the leg piece. Repeat on the opposite side to remove the second leg.

Use the tip of your knife to find the point where the thigh and drumstick meet and cut through the joint to separate into two pieces.

Use the tip of the knife to cut half of the breast off the breastbone. Pull the meat gently away from the carcass as you cut.

Remove the wing from the breast half at the joint then slice the breast piece for serving. Repeat with the other side.

1 Tuck the wing tips under the upper wing.

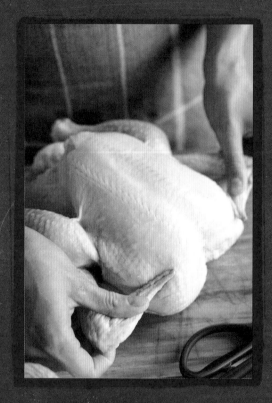

2 Wrap a piece of kitchen twine in a figure eight around the bottom of the legs.

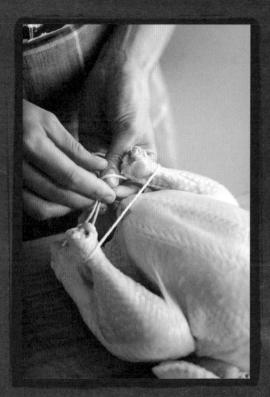 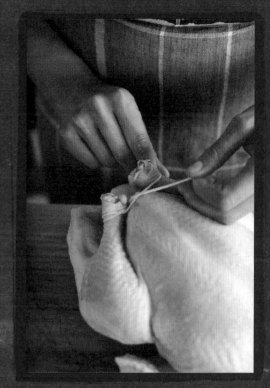

3 Tie to secure the string.

CUTTING A CHICKEN INTO EIGHT PIECES

1   Place the chicken, breast-side up, on the work surface. Score the skin between leg and breast to separate the two pieces.

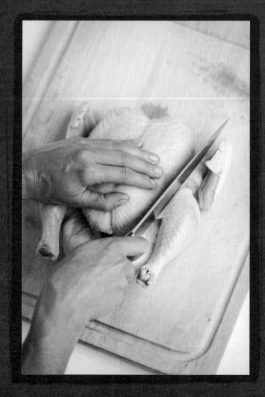

2 Pull the leg away from the body and, holding from behind the thigh, open the leg like a door, until the thigh pops out of the socket. Cut between the joints while pulling away the leg to detach it.

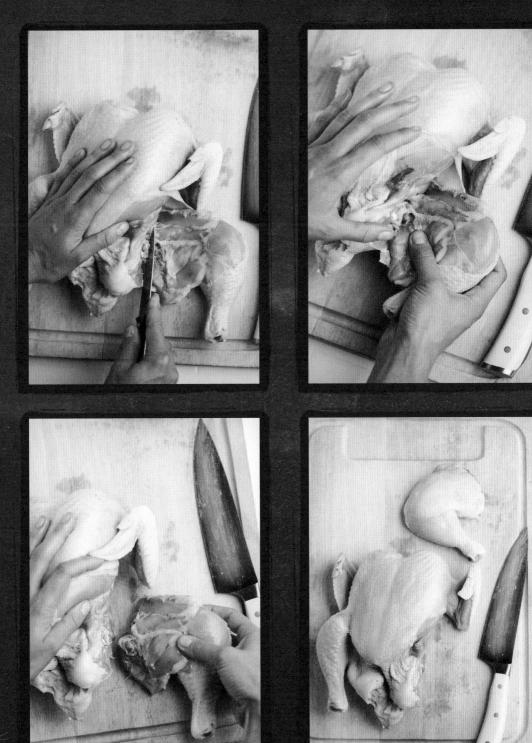

Repeat on other leg.

 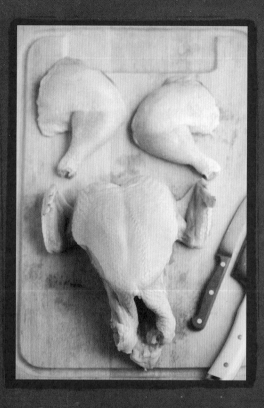

Pull the wing tip so the wing is fully extended and score at the joint attached to the breast. Place tip of the knife in the joint and twist gently until joint opens up; repeat on other wing.

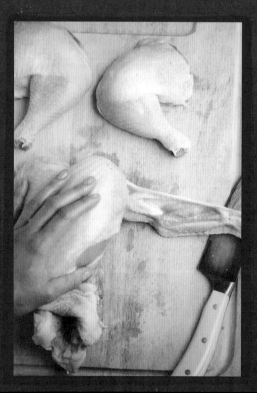 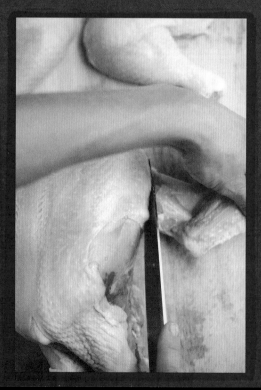

5 Rotate the chicken so it's breast-side up but perpendicular to the bottom of the counter. Pull up the end of the breast, and, using poultry shears, cut between the back of the breast and backbone to remove. Use shears as needed to remove any sinew.

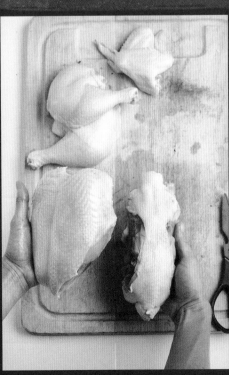

Flip the chicken, breast-side down, and score along the center of the breastbone with the tip of your knife. Push down on cartilage to break it, then crack it open with your hands. Cut through cartilage to split breast into two breast halves.

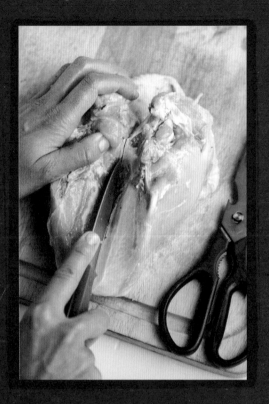

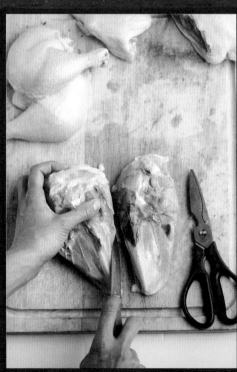

7 Cut legs at the joint along the white fat line to separate the drumstick from the thigh.

SEAFOOD

PEELING AND DEVEINING SHRIMP

Hold shrimp by the tail and peel off the shell. Using a paring knife, run the blade from head to tail along the back of the shrimp to expose the vein. Use the tip of the knife to pull out the vein.

SHUCKING AN OYSTER

Place a towel in your hand and hold the oyster, hinge-side outward. Wedge an oyster knife into the hinge and twist like a doorknob until you feel it pop. Slide the knife against the inside of each shell to detach the oyster.

SHUCKING A CLAM

Place a towel in your hand and hold the clam, hinge-side inward. Starting opposite the hinge, carefully slide a thin knife between the two half shells. Work the knife down toward the hinge and twist like a doorknob. Slide the knife against the inside of each shell to detach the clam.

FILLETING A FLAT FISH

Trim off the fins with kitchen scissors. Make a slit across the base of the tail. Place a knife under the tail and run it along the center to the head, keeping the knife as close to the bones as possible and lifting as you go. Repeat on the opposite side. Trim off the outer edge from each fillet.

FILLETING A ROUND FISH

Trim off the fins with kitchen scissors. Cut through the belly and around the gills but don't cut off the head. Insert a knife behind the fillet and cut along the length of the body, keeping the knife as close to the bones as possible. Lift up the meat and slice to separate from the bones. Turn over and repeat.

REMOVING PIN BONES FROM FISH

If you buy a large piece of fish, such as a side of salmon, be on the lookout for larger, inch-long bones, known as pin bones, which should be removed. To better expose the bones, drape a fillet or side over an inverted mixing bowl, flesh-side up. The tips of the pin bones will pop up and out, so they are easier to locate by eye or feel and to pull out by grasping with tweezers or needle-nose pliers.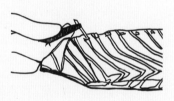

TIP: Pull out pin bones at an angle so you don't tear the fish flesh.

SKINNING A FISH FILLET

Set fish on the work surface, skin-side down. Take a sharp, thin knife (such as a fillet knife) and angle it away from you toward the skin and just begin to slice it away from the flesh. When you've pulled off a few inches, flip the fillet over. Use a paper towel to hold on to the fish skin with your free hand. With the blade of the knife angled toward the skin, push the knife away from you and pull the skin toward you. Move the skin and your knife in a fanning motion until the skin is removed.

FILLETING A WHOLE, COOKED FISH

1 Using a spoon, make notches behind the head and at the tail end of the fish.

2 Using a thin, flexible knife and a spoon, lift off the skin, then, with a serving spoon, push the fish down away from the backbone in one piece.

3 Lift off fillet, flip it over, and place it on serving platter, being sure to remove any excess bones.

4 Insert the knife under the bones at the tail and lift to remove the bone in one piece.

5 Scrape the bottom fillet free of any bones, peel off the bottom skin, and serve.

Fundamental Recipes

Each of these basic recipes provides a foundation for many meals, as well as a small tutorial on cooking to help you on your way.

CHICKEN STOCK

METHOD: Place a **chicken carcass** (any parts except the liver) in a stockpot and cover with a few inches of **water**. Bring to a boil and skim off any impurities. Decrease the heat so the liquid is at a simmer, and add any **vegetable scraps** you have on hand (such as carrots, celery, onion), a few **peppercorns**, and a **bay leaf**. Simmer until the liquid is the desired strength, anywhere from 1 to 3 hours. Pass the stock through a sieve and discard the solids.

TIP: Put the stock into small containers (or nest in an ice bath) so it can cool down within 2 hours. Skim off any fat, divide into manageable portions, and refrigerate or freeze as desired.

BOILED POTATOES

Boil potatoes in their skins as they will hold together better, and you can use the skins in the final dish. You can use this same technique for other roots and tubers like carrots, parsnips, sweet potatoes, turnips, and rutabaga.

METHOD: Place **potatoes** in a large pot and add enough cold **water** to cover by at least 1 inch. Add enough **salt** to give the water a salty taste and bring to a boil. Boil until the potatoes are knife-tender, anywhere from 10 to 15 minutes for smaller potatoes and up to 45 minutes for larger potatoes.

FLAVOR: It's hard to beat the classic—simply tossing the potatoes with butter, salt, and fresh herbs. Other options include tossing them with butter browned with herbs (see Browning Butter, page 93); garlic-infused oil; roasted red peppers and cilantro; or lemon juice, cumin, and chopped chiles.

TIP: You can store boiled, drained potatoes in the refrigerator for up to 2 days—ideal for potato salad. Or warm them back up by dunking in boiling water or in the microwave (be sure to pierce first) until heated through.

BAKED POTATO

This technique is for baking one or multiple potatoes at a time, and can also be used for roasting other root and tuber vegetables like sweet potatoes, beets (though you'll want to remove the skin after roasting), turnips, and rutabaga.

METHOD: Arrange a rack in the upper third of the oven and heat to 400°F/200°C/gas 6. Score an X on one side of the **potato**, wrap the potato in aluminum foil, and place on the oven rack. Bake until a fork can easily pierce the potato (it should be as soft as room-temperature butter). Remove the foil and serve.

TIP: If you're baking sweet potatoes, the juices may bubble up through the foil and drip on the oven so you may want to place a cookie or rimmed baking sheet one rack below the potatoes.

ROASTED POTATOES

Ever in search of a potato that is crisp on the outside and soft in the middle, I came up with this technique that yields amazing texture.

METHOD: Arrange a rack in the bottom of the oven and heat to 450°F/230°C/gas 8. Meanwhile, wash and dry the **potatoes** thoroughly. Dice the potatoes (skin on), toss with enough oil to coat them, and season with **salt** and freshly ground **black pepper**. When the oven is heated, coat the bottom of a roasting pan or baking dish with **oil**, then

heat briefly in the oven (the oil's surface will have a shimmering appearance when it's ready). Add the potatoes to the pan and carefully turn to coat. (This is the scariest part of the process because the pan is hot, so be careful.) Arrange the potatoes in one layer in the pan and place in the oven on the bottom rack. Roast the potatoes, checking them every 10 minutes, and, using a flat-sided spatula, scrape and turn them so they get well roasted on all sides (the goal is for a crisp skin on the outside and fluffiness within so do your best not to mess up the potato crispy bits). The potatoes are done when a fork can easily pierce the potato (it should be as soft as room-temperature butter), about 45 minutes total.

TIP: This technique works with other root vegetables such as parsnips and carrots.

You can make these potatoes up to 1 hour in advance; just rewarm before serving.

MASHED POTATOES

There are countless ways to make good mashed potatoes and to flavor them, so it's the perfect place to flex your experimental muscles. Here is a no-fail technique that's begging to be riffed.

METHOD: Steam, boil, or bake (at 350°F/180°C/gas 4) 2 lb/910 g of a good **baking potato** such as russet, Idaho, or Yukon gold (they'll hold their shape best during cooking) until tender. Drain, as needed, and return to the pot or place in a large bowl. Depending on the texture you want, you can mash them with a potato masher (for a coarser texture) or remove the skins and pass them through a potato ricer (for an airy texture) or a food mill (for a smooth texture). Once the potatoes are mashed, drizzle in

4 tbsp/55 g melted **unsalted butter** or **olive oil** and fold in gently until just combined. Add 1 cup/240 ml warmed **chicken or vegetable broth or half-and-half** and stir until just combined. Season with **salt** and freshly ground **black pepper**.

TIP: Mashed potatoes are best served fresh but can be made up to 1 hour in advance by covering with aluminum foil and placing in a water bath (see Melting Chocolate, page 93) over a low burner. Alternatively, smooth in a buttered baking dish, drizzle melted butter over the top, cover with foil, and hold in a 300°F/150°C/gas 2 oven.

POT BEANS

To soak or not to soak? That is the eternal bean question. How fresh the beans are is the determining factor. If you're using dried beans from the farmers' market, you don't really need to soak them, but if they've been sitting on some market shelf too long to admit, then soak away to get rid of any unwanted side effects. Whatever you decide, just do your best to stay away from the canned variety as they're often lacking in the texture department.

To soak, place the beans in enough water to cover by 2 in/5 cm and let sit at room temperature for at least 2 hours, but not more than 24 hours.

METHOD: Heat a medium pot over medium heat and add enough **oil, bacon drippings, or lard** to coat the bottom of the pot. When the oil shimmers, add ½ diced **onion** and two smashed **garlic** cloves, season with a pinch of **salt**, and stir to coat in the oil. Cook, stirring once or twice, until the onion is translucent and softened, about 5 minutes.

Add the **beans** and their soaking liquid and bring to a boil. When it boils, skim the surface of any impurities. Decrease the heat to low and let the beans just simmer, uncovered. Let them simmer until they are tender and easy to bite through, anywhere from 30 minutes to 1½ hours, depending on the bean variety. At this point you can season with salt and add acidic ingredients like molasses, tomatoes, or vinegar.

TIP: Anything you put into the bean cooking liquid will flavor the final dish. The most classic would be a bay leaf, some onions studded with a few cloves, some garlic, and a few peppercorns, but try other spices, herbs, and aromatics like cinnamon, star anise, rosemary, thyme, carrots, or even dried chiles.

The bean cooking liquid (a.k.a. liqueur) has tons of flavor so don't throw it out. Instead add some of it to your bean recipes from soups to pastas to purees for a deeper bean flavor in the final dish.

COOKING PASTA

METHOD: Cook **pasta** in a large pot with enough water for it to move around freely (about 1 lb/455 g pasta to 3 to 4 qt/3 to 4 L of water). Add enough **salt** so that the water just tastes salty and bring to a boil. Add the pasta and stir a few times so it doesn't stick together. Cook, uncovered, at a boil until the pasta is al dente—firm, but with no starchiness. Drain, but don't rinse.

TIP: Reserve a few cups of the pasta water before draining the pasta. When mixing the pasta into the sauce add the reserved cooking water as needed to help the sauce coat the pasta.

COOKING LONG-GRAIN WHITE BASMATI OR JASMINE RICE

RATIO: 1 cup/215 g rice to 1¾ cups/420 ml water or broth

METHOD: Bring 1¾ cups/420 ml **water** to a boil with ½ teaspoon **kosher salt** in a medium saucepan. Add 1 cup/215 g **rice**, stir briefly, cover, and cook over lowest heat until all the water is absorbed, 15 to 20 minutes (the rice will show steam holes when done). Let sit, covered, for 5 to 10 minutes before serving. Fluff with a fork and serve.

LONG-GRAIN BROWN RICE

Bring 2¼ cups/600 ml **water** to a boil with ½ teaspoon **kosher salt** in a medium sauce-pan. Add 1 cup/215 g **brown rice**, stir briefly, cover, and cook over lowest heat until all the water is absorbed, 30 to 40 minutes (the rice will show steam holes when done). Let sit, covered, for 5 to 10 minutes before serving. Fluff with a fork and serve.

BASIC PILAF

This method dates back to ancient Persia and is used in recipes throughout the Middle East. This is the dish at its most basic but it lends well to variety.

Heat **oil** in a frying pan over medium heat. Add chopped **onion** and cook until browned. Add some **ground spices** (such as cumin, coriander, mustard, or ginger) and cook until fragrant. Stir in the **grain**, such as long-grain white rice, pearled barley, or semi-pearled farro, and add the **liquid** needed to cook that grain (2 parts liquid to 1 part grain works for most grains). Cover and simmer until the liquid is absorbed.

BASIC RISOTTO

This is essentially a twist on a pilaf, so once you've got that down, it's just a few more stirs to make risotto. Try this out on your own time before attempting it in front of guests. You'll gain confidence when you realize that it's really not all that difficult.

METHOD: Heat 1 qt/1 L **stock or broth** in a saucepan over low heat and keep warm. In a separate saucepan, heat a glug of **oil** over medium-low heat. Add finely chopped **onion** and **garlic** and cook until soft but not colored. Add 2 cups/375 g **medium-grain rice** (such as Arborio) or a grain (try barley or farro) and stir until the grain is coated and, if rice, slightly translucent. Add a glass of **wine or water** to deglaze the pan and cook until the alcohol smell has cooked off. Add 1 ladle of warm stock and stir frequently, until the liquid is almost totally absorbed. Continue adding stock until the rice is al dente (soft, but with texture). Remove from the heat and stir in a few tablespoons of **olive oil or butter** and some grated **Parmesan**. Cover and let sit a few minutes before serving.

TIPS: Don't wash your rice before cooking or it will take away the starch that gives the dish its texture.

Make sure to use medium-grain rice.

Cook risotto in a medium, heavy-bottomed saucepan.

COOKING ANY WHOLE GRAIN

Cook absolutely any grain as you would pasta, in lots of salted simmering water. The grain is done when it's al dente (firm, but with no starchiness). Most grains cook in10 to 20 minutes by this method.

TIP: Grains are known for their versatility so experiment away. A lot of the same flavor combinations you'd use for rice will work with these grains. Just know that the larger grains have a heartier flavor so they will hold up to bold flavors. Grains can be made in advance and used as needed. The heartier grains, such as barley, bulgur, farro, and spelt travel well so they're best for picnics. And don't just think of grains as sides. With just a little added protein, they can make a hearty meal.

COUSCOUS

RATIO: 1 cup/100 g couscous to 1½ cups/ 360 ml liquid (water or broth)

YIELD: 1 cup/100 g yields 2 servings

METHOD: Bring 1½ cups/360 ml **water or broth** to a boil with a pinch of salt, a drizzle of **oil**, and, as desired, a smashed clove of **garlic** and any **spices** (a pinch of paprika, cumin, or coriander are classic). Place **couscous** in a bowl and when the water boils, stir the boiling water into the couscous (you can add some dried fruit if you like at this point). Cover and let steam for a few minutes until the water is absorbed. Fluff with a fork and add in any other ingredients (toasted nuts or herbs) and serve.

POLENTA

RATIO: 1 cup/100 g corn grits (a.k.a. polenta) to 3 cups/720 ml water or broth

YIELD: 1 cup/100 g yields 2 to 3 servings

METHOD: Bring **water or broth** to a boil in a large saucepan and add a pinch of **salt**. Stirring constantly, pour in the **polenta** and decrease the heat to low. Simmer, partially covered, stirring every few minutes to make sure it doesn't stick, until the polenta is very thick. Stir in a nob of **butter or a drizzle of oil** and, if desired, serve topped with tomato sauce and grated cheese.

TIP: Many recipes say you need to constantly stir polenta while it cooks. Instead, I partially cover it and stir it every few minutes and still get top-notch results.

STEAMED VEGETABLES

Steaming is often overlooked, although it is the simplest and healthiest way to cook.

METHOD: Place a few inches of water in a pot with a tight-fitting lid. Bring the **water** to a simmer over medium-high heat. Place **veggies** to be steamed in a steamer basket, a steamer inset, or in a sieve, cover, and steam until the vegetables are al dente (easily pierced with a knife).

TIP: Don't let the water boil or the vegetables will cook unevenly.

ROASTED VEGETABLES

METHOD: Heat the oven to 450°F/230°C/gas 8 and arrange a rack in the middle. Place diced **vegetables** on a rimmed baking sheet, drizzle with **oil**, season well with **salt** and freshly ground **black pepper**, and toss to coat. Roast until golden brown and tender when pierced with a knife, 15 to 45 minutes.

VEGETABLE SOUP

METHOD: Heat **olive oil** in a large saucepan or Dutch oven over medium-high heat until shimmering. Add chopped **onion**, season with **salt** and **pepper**, and cook, stirring occasionally, until translucent. Add chopped **celery, carrots,** and **garlic**, season with **salt** and **pepper**, and cook, stirring occasionally, until the garlic is fragrant, about 2 minutes. Add any **hearty vegetables** (such as cabbage and fennel) and a **bay leaf**. Season again with salt and pepper and cook an additional 5 minutes. If using, add **wine or vermouth** (for some acidity) and cook, stirring occasionally, until the alcohol smell has cooked off, about 2 minutes. Add diced potatoes (if using), some **broth or water** to cover, and let the soup come to a boil. Decrease the heat to low and gently simmer, uncovered, until the potatoes can be easily pierced with a fork. Stir in any quick-cooking vegetables such as peas and cook until tender. Stir in any herbs, season with salt and pepper, and serve.

WILTED GREENS

METHOD: Heat olive oil in a large pot over medium heat. Add **greens** in batches, cover, and cook until wilted. You'll need about 1½ to 2 lb/680 to 900 g for 4 servings.

TIP: You can do this with almost any green, like spinach, chard, or escarole.

QUICK BRAISED GREENS

METHOD: Bring a large pot of heavily **salted water** to a boil. Add a few handfuls of stemmed **greens** and cook until wilted and tender, about 5 minutes. Drain, coarsely chop, and set aside. Meanwhile, heat **oil** in a large frying pan over medium heat. Add chopped **onion** and cook until softened, about 4 minutes. Add the greens and turn to coat well. Add enough **broth** to cover the greens and cook until the greens are very tender. Season with **salt** and freshly ground **black pepper** and serve.

ROASTED GARLIC

METHOD: Heat the oven to 400°F/200°C/gas 6 and arrange a rack in the middle. Lop off the top of a **garlic head** so that cloves are just exposed. Wrap the garlic head in aluminum foil, drizzle with some **oil**, and close foil around garlic. Roast until the garlic cloves pop out of their skins when pushed and are golden brown.

CARAMELIZED ONIONS

METHOD: Heat some **oil** in a medium sauce-pan over medium heat. When it shimmers, add 1 or 2 thinly sliced **onions** and cook, undisturbed, until the onions are translucent and soft. Season with a big pinch of **salt** and continue to cook, stirring rarely, until the onions are very browned and soft.

TIP: If the onions stick, hit them with a little water, broth, or wine, and scrape up the pan to incorporate any browned bits.

BASIC TOMATO SAUCE

METHOD: Add enough **oil** to a medium saucepan to coat the bottom then place over medium heat. When it shimmers, add ½ diced **onion**, season well with **salt** and freshly ground **black pepper**, and cook until soft and translucent. Add a few cloves of sliced **garlic** and cook, stirring occasionally, until fragrant. Add a **can of diced tomatoes with juice or pureed tomatoes** and bring to a boil. Decrease the heat to a simmer, and cook, stirring occasionally, until the sauce is slightly thickened and flavors are melded, 15 to 20 minutes.

BAKED EGGS

METHOD: Heat the broiler and arrange a rack in the middle of the oven. Coat the insides of ramekins with **butter**, then crack an **egg** into each. Top with a drizzle of **cream**, place them on a rimmed baking sheet and bake, rotating pan halfway through baking, until the whites are just set but yolks are still runny, 5 to 8 minutes.

TIP: Add wilted greens, Canadian bacon, smoked fish, or diced tomatoes to the ramekins before adding the eggs. Instead of cream, top with pesto or some cheese before broiling.

BOILED EGGS

METHOD: Place an **egg** in a saucepan and cover with 2 in/5 cm of **water**. **Salt** the water then bring to a boil over medium heat. As soon as the water boils, turn off the heat, and cover the saucepan. Let sit 4 minutes for a soft-boiled egg and 10 to 12 minutes for a hard-boiled egg. Drain the cooked eggs and return them to the pan. Cover the pan and shake it to crack the shell. Dunk in an ice water bath for a few minutes, then peel. The method and timing are the same if you are boiling more than one egg at at time.

TIP: Older eggs (at least 1 week old) peel better than fresher eggs because there's less air in the shell.

FRIED OR OVEREASY EGGS

METHOD: Heat **oil** in a small nonstick frying pan over medium-low heat. When it shimmers, crack an **egg** into the pan, cover, and cook until set on the bottom. For overeasy eggs, carefully flip the egg and cook until just set.

POACHED EGGS

METHOD: Bring about 8 cups/2 L (at least 2 in/5 cm) of **water** to a simmer in a medium frying pan and add a capful of **vinegar**. Break each **egg** into a separate small cup or ramekin. Gently slide the eggs into the simmering water, one at a time. Cook 2 eggs at a time. Cook until the whites are just set, about 3 minutes.

TIP: To reheat poached eggs, place in gently simmering water for a few minutes until heated through.

SCRAMBLED EGGS

METHOD: Combine **eggs**, a drizzle of **half-and-half**, and **salt** in a medium bowl and whisk until very smooth. Melt **butter** in a large nonstick frying pan over medium-high heat. When foaming subsides, add the egg mixture. Cook while gently pushing, lifting, and folding from one side of the pan to the other until the eggs are set but still slightly wet. Add any cooked or fresh **veggies** to the pan, sprinkle with **herbs** and **cheese** (if using), and gently mix through. Season with **salt** and freshly ground **black pepper** and serve.

TIP: Plan on 3 eggs per person.

OMELET

METHOD: Combine **eggs, half-and-half,** and **salt** in a medium bowl and whisk until very smooth. Melt **butter** in a large nonstick frying pan over medium-high heat. When foaming subsides, add the egg mixture and swirl to coat the pan. As the eggs start to set, use a rubber spatula to gently push aside a small patch of cooked egg and tilt the pan so that uncooked egg fills in the gap. Repeat, working your way around the pan until the eggs have reached the consistency you like. Add the **filling** to one side of the eggs, season with **salt** and freshly ground **black pepper**, sprinkle **cheese** and chopped fresh **cilantro** (if using) over the filling, and fold the omelet over the top. Slide onto the plate and serve.

TIP: Plan on 2 eggs per person.

FRITTATA

METHOD: Heat the broiler to high and arrange a rack in the upper third of the oven. In a large bowl, whisk together **eggs**, some grated **cheese** (as desired), **salt**, and freshly ground **black pepper** until thoroughly combined. In a large ovenproof frying pan, heat some oil or butter over medium-high heat. When it foams, add **onion, garlic, or any other vegetables**, season well with **salt** and freshly ground **black pepper**, and cook, stirring occasionally, until cooked through, about 5 minutes. Stir in **herbs**, decrease heat to low, pour in the egg mixture, and cook until a 1-in/2.5-cm border of egg mixture is set. Place the pan in the oven and broil until some spots are browned and eggs are just set, about 2 minutes.

POACHED CHICKEN

METHOD: Put 4 to 5 lb/1.8 to 2.3 kg of **chicken parts** in a large pot and cover with **water** by a few inches. Add a few **peppercorns**, a **bay leaf**, a smashed **garlic clove**, ½ **onion**, a roughly chopped **carrot, celery stalk**, and a few **parsley stems**. Bring to a boil over medium-high heat. Decrease the heat to low, cover, and simmer until the chicken's juices are running clear, the meat is no longer pink, and an instant-read thermometer inserted into the thickest part of the meat (without touching bone) reads 165°F/74°C. Remove from the heat and use as desired.

ROAST CHICKEN

In a small bowl, mix together ¼ cup/120 ml **oil** and 1 tablespoon **kosher salt**. Put a 4- to 6-lb/2- to 3-kg **chicken** in a large baking dish or plastic bag, loosen the skin from the breast and legs of the chicken and, using your hands, spread a good part of the salt mixture across the meat under the skin. Rub the remaining mixture inside the chicken cavity and over the skin. Tie the legs together with kitchen twine. Loosely cover, refrigerate, and let marinate 30 minutes or up to 24 hours. Arrange a rack in the middle of the oven and heat the oven to 400°F/200°C/ gas 6. Remove the chicken from the refrigerator and pat dry with paper towels. Let the chicken sit at room temperature while the oven warms up, 20 to 30 minutes. When the oven is ready, place the chicken, breast-side up, on a roasting rack (or a bed of halved onions or heads of garlic) in a roasting pan

and roast until the skin is golden brown, about 1 hour. Rotate chicken and continue roasting until the chicken is well browned, juices run clear when the inner thigh is pierced with a knife, the legs move easily in the joint, and an instant-read thermometer inserted into the thickest portion of the thigh registers 160°F to 165°F/70°C to 74°C, another 40 to 50 minutes. Let the chicken rest at least 10 to 15 minutes before carving and serving.

SEARED STEAK

METHOD: Pat the **steak** dry with paper towels, coat with **oil**, and set aside at room temperature for at least 5 minutes. Heat a large, seasoned cast-iron skillet or large frying pan over medium-high heat until hot, but not smoking. Place the steak in the pan and cook, undisturbed, until well-browned on the first side. Flip and cook to desired doneness (see page 85). Remove steak to a dish and let rest 10 minutes before serving.

GRILLED MEAT

METHOD: Pat **meat** dry with paper towels, coat with **oil**, and set aside to come to room temperature, at least 5 minutes. Heat a lightly oiled grill or grill pan to medium-high heat. When heated, add meat and cook, undisturbed until well browned on the first side. Flip and cook to desired doneness (see page 85). Remove steak to a dish and let rest 10 minutes before serving.

ROAST MEAT

Heat the oven to 450°F/230°C/gas 8 and arrange a rack in the middle of the oven. Remove the **meat** from the refrigerator, season with **oil, salt**, and freshly ground **pepper**, and let rest at room temperature while the oven heats up. When the oven is ready, put the meat in a roasting pan and roast until golden-brown and cooked to desired doneness (see page 85).

BRAISED MEAT

Heat some **oil** in a 3- to 4-qt/3- to 4-L Dutch oven or saucepan over medium heat. When the oil is hot but not smoking, add the **meat** and cook until well browned. Flip and repeat on the other side. Transfer the meat to a plate and drain off all but 1 tablespoon of the drippings. Return the pan to the stove on medium heat, add chopped **onions or garlic** (or both), season with **salt** and freshly ground **black pepper**, and cook until golden and softened. Add **liquid** (wine, water, or broth) and scrape the pan to incorporate any browned bits. Add meat, bring to a boil, and then decrease the heat to medium-low. Cover and cook until the meat is cooked through and shreds easily with a fork.

SEARED FISH

METHOD: Liberally season **fish fillets** (with skin) with **oil, salt**, and **pepper**. Heat a large heavy-bottomed pan over high heat. (The pan is heated when the fish sizzles loudly as it hits the pan.) Place the fish in the pan, skin-side down, and decrease the heat to medium. Do not move fillets. Cook until well browned and cooked about three-fourths of the way through. Turn fillets and cook just until opaque in the center.

CARAMEL SAUCE

METHOD: Combine 1 cup/200 g **granulated sugar** and ¼ cup/120 ml **water** in a large saucepan and stir until the mixture resembles wet sand. Place over medium-high heat and bring to a boil. Let boil until the mixture turns dark amber in color and smells toasted, 5 to 7 minutes. Immediately remove from the heat, carefully pour in a few spoonfuls of **heavy cream**, and whisk until evenly incorporated. Return the saucepan to the stove and place over medium-low heat to keep warm. The caramel can crystallize while cooking. To avoid this, make sure all the utensils are clean; don't stir the caramel once the sugar dissolves (just swirl the pan to help it cook evenly); and, for extra insurance, you can wash down the sides (inside) of the pan with a brush dipped in water.

TOASTING NUTS OR COCONUT

METHOD: Preheat the oven to 350°F/175°C. Spread the nuts or coconut evenly on a baking sheet. Bake, stirring once or twice, until browned, 5 to 8 minutes for coconut, or 8 to 12 minutes for nuts. Set aside to cool.

COOKING CAPERS CRACKED

No matter how well you plan and prepare for cooking, there may still be a few snafus from time to time. From what to do when you run out of an ingredient to how to stop food from sticking to the pan, here are the solutions to common cooking problems.

SUBSTITUTIONS

SPICES AND HERBS

To swap dried herbs for fresh, use a 3:1 ratio:
1 tablespoon fresh herbs = 1 teaspoon dried.

The best way to swap herbs and spices is to understand their flavors (see pages 42 and 47) and use similarly flavored ingredients. For herbs, generally, you want to swap tender herbs for other tender herbs and woody herbs for other woody herbs.

Complementary herb substitutions

- Basil and mint
- Rosemary and sage
- Marjoram and thyme
- Fennel fronds and dill
- Parsley and chervil

OIL

Flavor and smoke point (see page 56) are the most important considerations when choosing which oil to use. An olive oil with assertive flavor will overwhelm a recipe with delicate flavors. Likewise, don't use olive oil for frying because its low smoke point means it would break down and have off flavors.

DAIRY

BUTTERMILK If you don't have buttermilk, stir together 1 cup/240 ml whole milk with 1 tablespoon lemon juice or vinegar and let it sit a few minutes before using.

WHOLE MILK If you don't have whole milk, you can substitute equal parts skim milk and half-and-half.

HALF-AND-HALF If you can't find half-and-half, use a combination of 3 parts whole milk and 1 part heavy cream.

SOUR CREAM Whole milk yogurt can be used in place of sour cream in recipes. Use Greek yogurt in recipes where the dish should have a thick texture (such as dips).

SALT

For types of salt, check out page 57. Remember that different salts vary in their levels of saltiness so be careful when substituting.
1 tablespoon kosher salt =
1 teaspoon table salt or 1½ teaspoons sea salt.

SUGAR

BROWN SUGAR Mix together 1 cup/200 g granulated sugar with 1 tablespoon molasses.

POWDERED SUGAR In a food processor, pulse together 1 cup/200 g granulated sugar with 1 tablespoon cornstarch until blended and fine textured.

COMMON COOKING ISSUES

You know how it goes, the best laid plans don't always turn out. So, if you've hit a culinary hiccup, check these fixes to common cooking issues before throwing it all away.

BROKEN MAYONNAISE OR OTHER EMULSIFIED SAUCE To fix a broken emulsion (it will seem curdled), put 1 teaspoon water in a bowl. Whisk the broken sauce into the water until it's smooth and creamy. (Use cold water if the sauce is warm and warm water if it's cold.)

CREAM IS CODDLED Not the most elegant solution but it works: place the sauce in a blender and puree until the sauce comes back together. Run it through a sieve to get rid of any overcooked bits.

OVER-WHIPPED CREAM Your cream is over-whipped if it looks grainy and separated. To fix it, add a few tablespoons of cream to the beaten cream and carefully whip by hand until it is back to the proper consistency.

FOOD STICKS TO THE PAN This is usually a result of adding food to the pan before the pan is properly heated. Let the pan warm up (without any fat or anything) for at least 3 minutes so the metal can expand, which helps prevent the food from sticking.

FOOD WON'T BROWN Most likely this is due to one of three things: the pan isn't adequately hot; you've overcrowded the pan so your food is steaming instead of browning; or you keep moving the food so it doesn't have a chance to do its thing.

SAUCE IS LIQUIDY You can reduce it down if it's a sauce or something else that you've been simmering. (Just remember that saltiness and flavors will intensify as you reduce, so you'll have to balance them out.) If you just want thickness and like the flavor as is, whisk in a slurry, which is a mixture of 1 tablespoon flour with 2 tablespoons water for every 2 cups/480 ml of liquid, and boil to thicken. If the dish needs more richness, stir in some cream and simmer until desired thickness.

FINISHED PASTA DISH IS DRIED OUT Save a few cups of the pasta cooking water and add it to the sauce when mixing the pasta for a better-coating sauce that won't dry out as easily. Add more liquid than you think you'll want and cook the pasta briefly in the sauce so that the liquid just coats the pasta but a bit of liquid is pooling in the bottom of the pot.

MEAT DIDN'T COOK EVENLY Be sure to let meat and poultry (especially large roasts and birds) sit at room temperature before cooking. Steaks can sit 5 to 10 minutes while roasts can sit 20 to 30 minutes, while the oven or grill heats up.

ROAST LOST ALL ITS JUICES The meat most likely didn't rest before it was sliced so dip sliced meat in pan juices, sauce, or broth before serving. Let steaks rest 5 minutes before serving and roasts 15 to 30 minutes (tent with aluminum foil to keep warm).

BRAISED MEAT WAS DRY Again, toss it with braising liquid, sauce, or broth. Next time, let the meat cool off in the liquid or it may get dry.

TOO SALTY You have a few options. If you've just dumped in salt by mistake, then try to fish it out. If it's too salty when you're taste testing, then you can balance it out with something acidic (such as lemon juice, vinegar, or yogurt). If it is a sauce, soup, or some other liquid, you can dilute it with more water or (non-salty) liquids.

COOKIE ALTERATIONS

FOR CHEWIER COOKIES Use melted butter in place of other fats.

FOR THIN COOKIES Add more sugar for a crisp, brittle texture.

FOR CAKEY COOKIES Add more egg yolks for a richer texture and more egg whites for a drier, puffier cookie.

PART 3
THE RECIPES

Now that you've mastered shopping, storing, and shucking, it's time to fire up the stove.

Within these chapters is an assortment of recipes I crafted to both teach and inspire you. True to my food philosophy, the recipes are healthful, based on seasonal ingredients, and have a variety of flavor combinations that draw from my life experiences.

Each chapter focuses on a different food and each recipe centers on a different technique. Before you start worrying this is going to be antiseptic basic cooking, don't worry, because it's not. Some recipes teach a basic technique but are loaded with interesting ingredients and flavors, while others use more quotidian ingredients in a creative way.

I've put a lot of thought into the wheres, whys, and hows of these recipes, but there's only so much I can write and encourage before it's up to you to get into the kitchen and have fun with it.

So, peruse the recipes, read the pointers, and, most importantly, enjoy the process. As with anything else in life, if you can't laugh at yourself while doing it, you're taking it too seriously.

Oh, and know that there is an underlying goal in this part of the book. If you cook your way through these recipes, you'll not only become deft in the kitchen, but also daring, because there is an assortment of techniques, ingredients, and recipes that aim to be both approachable and aspirational.

So, cook away, and once you're feeling comfortable with your whisking and weighing, head to the last section of the book, where you'll learn to take what you know and make it your own.

DIFFICULTY
Easy/Medium

YIELD
6 to 8 servings

TOTAL TIME
50 minutes

HANDS-ON TIME
25 minutes

Admit it, you've eaten your fair share of last night's pizza for breakfast. Instead of warming up leftovers, get a fresh start with this breakfast pizza. And, if the urge for reheated pizza hits you, there's always lunch.

TAKEAWAYS: How to make pizza; how to render pancetta.
RECIPE WITHIN A RECIPE: Use the wilted spinach mixture as a simple side.

If possible, buy a 5-oz/142-g piece of pancetta because you'll be able to cut it as desired. To make it easier to handle, freeze the pancetta briefly (5 to 15 minutes), then dice with a sharp knife.

🕐 If you have the time, make your own pizza dough (page 163); though, if you're in a time crunch, store-bought dough will work perfectly well.

"BACON" AND EGG BREAKFAST PIZZA

1 tbsp **olive oil**, plus more for the baking sheet

5 oz/142 g piece **of pancetta, cut in small dice** (about 1 cup)

½ **yellow onion, halved and thinly sliced**

Kosher salt and freshly ground black pepper

5 oz/142 g **cremini or button mushrooms, stemmed and thinly sliced**

5 oz/142 g **baby spinach, chard, or beet greens (stemmed and finely chopped)**

Flour, for rolling the dough

1 lb/455 g **fresh pizza dough**

5 oz/142 g **Fontina or Taleggio cheese, shredded**

1 **large egg, for garnish (optional)**

Heat the oven to 450°F/230°C/gas 8 and arrange a rack in the middle. Line a plate with paper towels and set aside. Meanwhile, heat the oil in a large frying pan over medium heat. Add the pancetta and cook, stirring occasionally, until crisp and browned, about 10 minutes. Remove the pancetta to the prepared plate (reserve any drippings in the pan) and set aside to drain.

Discard all but 1 tablespoon of drippings (save extra drippings if making the egg garnish), return the pan to the stove over medium heat, and add the onion. Season with salt and pepper and cook, stirring occasionally, until the onion is golden brown. Stir in the mushrooms and cook, stirring occasionally, until browned, about 5 minutes. Stir in spinach, chard, or beet greens, cover, and cook briefly until wilted. Remove from the heat, stir in the pancetta and season with salt and freshly ground black pepper.

Drizzle olive oil on a baking sheet; set aside. On a clean, lightly floured surface, using a lightly floured rolling pin, roll the pizza dough on parchment paper into a 9-in/23-cm round or oval. Use the parchment to transfer the dough onto the prepared baking sheet. If you have time, let the dough rest for a few minutes before topping it. This will prevent it from shrinking during cooking. Pierce the dough in several places with a fork to prevent it from bubbling up unevenly.

Sprinkle the dough with cheese, then spread the pancetta mixture evenly on top of the cheese. Bake until the cheese is melted and the pizza is browned on the bottom, 20 to 25 minutes.

If desired top with a sunnyside-up egg: heat the reserved pancetta fat in a small frying pan and cook the egg, covered, over medium heat until set as desired, 3 to 5 minutes.

To serve, place the egg (if using) on top of the pizza, cut into slices and serve.

ROLLING PIN
Lightly flour the rolling pin before rolling the dough.

Use kitchen scissors, a pizza cutter, or a large sharp knife to slice the pizza easily.

RIFFS
- Swap Canadian bacon for the pancetta to make it a bit healthier.
- Use thinly sliced squash in place of the mushrooms.
- Lighten it up by nixing the meat and adding tomatoes.
- Replace the cheese with blue cheese.

DIFFICULTY
Medium

YIELD
4 to 6 servings

TOTAL TIME
1 hour

HANDS-ON TIME
25 minutes

Oatmeal gets a dash of refinement in this soufflé that's a heartier take on the French classic. With melty cheese, chewy oats, and chives, this is a soufflé that's both unexpected and comforting.

TAKEAWAY: How to make a soufflé
GOES WELL WITH: Serve on its own or with a simple green salad for lunch or dinner.

OATMEAL BREAKFAST SOUFFLÉ

4 tbsp/50 g **unsalted butter, plus extra for coating the dish**
Flour, for coating the dish
1½ cups/360 ml **whole milk**
1½ tsp **kosher salt**
1¼ cups/105 g **old-fashioned rolled oats**
1⅓ cups/115 g **grated aged Gouda or aged Cheddar cheese**
1 tsp **ground nutmeg**
½ cup **thinly sliced fresh chives**
4 **large egg yolks, at room temperature**
6 **large egg whites, at room temperature**

Make sure to buy old-fashioned rolled oats and not instant.

Older eggs whip up more easily and consistently than fresher eggs.

Using more egg whites than yolks makes the soufflé more stable and less likely to fall (see page 254).

Heat the oven to 375°F/190°C/gas 5, arrange a rack in the lower third of the oven, and place a baking sheet on the rack. Generously coat the inside of a 2-qt/2-L baking dish or a 6-cup/1.5-L soufflé dish with butter. Add a pinch of flour, rotate the dish to fully coat the inside with flour, then turn over and tap to get rid of any excess flour; set aside. (If it's particularly hot out, place the dish in the refrigerator until ready to use.)

Combine the milk, remaining 4 tablespoons of butter, and 1 teaspoon of the salt in a small saucepan and heat over medium-high until it just comes to a boil, about 5 minutes. Immediately add the oats and cook, stirring constantly, until thickened and oats are tender, about 5 minutes.

CONTINUED

Remove from the heat and add the cheese, the remaining ½ teaspoon of salt, nutmeg, and chives, stirring until the cheese is melted. Beat the yolks until smooth and slowly stir into the oatmeal mixture.

The bowl and whisk you use for the egg whites must be impeccably clean as any fat or oils will keep the whites from holding air.

Place the egg whites in the bowl of an electric mixer fitted with the whisk attachment and beat on medium speed until soft peaks form, about 3 minutes. Increase the speed to high and beat until the whites are glossy and peaks are droopy but hold onto a spatula (see page 92), about 1 minute more.

Add one-third of the beaten whites into the cheese mixture and stir until blended with no visible white streaks. Add the remaining whites and gently fold until just combined. Gently turn into the prepared dish.

Place the soufflé on the heated baking sheet. Bake until it is well risen, the top is browned, the edges appear dry, and the center is set (it doesn't move if lightly touched), about 30 minutes. Serve immediately.

My all-time favorite chocolate flavor is gianduja, a Northern Italian specialty made of hazelnut paste and chocolate. Here those nutty, cocoa-y flavors are mixed with Italian cream cheese for a decadent twist on French toast.

TAKEAWAY: How to make French toast.
RECIPE WITHIN A RECIPE: Use the filling anywhere you'd like a sweet cream cheese spread.

DIFFICULTY
Easy

YIELD
6 servings

TOTAL TIME
30 minutes

HANDS-ON TIME
10 minutes

HAZELNUT-COCOA FRENCH TOAST SANDWICHES

HAZELNUT-MASCARPONE FILLING

4 oz/115 g **mascarpone or cream cheese**

⅓ cup/120 g **hazelnut-cocoa spread**

1 tsp **pure vanilla extract**

¼ tsp **kosher salt**

¼ tsp **ground cinnamon**

12 slices **French bread, stale or toasted, each ½ in/12 mm thick**

CUSTARD

6 **large eggs**

1½ cups/360 ml **half-and-half**

¼ cup/50 g **granulated sugar**

1 tsp **pure vanilla extract**

½ tsp **kosher salt**

3 tbsp **unsalted butter, for cooking**

Toasted hazelnuts, for garnish

Maple syrup, for garnish

Whipped cream, for garnish

Mascarpone is an Italian cream cheese. If you can't find it, use regular cream cheese.

Get the best hazelnut spread you can find, as some varieties can be overly sweet and full of stabilizers. If you use a sweeter brand, like Nutella, add a bit more salt to balance out the filling flavor.

CONTINUED

Heat the oven to its lowest setting and place a baking sheet on the middle rack.

FOR THE HAZELNUT-MASCARPONE FILLING

In a bowl, stir the mascarpone with a spatula until spreadable then mix in the hazelnut-cocoa spread, vanilla, salt, and cinnamon until thoroughly combined. Spread the mixture evenly among 6 slices of the bread then top with the remaining 6 slices. Lay the "sandwiches" in a pan or dish large enough to hold them all snugly.

FOR THE CUSTARD

Whisk together custard ingredients until the eggs are broken up and evenly blended. Pour over the sandwiches and set aside until the majority of the custard has been soaked up, about 5 minutes. Rotate or flip the sandwiches as needed to evenly coat.

Melt 1 tablespoon of the butter in a large frying pan over medium-high heat. When the foaming subsides, add 2 of the sandwiches to the pan. Fry until golden brown on one side, flip with a spatula, and fry the other side. As the sandwiches are finished, move them to the oven while the rest are cooking. Repeat to cook the remaining sandwiches, using 1 tablespoon butter per batch for the pan.

Remove the baking sheet from the oven and transfer the French toast to plates. Serve topped with hazelnuts, maple syrup, and whipped cream, as desired.

Filling can be made up to 2 days ahead and refrigerated in an airtight container.

DIFFICULTY
Medium

YIELD
12 crêpes

TOTAL TIME
**40 minutes,
plus resting time**

HANDS-ON TIME
1 hour

This is a recipe for that short cross-season period in March and April when the last Meyer lemons are still around and the first berries are coming to market. It's a pitch-perfect combination of flavors, so be sure to celebrate it while you can.

TAKEAWAY: How to make crêpes and citrus curd.
RECIPE WITHIN A RECIPE: The curd can also be spread on scones (page 176), or shortcakes (page 362), or as a filling for fruit tarts.

CRÊPES WITH MEYER LEMON CURD AND FRESH BERRIES

MEYER LEMON CURD

6 **large egg yolks**

⅔ cup/130 g **granulated sugar**

1 tbsp **finely grated Meyer lemon zest**

½ cup/120 ml **freshly squeezed Meyer lemon juice**

¼ tsp **kosher salt**

½ cup/115 g **unsalted butter, cut into pieces**

CRÊPES

3 **large eggs, beaten**

4 tbsp/50 g **unsalted butter, melted**

1½ cups/360 ml **whole milk**

1½ cups/185 g **unbleached all-purpose flour**

½ tsp **kosher salt**

1 tsp **pure vanilla extract**

Canola, grapeseed, or peanut oil, for cooking the crêpes

4 cups (about 1 lb/455 g) **assorted berries**

Whipped cream, crème fraîche, or heavy cream, for garnish (optional)

Meyer lemons are a hybrid between a lemon and a mandarin or orange and are becomingly increasingly popular. If you can't find them, use equal parts lemon juice and either mandarin or orange juice.

Crème fraîche is a thickened cream that has a nutty, tangy flavor. If you can't find it, use a good-quality sour cream, or make your own.

FOR THE CURD

Combine the yolks, sugar, zest, juice, and salt in a medium saucepan and whisk until evenly combined. Cook over medium-low heat, stirring constantly, until thick enough to coat the back of a spoon, about 8 minutes. (When you draw your finger across the spoon, it should make a mark through the custard, which should not run back in on itself.)

Remove from the heat, transfer to a bowl, and stir in the butter, piece by piece, until fully melted and well combined. Cover with plastic wrap and refrigerate until cold, at least 1 hour. Meanwhile, make the crêpe batter.

FOR THE CRÊPES

Place the eggs in a large bowl and whisk until broken up. Add the melted butter, milk, flour, salt, and vanilla and whisk until moistened through and evenly combined, about 30 strokes. Cover and refrigerate for at least 30 minutes and up to 12 hours.

Heat a large nonstick pan over medium heat. Rub the pan with a paper towel dipped in oil. To check that the pan is properly heated, sprinkle the pan with a few drops of water—the water should "dance" around before evaporating.

Add ¼ cup/60 ml of batter, tilting the pan to evenly cover or spread out in a circle using the back of a spoon. Cook until just set and browned, 1 to 2 minutes. Flip and cook until the second side is lightly browned, about 1 minute more. Remove from the heat and repeat with remaining batter.

To serve, spread some curd over one-fourth of a crêpe and fold into fourths. Top with a scattering of berries and, if desired, whipped cream, crème fraîche, or a drizzle of cream.

Don't let the curd boil or overcook or the texture will be compromised.

The curd can be made up to 4 days ahead and refrigerated in an airtight container until ready to use.

The crêpes can be made up to 1 month ahead. Stack them and store, well wrapped in plastic wrap and enclosed in a zipper top bag or airtight container, in the freezer. Defrost and heat in a 300°F/150°C/gas 2 oven before using.

RIFFS

- Add a tropical fruit such as mango, papaya, or pineapple to the berries.
- Add a pinch of ground nutmeg, ginger, cinnamon, or allspice to the crêpe batter.
- Swap the hazelnut-mascarpone filling from the French toast (page 129) for the curd.
- Swap a flavored whipped cream such as the one used with the waffles (page 134) for the curd.
- Top with a scoop of vanilla ice cream (page 378) or fruit sorbet for a dessert version.

DIFFICULTY
Medium

YIELD
*4 to 6 servings
(12 Belgian-style
waffles)*

TOTAL TIME
*30 minutes, plus
8 to 24 hours
rising time*

HANDS-ON TIME
30 minutes

Yeasted waffles have fallen out of fashion because they require more planning and patience than other batters. But don't let that stop you, because they can be assembled the night before and left to rise while you sleep. It's well worth the wait because the long rise rewards you with an addictively crisp exterior, custardy interior, and a slight malty flavor.

TAKEAWAY: How to make yeast-raised waffles.

RECIPE WITHIN A RECIPE: Use the whipped cream for topping other sweet breakfast dishes like French toast (page 129) or desserts such as berries or grilled bread with chocolate.

CRISP YEASTED WAFFLES WITH COCOA WHIPPED CREAM

YEASTED WAFFLES

2 cups/480 ml **whole milk**

1 tbsp **sugar**

¼-oz packet **active dry yeast** (2¼ tsp)

2 cups/255 g **unbleached all-purpose flour**

6 tbsp/85 g **unsalted butter, melted**

1 tbsp **pure vanilla extract**

2 **large eggs, beaten**

2 tsp **kosher salt**

Make sure to get instant or active dry yeast. Don't use rapid rise yeast or the recipe will be off.

COCOA WHIPPED CREAM

1 cup/240 ml **cold heavy cream**

2 tbsp **Dutch-process cocoa powder**

1 tbsp **sugar**

2 tsp **pure vanilla extract**

Dutch-process cocoa powder is treated with alkali, which makes it more mellow in flavor and also gives it a richer texture.

Maple syrup, for serving

1½ cups/225g **fresh berries, for serving**

FOR THE WAFFLES

Heat the milk in a medium saucepan over low heat to 100°F/38°C to 115°F/45°C, about 5 minutes. Remove from the heat, pour into a small bowl, and stir in sugar and yeast; set aside until the mixture bubbles, about 5 minutes. (If the mixture does not bubble, either the liquid was not at the correct temperature or the yeast has expired and you need to replace it.)

Place the flour in a bowl large enough to let the batter double in size. Add the milk mixture, butter, and vanilla and whisk until thoroughly moistened and smooth. Cover with plastic wrap and refrigerate 8 hours or up to 24 hours.

When ready to use, remove batter from refrigerator and whisk in the eggs and salt. Let sit out at room temperature while you heat the waffle iron, at least 15 minutes.

Heat a waffle iron to medium heat according to the manufacturer's instructions. Cook the waffles until they are golden brown and cooked through, 4 to 5 minutes for each waffle. Repeat to use all batter. Meanwhile, make the topping.

FOR THE WHIPPED CREAM

Combine all ingredients in a stand mixer fitted with the whisk attachment and whip on low speed until smooth, about 30 seconds. Increase the speed to high and beat until medium peaks form, about 1 minute.

To serve, top waffles with maple syrup, whipped cream, and berries.

RIFF: Make with white whole-wheat flour for a healthier, nutty-flavored waffle.

You'll need to give yourself time to let these waffles rise adequately. Though it may seem like a long time to wait, it actually makes things easier since you can make the batter the night before and have it ready to go first thing in the morning.

Waffles are best eaten as they're made, but you can store them in a 200°F/95°C oven while you cook them all up.

WAFFLE IRON
Preheat the waffle iron for at least 15 minutes before using.

DIFFICULTY
Easy

YIELD
*Twelve ½-cup/
120 ml or twenty-
four ¼-cup/60-ml
pancakes*

TOTAL TIME
35 minutes

HANDS-ON TIME
30 minutes

Tangy, spiced, and nutty, these pancakes have everything you need to get your day started, including a caffeinated syrup.

TAKEAWAY: How to make pancakes.

TOASTED WALNUT PANCAKES WITH RED-EYE MAPLE SYRUP

RED-EYE MAPLE SYRUP

2 cups/480 ml **maple syrup**

4 tsp **coffee grounds**

BUTTERMILK-WALNUT PANCAKES

2 cups/255 g **unbleached all-purpose flour**

3 tbsp **sugar**

2 tsp **baking powder**

2 tsp **kosher salt**

½ tsp **baking soda**

½ tsp **ground cloves (optional)**

3 cups/720 ml **buttermilk, at room temperature**

6 tbsp/85 g **unsalted butter, melted**

2 **large eggs, at room temperature**

3 tbsp **unsalted butter, for cooking pancakes**

¾ cup/85 g **toasted walnuts, roughly chopped, for garnish**

FOR THE SYRUP

The syrup can be made up to 1 week in advance. Store, refrigerated, in an airtight container and warm before using.

Combine the maple syrup and coffee grounds in a medium pan. Bring to a simmer over medium heat and cook until warmed through, 2 to 3 minutes. Remove from the heat, strain through a fine mesh strainer, and serve warm.

FOR THE PANCAKES

Combine the flour, sugar, baking powder, salt, baking soda, and cloves, if using, in a large bowl and aerate with a whisk or fork to remove any lumps.

Combine the buttermilk, the 6 tablespoons melted butter, and eggs in a medium bowl and whisk until the eggs are broken up and smooth. Add the milk mixture to the dry ingredients and stir until just moistened through (there will be a few lumps left).

Heat a large seasoned cast-iron skillet, frying pan, or griddle over medium heat. To check that the pan is properly heated, sprinkle a few drops of water on the hot pan—the water will "dance" around before evaporating.

Periodically check the heat of the pan to be sure the pancakes cook evenly.

Melt ½ tablespoon of the remaining butter in the pan, then ladle ½ cup/120 ml batter for each pancake. Cook until bubbles cover the top of the pancakes, 2 to 3 minutes. Flip and cook until golden brown, another 1 minute. Repeat with remaining batter, add butter with each batch to the pan. Serve immediately topped with walnuts and Red-Eye Maple Syrup.

Pancakes are best eaten as they're made, but you can store cooked pancakes on a baking sheet in a low (200°F/95°C) oven to keep warm while making the whole batch.

RIFFS
- Add dried fruit, sliced fresh fruit, or toasted nuts to the batter.
- Use the batter to make waffles.
- Add berries to the syrup, cook until simmering, and strain.

DIFFICULTY
Easy

YIELD
1 serving

TOTAL TIME
5 minutes

HANDS-ON TIME
5 minutes

A departure from the ubiquitous berry parfait, this one gets a tropical slant from the combination of mango, blueberries, toasted almonds, and coconut.

TROPICAL YOGURT PARFAIT WITH TOASTED COCONUT AND ALMONDS

¾ cup/180 ml **vanilla whole-milk yogurt**

⅓ cup/25 g **fresh blueberries**

¼ cup/90 g **small-dice ripe mango**

3 tbsp **toasted, sliced almonds (page 119)**

3 tbsp **toasted, unsweetened flaked coconut**

Honey or agave nectar, for garnish

Ground cinnamon, for garnish

Look for unsweetened raw coconut in the bulk section or health aisle of the grocery store. If you can't find it, use a dried fruit such as diced dates and go easy on the honey.

In a small bowl or parfait glass, layer ¼ cup/60 ml of the yogurt, half of the blueberries, and half of the mango. Top with another ¼ cup/60 ml yogurt, then all of the almonds and the remaining ¼ cup/60 ml yogurt, followed by all the remaining fruit and the coconut.

Drizzle with honey, sprinkle with a pinch of cinnamon, and serve.

DIFFICULTY
Easy

YIELD
1 sandwich and 2 cups/480 ml pesto

TOTAL TIME
15 minutes

HANDS-ON TIME
10 minutes

If Dr. Seuss were Italian, I imagine his version of green eggs and ham would resemble this open-faced sandwich—crusty country bread, slathered with peppery pesto, and topped with crisp cured ham.

TAKEAWAY: How to cook an egg over-easy.

RECIPE WITHIN A RECIPE: Use the leftover pesto to top roasted or grilled fish or chicken, stirred into vegetable soup, or in place of tomato sauce on a pizza or pasta.

ARUGULA PESTO "GREEN EGGS AND HAM" SANDWICH

ARUGULA PESTO

5 oz/140 g **baby arugula**

6 tbsp/90 ml **olive oil**

½ cup/55 g **toasted pine nuts**

3 **garlic cloves, smashed**

1 tbsp **freshly squeezed lemon juice**

⅓ cup/40 g **grated Parmigiano-Reggiano cheese**

Kosher salt

1 to 2 tbsp **water, as needed**

SANDWICH

1 tbsp **olive oil**

1 **large egg**

2 thin slices **prosciutto or Serrano ham**

2 tbsp **Arugula Pesto**

Slices of country bread, cut 1½-in/4-cm thick and toasted

CONTINUED

**BLENDER OR
FOOD PROCESSOR**
The pesto can be made in a
blender or food processor.

The pesto can be made up
to 2 days ahead. Place in an
airtight container, lay plastic
wrap against the pesto surface, cover, and refrigerate
until ready to use.

FOR THE PESTO

Place the arugula in a bowl of ice water and set aside to soak
briefly, at least 5 minutes.

Meanwhile, combine the oil, half of the pine nuts, garlic, and
lemon juice in a food processor fitted with the metal blade and
process until the mixture is very smooth. Drain the soaked
arugula, shake off excess water but don't pat dry (you want some
of that water in the pesto), and add to the food processor. Pulse
until the arugula is just incorporated, about 5 pulses. Add the
cheese and remaining pine nuts, season well with salt, and pulse
a few times to break up the pine nuts and mix in the seasoning.
(If the mixture is very thick, stir in 1 to 2 tablespoons of water.)
Taste the pesto and adjust the seasoning as desired.

FOR THE SANDWICH

Heat the oil in a small nonstick frying pan over medium-low
heat. When it shimmers, crack the egg into the pan and cook
until set on the bottom, about 3 minutes. Using a nonstick
spatula, carefully turn the egg over and cook until just set, about
1 more minute. Remove to a plate. Add the prosciutto to the pan
and cook until just crisp, about 1 minute.

Spread the pesto on the toasted bread, top with egg and prosciutto,
and serve.

━━━━━

RIFFS

- Use fresh basil, cilantro, or parsley in place of the arugula.
- Top with another cured meat, such as bresaola, or use some crisped
  speck or bacon for a smokier note.
- To make it meatless, swap the prosciutto for a grated hard cheese
  like Cheddar, Fontina, Gouda, or Gruyère and place under the broiler
  until melty.

Everyone should have the skills to make a scramble as it's a quick, crowd-pleasing dish that can be served any time of day. This one is as visually appetizing as it is tasty and a cinch to throw together.

TAKEAWAY: How to scramble eggs.
RECIPE WITHIN A RECIPE: Serve the sautéed asparagus as a simple side.

ASPARAGUS, TOMATO, AND FETA SCRAMBLE

6 **large eggs**

⅓ cup/75 ml **half-and-half**

Kosher salt and freshly ground black pepper

2 tbsp **unsalted butter**

1 **shallot, minced**

1½ cups/155 g **thinly sliced asparagus (tips in 1-in/2.5 cm pieces, stalks in ¼-in/6 mm pieces)**

½ **Fresno or jalapeño chile, seeded and thinly sliced (optional)**

½ cup/70 g **halved cherry or grape tomatoes**

⅓ cup/45 g **Cotija or feta cheese**

Hot sauce, for serving (optional)

Combine the eggs, half-and-half, and a pinch of salt in a medium bowl and beat with a fork until very smooth and even in color.

Melt 1 tablespoon of the butter in a 10-in/25-cm nonstick frying pan over medium-high heat. When the foaming subsides, add the shallot, asparagus, and chile, season with salt, and cook until softened, about 5 minutes. Transfer to a plate and set aside.

Wipe out the pan and return to the stove over medium heat. Add the remaining 1 tablespoon of butter. When the foaming subsides, add the egg mixture and tomatoes. Let sit until eggs start to set up at the very edges. Cook, using a rubber spatula, to gently push, lift, and fold the mixture from one side of the pan to the other until set but still slightly wet, 2 to 5 minutes. Return the asparagus mixture to the pan, sprinkle with cheese, and gently mix through. Season with salt and pepper and serve with the hot sauce.

RIFF: The variations are pretty much endless although delicious additions would be fresh herbs, mushrooms, spinach, or Canadian bacon.

DIFFICULTY
Easy

YIELD
2 servings

TOTAL TIME
15 to 20 minutes

HANDS-ON TIME
15 to 20 minutes

You can use milk or water in place of the half-and-half, although it will not yield as rich a texture.

When I make eggs as a part of a larger meal (such as a brunch), I cook them until they are still slightly wet then remove from the heat. (Eggs continue to cook when you take them off the heat.) Then cover and set aside until ready to serve, no more than 10 minutes.

This is a loose scramble, but if you prefer the eggs and vegetables to cook together, add the asparagus mixture back to the pan with the eggs and tomatoes.

YIELD
8 to 12 servings

TOTAL TIME
**2 hours, plus
setting time**

HANDS-ON TIME
25 minutes

*Loaded with Cajun flavors, this strata is like The Big Easy in a
baking dish—a savory and spicy addition to any brunch or buffet.*

TAKEAWAY: How to make a strata (savory bread pudding).
GOES WELL WITH: A simple green salad is all you need to make this
a one-dish meal.

CAJUN STRATA WITH MUSTARD SOUR CREAM

Andouille is a spicy, smoked
sausage from Cajun country.
If you can't find it, use
kielbasa, smoked bratwurst,
or Spanish dry chorizo.

Plum tomatoes aren't as juicy
as other types, which gives
them a more-concentrated
flavor. Well-known varieties
include Roma and San
Marzano, which are used
for tomato paste and sauce.
If you can't find plum, use a
slicing tomato, but discard
excess juices and seeds
before using.

CAJUN STRATA

1 tbsp **unsalted butter, plus
more for coating the pan**

1 lb/455 g **andouille or
kielbasa sausage, casings
removed**

1 **yellow onion, roughly
chopped**

1½ tsp **kosher salt, plus more
for seasoning**

2 **celery stalks, finely
chopped**

1 **red, orange, or yellow bell
pepper, roughly chopped**

1 **green bell pepper, roughly
chopped**

4 **garlic cloves, thinly sliced**

Freshly ground black pepper

4 **plum tomatoes, seeded and
roughly chopped**

10 **large eggs**

2 cups/480 ml **half-and-half**

1 tbsp **Dijon mustard**

2 tsp **cayenne pepper**

1 lb/455 g **loaf French bread,
stale or toasted, sliced ½ in/
12 mm thick**

2½ cups/195 g **shredded
Cheddar cheese**

1 cup/40 g **roughly chopped
fresh Italian parsley, plus
more for garnish**

MUSTARD SOUR CREAM

1 cup/240 ml **sour cream**

¼ cup/60 g **Dijon mustard**

2 tsp **cayenne pepper**

FOR THE STRATA

Thoroughly coat the inside of a baking dish that measures
13 by 9 in/33 by 23 cm with butter and set aside. Line a plate with
paper towels and set aside. Crumble the sausage in a large nonstick
frying pan and cook over medium heat, stirring to break up, until
browned, 10 to 15 minutes. Remove to the prepared plate and discard all but 1 tablespoon of the drippings.

Return the pan to the stove, add the 1 tablespoon butter, and melt over medium heat. When it foams, add the onion, season with salt, and cook until just softened. Add the celery, bell peppers, and garlic, season with salt and pepper, and cook until they begin to soften. Stir in the tomatoes and cook until they just begin to break down; remove from the heat, mix in the sausage and set aside.

Whisk the eggs, half-and-half, mustard, cayenne, and salt in a large bowl until evenly combined and smooth. Arrange half of the bread in the bottom of the prepared dish. Evenly layer in 1 cup/80 g of the cheese, half of the bell pepper mixture, and half of the parsley. Pour over half of the egg mixture. Repeat layering with remaining bread, another 1 cup/80 g of the cheese, and the remaining bell pepper mixture and parsley. Pour the remaining egg mixture over the top.

Push down to ensure that the bread is submerged in the egg custard, cover with plastic wrap, weight with a 1-lb/.5 kg weight set on a plate (a large can of tomatoes or rice in a resealable plastic bag works well), and refrigerate for 1 to 12 hours.

When ready to bake, heat the oven to 325°F/165°C/gas 3 and arrange a rack in the middle. Let the strata sit at room temperature while the oven heats, at least 20 minutes. Sprinkle the strata with the remaining cheese and bake until puffed and the edges pull away slightly, 50 to 55 minutes. Cool for at least 5 minutes before serving.

FOR THE SOUR CREAM

Meanwhile, mix together the sour cream ingredients until well combined.

Serve the strata with a dollop of sour cream.

You can prepare the strata up to baking as much as 12 hours ahead—convenient.

Stratas are the ideal make-ahead dish because they hold up. You can bake it and enjoy it for the next 3 days—just reheat and serve.

Use an oven thermometer (see page 64) to make sure your oven is at the correct temperature. If your oven's too hot you risk overcooking and curdling the eggs.

RIFFS
* Swap mixed mushrooms for the sausage and cook them until they are thoroughly browned.
* Add some sun-dried tomatoes to the veggie mixture.
* Stir some pesto sauce into the egg mixture.

A departure from heavy, greasy diner hash, what this sweet potato version lacks in tradition, it makes up for in flavor. It's a vegetarian breakfast that will satisfy even the most devout meat-lovers.

TAKEAWAY: How to poach an egg.

CHIPOTLE–SWEET POTATO HASH WITH POACHED EGGS AND AVOCADO

The vinegar helps the eggs set up. Also, fresh eggs will poach best, so use the freshest you can find.

The eggs can be poached up to 2 days ahead and stored in water in the refrigerator. To reheat the poached eggs, place in gently simmering water for a few minutes until heated through.

Chipotles in adobo are canned smoked jalapeños in sauce. If you can't find them, use 1 finely chopped fresh jalapeño or a few dashes of hot sauce.

POACHED EGGS

8 cups/2 L **water**

1 tsp **vinegar (optional)**

4 **large eggs**

HASH

2 tbsp **olive oil**

1 **yellow onion, cut into small dice**

Kosher salt and freshly ground black pepper

1 **green bell pepper, cut into small dice**

1 lb/455 g **sweet potatoes, cut into small dice**

1 **garlic clove, minced**

1 **canned chipotle chile in adobo, minced**

½ cup/120 ml **low-sodium vegetable broth or water**

1 tsp **fresh thyme leaves, minced (or ¼ tsp dried)**

1 medium **ripe avocado, sliced (for garnish)**

Sour cream, for garnish (optional)

CONTINUED

FOR THE EGGS

Bring about 8 cups/2 L (you need at least 2 in/5 cm) of water to a simmer in a medium frying pan and, if using, add the vinegar. Break each egg into a separate small cup or ramekin. Gently slide the eggs into the simmering water, cooking 2 at a time. Cook until the whites are just set, about 3 minutes.

Using a slotted spoon, carefully lift the eggs out of the water. Place in a bowl of warm water to hold their heat while finishing the hash.

FOR THE HASH

Heat the oil in a large frying pan over medium-high heat. When it shimmers, add the onion, season with salt, stir to coat the onion pieces in oil, and cook until softened and translucent, about 3 minutes. Stir in the bell pepper and cook until soft, about 5 minutes.

Add the sweet potatoes and stir to coat in oil. Cook, stirring occasionally, until the sweet potatoes just begin to brown, about 3 minutes. Stir in the garlic and chipotle and cook until fragrant, about 30 seconds. Add the broth or water, cover, and cook until the potatoes are fork-tender, about 5 minutes.

Remove the cover and cook until the liquid has almost completely evaporated (the bottom of the pan should have a film of liquid), about 3 minutes. Stir in the thyme, season generously with salt and pepper, and stir to combine.

Serve the hash topped with 1 or 2 poached eggs for each serving and garnish with sliced avocado and, if desired, a dollop of sour cream.

Known around my parts as "eggs with etiquette," these single-serving dishes are the perfect addition to a Sunday brunch or Mother's Day celebration.

TAKEAWAY: How to bake eggs.

DIFFICULTY
Easy

YIELD
6 servings

TOTAL TIME
15 minutes

HANDS-ON TIME
5 minutes

CREAMY BAKED EGGS WITH HOT-SMOKED SALMON

Butter, for coating the ramekins and for bread

4 oz/110 g **hot-smoked salmon, flaked into small pieces**

1 **ripe tomato, seeded and cut into small dice**

3 tbsp **thinly sliced green onions**

6 **large eggs**

⅓ cup/80 ml **heavy cream**

Freshly ground black pepper

6 slices **country bread**

1 tbsp **minced fresh parsley or dill, for garnish**

Heat the oven to broil and arrange a rack in the middle (the rack should be at least 6 inches away from the heat source). Thoroughly coat the inside of six 6-oz/180-ml ramekins with butter; set aside.

Evenly divide the salmon, tomatoes, and green onions among the ramekins. Crack an egg into each ramekin, drizzle cream over each egg, and season with pepper.

Place the ramekins on a rimmed baking sheet and broil, rotating the pan halfway through baking, until the egg whites are just set but the yolks are still a touch runny, 5 to 8 minutes.

Meanwhile, toast and butter a few slices of the country bread. When the eggs are ready, top with herbs and serve with buttered toast.

RIFF: Swap Canadian bacon or crab for the salmon. Lay pieces of prosciutto or other thinly sliced cured meat in the bottom of each ramekin and let some hang over the edge so it gets crispy as it cooks.

Hot-smoked salmon is less common than regular (cold-smoked) salmon, but is worth the search for its meaty, smoky note. If you can't find it, use another smoked fish, like trout.

RAMEKINS
Small ceramic ramekins work well in this recipe. If you don't have them, use oven-proof 6-oz/180-ml dishes or muffin tins though know the cooking time may vary.

Keep watch on the eggs because they will cook quickly and continue to cook after removed from the broiler.

DIFFICULTY
Medium

YIELD
8 to 10 servings

TOTAL TIME
40 minutes

HANDS-ON TIME
35 minutes

In Spain, tortillas are open-faced omelets traditionally made with lots of olive oil, even more potatoes, and eggs. This is a lesser-known, rustic version with a variety of ingredients. With a piece of crusty bread, this makes a meal any time of day.

TAKEAWAY: How to make a Spanish tortilla.
GOES WELL WITH: A simple green salad and some crusty bread.

COUNTRY-STYLE SPANISH TORTILLA

4 oz/115 g **dry Spanish chorizo**
½ cup/120 ml **olive oil**
1 lb/455 g **red-skin or Yukon gold potatoes, thinly sliced**
Kosher salt
½ **red onion, halved and thinly sliced**
1 **roasted red bell pepper, thinly sliced**
1 cup/135 g **fresh or frozen baby peas**
8 **large eggs**
½ tsp **smoked paprika**

There are two types of chorizo: Mexican chorizo, which is uncooked, and Spanish chorizo (the one used here), which is cured and dry. If you can't find Spanish chorizo, use another spicy dry salami.

Cut the chorizo into ¼-in/6-mm coins and then quarter; set aside. Rest a colander in a bowl; set aside. Line a plate with paper towels; set aside.

Heat the oil in a 10-in/25-cm nonstick frying pan over medium-high heat, about 3 minutes. (The oil is ready when you dip in a potato slice and bubbles form all around it.) Add the potatoes and cook, turning gently so they don't break, until the potatoes are translucent and knife-tender, about 5 minutes. Transfer the potatoes and oil to a colander set inside a bowl, toss with a pinch of salt, and set aside to drain. Reserve the drained oil.

Return the pan to stove over moderate heat, add 1 tablespoon of the drained oil and the chorizo. Cook until the chorizo is just crisp, about 2 minute. Using a slotted spoon, transfer the chorizo to the prepared plate. Add the onion and cook until softened. Stir in the bell pepper and peas and cook until the peas are bright green. Remove from the heat and set aside. Combine the eggs and paprika in a large bowl and whisk until smooth. Stir in all the potatoes, other vegetables, and the chorizo.

Add 1 tablespoon of the drained oil to the pan, then add the egg mixture and cook over low heat, covered, until the edges are set but the center is still loose, 15 to 20 minutes. Occasionally shake the pan gently to make sure the tortilla is not sticking (if it is sticking, loosen with a heatproof spatula). Flip the tortilla by holding a large flat plate over the pan, and inverting the frying pan over the plate. Slide the tortilla, cooked side up, back into the pan. Round off the edge of the tortilla with a heatproof spatula and cook over low heat, covered, until the egg on bottom of tortilla is set, about 3 minutes more.

Remove from the heat and let sit 5 minutes before serving. Slide the tortilla onto a plate and serve warm or cold, cut into wedges.

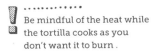

Be mindful of the heat while the tortilla cooks as you don't want it to burn .

This tortilla can be served warm or at room temperature.

DIFFICULTY
Medium

YIELD
1 serving

TOTAL TIME
15 minutes

HANDS-ON TIME
15 minutes

While traveling through India, I ate a variation of a Masala omelet in almost every city I visited. Once I returned, I crafted this recipe and I eat it on a regular basis, serving it as is or wrapped in a flatbread for a variation on a breakfast burrito.

TAKEAWAY: How to make an omelet.
RECIPE WITHIN A RECIPE: The filling can be used for scrambles.

MASALA-SPICED SPINACH OMELET

2 **large eggs**

1 tbsp **canola, grapeseed, or peanut oil**

2 **green onions (white and pale green parts), thinly sliced crosswise**

1 tbsp **seeded and finely chopped serrano chile**

1 medium **garlic clove, thinly sliced**

¾ tsp **curry powder**

1 **tomato, seeded and finely chopped**

1 handful (about 1 oz/30 g) **baby spinach or finely chopped chard leaves (from 1 cup/25 g packed leaves)**

Kosher salt and freshly ground black pepper

2 tbsp **crumbled feta or Cotija cheese**

1 tbsp **finely chopped fresh cilantro**

Omelets can be easily made for brunch. To do so, make the desired amount of filling ahead of time, whisk together the eggs, and store filling and eggs separately in the refrigerator until ready to use. When ready to cook, heat the pan, and continue with the recipe.

Crack the eggs into a small bowl and use a fork to beat until smooth and evenly combined; set aside. Place half of the oil in a small nonstick frying pan over medium heat. When it shimmers, add the green onions, chile, garlic, and curry powder and cook until fragrant, about 30 seconds. Add the tomato and spinach or chard, season with salt and pepper, and cook, stirring until wilted, about 1 minute. Remove the spinach mixture to a plate and wipe out the pan with a paper towel.

Return the pan to medium heat and add the remaining ½ table-spoon oil. Add the egg mixture and swirl to coat the pan. As the eggs start to set, use a rubber spatula to gently push aside a small patch of cooked egg then tilt the pan so that uncooked egg fills the gap. Repeat, working your way around the pan until the eggs have reached the consistency you like.

Spread the filling over half of the omelet, season with salt and pepper, then sprinkle the cheese and cilantro over the filling. Using a rubber spatula, gently fold the other half of the omelet over the filling. Slide onto a plate and serve.

A perfect omelet has no brown spots on the egg so pay special attention to the heat and cook the eggs until set, but no further.

EGGS

DIFFICULTY
Easy

YIELD
6 to 8 servings

TOTAL TIME
30 minutes

HANDS-ON TIME
30 minutes

I've always considered frittatas the chilled-out version of the omelet, as there's none of the fussiness of folding the egg over the filling. But that simplicity doesn't take away from how stellar a well-made frittata can be.

TAKEAWAY: How to make a frittata.
GOES WELL WITH: A simple green salad and toast.

SWISS CHARD, OYSTER MUSHROOM, AND RICOTTA FRITTATA

Use a good ricotta here as the commercial stuff is flavorless and rubbery. If you can't find ricotta, goat cheese will work well.

8 **large eggs**

¾ cup/140 g **ricotta cheese**

⅓ cup/40 g **grated Parmigiano-Reggiano cheese**

2 tbsp **unsalted butter**

2 **shallots, finely chopped**

1 tsp **kosher salt**

3 tbsp **fresh thyme leaves, minced (or 1 tbsp dried thyme)**

8 oz/225 g **oyster mushrooms, stemmed and thinly sliced**

8 oz/225 g **Swiss chard or spinach, stemmed and finely chopped**

1 tbsp **olive oil**

Heat the broiler to high and set a rack in the upper third. Combine the eggs and half of the cheeses in a medium bowl and whisk until the mixture is broken up and smooth; set aside.

Heat the butter in a medium nonstick frying pan over medium heat. When the foaming subsides, stir in the shallots, season with salt, and cook until softened, about 3 minutes. Stir in the thyme and cook until fragrant, about 30 seconds.

Stir in the mushrooms and cook, stirring rarely, until golden brown, about 3 minutes. Decrease the heat to medium-low, stir in the chard or spinach, cover, and cook until tender, about 4 minutes. Transfer the mixture to a plate.

Wipe out the pan and return to the stove. Add the olive oil to the pan and swirl to coat. Pour in the egg mixture then add the chard or spinach mixture, distributing evenly. Cook until the eggs are almost totally set (only the middle 2 inches should still be liquid), 5 to 7 minutes.

Scatter the remaining cheese over the top and push the cheese down into the egg mixture. Place the pan under the broiler and broil until the top of the frittata is set (none of it will look liquidy), about 2 minutes. Turn the frittata onto a platter and serve.

The frittata can be served hot or at room temperature.

DIFFICULTY	
Hard	

YIELD
12 servings

TOTAL TIME
3 hours, plus overnight rising time

HANDS-ON TIME:
30 minutes

Toasted almonds, honey-cream glaze, and buttery brioche stand in for the classic sticky bun dough. The long rise time requires some advance planning and patience but the payoff is an extra-tender, extra-indulgent take on the classic breakfast pastry.

TAKEAWAY: How to make brioche and sticky buns.

RECIPE WITHIN A RECIPE: The base dough for this recipe is a buttery brioche and it can be used—without the filling, sauce, and nuts—as you would in any recipe that calls for brioche dough. Brioche dough tends to be sticky and a bit hard to work with—the overnight rise alleviates that for a very workable dough.

ALMOND BRIOCHE STICKY BUNS

Make sure to get instant or active dry yeast. Don't use rapid rise yeast in this recipe because it won't produce the same results.

BRIOCHE DOUGH

1 cup/240 ml **whole milk (heated to 100°F/38°C to 115°F/45°C)**

¼ cup/50 g **granulated sugar**

¼-oz packet **active dry yeast (2¼ tsp)**

6 tbsp/85 g **unsalted butter, cut into small pieces, at room temperature, plus melted butter for coating the bowl and pan**

1 tbsp **kosher salt**

1 tsp **grated lemon zest**

3 **large eggs (at room temperature), lightly beaten**

1 tbsp **pure vanilla extract**

4 cups/500 g **unbleached all-purpose flour**

SPICE FILLING

½ cup/100 g **granulated sugar**

2½ tsp **ground cinnamon**

¾ tsp **ground cloves**

½ tsp **kosher salt**

HONEY-CREAM GLAZE

½ cup/115 g **unsalted butter**

1 cup/200 g **packed light brown sugar**

2 tbsp **honey or agave nectar**

¼ tsp **kosher salt**

¼ cup/60 ml **heavy cream**

2 tbsp **unsalted butter, at room temperature**

1 cup/115 g **toasted sliced almonds (page 119)**

CONTINUED

FOR THE DOUGH

Place the milk and sugar in the bowl of a stand mixer fitted with the dough hook and sprinkle with the yeast. Set aside to rest until the mixture bubbles, 5 to 10 minutes. Coat the inside of a large bowl with butter and set aside.

Add the salt, zest, eggs, and vanilla and mix until evenly incorporated. Add the flour little by little until the dough is moistened throughout and starts to come together. Mix on medium speed until the dough completely pulls away from the sides of the bowl to form a ball, and is smooth and elastic, about 5 minutes.

Add the 6 tablespoons/85 g butter piece by piece, letting each fully incorporate before adding the next. Place the dough in the prepared bowl, turn to coat in butter, and cover with a clean, damp kitchen towel or plastic wrap. Set aside in a warm place until it doubles in volume, about 1 hour.

When the dough has doubled in size, fold it onto itself, cover, and place it in the refrigerator overnight to rise, 12 to 36 hours.

FOR THE FILLING

In a small bowl, combine the granulated sugar, cinnamon, cloves, and salt and mix well; set aside.

FOR THE GLAZE

Combine the butter, brown sugar, honey, and salt in a medium pan over medium heat and stir until the sugar is dissolved. Cook, without stirring, until fluid and well combined (swirl the pan as needed to help everything cook evenly). Remove from the heat, pour in the cream and swirl to combine. Set aside until ready to use.

If the yeast mixture does not bubble in the first step, either the milk is not at the correct temperature or the yeast is old.

Instead of an overnight rise, you can let the buns go through their second rise at room temperature for 1 to 2 hours and then bake them. However, be forewarned that the dough will be a bit sticky and harder to work with and the buns won't have quite the same texture as the slow-rise version.

The glaze can make up to 1 day ahead and refrigerated in an airtight container until ready to use. Heat the glaze over low heat until pourable before proceeding with the recipe.

When ready to assemble, remove the dough from the refrigerator and let rest at room temperature at least 15 minutes. On a lightly floured work surface with a lightly floured rolling pin, roll the dough into an 18-by-8-in/45-by-20-cm rectangle (see page 160). Spread the butter evenly over the dough, sprinkle with filling, and press to ensure it adheres to the dough.

Starting at the long edge closest to you, roll up into a cylinder (as necessary, stretch dough to ensure that it rolls up evenly). Using a sharp knife coated lightly in cooking spray or oil, trim off uneven bits at the end then slice the cylinder into 12 (1½-in/4-cm) buns.

Coat a baking dish that measures 13 by 9 in/33 by 23 cm with butter then pour the glaze into the bottom. Scatter the almonds over the glaze, and place the buns in the pan. (At this point you can cover the buns with plastic wrap and refrigerate them overnight.) If baking immediately, set, uncovered, to rise until rolls are almost doubled in size and have risen into one another, about 30 minutes.

Meanwhile, heat the oven to 350°F/177°C/gas 4 and arrange a rack in the middle. (If the buns have been refrigerated, let them sit at room temperature for 30 minutes before baking.)

Bake the buns until they're puffed, golden brown, and an instant-read thermometer inserted into the center roll reads 190°F/90°C, 35 to 40 minutes. Remove from the oven and let sit 5 minutes before inverting onto a plate and serving immediately.

BAKING DISH
You'll need a baking dish that measures 13 by 9 in/ 33 by 23 cm.

INSTANT-READ DIGITAL THERMOMETER
An instant-read digital thermometer (page 64) is essential to ensure that the milk is at the correct temperature.

RIFFS
- Garnish with pine nuts, hazelnuts, walnuts, or pecans instead of almonds.
- Use ginger, cardamom, or nutmeg in place of cloves.
- Swap orange zest for the lemon zest.

DIFFICULTY
Medium

YIELD
1 pound/455 g
(6 to 8 servings)

TOTAL TIME
45 minutes

HANDS-ON TIME
15 minutes

Slightly salty with a perfect texture, this basic pasta dough is sturdy enough to be rolled into various shapes, yet tender enough to complement nearly any pasta sauce.

TAKEAWAY: How to make pasta.

BASIC PASTA DOUGH

5 **large egg yolks**

1 tbsp **olive oil**

2 cups/255 g **unbleached all-purpose flour**

2 tsp **kosher salt**

3 to 7 tbsp **water, as needed**

There is a range of water in this recipe because you'll need more or less depending on how humid or dry the weather is.

Combine yolks and olive oil in a small bowl and whisk until smooth; set aside.

In the bowl of a food processor fitted with the metal blade, add the flour and salt, and pulse briefly to combine. Add the egg mixture and continue pulsing until moistened through. Pulse in the water, 1 tablespoon at a time, until the dough is damp but not tacky and in pea-sized pieces.

The dough can be shaped, wrapped tightly in plastic wrap, and frozen up to 1 month before using.

Turn the mixture onto a clean, lightly floured surface and, using the heel of your hand, knead the dough until it is smooth and firm, about 5 minutes. Shape the dough into a flat disk, cover with a clean, damp kitchen towel or plastic wrap, and let rest in a cool, dry place for at least 30 minutes before using. Shape dough as desired.

For fettuccine, divide the dough into 6 pieces. On a clean, dry surface, roll the dough to a rectangle that is ⅛ in/3 mm thick and about 12 in/30.5 cm long. Briefly dust with flour then roll into a cylinder. Trim any jagged ends then slice into ½-in/12-mm strips. Unroll and spread out flat to dry, at least 1 hour, before cooking.

PASTA MACHINE
If you plan on making a lot of pasta, consider investing in a tabletop pasta machine or a pasta attachment for a stand mixer, if you have one.

Pizza dough is a confidence-builder as it's super easy to make from scratch—perfect for a beginner bread maker. But, even if you're a pizza-dough pro, try this recipe, as its slightly salty, doughy, yet crisp texture will earn you baking bragging rights.

TAKEAWAY: How to make pizza dough.

DIFFICULTY
Easy

YIELD
2 lb/910 g (enough for two 9-in/23-cm pizzas)

TOTAL TIME
45 minutes to 1 hour

HANDS-ON TIME
15 minutes

BASIC PIZZA DOUGH

1¼ cups/300 ml **warm water (heated to 100°F/40°C to 115°F/45°C)**

1½ tsp **sugar**

¼-oz packet **active dry yeast (2¼ tsp)**

3 cups/380 g **unbleached all-purpose flour**

2 tsp **kosher salt**

1 tbsp **olive oil, plus additional for coating bowl**

INSTANT-READ DIGITAL THERMOMETER
An instant-read digital thermometer (page 64) is essential to ensure that the water is at the correct temperature.

Put the water and sugar in the bowl of a stand mixer fitted with the dough hook and sprinkle the yeast on top; let rest until the mixture bubbles, about 5 minutes. Meanwhile, whisk together the flour and salt to aerate and break up any lumps. Drizzle a large bowl with olive oil and set aside.

When the yeast is ready, add the flour mixture and olive oil and mix on the lowest speed until the dough just comes together but looks shredded, about 2 minutes. Increase the speed to medium and mix until the dough is smooth and very elastic, about 6 minutes. (To test if the dough is ready, do the windowpane test: grab a piece of dough between your thumbs and forefingers and draw fingers apart to pull the dough into a 2-in/5-cm square—a "windowpane." If the dough stretches without breaking, you're good to go. Otherwise, keep mixing.)

Turn out the dough onto a clean surface, shape it into a ball, and place in the oiled bowl. Turn the dough to coat in oil then cover with a clean, damp kitchen towel or plastic wrap. Set aside in a warm place until it doubles in volume (it should not spring back when pressed), 30 to 45 minutes. Fold the dough onto itself and shape as desired. Once shaped, let rest at least 15 to 30 minutes before baking.

If the yeast mixture does not bubble in the first step, either the water is not at the correct temperature or the yeast is old.

Once the dough is made, you can wrap it tightly in plastic wrap and refrigerate up to 24 hours before using. If you have the time, this is preferable because it will allow the pizza to develop a more complex flavor.

The dough can be shaped, wrapped tightly in plastic wrap, and frozen up to 1 month before using.

This dough is very durable and can be used for grilled pizza as well.

DIFFICULTY
Medium

YIELD
*One 9½-in/
25-cm deep-dish
piecrust*

TOTAL TIME
*25 minutes, plus
chilling time*

HANDS-ON TIME
20 minutes

ROLLING PIN
You'll need a rolling pin.

*Store-bought pie dough pales in comparison to homemade,
especially when it's a buttery, flaky crust like this one.*

TAKEAWAY: How to make a piecrust.
RECIPE WITHIN A RECIPE: This piecrust can be used for sweet and
savory recipes alike, from pies and quiches to tarts, galettes, and pot pies.

While butter adds flavor to
doughs, shortening adds
flakiness. To get the best of
both worlds and for a workable, forgiving dough, I've
combined both fats in this
recipe.

The vodka helps to limit
gluten formation in the
finished dough. Unlike
bread doughs where gluten
provides structure, you want
minimal gluten formation
in a pie dough as it would
cause the texture to become
tough.

BASIC PIE DOUGH

1⅓ cups/165 g **unbleached all-purpose flour**

1 tbsp **sugar**

1 tsp **kosher salt**

½ cup/115 g **cold unsalted butter, cut into small pieces**

¼ cup/55 g **solid vegetable shortening**

1 tbsp **vodka**

2 to 4 tbsp **ice water**

Combine the flour, sugar, and salt in a large bowl and whisk
to aerate. Using clean hands, add half of the butter and the
shortening and toss until just coated. Rub butter and shortening between thumb and forefingers until mixture resembles
cornmeal.

Add the remaining butter, toss to coat in the flour, then rub into
the flour until the mixture forms pea-sized pieces (some big
chunks should remain) and comes together in fist-sized clumps
when squeezed.

Drizzle in the vodka and 2 tablespoons of the ice water and rake through mixture with fingers until just moistened. It will go from being a shaggy mess to coming together. The dough is moist enough when it is moistened through but not sticky when pressed. If the dough is not moist, drizzle in the remaining water, 1 tablespoon at a time, continuing to comb through the mixture with your fingers to moisten.

While rotating the bowl with one hand, push the dough between your other palm and the side of bowl to gather into a ball. Turn the dough onto a piece of plastic wrap, press it into a flat disk, and wrap securely. Refrigerate at least 1 hour or up to 2 days before rolling out.

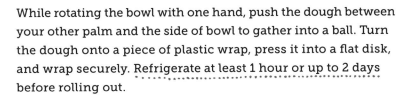

Roll out the dough on a lightly floured surface to a circle that is 11 in/28 cm in diameter and approximately ⅛ in/3 mm thick. Transfer the dough to a 9½-in/25-cm deep-dish pie plate and trim the edges so there is a ½-in/12-mm overhang. Use the excess dough to press the crust into the pie plate. Fold the overhang back on itself and press, as desired, into a decorative edge. Bake and use as desired.

DEEP-DISH PIE PLATE
This dough will fit in a 9½-in/25-cm or smaller deep-dish pie plate.

Piecrusts are hard to make in hot kitchens so try to work in a cool space. Chilling the dough between steps helps the gluten in the dough relax so it can remain flaky, so don't rush that step.

The dough can be made a few days ahead as desired. It can be rolled out and shaped in the pie dish up to 2 days ahead, covered, and stored in the refrigerator until ready to use. Alternatively, the dough can be shaped into a disk and frozen up to 1 month before defrosting and using.

If it is particularly hot outside, freeze the dough in the pie dish for 10 to 15 minutes before baking, to help prevent it from shrinking.

DIFFICULTY
Medium

YIELD
*One 9-by-5-in/
23-by-13-cm loaf*

TOTAL TIME
2 hours, 40 minutes

HANDS-ON TIME
15 minutes

This bread is a blank slate that's begging to be riffed on; but as is, it has a fine crumb, an impressive crust, and a slight sweetness that's suited to anything from sandwiches to French toast.

TAKEAWAY: How to make basic, yeasted sandwich bread.

Make sure to get instant or active dry yeast. Don't use rapid rise yeast or the recipe will be off.

BASIC YEASTED WHITE BREAD

1¼ cups/300 ml **warm water (heated to 100°F/40°C to 115°F/45°C)**

¼-oz packet **active dry yeast (2¼ tsp)**

3¼ cups/410 g **unbleached all-purpose flour, plus more for dusting**

4 tbsp/55 g **unsalted butter, melted, plus more for bowl and pan**

3 tbsp **honey or agave nectar**

2½ tsp **kosher salt**

Ice cubes

 If the yeast mixture does not bubble in the first step, either the water is not at the correct temperature or the yeast is old.

Place the water in the bowl of a stand mixer fitted with the dough hook and sprinkle yeast over the top. Let stand until the yeast bubbles, about 5 minutes.

Add the flour, butter, honey, and salt and mix on low until the dough comes away from the sides of the bowl and forms a shaggy, slightly sticky ball, about 2 minutes. Increase the speed to medium and mix until smooth and elastic but still slightly tacky, about 5 minutes more. (To test if the dough is ready, do the windowpane test: grab a piece of dough between your thumbs and forefingers and draw fingers apart to pull the dough into a 2-in/5-cm square—a "windowpane." If the dough stretches without breaking, you're good to go. Otherwise, keep mixing.)

LOAF PAN
You'll need a loaf pan that measures 9 by 5 in/23 by 13 cm.

Coat a large bowl with butter, shape the dough into a ball, transfer to the bowl, and turn to coat in butter. Cover with a clean, damp kitchen towel or plastic wrap. Set aside in a warm place until it doubles in volume (it should not spring back when poked), 45 minutes to 1 hour.

Coat a loaf pan that measures 9 by 5 in/23 by 13 cm with butter. Punch down the dough. Shape the dough into a rectangle and place in the pan. Dust the loaf with flour, cover with a clean, damp kitchen towel or plastic wrap, and set aside in a warm place until the dough rises about 1 in/2.5 cm above the top of the pan, 45 minutes to 1 hour.

Heat the oven to 400°F/200°C/gas 6 and arrange one rack in the upper third and a second rack in the lower third of the oven. Place a metal baking pan on the lowest rack.

When the dough is ready, decrease the oven temperature to 350°F/177°C/gas 4 and place the loaf pan on the upper rack. Add a few handfuls of ice cubes and immediately close oven.

Bake bread, rotating after 20 minutes, until the internal temperature of the bread is 190°F/87°C and the top is browned, 35 to 40 minutes. Transfer to a wire rack and let cool slightly, about 5 minutes. Turn out the loaf and let cool completely before slicing.

INSTANT-READ DIGITAL THERMOMETER
An instant-read digital thermometer (see page 64) is essential to ensure that the water is at the correct temperature.

Adding the ice cubes to the pan creates a steamy environment in the oven. This is done to encourage the "ovenspring" or the final rise of the bread before the crust develops.

This bread will last up to 5 days when stored at room temperature in an airtight container.

DIFFICULTY
Easy

YIELD
24 muffins

TOTAL TIME
35 minutes

HANDS-ON TIME
10 minutes

Somewhere, somehow, muffins got as sweet as cupcakes and no one seemed to be bothered. Except me. I like muffins to be just a tad sweet, very flavorful, and light as a feather—these muffins are all that and then some.

TAKEAWAY: How to make simple muffins.

BERRY MUFFINS WITH SPICED PISTACHIO STREUSEL

SPICED PISTACHIO STREUSEL

¼ cup/30 g **unbleached all-purpose flour**

1 tsp **ground ginger**

½ tsp **ground nutmeg**

¼ tsp **kosher salt**

½ cup/60 g **roughly chopped roasted, shelled pistachios**

⅓ cup/65 g **packed dark brown sugar**

4 tbsp/55 g **unsalted butter, cut into small pieces**

BERRY MUFFINS

3 cups/380 g **unbleached all-purpose flour**

2 tsp **baking powder**

½ tsp **baking soda**

¾ tsp **kosher salt**

1 cup/240 ml **plain whole milk Greek yogurt**

¾ cup/165 g **packed dark brown sugar**

½ cup/115 g **unsalted butter, melted**

3 **large eggs, at room temperature**

1 tbsp **pure vanilla extract**

1 tsp **pure almond extract**

2½ cups/312 g **fresh or frozen berries**

Greek yogurt is strained yogurt that is thicker and often more tangy than other yogurts. If you can't find it, use plain whole milk yogurt.

FOR THE STREUSEL

Combine the flour, ginger, nutmeg, and salt in a bowl and whisk to aerate and break up any lumps. Add the pistachios, sugar, and butter and rub between your fingers until the butter is incorporated and the mixture clumps together. Store in the refrigerator until ready to use.

The streusel can be made up to 2 days ahead and refrigerated in an airtight container.

FOR THE MUFFINS

Heat oven to 375°F/190°C/gas 5 and arrange a rack in the middle. Fill a 12-well muffin tin with cupcake liners or coat the wells with butter; set aside.

Whisk together the flour, baking powder, baking soda, and salt in a large bowl to break up any lumps and aerate the mixture; set aside.

Whisk together the yogurt, sugar, butter, eggs, vanilla extract, and almond extract in a medium bowl until smooth. Add this and the berries to the flour mixture and stir until just evenly mixed (a few lumps may remain), about 30 strokes. (Do not overmix; the batter should be thick, but the ingredients should be evenly incorporated.) Fill each muffin well with about ¼ cup/60 ml of mixture, then evenly sprinkle the streusel over top.

Bake until a toothpick inserted in the center comes out clean, 15 to 20 minutes. Let the muffins cool in the pan on a wire rack for 5 minutes. Remove from the pan and serve.

MUFFIN TIN
You'll need a 12-well standard muffin tin or mini muffin tins and paper cupcake liners.

These muffins last up to 5 days when stored at room temperature in an airtight container.

RIFFS

- Use pecans, walnuts, or almonds in place of the pistachios.
- Half-and-half can be used instead of the yogurt.
- Use any berry from blackberries to strawberries.
- Add some cinnamon to the streusel.
- Throw dried fruit such as currants, dates, or cranberries in the batter.
- Add a small amount of crystallized ginger or candied citrus zest to the streusel or the batter or both for a holiday slant.

YIELD
*Twenty-four
1½-in/4-cm
biscuits*

TOTAL TIME
45 minutes

HANDS-ON TIME
15 minutes

These ethereal buttermilk biscuits have a light crumb and a distinct crunch that would win many over on their own. But slathered with this sweet, salty, nutty butter, it's a match made in baking heaven.

TAKEAWAYS: How to handle biscuit dough; how to make brown butter.
RECIPE WITHIN A RECIPE: Use the black-pepper brown butter anywhere you'd slather regular butter, from corn on the cob to toast.

BUTTERMILK BISCUITS WITH BLACK PEPPER–BROWN BUTTER

BLACK-PEPPER BROWN BUTTER

½ cup/115 g **unsalted butter, at room temperature**

1 tbsp **honey or agave nectar**

2 tsp **coarsely ground black pepper**

½ tsp **kosher salt**

BUTTERMILK BISCUITS

2¾ cups/345 g **unbleached all-purpose flour**

1 tbsp **baking powder**

1 tsp **sugar**

1 tsp **kosher salt**

½ tsp **baking soda**

¾ cup/170 g **unsalted butter, frozen**

1¼ cups/300 ml **buttermilk, plus extra for brushing**

Keep a stick of unsalted butter in the freezer and you'll always be ready to make this recipe on a moment's notice.

FOR THE BROWN BUTTER

Melt the butter in a small frying pan over medium heat. Cook, swirling the pan to ensure evenly cooking, until the butter turns a nut brown color, about 5 minutes. Immediately remove from the heat, transfer to a bowl, and stir in the honey, pepper, and salt and set aside to cool to room temperature.

CONTINUED

🕐 The butter can be made up to 1 month in advance. Store it in an airtight container in the refrigerator or freezer until ready to use.

Stir to mix thoroughly and serve. Alternatively, transfer to an airtight container, cover, and freeze or refrigerate until ready to use.

FOR THE BISCUITS

Heat the oven to 425°F/220°C/gas 7 and arrange a rack in the middle. Combine the flour, baking powder, sugar, salt, and baking soda in a medium bowl and whisk to aerate and break up any lumps.

Using the large holes of a box grater, grate the butter into the flour mixture. Toss to coat the butter in flour then rub together with your fingertips until just combined but some pea-sized pieces of butter remain.

Add the 1¼ cups/300 ml buttermilk and stir until just moistened. Turn onto a clean, lightly floured surface, and knead briefly until evenly combined, about 30 seconds. Pat to a 1-in/2.5-cm thick rectangle. Using a very sharp knife, cut into 1½-in/4-cm squares. Place the biscuits in the freezer briefly to set up before baking, 15 to 30 minutes.

When ready to bake, arrange half of the biscuits on a rimmed baking sheet. Brush with the remaining buttermilk and bake until brown on the bottoms and golden on the tops, 15 to 18 minutes.

Serve immediately with the butter. Repeat to bake the remaining biscuits.

——

RIFFS
- Swap balsamic vinegar for the honey in the butter.
- Add ½ cup/60g grated aged cheese to the wet biscuit ingredients.
- Add a pinch of cayenne, paprika, nutmeg, or dry mustard to the dry biscuit ingredients.

This is my favorite childhood snack—peanut butter toast with bananas and brown sugar—turned into an adult treat with a good measure of allspice mixed in for a dash of refinement.

TAKEAWAY: How to make a quick bread.

DIFFICULTY
Easy

YIELD
*One 9-by-5-in/
23-by-13-cm loaf*

TOTAL TIME
1 hr, 10 minutes

HANDS-ON TIME
5 minutes

PEANUT BUTTER–BANANA BREAD

4 tbsp/55 g **unsalted butter, melted, plus more for greasing the pan**

1⅔ cups/200 g **unbleached all-purpose flour**

1½ tsp **baking powder**

1½ tsp **kosher salt**

1¼ tsp **ground allspice**

½ tsp **baking soda**

1½ cups/300 g **packed light brown sugar**

1¼ cups/500 g **mashed ripe banana (about 3 bananas)**

⅔ cup/170 g **crunchy natural peanut butter**

2 **large eggs**

1½ tsp **pure vanilla extract**

Heat the oven to 350°F/177°C/gas 4 and arrange a rack in the middle. Coat a loaf pan that measures 9 by 5 in/23 by 13 cm with butter and set aside.

Whisk together the flour, baking powder, salt, allspice, and baking soda in a bowl to aerate and break up any lumps; set aside.

In a stand mixer fitted with the paddle attachment, beat the sugar, bananas, peanut butter, and butter on medium speed until evenly combined. Add the eggs and vanilla and beat until just blended.

Add the flour mixture to the banana mixture and mix on low speed until just incorporated and there are no white streaks. Pour the batter into the prepared loaf pan and bake until a wooden pick inserted in the center comes out clean with just a few crumbs remaining, 55 to 70 minutes.

Remove from oven and let cool at least 5 minutes in pan. Remove the bread from pan and let cool completely on a wire rack.

Make this when you need to use up overripe bananas. Store ripe, unpeeled bananas in the freezer and thaw out as needed for this bread. They'll be mushy and brown but will work well.

Use natural peanut butter as it won't have stabilizers and other scary stuff.

Quick breads like this can be made by hand. But, because this bread has the addition of thick peanut butter, I chose to make it in a mixer to add an extra dose of airiness.

🕐 The bread will last up to 1 week when stored at room temperature in an airtight container.

RIFFS
- Use any nut butter such as almond or cashew butter.
- Add in 1 cup of toasted nuts, chopped; dried fruit; or chocolate chips.
- Add in some finely chopped crystallized ginger for a kick.

DIFFICULTY	
Easy	

YIELD
8 to 12 servings

TOTAL TIME
45 minutes

HANDS-ON TIME
15 minutes

There are many rules for making corn bread and this recipe doesn't follow any of them. Sweetened, it's Northern style. Made in a skillet, it's "Southern style." Bottom line is this: it would make a lot of traditionalists cringe. But the comforting, sweet maple and woodsy sage flavor more than makes up for the blasphemy.

TAKEAWAY: How to make skillet corn bread.

SAGE-MAPLE SKILLET CORN BREAD

½ cup/115 g **unsalted butter**

1½ cups/210 g **cornmeal, preferably stone ground**

1½ cups/185 g **unbleached all-purpose flour**

1 tbsp **kosher salt**

2 tsp **baking powder**

½ tsp **baking soda**

1½ cups/360 ml **whole milk, at room temperature**

3 **large eggs, at room temperature**

⅔ cup/165 ml **Grade B maple syrup**

20 **medium fresh sage leaves**

Buy stone-ground corn-meal, as anything more coarsely ground will give the corn bread a gritty texture.

Use a good-quality Grade B maple syrup here as it has an assertive flavor that is suited to baking.

 The butter quickly goes from brown to burnt so be sure to keep an eye out.

Heat the oven to 375°F/190°C/gas 5 and arrange a rack in the middle. Put the butter in a large cast-iron skillet and place in the oven to melt, 5 to 10 minutes.

Meanwhile, in a large bowl, whisk together the cornmeal, flour, salt, baking powder, and baking soda; set aside. Whisk together the milk, eggs, and syrup until smooth. Stir in the dry ingredients until moistened through.

When the butter is melted and golden brown but not burnt, use a dry towel or oven mitt to carefully (it's hot!) remove the skillet from the oven, and swirl to coat with the butter. Pour the melted butter into the batter and stir just until incorporated.

Scatter the sage leaves across the hot pan then pour in the batter. Return the skillet to the oven and bake until the bread is brown around the edge, springy to the touch, and a toothpick inserted in the center comes out clean with just a few crumbs, 25 to 30 minutes. Invert the bread onto a wire rack to cool. Slice into wedges and serve sage-side up.

CAST-IRON SKILLET
The even heat of a cast-iron skillet gives this an incredible crust, but you can make it in a baking dish that measures 8 by 8 in/20 by 20 cm.

RIFFS
- Use agave nectar, honey, or brown sugar instead of maple syrup.
- Use fresh rosemary, thyme, or marjoram instead of sage.
- Add ½ cup/60 g grated aged cheese to the wet ingredients.
- Stir in 1 cup hominy or sweet corn to the batter.

The bread will last up to 1 week when stored at room temperature in an airtight container—just reheat it briefly before eating.

Crumbly and moist with a hint of sweetness, these are a far cry from the sugar bombs sold in coffee shops these days. As any Scot would attest, they are simply delightful with a cup of tea.

TAKEAWAY: How to make scones.

TOASTED PECAN AND DATE SCONES

3 cups/380 g **unbleached all-purpose flour**

1 tbsp **baking powder**

1 tbsp **sugar**

2 tsp **kosher salt**

½ tsp **ground nutmeg**

½ cup/115 g **cold unsalted butter, cut into small pieces**

½ cup/110 g **pitted and roughly chopped dates**

¾ cup/80 g **toasted and roughly chopped pecans**

¼ cup/60 ml **honey or agave nectar**

⅔ cup/150 ml **heavy cream, plus more for brushing**

1 **large egg**

2 tsp **pure vanilla extract**

2 tbsp **sanding sugar, for dusting**

¼ tsp **ground nutmeg, for dusting**

Medjool dates are the best option here as they're moist and soft. If you can't find dates, most any other dried fruit such as figs, cherries, pineapple, or currants would also work.

Sanding sugar is a large-crystal sugar that is used for decorating baked goods. If you can't find it, granulated or turbinado sugar will work.

Heat the oven to 375°F/190°C/gas 5 and arrange a rack in the middle. Combine the flour, baking powder, sugar, salt, and nutmeg in a medium bowl; whisk to aerate and break up any lumps. Add the butter and toss to coat in the flour. Using clean hands, rub the butter into the flour until half the mixture is pea-sized with the rest resembling bread crumbs.

Stir in the dates and pecans. Whisk together the honey, cream, egg, and vanilla until smooth. Add the cream mixture to the dry ingredients and mix until just moistened through.

Turn the dough onto a clean, lightly floured surface and knead briefly until just combined, about 30 seconds. Using a rolling pin, roll out into a rectangle that is 1 in/2.5 cm thick.

Cut into 1½-in/4-cm squares and place on a rimmed baking sheet. Brush with additional cream and sprinkle with sanding sugar and nutmeg. Bake until the bottoms are golden and tops are blond, 15 to 20 minutes. Serve warm.

The scones will last up to 1 week when stored at room temperature in an airtight container.

RIFFS

- Half-in-half, whole milk, or soy milk can be substituted for the heavy cream.
- Agave or maple syrup can be used in place of the honey.
- Get creative and mix up the nuts and dried fruit combination.

DIFFICULTY
Easy

YIELD
6 to 8 servings (2 quarts/2 L soup)

TOTAL TIME
1 hour and 15 minutes

HANDS-ON TIME
20 minutes

Like a chowder in texture and a tortilla soup in flavor, this soup is a mash-up of flavors with no specific origin except that it comes from somewhere delicious.

TAKEAWAY: How to roast fresh chiles.

GOES WELL WITH: Serve as a start to a multi-course meal or as a light meal with a simple green salad.

CHARRED CHILE AND HOMINY CORN CHOWDER

Anaheim chiles are light green fresh chiles available in the produce section. If you can't find them, use poblano chiles or one 8-oz/225-g can green chiles.

1 **Anaheim chile**

7 ears **fresh corn**

2 tbsp **unsalted butter**

½ **yellow onion, finely chopped**

6 **garlic cloves, thinly sliced**

4 cups/1 L **low-sodium chicken broth**

1½ cups/360 ml **water**

One 28 oz/790 g **can hominy, drained**

1 cup/40 g **packed finely chopped fresh cilantro leaves, plus more for garnish**

Crema or sour cream, for garnish (optional)

1 **jalapeño chile, halved, seeded, and sliced paper thin, for garnish (optional)**

Tortilla chips, for garnish (optional)

Crema is a Mexican sour cream that is a bit thicker than regular sour cream. If you can't find it, go ahead and use regular sour cream.

BLENDER OR FOOD PROCESSOR
If you don't have a blender, use a food processor; otherwise, just eat it chunky.

Place the whole chile over open gas burner at medium heat. Alternatively, place on a baking sheet under a heated broiler. Char, turning occasionally, until the chile is black and blistered all over, 5 to 10 minutes total. Place the chile in a bowl and cover with plastic wrap for 5 minutes. Peel the chile by holding under running water and rubbing the skin with your hands. Trim off the chile top, remove the seeds, halve lengthwise, and cut into small dice. Set aside.

Prepare the corn by cutting the kernels from the cob (see page 81); reserve the cobs. (You should have about 6 cups/ 600 g corn kernels.) Melt the butter in a medium saucepan over medium heat. When the foaming subsides, add the onion and cook, stirring occasionally, until browned, about 5 minutes.

Add the garlic and corn kernels and cook, stirring constantly, until golden, about 5 minutes. Add the broth and water and scrape up any browned bits on the bottom of the pan. Add the reserved corn cobs and bring to a boil over high heat. Decrease the heat to low, cover, and simmer, stirring occasionally, until the broth is corn-flavored, 25 to 30 minutes.

Remove the soup from the heat, discard the cobs, and set aside to cool slightly, about 5 minutes. Fill a blender halfway with the soup and puree until very smooth, about 3 minutes. Repeat with the remaining soup.

Return the soup to the saucepan and stir in the toasted chile and the hominy, and cook over medium heat for 5 to 10 minutes, stirring occasionally to prevent burning. Stir in the cilantro; taste and adjust the seasoning. Serve, as desired, garnished with additional cilantro, crema, sliced jalapeño, and tortilla chips.

Be careful when blending hot liquids as the heat can cause them to explode out of the carafe. To avoid this, only fill the blender halfway, remove the plastic plug in the blender cover, and start blending on low for a few seconds before you kick it up to full speed.

The longer you puree the soup, the smoother it will be, so don't shortcut there. If the soup is still lumpy, strain it through a fine mesh sieve.

DIFFICULTY
Medium

YIELD
**8 to 10 servings
(3.5 quarts/
3.5 L soup)**

TOTAL TIME
**45 minutes, plus
2 hours for stock**

HANDS-ON TIME
15 minutes

Proof that going on a wild goose chase can be a good thing, this soup came about when my mother asked me to make "that deliciously interesting African soup." Armed with little info, I never found what I was looking for, but instead crafted this melting pot of a soup with flavors reminiscent of African and Thai food.

TAKEAWAY: How to make chicken stock.
GOES WELL WITH: This is a nice, filling comfort-food dish, perfect during colder weather. Serve with a simple green salad.

CURRIED CHICKEN SOUP WITH ROASTED PEANUTS

This stock is slightly different from others because you cook the whole bird for the first half. Traditionally, you would use only bones to make stock.

Curry powder varies in heat and flavor from brand to brand. Explore different brands to find one that suits you.

HOMEMADE CHICKEN STOCK

One 4 to 5 lb/1.8 to 2.3 kg **chicken, neck reserved and gizzards discarded**

8 cups/2 L **water**

2 **celery stalks, roughly chopped**

6 **garlic cloves, smashed**

6 **black peppercorns**

4 sprigs **thyme**

1 **bay leaf**

1 tbsp **kosher salt**

CURRIED CHICKEN SOUP

2 tbsp **canola, grapeseed, or peanut oil**

½ **yellow onion, thinly sliced**

Kosher salt and freshly ground black pepper

1 lb/453 g **sweet potato, cut into large dice**

1 lb/453 g **butternut squash, peeled and cut into large dice**

2 tbsp **curry powder**

2 tbsp **tomato paste**

1 tbsp **grated fresh ginger**

1 tbsp **grated garlic**

1 tbsp **minced fresh thyme**

2 tsp **Worcestershire sauce**

4 cups/1 L **Homemade Chicken Stock**

One 14-oz/414-g can **diced tomatoes**

One 14-oz/414-ml can **coconut milk**

⅓ cup/80 g **natural peanut butter**

1 to 2 tbsp **red wine vinegar**

½ cup/20 g **roughly chopped fresh cilantro**

6 **medium green onions, thinly sliced**

½ cup/55 g **coarsely chopped roasted peanuts, for garnish**

CONTINUED

FOR THE STOCK

In a large pot, combine the chicken, neck, water, celery, garlic, peppercorns, thyme, and bay leaf. Bring to a boil over high heat, then decrease the heat to low, cover partially, and simmer until the chicken is cooked, about 45 minutes.

Remove the chicken (leave the neck) to a plate and set aside to cool. Return the stock to the stovetop and continue to simmer over low heat, still partially covered. When the chicken is cool enough to handle, discard the skin and pull the meat off the bones. Add the bones to the simmering stock and shred the meat into bite-sized pieces. Season the meat with 1 teaspoon of the salt and refrigerate until ready to use.

Continue to simmer the stock until it's richly flavored, another 45 minutes to 1½ hours. Strain the stock (you should have about 7 cups/1.7 L) into a heatproof bowl and stir in the remaining 2 teaspoons of salt. Taste, adjust seasoning as desired, and use in the soup or set aside to cool for at least 1 hour before covering and refrigerating.

Stock can be made up to 4 days ahead and refrigerated in an airtight container until ready to proceed.

FOR THE SOUP

Heat the oil in a large heavy-bottomed pot with a tight-fitting lid or large Dutch oven over medium-high heat. When it shimmers, add the onion, season with salt, and cook until translucent, about 3 minutes.

Add the sweet potato and squash, season with salt and pepper, and cook over moderate heat, stirring, until softened, about 6 minutes. Stir in the curry, tomato paste, ginger, garlic, thyme, and Worcestershire sauce and cook until fragrant, about 1 minute.

Stir in 4 cups of the reserved stock, tomatoes (with juice), and coconut milk and bring to a boil. Decrease the heat to low, stir in the peanut butter and the reserved shredded chicken, season with salt, and simmer until the flavors are melded, about 20 minutes.

The soup can be made up to 2 days ahead and refrigerated in an airtight container.

Stir in the cilantro and green onions and cook until just heated through. Ladle into bowls, top with peanuts, and serve.

RIFF: If you don't have time to make the stock, you can shred the meat from a rotisserie chicken and use store-bought low-sodium chicken broth instead.

SOUPS

Also known as "faux pho" or "pho light" in my house, this shortcut version of the Vietnamese soup is by no means traditional. But it can be made in a fraction of the time and still delivers big on flavor.

TAKEAWAY: How to thinly slice meat.

CHEAT SHEET BEEF PHO (FAUX PHO BO)

PHO BROTH

2 tbsp **canola, grapeseed, or peanut oil**

2 **yellow onions, halved**

One 3-in/7.5-cm piece **fresh ginger, halved**

4 qt/4 L **beef stock or low-sodium broth**

One 3-in/7.5-cm **cinnamon stick**

3 **star anise pieces**

3 **whole cloves**

⅓ cup/90 ml **fish sauce**

3 tbsp **packed light brown sugar**

1 tbsp **kosher salt**

PHO

One 12-oz/340-g **package banh pho (flat rice noodles)**

1 lb/450 g **flank steak, London broil, sirloin, or eye of round, sliced as thin as possible**

2 to 3 **Thai chiles, trimmed and thinly sliced**

2 to 3 handfuls **bean sprouts**

1 bunch/50 g **fresh Thai basil**

1 bunch/50 g **fresh mint**

1 **white onion, sliced paper thin**

Chili-garlic hot sauce (such as Sriracha) or hoisin sauce (or both), for serving

2 **limes, cut into wedges, for serving**

CONTINUED

DIFFICULTY
Easy

YIELD
6 servings (3 quarts/3 L)

TOTAL TIME
50 minutes to 3 hours, 30 minutes

HANDS-ON TIME
20 minutes

• • • • • • • • • • • • •

Beef stock is more intensely flavored than beef broth, so use it if you make your own or happen to live near a store that sells it. Otherwise, a good-quality beef broth will do.

• • • • • • • • • • • • •

Asian fish sauce is a potent condiment that is made from salted, dried fish, which provides a rich flavor to the broth without making it fishy. You can find it in the ethnic aisle of grocery stores or in most Asian food markets.

• • • • • • • • • • • • •

For a more authentic version, use rock sugar in place of the brown sugar. Also, add 4 lb/ 2 kg blanched beef bones and 1 lb/550 g of beef stew meat to the broth. It will need to simmer for 1½ to 3 hours before being strained.

• • • • • • • • • • • • •

Banh pho are the typical pho noodles. If you can't find them, use any other rice noodle that you like.

• • • • • • • • • • • • •

Freeze the beef for 5 to 15 minutes before cutting and it will be much easier to slice thinly.

• • • • • • • • • • • • •

Thai chiles are quite hot. Use serranos or jalapeños instead if you want a milder spiciness.

• • • • • • • • • • • • •

Thai basil is purple-stemmed with a pretty assertive flavor. If you can't find it, use the more prevalent Italian (a.k.a. Genovese) basil or cilantro instead.

FOR THE BROTH

Heat the oil in a large pot over medium-high heat. When the oil shimmers, add the onion and ginger and cook, stirring occasionally, until browned and caramelized, about 10 minutes.

Add all the remaining broth ingredients and bring to a boil. Decrease the heat to low, partially cover, and simmer until the broth is infused with flavors, at least 30 minutes, for a very light flavor, and up to 3 hours for a richer flavor. Taste the broth, and add more fish sauce, salt, or sugar, as needed. (Because you are going to add unsalted ingredients at the end, go ahead and make this broth a touch salty.) Strain the broth and set aside until ready to use.

FOR THE PHO

Return the broth to the pot and place over medium-high heat. When the broth simmers, add the rice noodles and cook according to package directions or until tender.

Meanwhile, place the remaining ingredients on a serving platter. When ready to eat, fill soup bowls with the noodles and top with raw meat slices. Ladle broth into each bowl, serve, and let guests garnish the pho to their liking.

The broth can be put in a slow cooker and cooked on low for up to 8 hours. Strain before using.

The broth can be made up to 4 days in advance and refrigerated in an airtight container.

DIFFICULTY
Easy

YIELD
*8 to 10 servings
(4 quarts/4 L soup/
1 cup gremolata)*

TOTAL TIME
1 hour

HANDS-ON TIME
30 minutes

Two parts of Italian cuisine collide as a rustic springtime soup from Abruzzo is brought to life with a dollop of flavorful gremolata—a condiment normally reserved for braised dishes like osso bucco.

TAKEAWAY: How to make gremolata.

RECIPE WITHIN A RECIPE: Gremolata is a parsley, lemon, and garlic condiment that is made earthy and less assertive than usual here with the addition of pistachios. You could use gremolata in the traditional way with osso bucco, as a condiment like pesto, or as a pasta sauce.

FRESH PEA AND FAVA STEW WITH PISTACHIO GREMOLATA

Fava beans can be found fresh in the springtime. If you can't find them, use edamame and skip the blanching step.

Look for semi-pearled farro, a grain, in the bulk section or health food aisle of the grocery. If you can't find it, you can use soft (a.k.a. pastry) wheat berries or pearled barley, which don't need an overnight soak—just rinse and proceed.

Buy frozen artichoke hearts, if possible. Otherwise, use canned or jarred artichoke hearts and rinse before using.

PISTACHIO GREMOLATA

1 bunch **Italian parsley, stems removed and reserved for stew** (2 cups, packed/80 g of leaves)

1 cup/115 g **roasted, salted pistachios**

3 tbsp **olive oil**

1 tbsp **freshly squeezed lemon juice**

4 **medium garlic cloves, halved**

1 **tbsp water**

Kosher salt and freshly ground black pepper

1 tsp **finely grated lemon zest**

PEA AND FAVA STEW

12 oz/340 g **fresh fava beans (1½ cups shelled)**

2 tbsp **olive oil**

1 **yellow onion, halved and thinly sliced**

6 **garlic cloves, thinly sliced**

Freshly ground black pepper

2 cups/340 g **semi-pearled farro**

8 cups/2 L **low-sodium mushroom broth or vegetable broth**

1½ tsp **kosher salt, plus more for seasoning**

Reserved parsley stems from Gremolata

Rind from 2 oz/60 g **Parmigiano-Reggiano cheese**

12 oz/340 g **baby artichoke hearts, quartered**

1 lb/455 g **shelled fresh or frozen peas**

Olive oil, for garnish

Country bread, cut into 1-in/2.5-cm slices and toasted, for garnish

FOR THE GREMOLATA

Combine the parsley leaves, pistachios, olive oil, lemon juice, garlic, and water in a food processor fitted with the metal blade and process until the nuts are coarsely broken up and the mixture is well incorporated, about 1 minute. Season well with salt and pepper, stir in the lemon zest, and refrigerate until ready to use.

The gremolata can be made up to 2 days ahead. Place in an airtight container, lay plastic wrap against the surface, cover, and store in the refrigerator.

FOR THE STEW

Fill a bowl halfway with ice water and set aside. Bring a large pot of heavily salted water to a boil. Meanwhile, shell the fava beans. When the water is ready, drop the beans into the water, and boil for 1 to 2 minutes. Transfer to the ice water and let sit until cool. Drain, then remove the fava skins by splitting open the skin and squeezing out the bean. Set aside.

Heat the oil in a large, heavy-bottomed saucepan or Dutch oven over medium heat. When it shimmers, add the onion and garlic, season with salt and pepper, and cook until soft, about 4 minutes. Add the farro and stir to coat in oil. Add the broth and bring to a boil over high heat. Decrease the heat to low, stir in 1 teaspoon kosher salt, and cook until the farro is tender, about 15 minutes.

Tie the parsley stems together with kitchen string and add to the pot with the Parmesan rind (reserve the rest of the cheese for garnish), artichoke hearts, and ½ teaspoon kosher salt. Cook until the flavors are melded, about 10 minutes. Add the reserved fava beans and the peas, and cook until the peas and beans are bright green, about 2 minutes. Discard the parsley stems and cheese rind and adjust seasoning as desired.

Divide the soup into bowls, drizzle with a little olive oil, top with a dollop of gremolata and shavings of cheese, and serve with bread, additional cheese, and gremolata passed on the side.

DIFFICULTY
Easy

YIELD
*6 to 8 servings
(6 cups/1.5 L soup)*

TOTAL TIME
1 hour, 10 minutes

HANDS-ON TIME
20 minutes

Too many carrot soups are dull, flavorless, and just boring. Here the carrot flavor is concentrated by roasting and is elevated with the help of spices, lime juice, and toasted coconut.

TAKEAWAY: How to make a roasted vegetable soup.
GOES WELL WITH: Serve as a start to a multicourse meal or as a light meal with a simple salad.

**BLENDER OR
FOOD PROCESSOR**
If you don't have a blender, use a food processor; otherwise, just eat it chunky.

Unsweetened flake coconut lends a deep coconut flavor without extra sweetness. If you can't find it, use sweetened coconut but use it sparingly as it's very sweet.

ROASTED CARROT SOUP
WITH TOASTED COCONUT

5 tbsp/75 ml **olive oil**

8 **garlic cloves, smashed**

½ **yellow onion, cut into large dice**

2 lb/910 g **carrots, peeled and cut into ½-in/12-mm slices**

Kosher salt

2 cups/480 ml **carrot juice**

1 tsp **ground ginger**

½ tsp **finely ground black pepper**

2 cups/475 ml **low-sodium vegetable or chicken broth or water**

1 to 2 tbsp **honey or agave nectar**

2 to 3 tbsp **freshly squeezed lime juice**

⅓ cup/15 g **toasted, unsweetened flaked coconut, for garnish**

Sour cream or crème fraîche, for garnish

Heat the oven to 425°F/220°C/gas 7 and arrange a rack in the middle.

Combine 4 tbsp/60 ml of the oil with the garlic, onion, and carrots on a rimmed baking sheet and toss to coat. Season well with salt and roast, stirring occasionally, until they can easily be mashed with a fork, about 50 minutes.

Transfer the carrots to a large bowl. Carefully pour ½ cup/120 ml of the juice on the rimmed baking sheet and scrape up browned bits with a flat spatula.

Pour the juice and browned bits into a blender and add half the carrot mixture and half of the remaining carrot juice. Blend until very smooth. Pour into a medium bowl and repeat with remaining carrots and carrot juice. (Alternatively, use a stick blender in the pan.)

Meanwhile, heat the remaining 1 tablespoon of the oil in a large saucepan. When the oil shimmers, add the ginger and pepper and cook until fragrant. Add the pureed carrot mixture, broth, agave nectar or honey, and lime juice and bring to a simmer. Taste and add more honey, juice, or other seasoning, as desired. Serve topped with coconut and a dollop of sour cream.

The soup is better the next day so make it up to 2 days in advance.

RIFFS

- Just roast the carrots until knife-tender then serve as a side.
- Stir in some cooked grains or lentils to make it a heartier meal.
- Add diced apples or pears for a sweet note.
- Use another root vegetable, such as parsnips or yams, and swap vegetable broth for carrot juice.

Making broth from green tea may seem odd but it provides a subtle earthy background to this otherwise clean-flavored, light, and ultra-healthy soup.

RECIPE WITHIN A RECIPE: Slowly simmer any firm white fish in the broth until flaky for an impromptu poached fish.

GREEN TEA, TOFU, AND BARLEY SOUP

Look for pearl barley, semi-pearled farro, or soft (a.k.a. pastry) wheat berries in the bulk foods or health section of the grocery store. If you can't find them, you can use farro, spelt, hard (a.k.a. winter) wheat berries, or regular barley, but you'll want to soak them at least 8 hours before using so they'll cook faster.

Sake can be found in the ethnic aisle of your grocery store. If you can't find it, sherry or white wine will work.

Dried wakame seaweed can be found in the ethnic aisle of most grocery stores. If you can't find it, you can use a different dried seaweed or omit it.

BARLEY
Kosher salt
¾ cup/120 g **pearl barley**

GREEN TEA BROTH
1 tbsp **canola, grapeseed, or peanut oil**
1 **white onion, thinly sliced**
8 cups/2 L **water**
One 2-in/5-cm piece **fresh ginger, peeled and sliced into coins**
6 **green tea bags**
6 tbsp/100 ml **soy sauce**
1 tbsp **sake or white wine**
4 tsp **sugar**
2 tsp **sesame oil**

ADD-INS
8 oz/250 g **firm tofu, cut into large dice**
2 **carrots, trimmed and sliced paper thin**
4 **green onions, white and green parts separated, thinly sliced**
4 oz/115 g **shiitake mushrooms, trimmed and thinly sliced**
⅓ cup/15 g **dried wakame seaweed**
1 to 2 tsp **sesame seeds**

FOR THE BARLEY

Bring a pot of well-salted water to a boil. Add the barley and cook until swollen and tender, 15 to 20 minutes. Drain and set aside to cool.

FOR THE BROTH

Heat the oil in a large saucepan over medium heat. When it shimmers, add the onion and cook until golden brown, about 5 minutes.

Add the water and ginger and bring to a boil. Boil for 5 minutes then remove from the heat. Add the tea, soy, sake or wine, sugar, and sesame oil and steep until the tea flavor of the broth is the desired strength (it should taste like tea but should not be bitter or tannic), 3 to 5 minutes. Discard the tea bags, taste the broth, and adjust seasoning as desired.

Divide the barley and the add-ins evenly among bowls. At the table, pour tea broth into each bowl and serve.

🕐 The barley can be made up to 2 days ahead and refrigerated until ready to use.

RIFFS

- Add paper-thin slices of boneless pork chop, chicken breast, or shrimp to the bowl when adding broth.
- Use roasted rice green tea (genmaicha) for a nuttier, earthy flavor.

DIFFICULTY
Easy

YIELD
8 to 10 servings (3.5 quarts/3.5 L soup)

TOTAL TIME
3 hours, 30 minutes, plus bean soaking time

HANDS-ON TIME
20 minutes

If using dried beans, be sure to plan ahead because they'll have to soak at least 8 hours. Dried beans will have a better texture in the finished dish but may be hard to find—use canned black beans if you're in a bind.

Smoked beer is a style of beer that originated in Germany but is made by many microbreweries in the U.S. The top domestic beers are from Fort Collins Brewing, Maui Brewing, Sierra Nevada, and Allagash. If you can't find one, use a good porter and add an extra chipotle or two, keeping in mind it will spice things up quite a bit.

Chipotles en adobo are Mexican chipotle (smoked jalapeño) chiles sold in a can in sauce and can be found in the ethnic aisle of most grocery stores.

Crema is a thick Latin sour cream; sour cream is a good substitute.

I've nicknamed this "Midnight Chili" because thanks to the black beans and the spicy, smoky flavors, this looks and tastes black as night.

TAKEAWAY: How to make chili and/or cook stew meat.
GOES WELL WITH: Serve with corn bread (Sage-Maple Skillet Corn Bread, page 174) or a salad (Romaine Salad with Whiskey Onions, Corn Bread, and Buttermilk Dressing, page 209).

SMOKY BLACK BEAN, BEEF, AND GREEN PEPPER CHILI

3 cups/582 g **dried black (turtle) beans**

3 tbsp **canola, grapeseed, or peanut oil**

1½ lb/680 g **boneless beef round or chuck roast, cut into 1-in/2.5-cm pieces**

Kosher salt and freshly ground black pepper

1 **yellow onion, roughly chopped**

2 **green bell peppers, roughly chopped**

4 **garlic cloves, finely chopped**

1 tbsp **ground cumin**

1 **bay leaf**

One 12 oz/355 ml bottle **smoked beer**

3 cups/720 ml **low-sodium beef broth**

One 14.5 oz/411 g can **diced tomatoes with juice**

2 to 3 **chipotles en adobo, minced**

3 tbsp **finely chopped fresh oregano leaves**

1 to 2 tbsp **honey or agave nectar (optional)**

1 to 2 tbsp **red wine vinegar (optional)**

Avocado, for garnish

Crema or sour cream, for garnish

Sort and wash the beans, place them in a large bowl, and add enough water to cover the beans by 2 in/5 cm. Let sit at room temperature 8 hours or overnight.

Place the beans and their soaking water in a large saucepan; add enough additional water to cover the beans by 3 in/7.5 cm. Bring to a boil over high heat. Decrease the heat to low, skim the surface as needed, and simmer until tender, 1 to 1½ hours. Cool the beans in the cooking liquid and store, or drain and set beans aside.

Heat 1 tablespoon of the oil in a large Dutch oven over medium-high heat. Season the beef well with salt and pepper. When wisps come off the oil but it is not smoking, add half of the beef and cook until the pieces are very browned on all sides, 3 to 5 minutes. Remove the meat to a plate and repeat with the remaining beef.

Wipe out the pan, return to the stove over medium heat, and add the remaining oil. When it shimmers, add the onion, season with salt and pepper, and cook until golden brown, about 3 minutes. Add the bell peppers, garlic, cumin, and bay leaf and cook until fragrant, about 30 seconds. Add the beer and cook until any alcohol smell is cooked off, about 3 minutes. Add the beans, broth, and tomatoes (with juice) and bring to a boil.

Decrease the heat to low and simmer until the meat is fork-tender and flavors are melded, 1½ to 2 hours. Stir in the chipotles and oregano and simmer another 5 to 10 minutes. Taste, and add salt, pepper, honey or vinegar as needed. Serve topped with avocado and crema.

If you have a slow cooker, this is the time to pull it out. After the meat has been browned, combine everything and cook on low heat for about 6 hours.

The beans can be made up to 2 days in advance and refrigerated in the cooking liquid.

Use the bean cooking liquid in place of some of the broth to give the chili more body.

DIFFICULTY
Easy

YIELD
*4 to 6 servings
(5 cups/1.2 L soup)*

TOTAL TIME
45 minutes

HANDS-ON TIME
20 minutes

Don't be frightened by the addition of orange juice; it breathes new life into this classic comfort food. Topped with cheese toasts— as if your grilled cheese jumped into your soup—it's the perfect bridge between old and new.

TAKEAWAY: How to make pureed vegetable soup.
GOES WELL WITH: Serve as a start to a more formal dinner or as a light meal with a simple green salad.

TOMATO-ORANGE SOUP WITH GRILLED CHEESE CROUTONS

TOMATO-ORANGE SOUP

4 tbsp/55g **unsalted butter**

1 **red onion, finely chopped**

2 tsp **kosher salt**

4 **garlic cloves, roughly chopped**

1 tbsp **fresh thyme leaves (or 1 tsp dried thyme)**

½ tsp **ground cinnamon**

One 28 oz/795 g can **diced tomatoes with juice**

1 cup/240 ml **water**

1 cup/240 ml **freshly squeezed orange juice**

1 tsp **sherry vinegar**

CHEESE CROUTONS

8 slices **country bread, cut 1 in/2.5 cm thick**

6 oz/175 g **Gruyère, aged Cheddar, or aged Gouda, sliced paper thin**

CONTINUED

**BLENDER OR
FOOD PROCESSOR**
If you don't have a blender,
use a food processor; otherwise, just eat it chunky—the
soup is still tasty.

Be careful when blending
hot liquids as the heat can
make them explode out of
the blender carafe. To avoid
this, only fill the blender
halfway, remove the plastic
plug in the blender cover,
and start blending on low
for a few seconds before you
kick it up to full speed.

The soup can be made up to
2 days ahead of time and
refrigerated in an airtight
container.

FOR THE SOUP

Melt the butter in a medium saucepan over medium-high heat.
When the foaming subsides, add the onion and salt and cook
until softened and translucent, about 5 minutes. Stir in the garlic,
thyme, and cinnamon and cook until fragrant, about 30 seconds.
Add the tomatoes with juice, 1 cup water, and orange juice, and
bring to a boil.

Decrease the heat to medium-low and cook, stirring occasionally, until the flavors are melded and the liquid is slightly reduced,
20 to 25 minutes. Process in a blender or food processor in
batches until the soup is smooth and aerated. Return the puree
to the saucepan and place over medium-low heat. Add the sherry
vinegar and cook until heated through, 2 to 3 minutes. Taste and
adjust seasoning, as desired.

FOR THE CROUTONS

Meanwhile, heat the broiler and arrange a rack in the top. Alternatively, use a toaster oven. Toast one side of the bread for 30 to
60 seconds, then remove from the oven and flip over. Top each
bread slice with 2 cheese slices and broil until the cheese is melted
and bubbly, about 1 minute.

Ladle the soup into bowls, and serve with 2 cheese croutons for
each serving.

SOUPS

Raita, a yogurt-based condiment, is used to cut the spice in many an Indian dish. Here those spicy and cool elements get whirled together for a refreshing chilled soup that's a welcome source of relief from the stove during the dog days of summer.

TAKEAWAYS: How to make a no-cook soup; how to make cucumbers less bitter.

GOES WELL WITH: Serve as a start to a more formal meal or as a light meal with a simple salad.

DIFFICULTY
Easy

YIELD
6 to 8 servings

TOTAL TIME
1 hour

HANDS-ON TIME
20 minutes

COLD CUCUMBER RAITA SOUP

1 lb/455 g **unpeeled Persian cucumbers, roughly chopped**

2 tsp **kosher salt**

½ **red onion, roughly chopped**

2 **medium garlic cloves, smashed**

3 tbsp **red wine vinegar**

1 **avocado, peeled, pitted, and roughly chopped**

4 cups/1 L **buttermilk, well-shaken**

⅓ cup/5 g **packed fresh mint leaves**

1½ tsp **ground coriander**

1½ tsp **sugar**

¾ tsp **ground cumin**

¼ tsp **finely ground black pepper**

4 **medium green onions (white and pale green parts), trimmed and thinly sliced crosswise, for ganish**

4 **medium radishes, trimmed, halved, and thinly sliced, for garnish**

Toasted pita bread or naan, for serving

Persian cucumbers have a clean flavor and no seeds. If you can't find them, use Japanese or English hot-house cucumbers.

Naan is a charred Indian flatbread that is becoming more widely available. If you can't find it, you can use another flatbread or pita chips.

Sprinkle the cucumbers with salt, toss to coat, and place in a colander over a plate. Let sit 30 minutes then drain excess water. Meanwhile, combine the onion and garlic in a small nonreactive bowl, cover with the vinegar, and set aside for 10 to 30 minutes.

Combine cucumber, onion mixture, avocado, buttermilk, mint, coriander, sugar, cumin, and black pepper in a blender or food processor (you may have to do this in batches). Process on high until very well blended, smooth, and aerated, about 5 minutes. Pass the mixture through a fine mesh strainer into a nonreactive bowl.

Refrigerate until thoroughly chilled, at least 30 minutes. Before serving, whisk, taste and adjust seasoning as desired. Serve topped with green onions and radishes, with pita alongside.

🕐 The soup can be made up to 2 days ahead and stored refrigerated in an airtight container.

DIFFICULTY
Easy

YIELD
4 servings (¼ cup/ 60 ml vinaigrette)

TOTAL TIME
25 minutes

HANDS-ON TIME
10 minutes

Nutty squash, sweet currants, and toasted pine nuts combine with a mustardy balsamic vinaigrette in this cold-weather salad. It's light enough to be eaten without guilt but flavorful enough to help you escape the worst of winter doldrums.

TAKEAWAYS: How to make a vinaigrette; how to roast squash.

GOES WELL WITH: Serve this as an accompaniment to a roast or grilled meats or, for a main course salad, top it with sliced seared steak or roast chicken.

ARUGULA SALAD WITH ROASTED SQUASH, CURRANTS, AND PINE NUTS

BALSAMIC-MUSTARD VINAIGRETTE

2 tbsp **balsamic vinegar**

1 tbsp **red wine vinegar**

2 tsp **Dijon mustard**

1 tsp **packed light brown sugar**

1 tsp **Worcestershire sauce**

2 tbsp **extra-virgin olive oil**

Kosher salt and freshly ground black pepper

ARUGULA SALAD

1 lb/455 g **butternut or delicata squash, trimmed, halved lengthwise, and seeded**

1 tbsp **olive oil**

½ tsp **kosher salt**

Freshly ground black pepper

2 oz/60 g **(about 2 handfuls) baby arugula leaves**

⅓ cup/40 g **toasted pine nuts (page 119)**

¼ cup/40 g **dried currants**

Pretty much any hard winter squash will work here. If you get a bigger squash, just cut it into half-moons instead of rounds. See Chopping a (Hard) Winter Squash, page 80.

FOR THE VINAIGRETTE

Combine the vinegars in a large nonreactive bowl with the mustard, brown sugar, and Worcestershire and whisk to evenly combine. Set aside to let the flavors meld, at least 5 minutes. Slowly whisk in the olive oil until completely combined. Season with salt and pepper and serve.

FOR THE SALAD

Heat oven to 450°F/230°C/gas 8 and arrange a rack in the middle. Cut the squash halves crosswise into semicircles that are ½ in/ 12 mm thick (you'll have about 8). Toss the squash with the oil, salt, and pepper, and spread out on a rimmed baking sheet. Roast until the undersides are browned and slightly blistered, 10 to 15 minutes.

To assemble, place a portion of greens in each serving bowl, top with a scattering of pine nuts and currants, then add a couple squash pieces. Finish with a few cranks of freshly ground black pepper, as desired. Drizzle with a few teaspoons of dressing and pass the extra on the side.

You can make the dressing up to 2 days ahead and refrigerate in an airtight container. Dressing can be made in a jar, too (see page 91).

RIFFS
- Swap sweet potatoes for the squash.
- Top with some crumbled feta, goat cheese, or blue cheese.
- Add some sautéed mushrooms.

DIFFICULTY
Easy

YIELD
*4 servings (¾ cup/
180 ml dressing)*

TOTAL TIME
10 minutes

HANDS-ON TIME
10 minutes

A combination of avocado, sprouts, and a nutty and sweet, almost hummus-esque dressing breathes new life into the classic green side salad.

TAKEAWAY: How to make a basic green salad.
GOES WELL WITH: Use this salad in place of a classic green salad.

BUTTER LETTUCE SALAD WITH TAHINI-HONEY DRESSING

TAHINI-HONEY DRESSING

½ cup/120 g **tahini**

5 tsp **freshly squeezed lemon juice**

2 tbsp **honey or agave nectar**

2 **garlic cloves, halved**

¾ cup/180 ml **water**

Kosher salt and freshly ground black pepper

BUTTER LETTUCE SALAD

7 oz/210 g **butter lettuce**

1 **avocado, peeled, pitted, and thinly sliced**

1 **Persian cucumber, halved and thinly sliced** (about 1 cup/100 g)

1 **carrot, grated on large holes of box grater**

1 cup/35 g **sprouts (such as sunflower, pea, or radish), for garnish**

Tahini is a sesame paste that can be found in the ethnic aisle of the grocery store. Use it to make hummus or in place of peanut butter in marinades and sauces.

The dressing can be made up to 2 days ahead and refrigerated in an airtight container. Dressing can also be made in a jar (see page 91).

BLENDER OR MINI FOOD PROCESSOR
If you don't have a blender, use a food processor; otherwise, just put ingredients in a jar and shake until combined.

FOR THE DRESSING

Combine all ingredients in a blender or mini food processor and process until smooth. Taste and add additional salt and pepper as desired.

FOR THE SALAD

Place the lettuce in a bowl and scatter avocado, cucumber, carrot, and sprouts on top. Drizzle with dressing and serve.

RIFFS

- Use almond, cashew, or peanut butter in place of the tahini.
- Stir minced parsley, chives, or cilantro into the dressing.
- Add a chopped fresh chile or green onions to the dressing.
- Blend the dressing with some plain whole milk yogurt.
- Add radishes, tomatoes, or sunflower seeds to the salad.

Persimmons are one of my favorite fruits and the firm Fuyu is a welcome addition to salads. Earthy, filling, and sweet, this autumn salad shows why fall is my favorite of the food seasons.

TAKEAWAY: How to make a vinaigrette in a blender.
GOES WELL WITH: Autumn roasts or stews.
RECIPE WITHIN A RECIPE: Use the dressing on other salads or drizzle on steamed or blanched vegetables.

DIFFICULTY
Easy

YIELD
6 to 8 servings (⅓ cup/75 ml vinaigrette)

TOTAL TIME
10 minutes

HANDS-ON TIME
10 minutes

SPINACH SALAD WITH PERSIMMONS AND HAZELNUTS

CHIVE VINAIGRETTE

2 tbsp **cider vinegar**

1 tsp **Dijon mustard**

½ tsp **sugar**

¼ tsp **kosher salt**

2 tbsp **nut or squash oil**

2 tbsp **extra-virgin olive oil**

3 tbsp **thinly sliced fresh chives**

SPINACH-PERSIMMON SALAD

4 oz/110 g **baby spinach (about 4 handfuls)**

2 **medium ripe Fuyu persimmons, halved, seeded, and thinly sliced**

½ cup/60 g **crumbled feta cheese**

¼ cup/60 g **roughly chopped toasted hazelnuts**

Using a nut or squash oil in the dressing underscores the flavors of the salad. Hazelnut and acorn squash oils work particularly well. If you can't find the oils, just use olive oil.

Fuyu persimmons are tomato-shaped fruit that are best eaten when firm; they are in season in the fall.

FOR THE VINAIGRETTE

Combine the vinegar, mustard, sugar, and salt in a small blender or mini food processor. With the motor running, add the oils in a thin stream until smooth. Stir in chives then taste and adjust the seasoning as desired.

FOR THE SALAD

Combine the spinach and persimmons in a large nonreactive bowl. Drizzle with half of the dressing and toss to combine. Divide the salad between individual plates, scatter with feta and hazelnuts, and drizzle with additional dressing, as desired.

The dressing can be made by hand though it will not be as emulsified.

🕐 The dressing can be made up to 2 days ahead without the chives and refrigerated in an airtight container. Stir in chives just before using.

RIFFS

- Use pears instead of persimmons.
- Swap the cheese for dried fruit.
- Add caramelized onions to the salad before serving.

DIFFICULTY	
Easy	
YIELD	
6 to 8 servings	
TOTAL TIME	
30 minutes	
HANDS-ON TIME	
15 minutes	

I know, you see the words "raw kale" and you're a tad scared, aren't you? Well, don't be, because the kale gets combined with salt and lemon juice for a boost of flavor and an improved texture. This dish (pictured on pages 204–205) requires nothing more than some chopping, stirring, and a bit of patience. It pays back with a flavorful and filling salad that's easily one of the healthiest recipes you'll ever come across.

TAKEAWAY: How to make "massaged" raw kale.
GOES WELL WITH: Serve as a filling salad or as an accompaniment to a roast or stew.

RAW KALE SALAD WITH HEIRLOOM TOMATOES AND ROASTED CASHEWS

2 **large bunches kale** (about 1 lb/455 g)

2 tbsp **freshly squeezed lemon juice**

1½ tsp **kosher salt, plus more for seasoning**

3 **carrots, peeled**

3 **heirloom tomatoes** (about 1 lb/455 g)**, cut into medium dice**

6 **green onions, (white and pale green parts), trimmed and thinly sliced crosswise**

2 tbsp **freshly squeezed orange juice**

2 tbsp **cider vinegar**

3 tbsp **extra-virgin olive oil, plus more for garnish**

1 tsp **grated orange zest**

2 tbsp **toasted sesame seeds**

1 cup/115 g **roasted, salted cashews, roughly chopped**

Fold each kale leaf in half lengthwise and pull out and discard the center rib. Tear the leaves into 2-in/5-cm pieces and place in a large nonreactive bowl. Add the lemon juice and salt and, with clean hands, rub the kale between your forefingers until it is wilted and softened, about 5 minutes.

Use this technique whenever you want to eat kale raw, as it improves the texture.

Meanwhile, use a peeler to peel the carrots into ribbons that are 2 to 3 inches/5 to 7.5 cm long. Add the carrot strips, tomatoes, and green onions to the kale and toss to combine. Add the orange juice, vinegar, olive oil, and zest. Let sit 15 minutes at room temperature before adding the sesame seeds and cashews. Taste and adjust seasoning as needed. Serve garnished with a drizzle of olive oil.

The salad can be made up to 1 day ahead and refrigerated in an airtight container. The longer the salad sits, the more wilted the mixture becomes.

RIFFS

- Swap chard, turnip greens, or beet greens for the kale.
- When tomatoes aren't in season, use diced roasted beets or boiled new potatoes instead.
- Use almonds or sunflower seeds in place of, or in addition to, the cashews.
- Top with crumbled feta or goat cheese just before serving.

DIFFICULTY
Easy

YIELD
**6 to 8 servings
(⅔ cup/165 ml
dressing)**

TOTAL TIME
30 minutes

HANDS-ON TIME
10 minutes

Made with purple sweet potatoes and a sweet-tangy mustard-mayonnaise dressing, this is a welcome update to a classic potato salad. My brother was scared when he first saw the purple hue of the potatoes, but I took that as a good thing because it only left more for me!

TAKEAWAY: How to make potato salad.
RECIPE WITHIN A RECIPE: Use the dressing on salads or sandwiches.
GOES WELL WITH: This is perfect for a potluck or picnic.

PURPLE SWEET POTATO SALAD WITH GREEN BEANS AND PEAS

PURPLE SWEET POTATO SALAD

2 lb/1 kg **purple sweet potatoes, cut into 1-in/2.5-cm pieces**

1 lb/455 g **green beans, trimmed and cut into 1-inch pieces**

1 cup/150 g **fresh or frozen baby peas**

6 **green onions (white and pale green parts), trimmed and thinly sliced**

Kosher salt and freshly ground black pepper

MUSTARD-MAYO DRESSING

2 tbsp **mayonnaise**

2 tbsp **sour cream**

1 tbsp **Dijon mustard**

2 tbsp **brown-rice vinegar, plus more as needed**

1 tsp **kosher salt**

½ tsp **freshly ground black pepper**

½ tsp **sugar, plus more as needed**

The purple sweet potato is also known as a Japanese or Okinawan sweet potato. If you can't find it, you can use red-skinned, orange-fleshed sweet potatoes (often labeled yams).

If you can, make your own homemade mayonnaise (page 92) for this recipe or seek out a good-quality store-bought mayonnaise. The tang and sweetness factor of the mayonnaise will impact the final flavor of the dressing so you may need to add a pinch of sugar or a dash of vinegar to balance things out.

⏱ You can make the salad, without the green onions, up to 1 day ahead and refrigerate in an airtight container. Bring to room temperature and stir in the green onions before serving.

FOR THE POTATO SALAD

Place the potatoes in a large pot, cover with cold salted water, and bring to a boil. Boil the potatoes until fork-tender, but still semi-firm (10 to 15 minutes after the water begins to boil). Add the green beans and peas and cook until bright, about 2 minutes.

Drain and submerge the potatoes, green beans, and peas in ice water to cool (5 to 10 minutes).

FOR THE DRESSING

While the vegetables cool, whisk together all of the dressing ingredients until smooth. Taste, and if the dressing is too tangy, add a pinch of sugar. If it is too sweet, add another capful of vinegar. Taste and season with salt and pepper as needed.

Drain the potatoes, green beans, and peas, combine with the green onions and dressing and toss to coat and mix well. (If the dressing clings too much to the potatoes, add a capful of vinegar or water to loosen it up.) Season with salt and pepper and serve.

The dressing can be made up to 2 days ahead and refrigerated in an airtight container.

RIFFS

- You could also make this with regular (not sweet) potatoes.
- You can make this a bit healthier by using yogurt for the mayo and sour cream in the dressing, but it will make the dressing looser.

DIFFICULTY
Easy

YIELD
*4 to 6 servings
(⅓ cup/75 ml
vinaigrette)*

TOTAL TIME
10 minutes

HANDS-ON TIME
5 minutes

*Truth be told, I was first drawn to this salad because I liked the way the word **fattoush** sounds when said out loud. But then I had it prepared for me fresh and it was love at first bite. Everyday ingredients get recombined in this classic Middle Eastern dish for a refreshing twist on the standard green salad.*

TAKEAWAY: How to make vinaigrette in a jar.
GOES WELL WITH: Make this your go-to salad when you want something that adds flavor without stealing the spotlight from the main course.

FATTOUSH SALAD WITH PITA CRISPS

Sumac is a berry that is ground and used in many Middle Eastern dishes. It has a pleasant fruity, slightly sour taste and adds a lot to this dressing. It is often sold in gourmet and ethnic stores, but, if you can't find it, use some grated lemon zest.

Pomegranate molasses is a thick, sweet, and tart Middle Eastern condiment that is getting more and more popular. If you can't locate it, use reduced pomegranate juice, cranberry juice concentrate, or balsamic vinegar.

Persian cucumbers have a clean flavor and no seeds. If you can't find them, use Japanese or English hothouse cucumbers.

🕐 The vinaigrette can be made up to 2 weeks ahead and refrigerated in an airtight container. Bring to room temperature and shake before using.

HONEY-POMEGRANATE VINAIGRETTE

2 tbsp **extra-virgin olive oil**

1 **medium shallot, minced**

2 tsp **ground sumac**

1 tbsp **honey or agave nectar**

2 tsp **pomegranate molasses**

¼ cup/60 ml **red wine vinegar**

Kosher salt and freshly ground black pepper

FATTOUSH SALAD

8 oz/225 g **romaine lettuce hearts, torn into bite-sized pieces**

1 **plum tomato, roughly chopped**

2 **Persian cucumbers, halved lengthwise and sliced into half moons**

6 **radishes, halved and thinly sliced**

¼ cup/10 g **roughly chopped fresh mint leaves**

2 tbsp **roughly chopped fresh Italian parsley leaves**

2 cups/90 g **toasted pita chips**

3 oz/90 g **crumbled aged feta, for garnish**

FOR THE VINAIGRETTE

Place all ingredients in a jar and shake well to evenly combine. Set aside to let flavors meld, at least 5 minutes. Taste, adjust seasoning as desired, and shake to recombine before dressing the salad.

FOR THE SALAD

Place the lettuce in a bowl then scatter with tomato, cucumbers, radishes, mint, and parsley. Drizzle with the vinaigrette, top with pita chips and cheese, and serve.

SALADS

Smoky caramelized onions, crisp corn bread, tangy radishes, and an herb-packed buttermilk dressing meet up in this Southern-esque salad that's just as fitting served with molasses pork (page 312) as it is with panko-crusted tilapia (page 324).

TAKEAWAYS: How to make caramelized onions; how to make a quick pickle.
GOES WELL WITH: Smoky Black Bean, Beef, and Green Pepper Chili (page 192)

DIFFICULTY
Medium

YIELD
4 to 6 servings (⅔ cup/165 ml dressing)

TOTAL TIME
55 minutes

HANDS-ON TIME
25 minutes

ROMAINE SALAD WITH WHISKEY ONIONS, CORN BREAD, AND BUTTERMILK DRESSING

CORN BREAD CROUTONS

12 oz/340 g **corn bread**

PICKLED RADISH

1 **small watermelon radish (or 10 small breakfast radishes)**

¼ cup/60 ml **brown-rice vinegar**

2 tsp **sugar**

¼ tsp **kosher salt**

CARAMELIZED ONIONS

1 tbsp **unsalted butter**

1 **yellow onion, halved and thinly sliced**

1 tsp **sugar**

1 tbsp **whiskey, Scotch, or water**

BUTTERMILK DRESSING

¼ cup/60ml **buttermilk**

¼ cup/60 ml **crème fraîche**

¼ cup/10 g **minced fresh chives**

2 tbsp **minced fresh Italian parsley**

1 tbsp **brown-rice vinegar**

1¼ tsp **kosher salt, plus more for seasoning**

½ tsp **granulated sugar**

1 lb/455 g **romaine hearts, torn into bite-sized pieces**

Get corn bread from the store or make Sage-Maple Skillet Corn Bread (page 174) and use it here.

Crème fraîche is a tangier French take on sour cream. If you can't find it, use sour cream or crema Mexicana.

FOR THE CROUTONS

Heat the oven to 350°F/177°C/gas 4 and arrange a rack in the middle. Break up the corn bread into large pieces (about 1-in/2.5-cm squares) and place on a baking sheet. Toast until golden brown, about 15 minutes. Set aside.

The corn bread can be made up to 1 day ahead and stored at room temperature in an airtight container.

CONTINUED

FOR THE PICKLED RADISH

Meanwhile, using a mandoline or sharp knife, thinly slice the radish about ⅛ in/3 mm thick. In a nonreactive bowl, mix the vinegar, sugar, and salt together until dissolved. Add the radish slices and place in the fridge until ready to use, at least 10 minutes; stir before using.

FOR THE ONIONS

Meanwhile, add the butter to a large frying pan over medium-high heat. When it shimmers, add the onion and sugar and stir to combine. Cook, stirring occasionally, until deep brown, 15 to 20 minutes. Carefully add the whiskey and stir to incorporate and scrape up any browned bits in the pan. Set aside.

FOR THE DRESSING

Place all ingredients in a medium nonreactive bowl and whisk until smooth and evenly combined. Taste and adjust seasoning as desired. Set aside to help develop the flavor, at least 5 minutes.

FOR THE SALAD

Place the romaine in a serving bowl and scatter the caramelized onions, radish, and corn bread on top. Drizzle with ½ cup/120 ml of the dressing and serve.

RIFF: Add charred peppers, toasted corn, sautéed zucchini, shredded chicken, or crumbled blue cheese to the salad.

MANDOLINE
A mandoline will make quick work of slicing the radishes, but you could also use a sharp knife.

The onions can be made up to 2 days ahead. Refrigerate in an airtight container and warm to room temperature before using.

The dressing can be made without the herbs up to 2 days ahead and stored in an airtight container in the refrigerator; stir in herbs just before using.

DIFFICULTY
Easy

YIELD
*4 to 6 servings
(⅔ cup/75 ml
dressing)*

TOTAL TIME
1 hour

HANDS-ON TIME
15 minutes

Caraway is widely used in Eastern European cuisines, and lends a nutty, anise note. If you can't find it, use dill or anise instead.

Look for prepared horseradish in jars in the condiment aisle. Don't use horseradish cream as it has lots of added stabilizers and fat. If you can't find prepared horseradish, substitute prepared wasabi paste or spicy mustard.

Beets have such a bad rap, but when properly made, they're sweet, earthy, colorful, and complex all at once. This is a go-to when you need a salad that's a crowd-pleaser, can be made ahead, and transports well.

TAKEAWAY: How to roast beets.

ROASTED BEET SALAD WITH CREAMY CARAWAY DRESSING

CREAMY CARAWAY DRESSING

½ cup/120 ml **whole milk yogurt**

2 tbsp **extra-virgin olive oil**

2 tbsp **red wine vinegar**

1 tbsp **caraway seed**

1 tbsp **prepared horseradish**

1 tsp **kosher salt**

1 tsp **sugar**

½ tsp **freshly ground black pepper**

ROASTED BEET SALAD

1½ lb/680 g **beets**

3 heads **endive**

1 head **fennel**

2 tbsp **olive oil**

1 tbsp **red wine vinegar**

¾ tsp **kosher salt**

Freshly ground black pepper

⅓ cup/50 g **toasted walnuts, roughly chopped**

FOR THE DRESSING

Combine all ingredients in a small nonreactive bowl and whisk until smooth. Taste and adjust seasoning as desired. Refrigerate until ready to use.

The dressing and beets can be made up to 2 days in advance and refrigerated in an airtight container.

FOR THE SALAD

Heat the oven to 450°F/230°C/gas 8 and arrange a rack in the middle. Wrap the beets in aluminum foil, set directly on the middle rack, and roast until the beets are knife-tender, 45 to 50 minutes. When cool enough to handle, rinse the beets under water and rub off the skins. Halve beets then cut into ¼-in/6-mm slices.

Meanwhile, trim ends off the endive then cut the endive cross-wise into ½-in/12-mm rings and place in a large nonreactive bowl. Quarter the fennel lengthwise, cut out the core, then cut crosswise into ¼-in/6-mm slices.

The endive and fennel can be cut up to 4 hours ahead; store refrigerated in ice water.

Combine the endive, fennel, and beets in a bowl then toss with the olive oil, vinegar, salt, and pepper to coat.

To serve, place the beet mixture on a platter, drizzle with the dressing, scatter nuts over the top, and sprinkle with freshly ground black pepper.

RIFFS

- Stir in some cooked grains or lentils to make it a full meal.
- Add diced apples or pears for a sweet note.

DIFFICULTY
Medium

YIELD
**4 to 6 servings
(¼ cup/60 ml
vinaigrette)**

TOTAL TIME
15 to 20 minutes

HANDS-ON TIME
5 minutes

Salads tend to be thought of in warm-weather, but this one proves otherwise. With sweet fruit and tangy pickled fennel, this salad is so crisp and refreshing, it almost makes you happy that summer's over.

RECIPE WITHIN A RECIPE: Use the pickled fennel as a condiment.

FALL SALAD WITH CRISP APPLES AND PICKLED FENNEL

Whole-grain Dijon mustard has whole mustard seeds in it. If you can't find it, regular Dijon will work.

There are many types of cress, but I prefer the more mellow upland cress for this salad. If you can't find cress, use baby arugula or spinach leaves.

ORANGE VINAIGRETTE

¼ cup/60 ml **orange juice**

1 tbsp **whole-grain Dijon mustard**

2 tsp **cider vinegar**

Grated zest from 1 medium orange

½ tsp **kosher salt**

¼ tsp **freshly ground black pepper**

½ tsp **sugar**

¼ cup/60 ml **extra-virgin olive oil**

FENNEL-APPLE SALAD

1 **fennel bulb** (about 9 oz/255 g)

2 tbsp **cider vinegar**

2 tbsp **orange juice**

4 oz/120 g **upland cress leaves, washed** (about 4 cups lightly packed)

1 **medium Gala or Fuji apple, sliced paper thin**

3 tbsp **roasted, salted pumpkin seeds**

The vinaigrette can be made up to 1 week ahead and refrigerated in an airtight container. Shake or whisk briefly before using.

FOR THE VINAIGRETTE

Combine all the ingredients except the oil in a nonreactive bowl and whisk until the sugar is dissolved. Let sit for at least 5 minutes. Whisking constantly, slowly drizzle in the olive oil until completely incorporated. Taste and add salt and pepper as needed.

FOR THE SALAD

Trim the fennel bulb, quarter lengthwise, and cut out the core. Using a very sharp knife or a mandoline, cut the fennel quarters crosswise into ⅛-in/3-mm slices. Pour the vinegar and orange juice over the fennel and let marinate at least 5 minutes; drain before using.

If making the salad ahead, toss the apple with a capful of vinegar to prevent it from browning.

To arrange the salad, place the cress, then fennel, then apple on a plate. Scatter the pumpkin seeds over the top, then drizzle with the vinaigrette. Serve immediately.

The ultimate make-ahead dish (pictured on pages 216–217), this salad only gets more flavorful as it sits. Here I use a load of summer vegetables but feel free to mix it up according to what's in season.

TAKEAWAY: How to cook farro.

DIFFICULTY
Easy

YIELD
6 to 8 servings

TOTAL TIME
40 minutes

HANDS-ON TIME
15 minutes

SUMMER VEGETABLE–FARRO SALAD

1½ cups/280 g **semi-pearled farro, rinsed and drained**

2 **Persian cucumbers, thinly sliced**

1½ cups/225 g **halved Sweet 100 or grape tomatoes**

4 **medium green onions (white and pale green parts), ends trimmed, thinly sliced crosswise**

4 **medium breakfast radishes, thinly sliced**

¼ cup/10 g **finely chopped mixed fresh herbs (such as Italian parsley, chives, basil, and tarragon)**

3 tbsp **balsamic vinegar**

1 tbsp **extra-virgin olive oil, plus more for garnish**

2 tsp **kosher salt**

½ cup/60 g **crumbled feta cheese, goat cheese, or ricotta salata**

Bring a medium pot of heavily salted water to a boil over high heat, stir in the farro, decrease the heat to medium, and simmer until the farro is al dente (soft, yet retains structure), 15 to 20 minutes. Remove from the heat, drain any excess water, and set aside.

While the grains are cooling, make the rest of the salad. Combine all the remaining ingredients except the cheese in a large bowl and toss to coat thoroughly.

When the farro is at room temperature, add to the bowl and toss to combine. Taste and add more dressing or salt or both, as desired. Serve with a drizzle of olive oil and cheese scattered over the top.

Look for semi-pearled farro in the bulk section or health food aisle of the grocery. If you can't find it, you can use hard wheat berries or spelt, soft (a.k.a. pastry) wheat berries or pearled barley—just rinse and proceed.

Persian cucumbers are a sweet, delicate cucumber that is becoming more prevalent. If you can't find them, English hothouse cucumbers will work well.

This is the time to pull out the good balsamic and extra-virgin olive oil.

Ricotta salata is a sliceable, aged version of ricotta that should be more popular than it is.

The farro can be made up to 2 days ahead and refrigerated in an airtight container.

The salad can be made up to 2 days ahead but don't mix in the herbs and cheese until ready to eat. Just before serving, stir in the herbs and sprinkle cheese across the top.

DIFFICULTY
Easy

YIELD
4 servings (1 cup/240 ml pesto)

TOTAL TIME
30 minutes

HANDS-ON TIME
10 minutes

These days pesto sauce is so ubiquitous you may wonder why you should make your own. Well, because I can pretty much guarantee you haven't had a pesto like this. By blending the oil and nuts before adding the other ingredients, the sauce becomes so creamy and rich, people will swear you put cream in it.

TAKEAWAY: How to really make pesto.
RECIPE WITHIN A RECIPE: Though classically used for pasta, pesto is very versatile. Try it on a sandwich, mixed into soup just before serving, or dolloped on grilled meat or fish.

CREAMY PESTO PASTA WITH GREEN BEANS AND POTATOES

BASIL PESTO

2 oz/55 g (about 2 cups) **fresh basil leaves**

½ cup/70 g **pine nuts**

⅓ cup/75 ml **olive oil, plus more for drizzling**

1 **garlic clove**

½ tsp **kosher salt, plus more for seasoning**

½ cup/2 oz/55 g **grated Parmigiano-Reggiano cheese**

½ cup/2 oz/55 g **grated Pecorino cheese**

PASTA

¼ pound/120 g **marble or baby potatoes**

½ pound/230 g **gemelli, linguine, trenette, or trofie pasta**

¼ pound/120 g **haricot verts, trimmed and cut into 2-in/ 5-cm pieces**

Haricot verts are thin, French-style green beans. If you can't find them, use regular green beans and cook a minute or two longer.

Soaking the basil leaves helps to mellow their flavor and makes the final sauce more balanced. So don't skip that step.

FOR THE PESTO

Place the basil in cold water and set aside to soak briefly, at least 5 minutes.

Meanwhile, combine the nuts, oil, garlic, and salt in a food processor fitted with the metal blade and process until the mixture is very smooth.

Drain the soaked basil and shake off the water but don't pat dry (you want some of that water). Add the basil to the nut mixture in the food processor and process until just evenly combined and mixture is light green, about 5 pulses. Add the cheese and pulse until just combined, about 5 pulses.

Remove the pesto from the work bowl and taste. Add more salt as needed.

FOR THE PASTA

Place a large pot of heavily salted water over high heat. Add the potatoes and cook until fork-tender, about 8 minutes (start timing after the water boils). Use a slotted spoon to remove the potatoes to a colander and set aside.

Return the pot to high heat and return to a boil. Add the pasta and cook 2 minutes short of the package directions. With 1 minute left to go, add the haricots verts and cook until bright green, 30 seconds to 1 minute. Reserve 1 cup/240 ml pasta water and drain the pasta and haricots verts.

Use a warm pasta pot but don't put the pot back on the stove. Add the pesto and half of the pasta water and stir. Add the pasta and stir. Add more water as needed until each piece of pasta is well coated in the sauce. Taste and add more salt as needed. Serve with a drizzle of oil.

RIFFS

- Use walnuts, macadamia nuts, or pecans in place of the pine nuts.
- Swap fresh parsley, mint, cilantro, or arugula for the basil.
- Add fresh cut tomatoes to the finished pasta.
- Use asparagus in place of the green beans.

Pesto can be made up to 1 week ahead of time. To store, place in an airtight container, lay plastic wrap against the surface of the pesto, and refrigerate until ready to use.

BLENDER OR FOOD PROCESSOR
If you don't have a blender, use a food processor; otherwise, just eat it chunky.

DIFFICULTY
Easy

YIELD
6 to 8 servings

TOTAL TIME
20 minutes

HANDS-ON TIME
10 minutes

The first of spring's produce—sweet peas, delicate asparagus, and a mess of herbs—comes together in this light, herby, bright green pasta that cures even the worst bouts of spring fever.

PEA, ASPARAGUS, AND SPRING HERB PASTA

Shell-shaped conchiglie pasta is called for here, but other small pasta such as orecchiette, or even linguine will work well.

1 lb/455 g **conchiglie pasta**

4 tbsp **olive oil, plus more for garnish**

5 **shallots, quartered lengthwise, and sliced crosswise paper thin**

Kosher salt and freshly ground black pepper

1 lb/455 g **pencil-thin asparagus, trimmed and cut in ½-in/ 12-mm slices on bias**

2 **garlic cloves, thinly sliced**

2 cups/230 g **shelled fresh or frozen English peas**

⅔ cup/3 oz/75 g **grated Parmigiano-Reggiano cheese, plus more for garnish**

2 tbsp **unsalted butter**

2 tsp **freshly squeezed lemon juice**

2 tsp **grated lemon zest**

1 cup/40 g **roughly chopped mixed fresh herbs (such as chervil, chives, Italian parsley, mint, or tarragon)**

¾ cup/100 g **toasted pine nuts**

When you can find good-quality, in-season peas, take the extra time to shell them fresh. However, if they're not in good shape, go ahead and use frozen peas.

Bring a large pot of heavily salted water to a boil over high heat. Add the pasta and cook 2 minutes short of the package directions. Reserve 2 cups/480 ml pasta water and drain pasta.

CONTINUED

Meanwhile, heat the oil in a large frying pan over medium-high heat. When the oil shimmers, add the shallots, season with salt and pepper, and cook until golden brown, about 5 minutes.

Add the asparagus and garlic, season with salt, and cook until knife-tender and bright green, about 3 minutes. Stir in the peas and cook until peas are bright green, about 2 minutes.

Add the drained pasta and 1 cup/240 ml of the reserved pasta water and cook until the sauce starts to coat the pasta, about 2 minutes. Remove from the heat and transfer to a large serving bowl. Add the cheese and butter and stir to coat. Add more pasta water as needed so the sauce just clings to the pasta but is not dry.

Stir in the lemon juice, lemon zest, herbs, and pine nuts and stir to coat. Taste and adjust seasoning as desired. Garnish with freshly ground black pepper, a drizzle of olive oil, and freshly grated cheese and serve.

RIFFS

- Crisp 3 oz/85 g diced cured bacon, such as pancetta, in the frying pan then cook the shallot in the drippings for a smoky note.
- Use low-sodium vegetable or chicken broth in place of half of the pasta cooking water when finishing the sauce.
- Be indulgent and add a few tablespoons of heavy cream in place of the butter.

My mother loves pumpkin ravioli with brown butter-sage sauce but I don't always feel up to making them from scratch. This is the compromise dish with all the same flavors but without the strain.

TAKEAWAY: How to make brown butter.

RECIPE WITHIN A RECIPE: Omit the pasta and you have a satisfying roasted squash side dish. To finish it off, stir in the sage and shallots when it comes out of the oven and serve topped with a scattering of cheese and pumpkin seeds.

GOES WELL WITH: Use as a first course for a hearty meal, or serve with grilled or roasted meats for a one-course meal.

DIFFICULTY
Easy/Medium

YIELD
6 to 8 servings

TOTAL TIME
40 minutes

HANDS-ON TIME
15 minutes

ROASTED SQUASH PASTA WITH SAGE BROWN BUTTER

1 large (about 3 lb/1.4 kg) **butternut squash**

4 tbsp/60 ml **olive oil**

Kosher salt and freshly ground black pepper

1 lb/455 g **linguine or spaghetti pasta**

4 tbsp/60 g **unsalted butter**

15 to 20 **fresh sage leaves, thinly sliced**

4 **garlic cloves, thinly sliced**

½ cup/3 oz/60 g **grated Parmigiano-Reggiano cheese, plus more for garnish** (about 2 oz)

⅔ cup/70 g **roasted, salted pumpkin seeds, for garnish (optional)**

4 oz/115 g **Cotija, feta, or ricotta cheese, for garnish (optional)**

Butternut squash is the most common winter (a.k.a. hard-skinned squash), but you could also use pretty much any other commonly found hard-skinned winter squash. See page 80 for tips on how to safely open a winter squash.

Look for a high-quality ricotta as the cheaper stuff has a rubbery texture.

Heat the oven to 450°F/230°/gas 8 and arrange a rack in the middle. Trim the ends off the butternut squash, peel it, scrape out the seeds, and cut the flesh into ¾-in/2-cm cubes.

Combine the squash and 1 tablespoon of the oil on a rimmed baking sheet and toss with a generous pinch of salt and a few cranks of ground pepper. Roast, turning a few times, until knife-tender, about 20 minutes.

CONTINUED

Meanwhile, bring a large pot of heavily salted water to a boil. Add the pasta, stir, and cook 2 minutes short of the package directions. Reserve 1½ cups/360 ml of the pasta water, and drain the pasta and set aside.

Return the pasta pot to the stovetop over medium-low heat and add the butter. When the foaming subsides and the butter begins to brown, add the sage and cook until crisp and fragrant. Immediately remove the sage to a plate and set aside. Add the garlic and cook until golden brown, about 1 minute.

Immediately add the drained pasta and 1 cup/240 ml of the reserved pasta water and cook until the sauce just clings to the noodles. As necessary, add additional pasta water until there is a tiny pool of liquid in the bottom of the pot.

Remove from the heat, add the squash, the remaining oil, and Parmigiano-Reggiano and stir to coat. Taste and adjust seasoning as desired.

Serve immediately, topping each serving with grated cheese, a scattering of pumpkin seeds, a crumble of Cotija or feta or a generous dollop of ricotta, and freshly ground black pepper.

DIFFICULTY
Easy

YIELD
*12 to 16 servings
(11 cups/
2.75 quarts/2.6 L)*

TOTAL TIME
2 hours, 50 minutes

HANDS-ON TIME
50 minutes

A well-made ragù is my ultimate comfort food—slow cooked, layered with flavor, and seriously filling. This sauce fits that tab perfectly.

TAKEAWAY: How to make ragù.
GOES WELL WITH: Toss with pasta or use in a lasagna; this sauce makes enough for about 2 lb/910 g of pasta (like pappardelle), or for 1 large lasagna—just layer with noodles, Parmesan, ricotta, and mozzarella and bake. Balance out the ragù's richness by serving with a green salad.

REAL-DEAL PANCETTA AND PORK RAGÙ

If possible, buy a 4-oz/115-g piece of pancetta and you'll have more control over how it's cut. To cut, freeze 5 to 15 minutes then cut with a sharp knife.

¼ cup/60 ml **olive oil**

4 oz/115 g **pancetta, cut into small dice**

2 **yellow onions, finely chopped**

4 **garlic cloves, finely chopped**

Kosher salt and freshly ground black pepper

2 **carrots, finely chopped**

2 **celery stalks, finely chopped**

1 **bay leaf**

Ground veal has traditionally been the go-to in my family for ragù but it's been surrounded by plenty of controversy over the years. I now make mine with ground pork unless I can get the veal from a reputable farmer.

1½ lb/750 g **ground pork or veal**

¼ cup/60 g **tomato paste**

⅔ cup/160 ml **dry red wine**

One 28-oz/800-g can **tomato puree**

One 28-oz/800-g can **diced tomatoes, with juice**

1 cup/240 ml **whole milk**

2 tbsp **unsalted butter**

1 to 1½ tsp **sugar (optional)**

1 bunch **basil, leaves picked, plus more for garnish**

½ cup/2 oz/60 g **Parmigiano-Reggiano cheese, grated, plus more for garnish**

Look for a dry red wine, such as a Cabarnet Sauvignon, Merlot, Pinot Noir, Syrah, or Zinfandel. In terms of quality level, remember "If you wouldn't drink it, you shouldn't cook with it."

Line a plate with paper towels; set aside. Heat the oil in a large, heavy-bottomed pot or Dutch oven over medium heat. When the oil shimmers, add the pancetta and cook until crisp, about

6 minutes. If the pancetta lets off a lot of fat, discard all but 3 tablespoons of drippings. Remove the pancetta with a slotted spoon to the prepared plate and set aside.

Return the pot to the stove over medium heat, add the onion and garlic, season with salt and pepper, and cook until vegetables are translucent, about 5 minutes. Add the carrots, celery, and bay leaf, and cook until tender, about 5 minutes.

Add the ground meat and stir to break up. Once the meat starts to brown, after about 10 minutes, add the tomato paste and stir until evenly mixed. Add the wine, the tomato puree, and the diced tomatoes with juice and cook until the tomatoes start to simmer, about 10 minutes.

Add the milk, 1 tablespoon kosher salt, and butter and mix until thoroughly incorporated and bring to a simmer. Decrease the heat to very low, and simmer, uncovered, stirring occasionally, until the sauce is thick and reduced by about one-third, 1½ to 2 hours. Taste sauce and add the sugar if the sauce is sour. Stir in the sliced basil and cheese; taste, and adjust seasoning as desired.

Because the flavor really develops as this sits, if you can, make it up to 2 days ahead—just don't add the basil until you re-warm it.

DIFFICULTY
Easy

YIELD
8 servings

TOTAL TIME
45 minutes

HANDS-ON TIME
20 to 25 minutes

While most mac and cheese recipes have a thick roux (flour and butter) base, this one is made lighter but just as comforting with half-and-half and a mountain of melted cheese. The flavors are reminiscent of the classic Southern pimiento cheese spread but livened with a dash of paprika and a crunchy, herby bread crumb topping.

PIMIENTO MAC AND CHEESE

TOPPING

3 tbsp/45 g **unsalted butter, plus more for the baking dish**

1 cup/55 g **panko bread crumbs**

⅓ cup/15 g **finely chopped fresh Italian parsley**

1¼ tsp **paprika**

1 cup/4 oz/110g **grated Parmigiano-Reggiano cheese**

MAC AND CHEESE

1 pound/455 g **mini shell or elbow macaroni pasta**

½ **red onion, minced**

¾ tsp **Kosher salt, plus more for seasoning**

2 cups/475 ml **half-and-half**

One 7-oz jar **pimientos, diced** (about ¾ cup/140 g)

12 ounces/5 cups/350 g **shredded aged Cheddar cheese**

1 tbsp **Dijon mustard**

Panko bread crumbs are a Japanese cracker bread crumb. If you can't find them, use crushed melba toasts or saltine crackers.

Pimientos are sweet red chili peppers and are often sold jarred. If you can't find them, go ahead and use roasted red peppers.

Heat the broiler and arrange a rack in the upper third of the oven. Coat a 2-qt/1.9-L baking dish with butter and set aside.

FOR THE TOPPING

Melt 2 tbsp/30 g of the butter in a small pan over low heat. Transfer to a small bowl and add the panko, parsley, ½ teaspoon of the paprika, and ¾ cup/85 g of the Parmesan and toss to combine. Set aside.

🕐 The bread crumb topping can be made up to 2 days ahead of time. Store refrigerated in an airtight container until ready to use.

FOR THE MAC AND CHEESE

Bring a large pot of heavily salted water to a boil over high heat. Add the pasta and cook 2 minutes short of the package directions. Reserve ¼ cup/60 ml of the pasta cooking water and drain the pasta.

Return the pot to the stove over low heat and add the remaining butter. When the foaming subsides, add the onion, season with salt, and cook until golden, about 5 minutes. Stir in the half-and-half, pimientos, and remaining papika.

When the mixture just begins to simmer, add the Cheddar and whisk until smooth. Add in the remaining Parmesan and the mustard and whisk until melted. Add the pasta and ¾ teaspoon salt and stir to coat. Taste and season with additional salt as needed.

To assemble, pour the pasta mixture into the buttered baking dish and top with the panko mixture. Put under the broiler until the mixture bubbles and the top is browned, 1 to 2 minutes. Remove from the broiler and let cool for 5 minutes before serving.

You could serve the recipe at this point (without bread-crumbs and broiler time) for a stovetop mac and cheese.

RIFFS

- Mac and cheese is one of the most versatile dishes out there so feel free to let your imagination run wild—a good place to start is by adding a few pinches of your favorite spice blend (such as garam marsala, curry powder, or five-spice powder) to the onions.
- Change the flavor of the bread crumbs: use another herb such as chives, cilantro, or sage or add a pinch of ground spices per Rubs (page 411).

DIFFICULTY
Easy

YIELD
4 to 6 servings

TOTAL TIME
1 hour

HANDS-ON TIME
40 minutes

Fideos are nests of angel hair noodles that are used to make various Mexican and Spanish dishes. Here they're cooked in a paella-pasta hybrid for a take on chorizo and clams that leaves me wondering why this dish isn't on more menus.

TAKEAWAY: How to cook clams.

SAFFRON FIDEOS WITH CHORIZO AND CLAMS

5 tbsp/90 ml **olive oil**

1 **yellow onion, finely chopped**

Kosher salt and freshly ground black pepper

4 **garlic cloves, finely chopped**

One 28 oz/800 g can **pureed tomatoes**

Sugar (optional)

8 oz/225 g **fideos (dried vermicelli noodle nests) or angel hair pasta, broken into 2-in/5-cm pieces**

4 oz/113 g **Spanish chorizo, thinly sliced into coins**

1 **dried bay leaf**

Large pinch **of saffron threads (optional)**

1 cup/240 ml **dry sherry (such as fino)**

4 cups/1 L **low-sodium fish stock or chicken broth**

3 lb/1.4 kg **clams, scrubbed**

¼ cup/10 g **finely chopped fresh Italian parsley**

Fideos can be found in the pasta or ethnic aisle of the grocery store. If you can't find them, use vermicelli or angel hair pasta.

There are two types of chorizo out there. Mexican chorizo is wet and uncooked whereas Spanish chorizo (the one used here) is cured and dry. If you can't find the Spanish type, Mexican chorizo or another spicy dry salami will work.

Saffron adds a distinct earthy note to anything it's used in. Buy saffron threads that are bright orange from Iran, Spain, Morocco, or Kashmir.

The sauce can be made up to 2 days ahead and refrigerated in an airtight container. Warm before using.

Heat 1 tablespoon of the oil in a large, heavy-bottomed pot or Dutch oven over medium heat. When it shimmers, add the onion, season with salt and pepper, and cook until it begins to soften, about 3 minutes. Add the garlic and tomatoes and bring to a boil over high heat. Decrease the heat to medium and cook, stirring frequently, until the sauce is reduced and very thick, about 20 minutes. Taste and, if it is sour, add some sugar to balance it out. Set aside.

Heat 3 tablespoons of the remaining oil in a large frying pan over medium heat. When it shimmers, add the pasta and cook, stirring frequently, until well browned, 8 to 10 minutes. Using a slotted spoon, transfer the pasta to a plate and set aside.

Line a plate with paper towels. Add the remaining 1 tablespoon of oil to the pan and the chorizo, and cook until the chorizo is browned, about 2 minutes. Remove chorizo to the prepared plate and set aside.

Stir in the bay leaf, saffron (if using), sherry, and stock and bring to a boil, about 5 minutes. Add the clams and cook, covered, over moderate heat, until the clams are fully opened, about 5 minutes. (Discard any that remain unopened after 5 minutes.) Transfer the clams with a slotted spoon to a bowl and discard the bay leaf.

Add the clam cooking liquid and toasted pasta to the tomato sauce mixture and cook, stirring frequently, until the pasta is tender and has absorbed most of the liquid, 5 to 10 minutes. Taste, add salt and pepper as needed. Add the chorizo and clams and cook, tossing, until the clams are heated through, 1 to 2 minutes. Serve sprinkled with parsley and freshly ground black pepper.

Cook the fideos until they are al dente—firm but not chalky—even if it leaves you with a slightly soupier sauce.

RIFFS:

- Nix the seafood or use mussels, scallops, or shrimp instead.
- Before serving, stir in some finely chopped chard or spinach until wilted.

A veggie-on-veggie lasagna that solves the problem as to what to do with all the ever-abundant late summer squash and arugula out there.

TAKEAWAY: How to make lasagna.

RECIPE WITHIN A RECIPE: The sauce here could be used with any pasta.

SMOKED MOZZARELLA, ZUCCHINI, AND ARUGULA LASAGNA

SPICY TOMATO SAUCE

2 tbsp **olive oil**

½ **yellow onion, finely chopped**

Freshly ground black pepper

4 **garlic cloves, thinly sliced**

1½ tsp **red pepper flakes**

Two 28-oz/800-g **cans crushed tomatoes**

Kosher salt and freshly ground black pepper

ARUGULA-CHEESE FILLING

5 oz/140 g **baby arugula, tough stems removed**

3 **medium garlic cloves, smashed**

1 lb/455 g **ricotta cheese**

1 tsp **grated lemon zest**

1 tbsp **freshly squeezed lemon juice**

Kosher salt

LASAGNA

2 tbsp **minced fresh oregano leaves**

2 tbsp **olive oil, plus more for drizzling**

2 lb/910 g **summer squash (such as zucchini or pattypan squash), trimmed and thinly sliced crosswise**

Kosher salt and freshly ground black pepper

One 9 oz/255 g **box no-boil lasagna noodles**

8 oz/225 g **smoked mozzarella or provolone cheese, low-moisture mozzarella, cut into small dice, or fresh goat cheese (chèvre), crumbled**

2 cups/8 oz/235 g **finely grated Parmigiano-Reggiano cheese**

No-boil lasagna noodles are available in most stores these days. If you can't find them, use regular lasagna noodles but be sure to cook them according to package directions before assembling the lasagna.

As with all smoked cheeses, smoked mozzarella adds a distinct taste to the dish. If you don't like smoked foods, just use regular low-moisture mozzarella or fresh goat cheese (chèvre) instead.

FOR THE SAUCE

Heat the oil in a Dutch oven or a large, heavy-bottomed pot over medium-high heat. When it shimmers, add the onion, season well with salt and pepper and cook until just softened. Add the garlic and red pepper flakes and cook until fragrant.

Stir in the tomatoes and season with salt and more pepper. Cook until well mixed and tomatoes start to simmer. Decrease the heat to medium-low and simmer, stirring occasionally, until flavors meld, at least 20 minutes more.

FOR THE FILLING

Combine all the ingredients in a food processor fitted with the metal blade and process until evenly combined, about 2 minutes. Taste and season with salt as needed; set aside.

FOR THE LASAGNA

Heat the oven to 375°F/190°C/gas 5 and arrange a rack in the middle. Toss together the oregano, oil, and zucchini in a bowl and season well with salt and pepper.

To assemble the lasagna, spread 1 cup/240 ml of the tomato sauce in a thin base layer over the bottom of a baking dish that measures 13 by 9 in/33 by 23 cm. To start layering, arrange one-fourth of the noodles over the base sauce, top with 2 cups/480 ml sauce and spread it evenly. Dollop one-third of the ricotta mixture over the noodles. Scatter one-fourth of the zucchini mixture over the ricotta, then top with one-fourth each of the mozzarella and Parmigiano-Reggiano. Repeat to make 2 more layers.

For the final layer, top the lasagna with the last of the noodles, sauce, zucchini, mozzerella, and Parmigiano-Reggiano.

Cover with aluminum foil, place on a rimmed baking sheet, and bake until the liquids are bubbling and noodles are beginning to soften, about 40 minutes. Remove the foil and continue baking until the top is golden brown and noodles are completely tender, about 20 minutes more. Drizzle with some olive oil and allow to rest at least 15 minutes before serving.

RIFF: Brown some crumbled sausage and add it to the layers.

The tomato sauce can be made up to 2 days ahead. Store refrigerated in an airtight container until ready to use.

Lasagnas are better when made ahead because they take on more flavor as they sit. Just let the baked dish cool off and refrigerate it up to 2 days ahead until ready to use.

DIFFICULTY
Easy

YIELD
6 to 8 servings

TOTAL TIME
15 minutes, plus marinating time

HANDS-ON TIME
15 minutes

So simple, but so delicious. The tomatoes, garlic, oil, and red pepper flakes create a brag-worthy sauce made sublime by the addition of creamy burrata cheese (recipe pictured on pages 236–237).

TAKEAWAY: How to make a no-cook pasta sauce.

RECIPE WITHIN A RECIPE: The tomato mixture doubles as a bruschetta topping—just spoon over toasted country bread, drizzle with olive oil, sprinkle with salt, and serve.

FRESH HEIRLOOM TOMATO SAUCE WITH BURRATA

Top-quality tomatoes take this dish from good to great so buy ones that are fresh, ripe, and in season. When you cut the tomatoes, they'll release juice. Instead of discarding it, add to the sauce for extra flavor.

This dish also works well with any pasta that clings to the little puddles of sauce, like shell-shaped conchiglie or cup-shaped orecchiette.

Burrata is part cream, part mozzarella cheese that's pure indulgence. If you can't find it, buffalo mozzarella will work well.

3 lb/1.4 kg **heirloom tomatoes, cut into small dice, juice reserved**

⅓ cup/90 ml **extra-virgin olive oil, plus more for garnish**

2 **garlic cloves, thinly sliced (optional)**

2 tsp **kosher salt, plus more for seasoning**

1½ to 3 tsp **red pepper flakes**

15 **large fresh basil leaves**

1 lb/455 g **rigatoni, campanelle, conchiglie, or orecchiette pasta**

2 tbsp **finely chopped fresh Italian parsley**

12 oz/340 g **burrata cheese, cut into 6 or 8 pieces**

Combine the tomatoes, reserved juice, oil, garlic, salt, and red pepper flakes (use 1½ teaspoons if you don't like spicy and up to 3 teaspoons if you do) in a large nonreactive bowl. Stir gently to coat well, and let sit at room temperature at least 30 minutes or up to 3 hours before serving.

When the tomatoes are ready, tear the basil leaves into bite-sized pieces and stir into the tomato mixture. Meanwhile, bring a large pot of heavily salted water to a boil and cook the pasta according to the package directions. (If the tomatoes have not let off a lot of juice, reserve ½ cup/120 ml of the pasta cooking water before draining.)

Toss the pasta with the reserved pasta cooking water (as needed) and parsley and stir to mix. Add the tomato mixture, and stir to combine. (If using mozzarella, stir it in here.) Taste and season with salt and additional pepper flakes, as desired.

Divide the pasta into individual bowls, top each with some of the burrata cheese, a drizzle of olive oil, and a sprinkling of salt, and serve.

RIFFS
- Use tangy cheeses like goat cheese or feta in place of the burrata.
- Add chopped capers, olives, sun-dried tomatoes, roasted bell peppers, or anchovies to the tomato mixture.
- Mix with homemade pesto (see page 140, 218, and 314) for a chunky crossover sauce.

DIFFICULTY
Easy

YIELD
6 to 8 servings

TOTAL TIME
1 hour

HANDS-ON TIME
40 minutes

My father's all-time favorite comfort food, stroganoff was a standard family meal when I was growing up. In an effort to make it a bit healthier, the beef in this old-school dish gets replaced with loads of mushrooms and just as much flavor.

TAKEAWAY: How to temper a sauce.

TRIPLE-MUSHROOM STROGANOFF

12 oz/340 g **egg noodles**

5 tbsp **unsalted butter**

2 lb/910 g **assorted cremini, portobello (black gills removed), and oyster mushrooms, cut in ¼-in/6-mm slices**

1 **yellow onion, thinly sliced**

1 tbsp **packed brown sugar**

1 tbsp **tomato paste**

⅔ cup/160 ml **dry red wine**

2 tbsp **unbleached all-purpose flour**

1½ cups/360 ml **low-sodium mushroom broth**

½ cup/120 ml **sour cream or plain, whole milk Greek yogurt**

¼ tsp **ground nutmeg**

Kosher salt and freshly ground black pepper

1 tbsp **balsamic, sherry, or red wine vinegar**

⅓ cup/10 g **thinly sliced fresh chives**

The assortment of mushrooms adds layers of flavors and a distinct meatiness. Experiment with different types of mushrooms to find your favorite combination.

Use a spoon to scrape out the black gills on the undersides of the portobello mushroom caps.

Look for a dry red wine, such as a Cabernet Sauvignon, Merlot, Pinot Noir, Syrah, or Zinfandel. In terms of quality level, remember "If you wouldn't drink it, you shouldn't cook with it."

Mushroom broth helps underline the earthy flavor in the dish. If you can't find it, use vegetable or chicken broth.

🕐 Noodles can be cooked up to 2 days ahead of time. Toss with melted butter before proceeding.

Bring a pot of heavily salted water to a boil over high heat and cook the noodles according to the package directions. When they're ready, drain and toss with 2 tablespoons of the butter; set aside.

Meanwhile, melt 1 tablespoon of the remaining butter in a large, heavy-bottomed pot or Dutch oven over medium-high heat. When the foaming subsides, add half the mushrooms and cook, stirring rarely, until the liquid is cooked off and the mushrooms

NOODLES

are well browned, 8 to 10 minutes. Transfer the mushrooms to a bowl and set aside. Add another 1 tablespoon of butter, and repeat with the remaining mushrooms. Set aside.

Add the remaining 1 tablespoon of butter and melt over medium-high heat. When the foaming subsides, add the onion and cook until it is lightly browned, about 5 minutes. Stir in the sugar and tomato paste and cook until fragrant. Add the wine, scraping up any browned bits on the bottom of the pan, and cook until the liquid is slightly reduced and any alcohol smell is cooked off, about 1 minute.

Sprinkle the flour over the top and stir until just toasted, about 1 minute. Whisk in the broth and cook until the liquid is thickened and coats the back of a spatula, about 2 minutes; decrease the heat to low.

Stir some of the sauce into the sour cream to temper it then stir this mixture into the sauce and season with nutmeg. Season the mushroom mixture to taste with salt and pepper and stir into the sauce. Add the noodles, vinegar, and chives to the pot, toss well, and serve.

The mushrooms and sauce can be made up to 1 day ahead of time. To serve, heat the sauce over medium-low until heated through, then finish the recipe.

The sour cream can curdle if there's too much of a temperature difference between it and the broth. To prevent curdling, let the sour cream warm to room temperature before adding. As an extra precaution, the recipe calls for tempering the sour cream by mixing it with a small amount of the hot sauce. Finally, don't let the sauce boil once you've added the sour cream.

DIFFICULTY
Easy

YIELD
*6 servings
(4 cups/1 L sauce)*

TOTAL TIME
1 hour, 15 minutes

HANDS-ON TIME
40 minutes

Poor eggplant, it always seems to be typecast in the kitchen, being constantly fried or breaded. In this healthy yet hearty Mediterranean-flavored casserole, it combines with tangy yogurt, earthy pine nuts, nutty bulgur, and a sweet tomato sauce for a new starring role (recipe pictured on pages 242–243).

RECIPE WITHIN A RECIPE: Use the red pepper tomato sauce in place of normal tomato sauce.

GOES WELL WITH: Serve with a simple green salad and some crusty bread.

EGGPLANT CASSEROLE WITH PINE NUT–YOGURT SAUCE

BULGUR
¾ cup/180 ml **water**

½ tsp **kosher salt**

¾ cup/150 g **cracked bulgur wheat**

Cracked bulgur is cracked wheat that is the same size as cornmeal and is used to make tabbouleh. If you can't find it, you can use quinoa (cook according to package directions) or leave it out.

RED PEPPER TOMATO SAUCE
2 tbsp **olive oil**

½ **yellow onion, finely chopped**

Kosher salt and freshly ground black pepper

3 **roasted red peppers, minced**

6 **garlic cloves, finely chopped**

One 28-oz/800-g can **pureed tomatoes**

¾ cup/30 g **thinly sliced fresh basil or chopped Italian parsley, plus more for garnish**

⅓ cup/45 g **dried currants**

Sugar (optional)

Dried currants are a seedless grape that has been dried. It is not the same as the fruit that's related to the gooseberry.

EGGPLANT CASSEROLE
2 lb/910 g **eggplant, cut into ½-in/12-mm slices**

2 tbsp **olive oil**

Kosher salt

3 **garlic cloves, minced**

1 cup/240 ml **plain, whole-milk Greek yogurt**

½ cup/47 g **slivered almonds or pine nuts**

Greek yogurt is a strained yogurt that is thicker and tangier than regular yogurt. It has become more and more widely available, but if you can't find it, regular plain yogurt will work too.

FOR THE BULGUR

Combine the water and salt in a small saucepan and bring to a boil over high heat. Add the bulgur, stir to combine, and remove from the heat. Cover and let sit until the bulgur is tender and swelled up, 20 to 30 minutes. Meanwhile, make the sauce.

The bulgur can be made up to 2 days ahead. Store refrigerated until ready to use.

FOR THE SAUCE

Heat the oil in a medium saucepan over medium heat. When it shimmers, add the onion, season well with salt and black pepper, and cook until soft and translucent, about 5 minutes.

The sauce can be made up to 2 days ahead. Store refrigerated until ready to use.

Add the roasted peppers and cook, stirring occasionally, until they just begin to color, about 5 minutes. Add the garlic and tomato puree and bring to a boil. Decrease the heat to a simmer, and cook, stirring occasionally, until the sauce is slightly thickened and flavors are melded, 15 to 20 minutes. When the sauce is ready, stir in the basil and currants. Taste and, if necessary, season with sugar, salt, or pepper. Remove from the heat and set aside. Meanwhile, cook the eggplant.

FOR THE CASSEROLE

Heat the broiler and arrange a rack in the top of the oven. Brush the eggplant with oil and season with salt. Arrange the slices on a rimmed baking sheet and broil until golden brown, about 15 minutes. Remove from the oven and set aside. Decrease the oven temperature to 375°F/190°C/gas 5.

The casserole can be assembled up to 2 days before baking and can be baked up to 2 days ahead. Bring to room temperature before serving.

To assemble the casserole, spoon one-fourth of the sauce (about 1 cup/240 ml on the bottom of a 9-in/23-cm square baking dish. Lay one-third of the eggplant slices over the sauce. Spread all the bulgur over the eggplant. Repeat layering sauce and eggplant, ending with the sauce (you'll have 4 layers of sauce and 3 of eggplant, with a layer of bulgur in the middle).

Place the garlic on a cutting board and sprinkle a pinch of salt on top. Chop the mixture until it is a rough paste. Stir the garlic into the yogurt. Spread over the sauce in an even layer on top of the casserole. Scatter the nuts over the yogurt. Bake until cooked through but not bubbling, 20 to 25 minutes. Remove from the oven and let rest 5 minutes.

Serve hot or at room temperature.

RIFF: Replace the bulgur with 1½ cups/360 ml cooked ground meat.

DIFFICULTY
Hard

YIELD
8 to 12 servings

TOTAL TIME
1 hour

HANDS-ON TIME
35 minutes

This fennel tart (pictured on page 247) is a savory and earthy take on the classic dish known as Tarte Tatin. It is an elegant start to a meal or works as a main course when served with a salad.

TAKEAWAY: How to make caramel.

There are various anise-flavored liqueurs and any of them, including Pernod, Ricard, Herbsaint, or ouzo, will work well. If you can't find it, you can use dry vermouth or a sweet white wine, such as Riesling.

CARAMELIZED FENNEL TARTE TATIN

4 heads **fennel with fronds** (2¼ lb/1 kg)

2 tbsp **anise-flavored liqueur (such as Pernod)**

1 tbsp **freshly squeezed lemon juice**

4 **garlic cloves, thinly sliced**

Grated zest of 1 lemon

1 tsp **kosher salt, plus more for seasoning**

¼ tsp **freshly ground black pepper, plus more for seasoning**

⅓ cup/65 g **sugar**

2 tbsp **water**

3 tbsp **unsalted butter**

¼ cup/10 g **roughly chopped fresh Italian parsley**

1 sheet **store-bought frozen puff pastry (from a 17¼-oz/490-g package), thawed according to package directions**

Roughly chop a handful of fennel fronds, cover, and store in the refrigerator. Discard the remaining fronds or save for another use. Halve the fennel lengthwise. Place the halves on a board, cut-side down, and slice lengthwise into ½-in/12-mm slices. Combine the fennel, Pernod, juice, garlic, and zest in a large nonreactive bowl, season with salt and pepper, and toss to combine; set aside.

Heat the oven to 425°F/220°C/gas 7 and arrange a rack in the middle. Stir together the sugar and the water in a large oven-proof frying pan over medium-high heat. Cook, undisturbed, until the mixture turns amber in color, about 5 minutes. Immediately add the butter and swirl the pan to incorporate.

Drain the fennel slices. Arrange them snugly atop the caramel, pack them tightly (fennel may stick up above the rim of the frying pan), and decrease the heat to medium. Using tongs, rotate the fennel from bottom to top and cook, stirring every 5 minutes, until the fennel is knife-tender and golden throughout, and juices are deep golden and bubbling, about 20 minutes. Increase the heat to high, stir in the parsley, and cook until the caramel has reduced and thickened, about 5 minutes more.

With a floured rolling pin, roll the pastry into an 11-in/28-cm circle on a floured work surface (as shown on page 246). Brush off any excess flour, transfer to a baking sheet and refrigerate until ready to use.

When the fennel is ready, drape the pastry round over the top of the frying pan and tuck the edges into the pan around the filling (as shown on page 246). Bake the tart until the juices are deep brown and bubbly and the top of the pastry is browned, 20 to 25 minutes. Transfer the pan to a rack and cool at least 5 minutes.

Just before serving, place a rimmed platter over the frying pan and, using potholders to hold pan and platter tightly together, invert the tart onto the platter.

Garnish with reserved fennel fronds and serve immediately.

The caramel can crystallize while cooking. To avoid this: make sure all the utensils are clean; don't stir the caramel once the sugar dissolves (just swirl the pan to help it cook evenly); and, for extra insurance, you can wash down the sides (inside) of the pan with a brush dipped in water.

DIFFICULTY	
Easy	

YIELD
8 to 10 tacos

TOTAL TIME
30 minutes

HANDS-ON TIME
25 minutes

These tacos are the perfect solution for when you grow your own zucchini, only to wonder what to do with the seemingly never-ending supply come late summer. But, even if you don't have a garden, this is still a healthy, fresh veggie taco.

TAKEAWAY: How to char chiles.
RECIPE WITHIN A RECIPE: The veggies could also be served as a quick side dish.

CHARRED CHILE, CORN, AND ZUCCHINI TACOS

ZUCCHINI-CHILE FILLING

4 **poblano chiles**

2 tbsp **canola, grapeseed, or peanut oil**

¾ cup/75 g **fresh corn kernels**

Kosher salt and freshly ground black pepper

1 **yellow onion, finely chopped**

3 **garlic cloves, thinly sliced**

12 oz/350 g **zucchini, trimmed, halved lengthwise, and thinly sliced crosswise**

½ cup/120 ml **low-sodium vegetable broth or water**

2 tbsp **finely chopped fresh cilantro or oregano leaves**

TACOS

8 to 10 **small corn tortillas, warmed**

Tomatillo salsa, for garnish (optional)

Crumbled Cotija or feta cheese, for garnish (optional)

Crème fraîche, crema, or sour cream, for garnish (optional)

Avocado, for garnish (optional)

Poblano (often mistakenly labeled pasilla) chiles are more and more widely available. If you can't find them, go ahead and use Anaheim chiles, New Mexican green chiles, or green bell peppers instead.

This allows for 1 tortilla per taco, however, some people like to double their tortillas. So you could use 20 tortillas for 10 tacos.

Warm tortillas by either wrapping in aluminum foil and heating through in a 350°F/177°C/gas 4 oven, about 15 minutes. Or, place in a dry (no oil) pan over medium heat and warm briefly, about 30 seconds per side.

FOR THE FILLING

Heat the broiler and arrange a rack in the upper third. Place the chiles on a baking sheet and set under the broiler. Char, turning occasionally, until black and blistered all over, about 5 minutes. Place the chiles in a bowl and cover with plastic wrap for 5 minutes. Peel the chiles by rubbing the skins under running water. Trim off the chile tops, remove the seeds, halve lengthwise, and cut into strips that are ½ in/12 mm wide. Set aside.

Heat 1 tablespoon of the oil in a large frying pan over medium-high heat. When the oil shimmers, add the corn and cook, stirring rarely, until toasted, about 5 minutes. Season with salt and set the corn aside.

Return the pan to the stove over medium-high heat and add the remaining tablespoon of oil. When it shimmers, add the onion and cook until softened, about 3 minutes. Add the garlic, chiles, zucchini, and broth and bring to a boil. Decrease the heat to medium-low. Cook until the zucchini is fork-tender and the liquid reduces enough to just coat the vegetables, about 10 minutes.

Stir in the corn and herbs, season with salt and freshly ground pepper and remove from the heat.

FOR THE TACOS

Divide the mixture among warm tortillas and top, as desired, with your choice of garnishes.

The filling can be made up to 2 days ahead and refrigerated in an airtight container. Reheat before using.

DIFFICULTY
Easy

YIELD
8 to 10 servings

TOTAL TIME
1 hour, 30 minutes, plus overnight soaking time

HANDS-ON TIME
15 minutes

A meatless, dare I say light, take on bean ragout, this vegetarian dish has layers of subtle, earthy flavors yet is filling enough to leave you satisfied.

TAKEAWAY: How to make compound butter.
RECIPE WITHIN A RECIPE: The butter can be used to top baked potatoes, grilled meats, or toast.

While not essential, I prefer oil-cured olives for the flavored butter as they tend to have a more intense fruity olive flavor.

The beans need to be soaked before using. If you have time, cover with water and soak 8 hours to overnight. If you're crunched on time, you can do a quick soak (see page 112) or use canned beans.

Look for dried beans in the health or canned aisle of your grocery. Cranberry beans work really well here but cannellini beans, white beans, or Great Northern beans would all work well too. Just pay attention to the package directions as each bean has a slightly different cooking time.

Clean leeks thoroughly before using. To do so, trim leeks and halve lengthwise. Hold leeks under running water and pull back each layer to remove any dirt. Dry thoroughly before using.

Saffron adds a distinct earthy note to anything it's used in. Buy saffron threads that are bright orange from Iran, Spain, Morocco, or Kashmir.

CRANBERRY BEAN RAGOUT WITH OLIVE-CITRUS BUTTER

OLIVE-CITRUS BUTTER

½ cup/115 g **unsalted butter, at room temperature**

⅓ cup/50 g **minced pitted black olives**

2 tsp **grated lemon or orange zest**

CRANBERRY BEANS

1½ cups/300 g **dried cranberry or white beans**

4 **garlic cloves, smashed**

1 **bay leaf**

¼ tsp **black peppercorns**

8 cups/2 L **low-sodium vegetable or chicken broth or water**

RAGOUT

2 tbsp **unsalted butter**

1 **leek, trimmed, halved lengthwise and thinly sliced**

1 **carrot, minced**

1 **celery stalk, minced**

4 **garlic cloves, thinly sliced**

2 tbsp **roughly chopped fresh oregano leaves** (or 2 tsp dried), **plus more for garnish**

One 3-in/7.5-cm **cinnamon stick**

3 tbsp **tomato paste**

Pinch **of saffron threads (optional)**

3 cups/720 ml **reserved bean cooking liquid**

Kosher salt

2 to 3 tbsp **red wine vinegar**

Roughly chopped fresh Italian parsley, for garnish (optional)

FOR THE BUTTER

Using a spatula, beat the butter in a large mixing bowl until very spreadable. Add the olives and zest and stir to combine; place in a small bowl or crock, cover, and refrigerate until ready to use.

FOR THE BEANS

Place the beans in large bowl. Add enough water to cover by 3 in/ 7.5 cm; soak at room temperature at least 8 hours or overnight.

Drain the beans. Wrap the garlic, bay leaf, and peppercorns with a leek leaf and tie with kitchen twine to secure. Add the beans and broth to a large pot and bring to boil. Decrease the heat to a simmer and cook until the beans are tender but still hold their shape, stirring occasionally, 45 minutes to 1 hour. Drain, reserving 3 cups of the cooking liquid. Discard the leek packet.

FOR THE RAGOUT

Melt the butter in the pot used to cook the beans over medium heat. Add the leeks and cook until translucent, about 4 minutes. Add the carrot, celery, and garlic and cook until just softened. Add the oregano and cinnamon and cook until fragrant, about 30 seconds. Stir in the tomato paste and cook until fragrant.

Add the drained beans, saffron, and the 3 cups reserved cooking liquid and simmer until the beans are tender and flavors are melded together, 40 to 45 minutes. Season with salt, add 2 tablespoons vinegar, and let cook another 5 minutes. Taste and add more vinegar, as desired to brighten the flavor of the beans. Serve topped with olive butter and herbs, as desired.

The butter can be made up to 1 month ahead and stored tightly wrapped in the freezer. To facilitate slicing, let it sit at room temperature briefly before using.

The beans can be cooked up to 2 days ahead. To do so, let them cool in their cooking liquid then store, refrigerated, in the liquid. Use this liquid for thickening pasta sauces, in soups, or in the final bean dish.

Don't add salt to the bean cooking liquid; it lengthens the cooking time. Add salt once the beans are tender and let sit a few minutes to absorb.

RIFF: Add a piece of pancetta or ham hock to the beans as they cook for a porky flavor.

DIFFICULTY
Medium

YIELD
6 to 8 servings

TOTAL TIME
45 minutes

HANDS-ON TIME
15 minutes

Don't be intimidated by soufflés because with a few pointers and a few test runs, you can become an expert in no time. This herby and tangy soufflé is a reliable starter recipe and, hey, if the soufflé does fall, at least I can guarantee it will be tasty.

TAKEAWAY: How to make a soufflé.
GOES WELL WITH: A green salad and crusty bread.

HERBED GOAT CHEESE SOUFFLÉ

3 tbsp **unsalted butter, plus more for coating**

⅓ cup/1½ oz/40 g **grated Parmigiano-Reggiano cheese**

3 tbsp **unbleached all-purpose flour**

1 cup/240 ml **half-and-half**

1 tbsp **minced fresh thyme leaves**

1 tsp **kosher salt**

½ tsp **freshly ground black pepper**

4 **large egg yolks, at room temperature**

5 oz/140 g **fresh goat cheese (chèvre), crumbled**

6 **large egg whites, at room temperature**

Older eggs whip up more easily and consistently than fresher eggs.

Using more egg whites than yolks makes the soufflé more stable and less likely to fall.

Heat the oven to 375°F/190°C/gas 5, arrange a rack in the middle, and place a baking sheet on the rack. Generously coat a 2-qt/2-L baking dish or a 6-cup/1.4-L soufflé dish with butter and sprinkle it evenly with half of the Parmigiano-Reggiano to coat; set aside. Pour any excess cheese back with remaining cheese.

Melt the 3 tablespoons butter in a medium saucepan over low heat. When the foaming subsides, add the flour and stir occasionally until the flour has cooked slightly, about 3 minutes. Gradually whisk in the half-and-half, thyme, salt, and pepper and bring to a simmer, about 2 minutes. Remove from the heat and whisk in the egg yolks, one at a time, until well blended. Whisk in the goat cheese until evenly combined (it won't get totally smooth) and set aside to cool slightly.

Place the egg whites in the bowl of a stand mixer fitted with the whisk attachment and beat on medium speed until soft peaks form, about 2 minutes. Increase the speed to high and beat until the whites are glossy and peaks are droopy but hold onto a spatula, about 3 minutes more.

Fold one-third of the egg whites into the cheese mixture until blended and no white streaks are visible. Add the remaining whites and gently fold until thoroughly combined. Pour into the prepared dish and sprinkle the remaining Parmesan over the top.

Place the soufflé on the heated baking sheet and bake until it is well risen, the top is browned, the edges appear dry, and the center is set (it doesn't move if lightly touched), 25 to 30 minutes. Serve immediately.

Make sure the bowl and whisk you use for the egg whites are impeccably clean as any fat or oils will prevent the whites from keeping air.

Don't over-whisk the whites or they'll deflate while baking. Whisk whites until they hold onto the whisk when pulled out of the bowl.

RIFFS
- Use other woody herbs such as sage or oregano instead of thyme.
- Add a pinch of cayenne, paprika, or ground nutmeg to the egg yolks.

DIFFICULTY
Easy

YIELD
4 to 6 servings

TOTAL TIME
40 minutes

HANDS-ON TIME
20 minutes

I call these Indian burritos (though they're properly known as "kati rolls") because they're transportable treats rolled up in a flatbread. My version isn't particularly traditional, but it is quite delicious.

TAKEAWAY: How to make curry.
RECIPE WITHIN A RECIPE: Serve the curry on its own for a simple and flavorful side dish.

INDIAN "BURRITOS" WITH CURRIED CAULIFLOWER

CURRIED CAULIFLOWER

3 tbsp **canola, grapeseed, or peanut oil**

One 1-in/2.5-cm piece **fresh ginger, peeled and grated**

1 to 1½ tbsp **curry powder**

1 head **cauliflower** (about 1½ lb/680 g)**, florets cut into bite-sized pieces**

Kosher salt

1 **yellow onion, finely chopped**

4 **garlic cloves, thinly sliced**

1 **serrano chile, halved and seeded**

8 oz/225 g **red-skinned potatoes, cut into small dice**

1 cup/240 ml **low-sodium vegetable broth, chicken broth, or water**

1 cup/100 g **shelled fresh or frozen baby peas**

½ cup/20 g **roughly chopped fresh cilantro**

BURRITO

4 to 6 **soft whole-wheat flatbreads (such as roti, lavash, or tortilla), warmed**

Plain whole milk yogurt, for garnish

Chutney, for garnish

Curry powder is a spice mix and varies from brand to brand. I like the heat of Madras curry powder, but use more or less depending on how hot your powder is.

Any chutney works here. If you can't find chutney, use a small amount of apricot jam.

CONTINUED

The curry can be made ahead and warmed up before serving.

FOR THE CURRY

Heat 2 tablespoons of the oil in a large frying pan over medium-high heat. When the oil shimmers, add the ginger, half of the curry powder, and all of the cauliflower. Season with salt and cook, stirring occasionally, until fragrant and the cauliflower is golden brown, 6 to 8 minutes. Remove to a plate with a slotted spoon.

Wipe out the pan, return to the stove over medium heat, and add the remaining 1 tablespoon of oil. When it shimmers, add the onion, garlic, and chile, season with salt, and cook until softened, about 3 minutes. Stir in the remaining curry powder and cook until fragrant. Add the cauliflower, potatoes, and broth, and bring to a boil.

Decrease the heat to low, cover, and cook for 5 minutes. Remove the cover and stir through to coat all the cauliflower. Cover again and simmer until the potatoes are knife-tender, 12 to 15 minutes. Remove the cover, add the peas and cook until they are bright, about 3 minutes. Adjust the seasoning as desired, stir in the cilantro, and use to fill the burritos.

FOR THE BURRITOS

To make the burrito, place the curry in the middle of the flatbreads. Top with yogurt and chutney, fold in sides, then roll up into a burrito shape, and serve.

A meatless take on the diner classic, this version is just as decadent, loaded with a ton of onions, a mess of mushrooms, and lots of melt-y cheese.

TAKEAWAY: How to brown mushrooms.
RECIPE WITHIN A RECIPE: Use the caramelized onions to top pizzas, other sandwiches, or seared meat.

MUSHROOM "PATTY" MELT

2 **large portobello mushrooms, stemmed (stems discarded)**
2 tbsp **canola, grapeseed, or peanut oil**
1 tbsp **low-sodium soy sauce or Worcestershire sauce**
Kosher salt and freshly ground black pepper
1 **yellow onion, halved and thinly sliced**
½ cup/120 ml **good-quality pale ale**
4 slices **rye sandwich bread, sliced ½ in/12 mm thick**
4 oz/115 g **Gruyère, shredded on large holes of box grater**
2 tbsp **unsalted butter, at room temperature**

Use a spoon to scrape out the black gills on the undersides of the portobello mushroom caps.

Cut the mushroom caps into ½-in/12-mm slices then combine with 1 tablespoon of the oil, soy sauce or Worchestershire, salt, and pepper in a bowl, toss to coat, and set aside to marinate, at least 5 minutes.

Heat a large cast-iron skillet over medium-high heat and add the mushrooms. Cook, turning once, until the mushrooms are well browned and knife-tender, 7 to 10 minutes; set aside.

The mushrooms and onions can be made up to 2 days ahead and refrigerated in an airtight container.

Return the skillet to the stove, add the remaining 1 tablespoon oil, and cook over medium heat. When it shimmers, add the onion, season with salt, and stir to coat in oil. Cook, stirring rarely, until golden brown, about 10 minutes. Add the beer, scrape up any browned bits, and cook until any alcohol smell is cooked off and the liquid is almost all evaporated, about 3 minutes.

Top each of 2 slices of bread with half the onions, half the cheese, the mushrooms, then the remaining cheese and onions. Close each sandwich with the 2 remaining slices of bread. Spread butter on the outsides of both sandwiches.

Wipe out the skillet, return to the stove, and decrease the heat to medium-low. Cook the sandwiches until the cheese is melted, about 2 minutes per side. Slice in half and serve.

DIFFICULTY
Easy

YIELD
2 to 4 servings

TOTAL TIME
15 minutes

HANDS-ON TIME
15 minutes

To amp up the nutrition and flavor in fried rice, I started making mine with whole grains and it has become a favorite dish for my niece and nephew. Pretty much any cooked, day-old grain works here so keep this recipe in mind next time you're stuck with leftovers.

TAKEAWAY: How to make fried rice.
GOES WELL WITH: This makes a hearty side dish or a light lunch.

MUSHROOM AND EDAMAME FRIED "RICE"

If you don't have leftover grains and want to make this dish, cook grains according to the package directions, drain well, then spread out on a rimmed baking sheet and refrigerate to cool quickly.

Edamame is the Japanese name for soy beans. You can find them fresh from spring to fall or buy them frozen. If you can't find them, use peas instead.

3 cups/550 g **cooked grain (such as quinoa, cracked bulgur, or couscous), chilled**

1 tbsp **canola, grapeseed, or peanut oil**

6 **garlic cloves, thinly sliced**

4 **green onions (white and pale green parts), thinly sliced**

4 oz/125 g **shiitake mushrooms, stemmed (stems discarded), caps halved and thinly sliced crosswise**

Kosher salt

1 cup/125 g **shelled fresh or frozen edamame (soy beans)**

¼ cup/10 g **thinly sliced fresh basil or chopped cilantro leaves**

2 **large eggs, beaten**

1 tbsp **low-sodium soy sauce**

Chili oil or red pepper flakes, and additional soy sauce, for seasoning (optional)

Break up the cooked grain to remove clumps; set aside.

Heat the oil in a large nonstick frying pan over medium-high heat and swirl to coat the pan. When the oil shimmers, add the garlic and green onions and cook until aromatic, about 30 seconds. Add the mushrooms, season with salt, and cook, stirring rarely, until browned, about 5 minutes.

Add the grain, edamame, and basil, toss to coat with oil and heat through. Cook until the grain is golden brown, about 3 minutes.

Make a well in the center of the mixture, exposing the pan bottom. Put the egg and soy in the well and stir until just cooked through. Break up the egg mixture and stir into the grain-vegetable mixture, stir-frying until the eggs are golden, about 3 minutes. Taste and adjust seasoning with chili oil or red pepper flakes, and soy sauce. Serve immediately.

RIFFS
- Feel free to bulk up the veggies and add in peas, steamed broccoli, roasted peppers, or spinach.
- Add in some tofu, shredded chicken, or pork for a one-dish meal.

DIFFICULTY
Medium

YIELD
8 servings

TOTAL TIME
1 hour

HANDS-ON TIME
20 minutes

Stuffed peppers may take you back to family dinners of yesteryear but here they're modernized with quinoa and a dash of North African flavor.

TAKEAWAY: How to make quinoa.
RECIPE WITHIN A RECIPE: The quinoa filling works on its own as a side dish.
GOES WELL WITH: This is hearty enough to be a main course with a side salad or served alongside roasted or grilled meats.

SPICED QUINOA–STUFFED BELL PEPPERS

4 **red, yellow, or orange bell peppers** (1½ lb/680 g)

2 cups/480 ml **low-sodium vegetable broth or water**

1½ tsp **kosher salt, plus more for seasoning**

1 cup/170 g **quinoa, rinsed**

2 tbsp **olive oil**

½ **red onion, finely chopped**

Freshly ground black pepper

4 **garlic cloves, minced**

1½ tsp **ground coriander**

¼ tsp **ground cinnamon**

One 14.5 oz/225 g can **chickpeas, drained**

One 14.5 oz/225 g can **diced or crushed tomatoes, drained**

¼ **preserved lemon, pulp discarded, and rind diced** (2 tbsp/20 g)

⅓ cup/45 g **dried currants**

¼ cup/5 g **finely chopped fresh mint**

3 tbsp **toasted pine nuts (page 119)**

Quinoa is a whole grain (actually a seed) that is gluten-free, high in protein, and becoming increasingly popular. If you can't find it, use whole-wheat couscous or cracked bulgur. Skip the quinoa instructions here, use enough to yield 2 cups cooked, and cook grains according to package directions then use in the recipe.

Preserved lemon is pickled lemon and is commonly used in North African cuisine. It is not as tart as a fresh lemon yet has a really intense lemon flavor. If you can't find it, you can use grated lemon zest in its place.

Heat the oven to 400°F/200°C/gas 6 and arrange a rack in the middle. Halve the peppers lengthwise (cut the peppers so the stem is preserved on one of the halves for each pepper). Remove and discard the seeds. Bring a few inches of water to a simmer in a large pot fitted with a steam basket insert. Add the peppers, cover, and cook until just knife-tender, about 10 minutes; remove from the heat.

Combine 1½ cups/360 ml of the broth and half of the salt in a small saucepan and bring to a boil over high heat. Add the quinoa, stir to combine, cover, and decrease the heat to a simmer. Cook until tender and most of the liquid has been absorbed, about 10 minutes. Keep covered and remove from heat.

Heat the oil in a medium frying pan over medium-high heat. When it shimmers, add the onion, remaining salt, season with pepper, and cook, until softened, about 5 minutes. Add the garlic, coriander, and cinnamon and cook until fragrant, about 30 seconds.

Remove from the heat and add the quinoa, chickpeas, tomatoes, preserved lemon, currants, mint, and pine nuts. Mix well and season to taste with salt and pepper. Nestle the peppers in a baking dish that measures 13 by 9 in/33 by 23 cm and divide the mixture evenly between the peppers.

Add the remaining ½ cup/120 ml of broth to the bottom of the pan. Roast the stuffed peppers until the peppers are completely fork-tender, the edges have started to brown, and the filling is heated through, 35 to 40 minutes.

Serve hot or at room temperature.

STEAMER BASKET
If you don't have a steamer basket, use a metal rack, small colander, or sieve to elevate the peppers above the water. Alternatively, halve them and microwave them until knife-tender.

Every step of this recipe can be made ahead of time. You can steam the peppers, make the quinoa, or stuff the peppers up to 2 days ahead. Store, refrigerated, in an airtight container then finish the recipe when you're ready.

DIFFICULTY
Medium

YIELD
6 to 8 servings

TOTAL TIME
1 hour

HANDS-ON TIME
45 minutes

Not a true "risotto" as it's made with grains instead of rice, this whole-grain version is more nutritious but just as creamy and satisfying as the real deal.

TAKEAWAY: How to make a risotto.

Clean leeks thoroughly before using. To do so, trim the leeks and halve lengthwise. Hold the leeks under running water and pull back each layer to remove any dirt. Dry thoroughly before using.

Look for semi-pearled farro, barley or soft (a.k.a. pastry) wheat berries in the bulk foods or health section of the grocery store. If you can't find them, you can use farro, spelt, hard (a.k.a. winter) wheat berries, or regular barley, but you'll want to soak them at least 8 hours before using so they'll cook faster.

If your beets don't come with greens, you can use finely chopped baby spinach or stemmed and finely chopped chard.

WHOLE GRAIN "RISOTTO" WITH BEETS AND WILTED GREENS

4 cups/960 ml **low-sodium chicken or vegetable broth**

2 tbsp/30 g **unsalted butter**

2 **leeks, trimmed, halved, and thinly sliced**

Kosher salt and freshly ground black pepper

2 cups/350g **semi-pearled farro, pearl barley, or soft (a.k.a. pastry) wheat berries**

1 lb/455 g **beets, peeled and cut into small dice**

1 cup/240 ml **vermouth, dry white or red wine, or sherry**

4 oz/120 g **beet greens, finely chopped** (about 1½ cups)

Grated zest and juice of 1 lemon (about 1 tbsp juice)

½ cup/2 oz/55g **finely grated Parmigiano-Reggiano cheese**

½ cup **finely chopped fresh mixed herbs (such as chervil, chives, parsley, and/or tarragon)**

Crème fraîche, for garnish

Olive oil, for garnish

Place the broth in a small saucepan and keep warm over very low heat.

Heat the butter in a 4- to 6-qt/4- to 6-L heavy-bottomed saucepan over medium heat. When the foaming subsides, add the leeks, season with salt and pepper, and cook until translucent, about 5 minutes. Add the grains, stir to coat in the butter, and cook until the grain starts to make a crackly sound, about 1 minute. Add the beets and vermouth and cook until the alcohol smell is cooked off, about 3 minutes.

Decrease the heat to medium-low, add 1 ladleful (about 1 cup/ 240 ml) of the broth and simmer, stirring, until broth is nearly absorbed. Continue adding the broth 1 ladleful at a time, stirring occasionally (it should be at a simmer the whole time), until the broth is almost all absorbed and the grain is al dente (firm, but not chalky) and the risotto has a porridge-like consistency with a creamy-looking sauce, 30 to 35 minutes. Taste the grain to make sure it is cooked through and tender. If not, add 1 ladleful more broth (if you've run out of broth, use warm water) and cook until almost completely absorbed.

Make sure to keep the risotto at a simmer the whole time, otherwise the liquid will cook off too quickly and the dish will be undercooked.

Stir in the greens, season with salt and pepper, and stir until the greens are wilted. Add the lemon zest and juice, cover, and set aside to rest a few minutes. Remove from the heat, stir in the cheese and herbs, then taste and adjust seasoning.

Divide the risotto among serving bowls, top with a dollop of crème fraîche and a drizzle of olive oil, add freshly ground black pepper, and serve.

RIFF: You can make this with standard risotto rice (i.e. Carnaroli or Arborio) for a traditional risotto.

DIFFICULTY	
Easy	

YIELD
4 servings

TOTAL TIME
2 hours, 15 minutes

HANDS-ON TIME
20 minutes

A modern take on a Norman Rockwell family dinner, consider this roast chicken (pictured on page 267) for your next Sunday supper. The honey-balsamic glaze cooks into an onyx lacquer on the chicken and infuses the vegetables with its subtly spiced flavor.

TAKEAWAY: How to roast chicken.

RECIPE WITHIN A RECIPE: Try this glaze on tofu, beef tenderloin, salmon steaks, pork loin, or lamb chops.

GOES WELL WITH: The quintessential pairing would be a starch (roast potatoes, mashers, polenta) with a green salad, but I like this recipe with wilted greens (page 115) or green beans (page 347).

BALSAMIC CARAMEL CHICKEN WITH ROASTED EGGPLANT

One 4 to 5 lb/1.8 to 2.3 kg **roasting chicken**

2 tbsp **unsalted butter, cut into small pieces**

Kosher salt and freshly ground black pepper

1 **lemon, halved**

1 cup/240 ml **low-sodium chicken broth**

¼ cup/60 ml **balsamic vinegar**

2 tbsp **low-sodium soy sauce**

2 tbsp **honey or agave nectar**

6 **garlic cloves, peeled and thinly sliced**

One 1-in/2.5-cm piece **fresh ginger, sliced into coins**

10 **black peppercorns**

3 **red onions, cut into slices that are 1 in/2.5 cm thick**

1 lb/455 g (about 3) **Japanese eggplant, cut into 1-in/2.5-cm chunks, or** 1 lb/455 g **cherry, grape, or Sweet 100 tomatoes, halved**

1 tbsp **olive oil**

You can rub the chicken with butter, salt, pepper, and lemon up to 1 day ahead and store, covered, in the refrigerator. This technique—called dry brining—will result in a moist, flavorful chicken.

Be sure to let the bird rest at room temperature before roasting otherwise it will cook unevenly.

Heat the oven to 400°F/200°C/gas 6 and arrange a rack in the middle. Gently loosen the skin on the chicken's breast and stuff butter under the skin. Season all over with salt and pepper. Place ½ lemon inside the cavity, squeeze the other half over the top, and then rub that lemon half over the skin. Let the chicken sit at room temperature while the oven heats, 20 to 30 minutes.

Meanwhile, combine the broth, vinegar, soy sauce, honey, garlic, ginger, and peppercorns in a medium saucepan and bring to a boil. Decrease the heat to a simmer and cook until reduced to ½ cup/120 ml, about 10 minutes. Remove from the heat, strain, and discard the garlic, ginger, and peppercorns.

Arrange the onions in the center of a roasting pan or large baking dish and place the chicken on top (the onions will act like a makeshift roasting rack). Roast until the skin is golden brown, about 30 minutes.

Decrease the heat to 375°F/190°C/gas 5 and toss the eggplant or tomatoes with olive oil and season with salt and pepper. Scatter the vegetables around the chicken in the bottom of the roasting pan.

Continue roasting the chicken, brushing with glaze and any pan drippings from the bottom of the pan, every 10 minutes, until the chicken is cooked through, and an instant-read thermometer inserted in the thickest part of the thigh (avoiding bone), registers 165°F/74°C, another 30 to 45 minutes. Let rest 10 minutes; carve and serve.

 During the last 30 minutes of roasting, be sure to monitor the basting juices and to baste often as the juices can burn fairly easily.

RIFFS

- Swap 1 lb/455 g quartered round potatoes for the veggies.
- Use diced sweet potatoes, carrots, turnips, or squash and add them to the roasting pan in place of the eggplant.
- Use tangerines or blood oranges in the chicken instead of lemon.
- If you leave off the glaze and veggies, the pared down recipe is the technique for a classic roasted chicken—perfect for any food adventure you concoct.
- Roast on a bed of halved garlic heads.

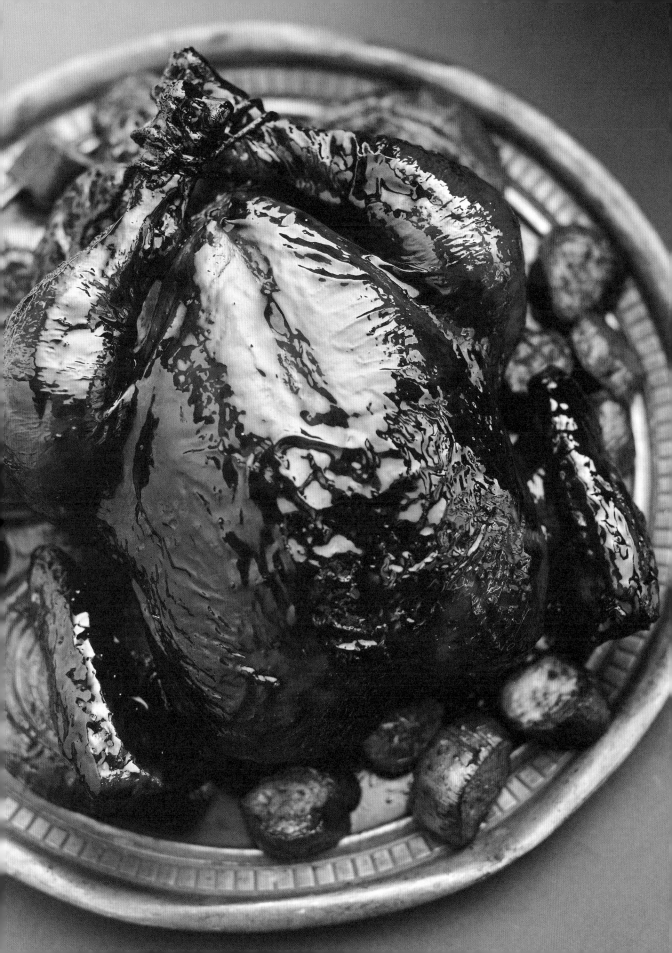

DIFFICULTY
Easy

YIELD
4 servings

TOTAL TIME
1 hour, 30 minutes

HANDS-ON TIME
20 minutes

Consider this mole light because you get many of the flavors of an almond mole, but without all the time-consuming work. It's quite a list of ingredients but the spicy-sweet-smoky end flavor more than justifies the means.

TAKEAWAY: How to make a quicker mole sauce.

Dried chiles are sold in the ethnic aisle of most markets. Ancho chiles (a.k.a. dried poblanos) are quite common, but, if you can't find them, use dried New Mexico chiles, dried pasillas, or mulatos. You can set the dried chiles in the water to soak up to 8 hours before proceeding.

Chipotles en adobo are chipotle (a.k.a. smoked jalapeño) chiles sold in a can in sauce and can be found in the ethnic aisle of most grocery stores. You won't use all the chipotles in this recipe, but there are plenty of other ways to use them, like Smoky Black Bean, Beef, and Green Pepper Chili (page 192); Chipotle—Sweet Potato Hash with Poached Eggs and Avocado (page 146); or blended into Buttermilk Dressing (page 209) for an added kick.

If you can't find bone-in, skinless chicken, buy it with the skin and pull it off. To get a better grip, grasp the skin with a paper towel and pull!

Fresh Mexican oregano has a mintier flavor than regular oregano. If you can't find it, use dried Mexican oregano.

BRAISED CHILE CHICKEN WITH RAISINS AND ALMONDS

4 **dried ancho chiles, torn into pieces**

¼ cup/60 ml **canola, grapeseed, or peanut oil**

1 **yellow onion, roughly chopped**

8 **garlic cloves, thinly sliced**

2 **chipotles en adobo, minced**

One 14.5 oz/415 g can **diced tomatoes, with juices**

1 cup/115 g **toasted whole almonds (page 119)**

1 stick **cinnamon**

¼ tsp **ground cloves**

Kosher salt, plus more for seasoning

Freshly ground black pepper

1 cup/240 ml **low-sodium chicken broth or water**

1 tbsp **red wine vinegar**

1 to 2 tbsp **honey or agave nectar**

3 lb/1.4 kg **bone-in, skinless chicken pieces (white and dark meat)**

¼ cup/40 g **roughly chopped fresh Mexican oregano leaves or** 1 tbsp **dried Mexican oregano**

½ cup/85 g **raisins**

Place the chiles in a dry (no oil) frying pan over medium heat and toast until charred and fragrant, 3 to 5 minutes. Remove from the heat, cover with water, and set aside to soak until soft and pliable, at least 30 minutes.

Heat half of the oil in a large, heavy-bottomed saucepan with a tight-fitting lid or Dutch oven over medium-high heat. Add the onion, garlic, and chipotles, season with salt, and cook until soft, about 3 minutes. Remove the stems and seeds from the soaked chiles then add to the pan along with the tomatoes with juices, half of the almonds, cinnamon, and cloves, and season with salt and pepper. Cook until the tomatoes break down, about 5 minutes.

Transfer to a blender or food processor (you may have to do this in batches), add the broth, and process until smooth and aerated, 2 or 3 minutes. Taste and add vinegar, honey, and salt, and pepper as needed. Meanwhile season the chicken well with salt and pepper and set aside.

Wipe out the saucepan or Dutch oven and return to the stove over medium heat. Add the remaining oil and, when it is hot but not smoking, add the chicken (you may have to do this in batches) and brown well, turning once, 3 to 4 minutes per side.

Return all chicken to saucepan and cover with the chile sauce. Bring to a boil then decrease the heat to low. Cover and simmer, stirring rarely, until the chicken is fork-tender, at least 40 minutes. Stir in the remaining almonds, the oregano, and raisins and cook another 5 minutes. Taste, adjust seasoning as desired, and serve.

Be careful when blending hot liquids as the heat can make them explode out of the carafe. To avoid this, only fill the blender halfway, remove the plastic plug in the blender cover, and start blending on low for a few seconds before you kick it up to full speed.

The sauce can be made and blended up to 2 days ahead. Store, refrigerated, in an airtight container then brown chicken and proceed with recipe when ready.

The dish can be made up to 2 days ahead. Cool the chicken in the sauce and refrigerate in an airtight container. Warm over medium-low until heated through before serving.

DIFFICULTY
Medium

YIELD
6 to 8 servings

TOTAL TIME
1 hour, plus broth cooking time

HANDS-ON TIME
20 minutes

My Lebanese brother-in-law considers this classic Middle Eastern stew his ultimate comfort food. I was drawn to it because it's surprisingly light for a stew, and the ingredients bring herb-y, meaty, and vegetal notes that harmonize beautifully.

TAKEAWAY: How to make chicken stock.

RECIPE WITHIN A RECIPE: The first part of the recipe makes a flavorful poached chicken. You could use the broth for chicken soup or just shred the chicken and serve topped with some of the cooking liquid.

CORIANDER CHICKEN, CILANTRO, AND CHARD STEW

Poaching the chicken in broth results in an amped-up chicken broth. It differs from a stock, which is made from scratch with bones.

Coriander is the dried seed of the cilantro plant; however, it has a different flavor from the fresh leaves.

White pepper gives this dish depth, so be sure to include it.

Only part of the broth is used in the final stew. Save the remaining broth for use in other soups, stews, and sauces.

If you can't find chard, you can use escarole, spinach, or beet greens.

CARDAMOM CHICKEN BROTH

10 whole **cardamom pods or** 1½ tsp **cardamom seeds**

1 whole 4 lb/2 kg **chicken, neck reserved, gizzards discarded**

10 **whole black peppercorns**

1 **stick cinnamon**

1 **bay leaf**

½ **lemon**

½ **red onion**

9 cups/2 L **low-sodium chicken broth or water**

1 tsp **kosher salt**

CORIANDER CHICKEN STEW

3 tbsp **unsalted butter**

1 head **garlic, cloves separated and minced**

2 tbsp **ground coriander**

1 tsp **kosher salt**

½ tsp **ground white pepper**

4 cups/120 g **roughly chopped fresh cilantro**

4 cups/1 L **Cardamom Chicken Broth**

½ **red onion, finely chopped**

1 tbsp **freshly squeezed lemon juice**

¼ cup/60 ml **red wine vinegar**

2 lb/910 g **chard, ribs removed and cut crosswise into 1-in/ 2.5-cm strips**

Steamed white rice, boiled potatoes, or pita bread, for serving

FOR THE BROTH

Tap the cardamom pods with the bottom of a pan to crack them. Add the cracked pods along with the remaining ingredients except salt to a large pot. Bring to a boil over high heat. Decrease the heat to medium-low and simmer until cooked through and easily fork-tender, 45 to 50 minutes.

Reserve the cooking liquid and remove the chicken to a cutting board. When cool enough to handle, remove and discard the skin, and shred the chicken into bite-sized pieces. Add the salt and toss to coat; set aside or refrigerate until ready to use. Meanwhile, prepare the rest of the dish.

FOR THE STEW

Heat 2 tablespoons of the butter in a large heavy-bottomed pot or Dutch oven over medium heat. When the foaming subsides, add the garlic, coriander, salt, and white pepper, and cook until fragrant. Add half of the cilantro and cook until wilted.

Decrease the heat to low and add 4 cups/1 L of the chicken broth and simmer until the broth is infused with the flavors, 15 to 20 minutes. Meanwhile, combine the onion with the lemon juice and vinegar in a bowl and set aside for at least 10 minutes.

Stir the chard, a few handfuls at a time, into the stock, waiting until each batch is wilted to add more; repeat until all the chard is added. Add the reserved chicken and simmer, 5 to 10 minutes.

Meanwhile, heat the remaining 1 tablespoon butter in a small frying pan or pot over medium heat. When it foams, add the remaining cilantro, and stir. Remove from the heat and pour into the chard mixture along with the onion mixture. Cook until heated through, taste, adjust seasoning as desired, and serve with rice, potatoes, or pita bread.

The broth and chicken can be made up to 2 days in advance and refrigerated in an airtight container.

Once you pull the meat off the chicken, freeze the carcass to use for homemade chicken stock.

Speed up this recipe by using previously homemade or storebought broth and a rotisserie chicken. It won't have the same complexity of flavor but works in a pinch.

Don't skip the onion garnish as it brings a whole other dimension to the dish.

DIFFICULTY
Easy

YIELD
4 to 6 servings

TOTAL TIME
1 hour, 30 minutes, plus marinating time

HANDS-ON TIME
15 minutes

"Huli huli" means "turn turn" in Hawaiian and refers to a smoky chicken that's slow-cooked on a rotisserie. Since most of us don't live in Hawaii and definitely don't own rotisseries, I crafted this DIY version with just as much flavor and half the effort.

TAKEAWAY: How to butterfly a chicken.
RECIPE WITHIN A RECIPE: Use this marinade on anything from tofu to pork loin.

GRILLED HULI HULI–STYLE CHICKEN

⅓ cup/80 ml **low-sodium soy sauce**

¼ cup/60 ml **pineapple juice**

¼ cup/50 g **packed dark brown sugar**

8 **garlic cloves, roughly chopped**

One 4-in/10-cm piece **fresh ginger, peeled and roughly chopped**

2 tbsp **brown-rice vinegar**

2 tbsp **Worcestershire sauce**

1 tbsp **tomato paste**

1 tbsp **toasted sesame oil**

¼ tbsp **finely ground black pepper, plus more for seasoning**

1 whole 4 lb/1.8 kg **chicken, neck and gizzards removed and discarded**

Kosher salt

Steamed rice, for serving

For tips on how to peel ginger, see page 79.

To make the marinade, combine everything except the chicken, salt, and rice in a blender and process until evenly combined.

Review page 97 for details on how to butterfly a chicken.

To butterfly the chicken, remove the backbone with a pair of sharp poultry shears or kitchen scissors and discard it. Press down along the center of the breast to flatten it. If it's not totally flat, flip the chicken, skin-side down, and score the cartilage on the back of the breastbone. Flip the chicken, skin-side up, and press down until the chicken is completely flat.

Place the chicken in a large, shallow dish and season generously with salt and pepper. Pour the marinade over the chicken and turn it several times until evenly coated. Cover and refrigerate to marinate 1 to 8 hours.

When ready to cook, heat a charcoal or gas grill to medium (about 350°F/177°C). Remove the chicken from the marinade (reserving the marinade), let excess liquid drip off, and let rest at room temperature while the grill heats, 20 to 30 minutes.

Place the chicken on the grill skin-side up, close the lid, and baste with marinade every 10 minutes. After basting the chicken 4 times (about 40 minutes of cooking), flip it over. Baste the chicken every 5 minutes until the internal temperature taken with an instant-read thermometer on the inside of the thigh registers 165°F/74°C (be sure the thermometer is not touching the bone) and, when pierced, the juices run clear, about 20 minutes more.

Let the grilled chicken rest on a cutting board for 10 to 15 minutes before serving. Meanwhile, boil the leftover marinade in a small pan over high heat until reduced and thickened, about 5 minutes. Strain and serve with the chicken along with steamed rice.

The recipe can also be made in the oven. To do so, heat the oven to 450°F/230°C/gas 8. Place the chicken in a roasting pan or baking dish fitted with a rack, and roast, basting every 5 minutes, until 165°F/74°C, about 50 minutes.

DIFFICULTY
Medium

YIELD
4 to 6 servings

TOTAL TIME
1 hour, 15 minutes

HANDS-ON TIME
25 minutes

I had this dish when I traveled to India for the first time a few years ago. Initially deterred by the name, I later realized that it's similar to the beloved chicken tikka masala and has only a few tablespoons of butter.

RECIPE WITHIN A RECIPE: The sauce has complex Indian flavors without a lot of work—try tossing it with shrimp, scallops, or tofu for a shortcut dish.

INDIAN-STYLE BRAISED "BUTTER" CHICKEN

"BUTTER" CHICKEN

1 cup/240 ml **whole-milk plain yogurt**

¼ cup/60 ml **freshly squeezed lime juice** (from 4 limes)

1 tbsp **grated garlic**

1 tbsp **peeled and grated fresh ginger**

1 **serrano chile, halved**

1 tbsp **kosher salt**

¾ tsp **ground coriander**

½ tsp **ground cumin**

½ tsp **ground cardamom**

¼ tsp **ground cinnamon**

2½ lb/1.3 kg **bone-in chicken thighs** (6 to 8)

MAKHANI SAUCE (TOMATO-SPICE SAUCE)

2 tbsp **unsalted butter**

1 **yellow onion, finely chopped**

Kosher salt

1 tbsp **peeled and grated fresh ginger**

1 tbsp **grated garlic**

½ cup/130 g **tomato paste**

1¼ cups/355 ml **low-sodium chicken broth or water**

¼ cup/6 g **roughly chopped fresh cilantro, for garnish**

¼ cup/21 g **thinly sliced green onions (white and pale green parts), for garnish**

> This recipe calls for a lot of spices but they each add depth of flavor to the dish. Check out the Index (page 433) for other recipes where you can use these spices.

FOR THE CHICKEN

Combine all ingredients except the chicken and mix thoroughly. Add the chicken and turn to coat. Cover and marinate at least 30 minutes at room temperature.

Meanwhile, heat the oven to 475°F/245°C/gas 9 and arrange a rack in the middle. Remove the chicken from the marinade, letting the excess drip off and reserving the marinade. Place the chicken on a rimmed baking sheet. Roast until the chicken is just beginning to brown, 15 to 20 minutes; remove from the oven and set aside. Meanwhile, make the sauce.

FOR THE SAUCE

Heat the butter in a large saucepan or Dutch oven over medium heat. When the foaming subsides, add the onion, season with salt, and cook until just softened. Stir in the ginger, garlic, and tomato paste and cook until fragrant, about 30 seconds. Add the broth and bring to a boil.

Decrease the heat to low, add the reserved marinade and the roasted chicken pieces. Cover and simmer until chicken is cooked through and fork-tender, 20 to 30 minutes. Taste and adjust the seasoning as desired. Stir in the cilantro and green onions and serve.

Don't let the sauce boil once you add the yogurt or it will curdle.

The chicken can be refrigerated and marinated for up to 24 hours before being cooked. If refrigerated, let the chicken sit out at room temperature at least 20 minutes before cooking.

As with all braised dishes, butter chicken makes for tasty leftovers.

RIFFS

- You can use heavy cream in place of the yogurt though it will obviously be heavier.
- Add some diced squash, sweet potatoes, potatoes, or cauliflower florets when simmering the chicken.

DIFFICULTY
Medium

YIELD
2 servings

TOTAL TIME
25 minutes

HANDS-ON TIME
25 minutes

Break the boredom of white meat chicken without any extra effort. This stuffed chicken has a range of Mediterranean flavors, from earthy to sweet, using easy-to-find ingredients that are likely already in your pantry.

TAKEAWAY: How to pan-roast chicken.
RECIPE WITHIN A RECIPE: Layer all the ingredients for the chicken stuffing to make a quick cheese spread.

PISTACHIO AND APRICOT GOAT CHEESE–STUFFED CHICKEN

2 tbsp **olive oil**

½ **red onion, cut into small dice**

2 tbsp **minced fresh Italian parsley**

Kosher salt and freshly ground black pepper

Two 8 oz/225 g **boneless, skinless chicken breasts**

2 oz/55 g **fresh goat cheese (chèvre)**

3 tbsp **roughly chopped shelled roasted pistachios**

2 tbsp **finely chopped dried apricots** (about 4)

¼ tsp **ground nutmeg**

To speed up softening of the goat cheese, place it in a small bowl and stir with a spatula or spoon until spreadable.

If you don't have an oven-proof pan, go ahead and place the browned chicken in a ovenproof baking dish and finish as directed in the recipe.

Heat the oven to 375°F/190°C/gas 5 and arrange a rack in the middle. Heat 1 tablespoon of the oil in a large pan with an oven-proof handle over medium heat. When it shimmers, add the onion and cook until soft and cooked through, about 6 minutes. Stir in the parsley, season with salt and pepper, and cook until just wilted. Remove the mixture from the pan and transfer to a bowl to cool. Wipe out the pan and set aside to cool.

Meanwhile, make pockets in the chicken by laying 1 piece on a cutting board and slicing horizontally about three-fourths of the way through the meat. Move the knife back and forth in a fanning motion to slightly enlarge the pocket (but don't cut all the way through). Season the chicken all over with salt and pepper and repeat with the other breast.

Stir goat cheese, pistachios, and apricots into the cooled onion mixture, taste, and adjust seasoning as desired. Divide the mixture between the chicken pockets and use toothpicks or butcher's twine to secure the chicken pockets closed.

Return the pan to medium-high heat and add the remaining 1 tablespoon of oil. When the oil shimmers, place the chicken breasts in the pan and cook, undisturbed, until golden brown, about 6 minutes. Turn the breasts over, transfer the pan to the oven, and bake until the filling is hot all the way through and the chicken is white but still juicy, 7 to 10 minutes.

▬▬▬

RIFFS
- Use cilantro and dates instead of parsley and apricots.
- Use fromage blanc or feta instead of goat cheese.
- Make with double-cut pork chops and roast until 155°F/68°C.

| DIFFICULTY |
| **Easy** |

| YIELD |
| **2 servings** |

| TOTAL TIME |
| **25 minutes** |

| HANDS-ON TIME |
| **25 minutes** |

The ultimate date night food, this dish (pictured on page 281) packs loads of Italian flavor, is practically impossible to overcook thanks to the prosciutto, and is quick enough to make that it will be ready by the time you've finished off your first glass of wine.

TAKEAWAY: How to pan-sauté meat.
GOES WELL WITH: Pairs well with wilted greens, sautéed broccoli rabe, or roasted root vegetables.

PROSCIUTTO-SAGE CHICKEN WITH PAN-ROASTED FIGS

Two 8 oz/225 g **boneless, skinless chicken breasts**

4 to 5 **firm-ripe fresh figs, halved**

2 tsp **sugar**

⅓ cup/44 g **unbleached all-purpose flour**

½ tsp **kosher salt, plus more for seasoning**

¼ tsp **freshly ground black pepper, plus more for seasoning**

6 **fresh sage leaves**

4 thin slices **prosciutto** (about 3 oz/85 g)

1 tbsp **unsalted butter**

1 tbsp **olive oil**

⅓ cup/75 ml **apple cider**

Put the prosciutto in the freezer for about 5 minutes before using to facilitate the wrapping step.

You can assemble the chicken breasts up to 4 hours ahead and keep refrigerated until ready to complete.

Place the chicken breasts between 2 sheets of plastic wrap or parchment paper. Using a frying pan or meat mallet, gently pound the meat to a 1 in/2.5 cm thickness. Toss the figs with sugar and set aside.

Combine the flour with the salt and pepper in a wide, shallow plate. Coat each breast by dredging it in the flour mixture then shaking off any excess. Place 3 sage leaves on each chicken breast then wrap 2 pieces of prosciutto around like a belt and tuck in the ends to secure (see page 280); set aside.

Melt the butter over medium heat in a large frying pan. When the foaming subsides, add the figs cut-side down and cook until browned, 3 to 4 minutes. Remove to a plate, season with salt and pepper and set aside.

Wipe out the pan, add the oil to the pan, and return to the stovetop over medium heat. When the oil shimmers, add the chicken and cook until golden brown, about 4 minutes per side. Stir in the cider and deglaze the pan by scraping the bottom with a spatula to incorporate any browned bits into the sauce.

Decrease the heat to low and cover. Cook, spooning the sauce over the chicken a few times, until the sauce is slightly thickened and the chicken is almost cooked through, 5 to 7 minutes (add a few splashes of water if the sauce gets too thick). Remove the cover, season with salt and pepper and serve with the figs.

RIFFS
- Use a boneless thin-cut pork chop in place of the chicken.
- Use 2 to 3 plums, apricots, persimmons, or pears in place of the figs.
- Top with a slice of melting cheese such as Fontina, Gruyère, or Gouda.

DIFFICULTY
Easy

YIELD
4 to 6 servings

TOTAL TIME
*1 hour, plus
marinating time*

HANDS-ON TIME
15 minutes

Crusty and crunchy with a tangy lemon and piney rosemary flavor, this oven-fried chicken has all the pluses of real-deal fried chicken without the cleanup.

TAKEAWAY: How to bread chicken.
RECIPE WITHIN A RECIPE: You could use the marinade for anything from chicken to pork chops, and just cook without coating.
GOES WELL WITH: A simple side salad and some mashed potatoes.

ROSEMARY-LEMON OVEN-FRIED CHICKEN

COOLING RACK
A cooling rack or toaster oven rack nested inside a rimmed baking sheet helps the chicken cook evenly because it allows the heat to circulate around the pieces.

• • • • • • • • • • • •

Buy bone-in, skin-on chicken thighs for this recipe. Remove the skin by grabbing it with a paper towel and giving it a good tug.

• • • • • • • • • • • •

To crush the cornflakes, place them in a resealable plastic bag and tap with a rolling pin, pan, or mallet until crushed. Alternatively pulse a few times in a mini food processor.

ROSEMARY-LEMON MARINADE

½ cup/120 ml **whole-milk plain yogurt or buttermilk**

¼ cup/60 ml **canola, grapeseed, or peanut oil**

¼ cup/60 ml **freshly squeezed lemon juice**

2 tbsp **roughly chopped fresh rosemary leaves** (2 tsp dried)

4 **garlic cloves, smashed**

2 tsp **grated lemon zest**

¾ tsp **cayenne pepper**

1 tsp **kosher salt**

8 **bone-in, skin-on chicken thighs** (about 2 lb/1 kg)**, skin removed**

CRISPY COATING

1½ cups/100 g **stone-ground cornmeal**

¾ cup/50 g **crushed cornflakes**

½ cup/2 oz/60 g **grated Pecorino cheese**

¼ cup/60 ml **canola, grapeseed, or peanut oil**

1½ tbsp **kosher salt**

½ tsp **finely ground black pepper**

¼ tsp **cayenne pepper**

3 **large eggs, beaten thoroughly**

CONTINUED

FOR THE MARINADE

Combine all the ingredients except the chicken until evenly combined. Add the chicken, turn to coat, cover, and refrigerate at least 2 hours and up to 6 hours.

When ready to cook, heat the oven to 425°F/220°C/gas 7 and arrange a rack in the upper third. Nest a cooling rack inside a rimmed baking sheet lined with aluminum foil; set aside.

FOR THE COATING

Combine the cornmeal, cornflakes, cheese, oil, salt, black pepper, and cayenne in a shallow bowl and mix until well combined; set aside. Whisk together the eggs in a shallow bowl until evenly combined; set aside.

To coat the chicken, remove it from the marinade and let any excess drip off. Dip the chicken in the beaten eggs then in the cornflake mixture, turning to coat all over and pressing to help it adhere. Place the chicken pieces on the prepared baking sheet and repeat with remaining chicken. Let the chicken rest on the baking sheet for 15 minutes before baking.

Bake until the coating is golden and crispy, the juices of the chicken run clear when poked, and the internal temperature is 160°F/71°C, 40 to 45 minutes.

Letting the excess marinade drip off helps let the chicken grab onto the egg and coating, so don't rush that step.

You can coat the chicken then return it to the fridge and let it sit for up to 4 hours before cooking. Just let it sit at room temperature to lose some of its chill for at least 15 minutes before baking so it cooks more evenly.

Not your typical chicken stir-fry, this has an eclectic mix of ingredients for a funky, slightly tropical take on the original.

TAKEAWAY: How to make a stir-fry.
GOES WELL WITH: Instead of rice, serve this over wide rice noodles.

DIFFICULTY
Easy

YIELD
4 servings

TOTAL TIME
20 minutes

HANDS-ON TIME
15 minutes

PAPAYA CHICKEN STIR-FRY

2 tbsp **low-sodium soy sauce**

1 lb/450 g **skinless, boneless chicken breasts or thighs, cut into 1-in/2.5-cm pieces**

¼ cup/60 ml **red wine vinegar**

¼ cup/60 ml **freshly squeezed orange juice**

1 tbsp **honey or agave nectar**

1 tbsp **canola, grapeseed, or peanut oil**

4 **shallots, halved lengthwise and thinly sliced crosswise**

Kosher salt and freshly ground black pepper

1 **serrano or Thai chile, thinly sliced**

4 **garlic cloves, thinly sliced**

1-in/2-cm **piece fresh ginger, peeled and grated**

1 **ripe papaya, peeled, seeded and cut crosswise into strips that are ½ in/12 mm wide**

1 cup/130 g **shelled and roasted cashews (page 119)**

1 tbsp **freshly squeezed lime juice**

¼ cup **thinly sliced fresh basil leaves**

Steamed rice or noodles, for serving

Mix together 1 tablespoon of the soy sauce and the chicken, toss to coat, and set aside.

Whisk together the remaining soy sauce, red wine vinegar, orange juice, and honey, and set aside.

Look for a papaya that is yellow, heavy for its size, and yields to gentle pressure. If you can't find papaya, you can use mango or pineapple.

The easiest way to slice basil is in a chiffonade. To do so, stack a few leaves, then roll them into a tight cigar shape. Using a sharp knife, slice into thin strips. Use quickly as they darken with time.

CONTINUED

Heat the oil in a large frying pan over medium-high heat. When the oil shimmers, add the shallots, season with salt, and cook until golden, about 2 minutes. Add the chile, garlic, and ginger and cook until fragrant, about 30 seconds. Add the chicken and cook, stirring rarely, until it is browned, 5 minutes.

Remove the chicken to a plate and return the pan to the stove. Add the reserved vinegar mixture and scrape the bottom of the pan to stir in any browned bits. Boil until slightly thickened, about 2 minutes.

Stir in the papaya and cook until just softened, about 2 minutes. Add the chicken and cashews and cook until heated through, about 2 minutes. Season with salt and pepper, as needed. Remove from the heat, stir in the lime juice and basil, and serve over rice.

RIFF: Use boneless pork chop or flank steak in place of the chicken.

 With stir-fries, cooking moves especially fast. So it's a must to have all your ingredients prepped before you start.

When you add the vinegar to the pan, open a window or turn on a fan because the fumes released may sting your eyes or make you cough.

DIFFICULTY
Easy/Medium

YIELD
4 servings

TOTAL TIME
30 minutes

HANDS-ON TIME
30 minutes

I was fortunate that homecooked meals were the norm in our family when I was younger. My mother would frequently make a version of this elegant but easy dish. For special occasions, she served it in puff pastry cups but it's amazing served with anything that can soak up the delicate cream sauce.

TAKEAWAY: How to make a one-pan chicken dish.

TARRAGON-CREAM CHICKEN WITH FRESH PEAS

2 lb/910 kg **skinless, boneless dark or white meat chicken, cut into strips that are 1 in/2.5 cm thick**

Kosher salt and freshly ground black pepper

1 tbsp **canola, grapeseed, or peanut oil**

1 tbsp **unsalted butter**

2 **shallots, finely sliced**

½ cup/120 ml **brandy**

½ cup/120 ml **low-sodium chicken broth or water**

½ cup/120 ml **heavy cream**

2 tbsp **whole-grain Dijon mustard**

6 oz/170 g **snap peas, stem ends trimmed**

1 cup/100 g **frozen or shelled fresh baby peas**

2 tbsp **chopped fresh tarragon leaves**

Steamed white rice, boiled potatoes, or noodles, for serving

Pat the chicken dry with paper towels and season thoroughly with salt and pepper. Heat the oil in a large, heavy-bottomed pan over medium-high heat until hot but not smoking. Add the chicken to the pan in a single layer, leaving at least ½ inch/ 12 mm between each piece (you may have do this in 2 or 3 batches). Cook until golden brown, but not cooked through, about 2 minutes per side. Transfer the chicken to a plate and repeat to brown all chicken.

Don't mess with the meat while it's browning. If it doesn't easily release from the pan, either the pan was too cold or the chicken is not cooked enough.

Discard any drippings, wipe out the pan, and return to the stove over medium heat. Add the butter and, when the foaming subsides, add the shallots, season with salt, and cook until soft and golden, 1 to 2 minutes.

Remove from the heat, add the brandy, and scrape up any browned bits on the bottom of the pan. Return to the stove and simmer until any alcohol smell is cooked off and the liquid is reduced, about 2 minutes. Whisk in chicken juices that have accumulated on the plate from the chicken, the broth, cream, and mustard and cook until the sauce is thick enough to coat the back of a spoon, about 5 minutes.

Return the chicken to the pan along with the peas and simmer until the chicken is cooked through and the peas are bright green, 2 to 3 minutes. Stir in the tarragon, adjust seasoning as desired, and serve with rice, potatoes, or noodles.

Be sure to remove the pan from the heat before adding the brandy, so as to prevent it from catching fire. Also, never add alcohol to a pan directly from a bottle but instead measure out the amount you need and add that.

RIFFS
- Basil is a good substitute if you can't find or don't like tarragon.
- Swap pork tenderloin for the chicken.
- Add mushrooms to the shallots and cook until golden brown.

DIFFICULTY
Easy

YIELD
8 servings

TOTAL TIME
2 hours, 45 minutes

HANDS-ON TIME
15 minutes

Flavors from all across the globe mash up in this subtly spiced, richly flavored braised pork. Its chameleon-like flavor makes it suitable to serve over rice, on tacos, as sliders, or even as a make-shift ragù.

TAKEAWAY: How to braise pork.
RECIPE WITHIN A RECIPE: The braising liquid doubles as a tasty marinade.
GOES WELL WITH: Serve it over a starch that can sop up the braising liquid—anything from polenta or potatoes to rice or noodles. Serve on toasted slider buns for pulled pork sandwiches. Serve as is over mashed potatoes or polenta. Toss with noodles for a twist on ragù.

BLOOD ORANGE–BRAISED PORK SHOULDER

¼ cup/50 g **packed light brown sugar**

1 tbsp **kosher salt**

One 3½- to 4-lb/1.4- to 1.8-kg **bone-in pork shoulder (Boston butt or picnic)**

2 tbsp **canola, grapeseed, or peanut oil**

1½ cups/360 ml **freshly squeezed blood orange juice (or tangerine or orange juice)**

1 cup/240 ml **low-sodium chicken broth or water**

½ cup/120 ml **whiskey**

½ cup/120 ml **low-sodium soy sauce**

½ cup/120 ml **balsamic vinegar**

12 **garlic cloves, smashed**

One 3-in/7.5-cm **cinnamon stick**

15 **black peppercorns**

1 bunch **fresh thyme**

2 **yellow onions, cut into eighths**

Try to find a bone-in pork shoulder as it will have more depth of flavor than a boneless cut. If you can't find one, use a boneless pork shoulder.

You can rub the pork shoulder in the salt and sugar and store refrigerated up to 1 day before cooking—just pat the meat dry with paper towels before using.

Heat the oven to 325°F/165°F/gas 3 and arrange a rack in the middle. Combine the brown sugar and salt in a bowl and mix well. Rub the mixture all over the pork and set aside at room temperature for 20 to 30 minutes.

When ready, heat the oil in an ovenproof Dutch oven or a large heavy-bottomed pot with a tight-fitting lid over medium heat until it is just beginning to smoke. Add the pork and cook, moving only to rotate, until all sides are well browned. Remove to a plate. Add the orange juice, broth, whiskey, soy sauce, and vinegar to the pot and scrape the bottom of the pot to incorporate any browned bits. When the liquid boils, decrease the heat to medium-low and add the garlic, cinnamon stick, peppercorns, thyme, onions, and the pork.

Once the liquid is at a simmer, cover, and place in the oven. Baste occasionally, until the pork is fork-tender, falling off the bone, and has an internal temperature of at least 155°F/68°C, 2 to 2½ hours.

Discard the cinnamon stick and peppercorns, then using 2 forks, pull the meat off the bone and shred. Discard the bone, stir the meat to coat in the sauce, and serve with braising juices poured over the meat.

 You can make the pork up to 2 days ahead of time. Cool in the cooking liquid to room temperature then refrigerate until ready to use. To serve, skim off any fat on the surface then warm through over medium-low heat.

Anytime you make a braise, cool and store the meat in its cooking liquid or it will dry out.

Everything all at once but no one thing more than the other, this dish is sweet, salty, and spicy, and borrows flavors from the Caribbean to the South Pacific.

DIFFICULTY
Medium

YIELD
4 servings

TOTAL TIME
40 minutes

HANDS-ON TIME
15 minutes

TAKEAWAY: How to pan-roast a pork chop.

RECIPE WITHIN A RECIPE: Use the rub on anything from chicken to salmon to steaks.

GOES WELL WITH: Serve over mashed sweet potatoes, with a big green salad, or with bell peppers with walnuts (page 338).

BROWN SUGAR PORK CHOPS WITH MANGO-HORSERADISH SAUCE

MANGO-HORSERADISH SAUCE

1 **ripe mango, peeled, pitted, and cut into small dice**

2 tbsp **prepared horseradish**

2 tsp **cider vinegar**

1 **garlic clove**

½ tsp **ground ginger**

1 tsp **packed light brown sugar**

½ **red bell pepper, cut into small dice**

2 **green onions (white and light green parts), trimmed and thinly sliced**

Kosher salt and freshly ground black pepper

Look for prepared horseradish in jars in the condiment aisle. Don't use horseradish cream as it has lots of added stabilizers and fat. If you can't find prepared horseradish, substitute prepared wasabi paste or spicy mustard.

BROWN SUGAR PORK CHOPS

4 **bone-in rib pork chops** (2.5 lb/1.2 kg), **cut 1 in/2.5 cm thick**

3 tbsp **packed light brown sugar**

1 tbsp **kosher salt**

1 tbsp **coarsely ground black pepper**

2 tsp **ground ginger**

1 tbsp **canola, grapeseed, or peanut oil**

Any pork chop will work here but I prefer the look and taste served up by a bone-in rib chop.

CONTINUED

FOOD PROCESSOR
I used a food processor here but a blender will also work fine.

🕐 The sauce can be made up to 2 days ahead but it becomes more spicy with time.

FOR THE SAUCE

Combine half of the mango with all the horseradish, vinegar, garlic, ginger, and brown sugar in a food processor fitted with the metal blade and process until smooth. Transfer to a nonreactive bowl and stir in the remaining mango, bell pepper, and green onions. Season with salt and black pepper and let rest at least 15 minutes before serving.

FOR THE CHOPS

Heat the oven to 425°F/220°C/gas 7 and arrange a rack in the middle. Rinse the pork chops and pat dry with paper towels. Combine the brown sugar, salt, pepper, and ginger in a small bowl and mix until evenly combined. Rub all of the spice mixture all over the pork chops and set aside at room temperature for 15 to 30 minutes before cooking.

Heat the oil in a large cast-iron pan or large, ovenproof frying pan over medium-high heat. When it shimmers, pat chops dry then cook on one side, undisturbed, until golden brown, about 4 minutes.

Flip the chops in the pan and place the pan in the oven. Cook until the chops are firm and at a 150°F/65°C internal temperature, 5 to 10 minutes. Place the chops on warm plates and let rest 2 minutes then serve with the sauce.

PORK, BEEF, AND LAMB

The classic Jamaican jerk flavors—fiery chiles, sweet onions, and hot spices—make up the rub for these glazed ribs. Yes, this does require a lot of time and a lot of ingredients, but that's what makes for tons of flavor in these fall-off-the-bone ribs.

TAKEAWAY: How to oven-braise ribs.
RECIPE WITHIN A RECIPE: Use the rub anytime you want to give a Jamaican flavor to grilled meats.

DIFFICULTY
Medium

YIELD
2 to 4 servings

TOTAL TIME:
3 hours, 20 minutes, plus marinating time

HANDS-ON TIME
20 minutes

CARIBBEAN JERK-STYLE SPARERIBS

CARIBBEAN JERK RUB

⅓ cup/65 g **packed dark brown sugar**

1 tbsp **ground allspice**

2 tsp **ground nutmeg**

2 tsp **kosher salt**

1½ tsp **freshly ground black pepper**

1 tsp **ground cinnamon**

3 lb/1.4 kg **rack pork spareribs**

PINEAPPLE-CHILE MARINADE

1 cup/240 ml **pineapple juice**

⅓ cup/80 ml **low-sodium soy sauce**

¼ cup/60 ml **freshly squeezed lime juice**

¼ cup/60 ml **cider vinegar**

2 tbsp **canola, grapeseed, or peanut oil**

1 bunch **fresh cilantro, trimmed**

8 **thyme sprigs**

8 **garlic cloves, smashed**

6 **green onions (white and pale green parts), cut into 1-in/ 2.5-cm pieces**

2 **Scotch bonnet or habanero chiles, thinly sliced**

Scotch bonnet chiles are traditionally used in this recipe, although habaneros are a good substitute as they're just as spicy. If you can't find either, you can use 4 halved serrano or Thai chiles.

 Use gloves or coat your hands with a thin layer of cooking oil before handling the chiles for this recipe as they are incredibly hot. And, by all means, make sure you don't touch your face while working with them or you'll be in serious pain.

CONTINUED

Place all the rub ingredients in a bowl and mix to combine. Coat the ribs with the rub, place in a resealable plastic bag, and add the marinade ingredients. Turn the ribs to coat, cover, and refrigerate at least 4 hours or overnight.

Heat the oven to 300°F/150°C/gas 2 and arrange a rack in the middle. Remove the ribs from the refrigerator and let come to room temperature while the oven is heating, at least 20 minutes. Meanwhile, line a rimmed baking sheet with aluminum foil.

Place the ribs on the prepared baking sheet, discard the solids from the marinade, and pour the marinade on the ribs. Close tightly with aluminum foil and cook until the ribs have at least a 155°F/68°C internal temperature and the bones move easily, 2 to 2½ hours.

Remove the foil and increase the oven temperature to 350°F/177°C/gas 4. Cook the ribs, basting every 10 minutes, until the ribs are glazed, 20 to 30 minutes. Let rest 5 minutes, then cut between the ribs and serve. Pour the pan juices into a small bowl and serve on the side.

You'll want to plan ahead for these ribs because they need to marinate for 4 hours before they cook.

BAKING SHEET
A good-quality, heavy-duty rimmed baking sheet is key here as it will not warp in the oven and will get hot enough to transform the marinade into a glaze in the last half hour.

You can cook the ribs through the last step up to 2 days ahead of time and then heat in the oven and glaze just before serving.

DIFFICULTY
Easy

YIELD
12 meatballs

TOTAL TIME
40 to 50 minutes

HANDS-ON TIME
15 to 20 minutes

These meatballs have flavors familiar to Italy but that don't hail from any particular region—it's what my family calls "Itai," a.k.a. bastardized Italian food. Despite their illegitimate origins, they'd give any traditional meatball a run for its money.

TAKEAWAY: How to make meatballs.

GOES WELL WITH: Stateside we usually see meatballs served with pasta but they're often served in Italy in a bowl, simply topped with a spoonful of tomato sauce (page 116) and some crusty bread alongside.

ITAI-STYLE MEATBALLS

½ **red onion, finely chopped**

½ cup/2 oz/60 g **grated Parmigiano-Reggiano cheese, plus more for serving**

3 tbsp **toasted pine nuts**

3 tbsp **sun-dried tomatoes, minced**

1 tbsp **Worcestershire sauce**

2½ tsp **kosher salt**

1½ tsp **red pepper flakes**

4 **garlic cloves, finely chopped**

2 **large eggs, beaten**

1 lb/455 g **ground chuck beef, chilled**

1 lb/455 g **ground pork, chilled**

⅔ cup/35 g **panko bread crumbs**

¼ cup/10 g **finely chopped fresh Italian parsley**

2 tbsp **minced fresh oregano**

Tomato sauce (page 116), for serving, optional

Oil-packed sun-dried tomatoes are preferred, though any kind will work.

Ground chuck is flavorful and has a not-too-fatty ratio of fat to meat (about 15 percent fat). Our family traditionally used a mix of veal and pork for our meatballs but we've converted to beef over the years.

Heat the oven to 375°F/190°C/gas 5 and arrange a rack in the middle.

Add the onion, cheese, pine nuts, sun-dried tomatoes, Worces-tershire, salt, red pepper flakes, garlic, and eggs to a blender or food processor fitted with the metal blade and process until very smooth. Transfer to a large bowl along with the beef, pork, bread crumbs, parsley, and oregano and gently mix until thoroughly combined, about 2 minutes.

Divide the meat mixture into twelve parts and roll between your dampened palms until compact, smooth, and round (about 2½ in/6 cm in diameter). Place the meatballs on a rimmed bak-ing sheet and repeat until you have used up all the meat mixture.

Bake until the meatballs are firm and just cooked through, with a 155°F/68°C to 160°F/71°C internal temperature, 25 to 30 minutes. Eat alone or serve with tomato sauce.

Once cooked through, the meatballs can be cooled and refrigerated in an airtight container for a couple of days or frozen for a few months.

RIFF: Form into a meat loaf and bake as directed on page 310.

DIFFICULTY
Easy

YIELD
4 servings

TOTAL TIME
30 minutes, plus marinating time

HANDS-ON TIME
15 minutes

A stellar way to showcase cherries when they're at their prime, this salsa pairs surprisingly well with meat and is a welcome departure from the classic pairing of mint jelly.

TAKEAWAY: How to panfry lamb chops

RECIPE WITHIN A RECIPE: Use this cherry salsa atop other grilled meats, on smoked meat sandwiches, spooned over goat or ricotta cheese as an appetizer, or as a dip with savory crackers.

LAMB CHOPS WITH FRESH CHERRY SALSA

FRESH CHERRY SALSA

2 cups/355 g **fresh cherries, pitted and halved**

1 **shallot, minced**

1 tbsp **Dijon mustard**

1 tbsp **red wine vinegar**

2 tbsp **olive oil**

½ cup/20 g **roughly chopped fresh mint, tarragon, or Italian parsley**

Kosher salt and freshly ground black pepper

ALLSPICE-RUBBED LAMB CHOPS

1 tbsp **kosher salt**

2 tsp **ground allspice**

1 tsp **freshly ground black pepper**

Eight ¾-in/2-cm-thick **rib lamb chops** (about 2 lb/910 g)

2 tbsp **olive oil**

There are two kinds of lamb chops out there: those from the rib and those from the loin. Either will work in this recipe, though the timing here is for rib chops so add a few minutes if you are using loin chops.

FOR THE SALSA

Combine the cherries, shallot, mustard, vinegar, and olive oil in a nonreactive bowl and stir to combine. Let marinate at room temperature 30 minutes to 3 hours. Meanwhile, prepare the chops. When ready to serve the salsa, stir in the herbs, taste, and season with salt and pepper as desired.

The salsa can be made without the herbs up to 1 day ahead and refrigerated in an airtight container. Stir in the herbs and adjust the seasoning when ready to use.

FOR THE CHOPS

Mix the salt, allspice, and pepper together in a small bowl until well combined. Drizzle the chops with 1 tablespoon of the oil then rub the meat all over with the salt mixture. Set aside to marinate at room temperature, 20 to 30 minutes.

Heat a large cast-iron skillet or heavy-bottomed frying pan over medium-high heat and add the remaining 1 tablespoon oil. When wisps come off the oil but it is not smoking, add lamb and cook, undisturbed, until well browned, about 3 minutes. Flip and cook until the lamb has a 130°F/54°C to 135°F/57°C internal temperature, another 3 to 5 minutes.

Remove from the heat, tent loosely with aluminum foil, and let rest a few minutes before serving topped with the cherry salsa.

RIFF: Use plums or pluots in place of the cherries.

DIFFICULTY
Easy

YIELD
4 servings

TOTAL TIME
30 minutes

HANDS-ON TIME
20 minutes

The versatility of miso paste goes well beyond soup. One of my favorite ways to use it is in a marinade, as it pays off in caramelized sweet, salty flavors that are irresistible.

Look for white miso paste in the ethnic aisle of the grocery store. It has a very long shelf life when stored in the refrigerator, although the flavor intensifies with time.

Shishito peppers are sweet, slightly spicy Japanese green peppers that are becoming more popular. If you can't find them, Anaheim chiles, banana peppers, or jalapeños will work too (though jalapeños are spicier).

If you use tomatoes, be careful as a few may pop while being grilled.

You can grill these skewers outdoors or cook them under a broiler.

The meat can hang out in the marinade for up to 1 day—just refrigerate in an airtight container.

MISO-MARINATED BEEF AND CHARRED VEGETABLE SKEWERS

MISO MARINADE

¼ cup/70 g **white miso paste**

2 tbsp **packed light brown sugar**

2 tbsp **low-sodium soy sauce**

2 tbsp **brown-rice vinegar**

1 tbsp **sugar**

1 tsp **toasted sesame oil**

6 **garlic cloves**

1 tbsp **water**

PEPPER-BEEF SKEWERS

2 lb/1 kg **sirloin or New York strip steak, trimmed and cut into large dice**

1 lb/450 g **shishito peppers or cherry tomatoes**

1 tbsp **toasted sesame oil**

Kosher salt and freshly ground black pepper

TO COOK ON AN OUTDOOR GRILL:

Heat a grill to medium-high heat.

Meanwhile, combine all the marinade ingredients in a blender and process until smooth. Reserve ¼ cup/60 ml. Toss the meat in the remaining marinade then thread 5 pieces of meat on each of 8 skewers.

Toss the peppers with the sesame oil, season with salt and black pepper and thread on the remaining 8 skewers.

Grill the meat and vegetable skewers undisturbed, for 3 minutes. Brush the meat with the remaining miso marinade, flip the meat and vegetables, and grill until the vegetables are charred and meat is caramelized, about 2 more minutes. Season with additional salt and pepper to taste, and serve.

TO COOK INDOORS:

Alternatively, heat a broiler to high and arrange a rack in the middle. Scatter the vegetables on a rimmed baking sheet and broil until charred. Lightly coat a grill pan or large, heavy skillet and heat over medium-high. When wisps of smoke come off the oil, grill the skewers in the pan (in 2 or 3 batches), turning once, until the steak is charred, about 5 minutes. Serve immediately.

METAL SKEWERS
You'll need sixteen 10-in/ 25-cm skewers for this recipe. If you're frequently firing up your grill, you may want to buy a set of metal skewers. Otherwise, use wooden skewers but be sure to soak them in water at least 20 minutes before using so they don't catch fire.

A departure from the everyday stir-fry, this dish gets a distinct Thai vibe from the lemongrass and fish sauce, making it a welcome change from beef and broccoli.

TAKEAWAY: How to make a stir-fry.

Buy lemongrass that is free of blemishes. You need to bruise lemongrass to bring out its flavor. To do so, tap on the stalk with a wooden handle a few times to lightly crush it.

Fish sauce can be found in the ethnic aisle of your grocery store.

The beef will be much easier to slice thinly if you freeze it for 10 to 15 minutes before cutting.

If you can't find mustard greens, anything from collard greens to kale to dandelion greens would work too.

MUSTARD GREENS AND LEMONGRASS BEEF STIR-FRY

MARINADE

1 **lemongrass stalk, bruised, outer leaves discarded, ends trimmed, and minced**

3 tbsp **Asian fish sauce**

3 tbsp **packed light brown sugar**

1 tbsp **freshly squeezed lime juice, plus more for serving**

1 tbsp **low-sodium soy sauce**

4 **garlic cloves, minced**

1 **serrano chile, sliced**

STIR-FRY

12 oz/340 g **flank steak, trimmed and frozen briefly (10 to 15 minutes)**

12 oz/340 g **mustard greens, stemmed, and leaves chopped into 3-in/7.5-cm pieces**

2 tbsp **canola, grapeseed, or peanut oil**

2 tbsp **water**

½ **yellow onion, halved and thinly sliced**

Steamed rice or noodles, for serving

FOR THE MARINADE

To make the marinade, mix together the lemongrass, fish sauce, brown sugar, lime juice, soy sauce, garlic, and chile. Cut the meat across the grain into strips that are ½ in/12 mm by 2 in/5 cm. Combine with the marinade, toss to coat, and set aside to marinate 10 to 15 minutes. Meanwhile, prepare the mustard greens.

FOR THE STIR-FRY

Place the chopped mustard greens in a colander, wash, and set aside. When the meat is ready, transfer to a plate and reserve the marinade.

Heat 1 tablespoon of the oil in a large 12-in/30.5-cm frying pan over high heat. When wisps come off the oil, but the oil isn't smoking, add half the meat and cook, turning once, until browned on both sides, about 3 minutes total. Remove to a plate and repeat with the remaining meat. Add the 2 tablespoons water to the pan; stir up browned bits with a wooden spoon and pour into the reserved marinade.

Wipe out the pan, add the remaining 1 tablespoon of oil, and return to the stove over high heat. When the oil shimmers, add the onion and cook until fragrant, about 30 seconds. Add the greens and cook, tossing occasionally, until wilted, about 30 seconds. Add the beef and the reserved marinade mixture and cook until well mixed and the sauce is thick enough to coat everything, 30 to 60 seconds. Serve with rice or noodles and a squeeze of lime juice.

The beef can marinate up to 8 hours in advance.

Check out the meat and you'll notice that, similar to wood, it has a grain. Always slice at a 90-degree angle, perpendicular, to the grain.

RIFFS
- Swap pork or chicken for the beef.
- Use another hearty winter green—such as kale—in the stir-fry.

DIFFICULTY
Easy

YIELD
4 to 6 servings

TOTAL TIME
20 minutes

HANDS-ON TIME
20 minutes

*I'd love to lay claim to this dish but it's a classic Peruvian specialty. Known as **lomo saltado**, it's a form of **chifa** cuisine—Chinese food with a Latin slant created by Chinese immigrants to Peru.*

RECIPE WITHIN A RECIPE: Use the spice rub on grilled meats for a twist.

GOES WELL WITH: Traditionally served over rice with some French fries, but any starch will do.

PERUVIAN SKIRT STEAK STIR-FRY

1½ lb/680 g **skirt steak**

2½ tsp **ground cumin**

1 tsp **kosher salt, plus more for seasoning**

½ tsp **ground cinnamon**

2 tbsp **canola, grapeseed, or peanut oil**

½ **red onion, cut into ½-in/12-mm slices**

2 tbsp **sliced garlic**

1 **serrano chile, thinly sliced**

1 tbsp **red wine vinegar**

4 **plum tomatoes, quartered**

2 tbsp **low-sodium soy sauce**

¼ cup/10 g **finely chopped fresh cilantro**

Freshly ground black pepper

Steamed rice, French fries, or boiled potatoes, for serving

If you can't find skirt steak, you can use hanger or flank steak.

Check out the meat and you'll notice that, similar to wood, it has a grain. Always slice at a 90-degree angle, perpendicular, to the grain.

Don't cook the meat any-more than indicated in the recipe or the meat will be really tough.

When you add the vinegar to the pan, open a window or turn on a fan because the fumes released may sting your eyes or make you cough.

Freeze the beef for 10 to 15 minutes. Cut the beef against the grain into strips about 2 in/5 cm long and 1 in/2.5 cm thick. Toss with cumin, salt, and cinnamon until well coated.

Heat 1 tablespoon of the oil in a large frying pan over medium-high heat until wisps of smoke come off the pan. Add one-third of the steak and stir-fry until it is just cooked through, 1 to 2 minutes. Remove to a plate and set aside; repeat until all of the steak is cooked.

Add the remaining 1 tablespoon of oil and return the pan to medium-high heat. Add onion and cook until softened, 3 to 4 minutes. Add the garlic and chile, and cook until browned and softened, 2 to 3 minutes. Carefully add the vinegar and stir until the smell is cooked off, about 30 seconds.

Add the tomatoes and cook until they are softened, just broken down, and have released some juices, about 2 minutes. Return the meat and any collected juices to the pan, add the soy sauce, and stir to heat through. Add the cilantro, season as needed with pepper and additional salt, and serve with rice, French fries, or potatoes.

DIFFICULTY
Easy

YIELD
6 to 8 servings

TOTAL TIME
1 hour, 30 minutes

HANDS-ON TIME
20 minutes

In this roast, Thai flavors combine in a decidedly non-Thai technique. The chile-coconut carrots and red curry beef are tasty on their own but taste even better together.

RECIPE WITHIN A RECIPE: Make the carrots without the meat for a low-fuss Thai-flavored side dish.

Thai red curry paste is found in the ethnic aisle of the market. If you can't find it, green curry paste will also work well.

Tri-tip is a cut that originated on the West Coast and is becoming more popular nationwide. If you can't find it, a sirloin strip or shell steak will make a good substitute but keep an eye on the meat temperature as they will cook at different rates.

 This is a pretty spicy dish. If you want it less so, take the seeds out of the chile.

RED CURRY ROAST WITH COCONUT-CHILE CARROTS

RED CURRY MARINADE

¼ cup/50 g **packed dark brown sugar**

¼ cup/60 ml **low-sodium soy sauce**

2 tbsp **Thai red curry paste**

One 1-in/2.5-cm piece **fresh ginger**

1 **tri-tip roast** (1½ to 2 lb/680 to 910 g)

1 tbsp **canola, grapeseed, or peanut oil**

COCONUT-CHILE CARROTS

1 tbsp **canola, grapeseed, or peanut oil**

2 tbsp **packed light brown sugar**

1 tbsp **freshly squeezed lime juice**

1 tbsp **Asian fish sauce**

1 cup/240 ml **coconut milk**

1½ lb/680 g **carrots, peeled, and cut into 3-in/7.5-cm lengths**

½ **red onion, cut into ½-in/12-mm slices**

1 **serrano chile, stemmed and sliced into rings**

Kosher salt

¼ cup/10 g **tightly packed roughly chopped fresh cilantro**

Heat the oven to 450°F/230°C/gas 7 and arrange a rack in the middle.

FOR THE MARINADE

Combine the sugar, soy sauce, curry paste, and ginger in a small pan and heat over medium until the sugar is dissolved. Let the marinade cool slightly. Place the meat in a nonreactive container, rub with oil, and pour the marinade over the meat. Turn the meat to coat and let sit to marinate and come to room temperature while the oven warms up, at least 45 minutes. Meanwhile, marinate the carrots.

FOR THE CARROTS

Combine the oil, sugar, lime juice, fish sauce, and coconut milk in a large nonreactive bowl and whisk to combine and dissolve the sugar. Add the carrots, onion, and chile, season with salt, and toss well to coat. Let sit while oven heats up, at least 15 minutes.

Heat a large heavy-bottomed pan over medium-high heat. When heated, add the roast, top-side down, and cook until browned, about 5 minutes.

Scatter the carrots in a roasting pan and nestle the roast in the middle. Roast, basting the meat and turning the carrots occasionally, until the internal temperature of the roast registers 130°F/54°C on an instant-read thermometer, 35 to 45 minutes.

Remove the roast from the oven and transfer it to a cutting board. Tent it with aluminum foil and allow the meat to rest for 5 to 10 minutes before slicing.

If the carrots are fork-tender, remove from the oven; otherwise, continue to cook while the meat rests, about 10 more minutes. Carve the meat and transfer to a serving platter. Serve with the carrots and onions, sprinkle with cilantro, and serve.

RIFFS

- Swap sweet potatoes or squash for the carrots.
- Try a pork loin or butterflied whole chicken (see pages 97 and 272) instead of the beef.
- Grill the meat during the warmer months to add a charred note.

The longer the better when it comes to marinating the meat and carrots so feel free to marinate them, refrigerated, for up to 1 day.

Adequate marinating time and minimal cooking keep the tri-tip tender. Don't take this meat beyond medium or it will be tough and chewy.

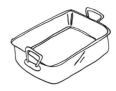

ROASTING PAN
A heavy roasting pan helps the carrots get really brown. If you don't have one, you can use a rimmed baking sheet or baking pan, but the carrots will not caramelize as much.

DIFFICULTY
Easy

YIELD
8 to 10 servings

TOTAL TIME
1 hour, 30 minutes

HANDS-ON TIME
15 minutes

Meat loaf is as American as apple pie and there are countless versions of it. This meat loaf mixes pork and beef for a balance of flavor that's tied together with flavors reminiscent of the Spanish red pepper sauce known as romesco.

TAKEAWAY: How to make meat loaf.

RED PEPPER AND SMOKED PAPRIKA MEAT LOAF

1 tbsp **canola, grapeseed, or peanut oil**

1 **red onion, finely chopped**

4 **garlic cloves, finely chopped**

1½ tsp **kosher salt, plus more for seasoning**

1 tsp **freshly ground black pepper, plus more for seasoning**

2 **roasted red peppers (see page 310), roughly chopped**

¼ cup/60 g **tomato paste**

2 tbsp **Dijon mustard**

2 tbsp **Worcestershire sauce**

1½ tsp **smoked paprika**

2 **large eggs, beaten**

½ cup/20 g **finely chopped fresh Italian parsley**

½ cup/55 g **panko bread crumbs**

1 lb/455 g **ground pork**

8 oz/225 g **ground beef chuck**

8 oz/225 g **sweet Italian sausage, casing removed and crumbled**

Smoked paprika adds a distinct Spanish note but go ahead and use regular paprika if you can't find it.

Panko bread crumbs are a Japanese cracker bread crumb. If you can't find it, use crushed melba toasts or saltine crackers.

Sweet Italian sausage can be replaced with bratwurst or other mild uncooked sausage.

This also works well shaped as meatballs and baked until cooked through.

Heat the oven to 350°F/177°C/gas 4 and arrange a rack in the middle. Heat the oil in a medium pan over medium heat. When it shimmers, add the onion and garlic, season to taste with salt and black pepper and cook until softened, about 3 minutes; set aside.

Combine the onion mixture, roasted red peppers, tomato paste, mustard, Worcestershire, paprika, 1½ teaspoons salt, and 1 teaspoon black pepper in a food processor fitted with the metal blade and process until smooth. Turn the puree into a large bowl and add the eggs, parsley, bread crumbs, pork, beef, and sausage. Using clean hands, gently mix all together until thoroughly combined (don't squeeze the mixture).

Dampen your hands and put the meat on a rimmed baking sheet. Form the meat into a loaf that measures 9 by 5 in/23 by 13 cm. Bake until the internal temperature registers 150°F/66°C to 155°F/68°C on an instant-read thermometer, 55 minutes to 1 hour. Remove from the oven and let cool for 10 to 15 minutes before serving.

——

RIFFS: Form into meatballs and cook as indicated on pages 298–299.

DIFFICULTY
Easy

YIELD
4 servings

TOTAL TIME
40 to 45 minutes

HANDS-ON TIME
15 minutes

This falls into the category I call "weeknight meal with jazz hands" as it's simple enough for a Tuesday but has enough flair to serve for company.

TAKEAWAY: How to pan-roast a pork tenderloin.
GOES WELL WITH: The saucy sauce begs for something that will soak it up like mashers, grits, polenta, or barley.

PAN-ROASTED PORK TENDERLOIN WITH ORANGE-MOLASSES GLAZE

1 tsp **kosher salt**

½ tsp **freshly ground black pepper**

1 **pork tenderloin** (1¼ to 1½ lb/ 570 to 680g)

1 tbsp **canola, grapeseed, or peanut oil**

⅓ cup/80 ml **apple brandy**

⅓ cup/100 g **orange marmalade**

¼ cup/60 ml **freshly squeezed orange juice**

1 tbsp **Dijon mustard**

2 tsp **molasses**

10 **fresh sage leaves**

Any brandy will do the trick but an apple brandy, such as applejack or Calvados, underlines the fruity notes in the dish.

Heat the oven to 400°F/200°C/gas 6 and arrange a rack in the middle.

Rub salt and pepper on the tenderloin. Heat the oil in a large, cast-iron pan or heavy-bottomed ovenproof frying pan over medium-high heat. When wisps come off the oil but it is not smoking, add the tenderloin and sear until well browned on one side, about 5 minutes; transfer to a large plate.

Be sure to remove the pan from the heat before adding the brandy, so as to prevent it from catching fire. Also, never add alcohol to a pan from a bottle but instead measure out the amount you need and add that.

Take the pan off the heat, and add the brandy, marmalade, juice, mustard, molasses, and sage to the pan. Return to heat and stir until the mixture is thick enough to coat the back of a spoon, 2 to 3 minutes. Add the tenderloin, seared-side down, and spoon sauce over the top. Put in the oven and roast, basting occasionally, until it has a 145°F/63°C internal temperature, 15 to 20 minutes. Discard the sage.

Check out the meat and you'll notice that, similar to wood, it has a grain. Always slice at a 90-degree angle, perpendicular, to the grain.

Remove the meat to a cutting board, tent with aluminum foil, and let rest for 5 to 10 minutes. Slice across the grain into thin slices, spoon glaze over the top, and serve.

DIFFICULTY
Easy

YIELD
8 servings

TOTAL TIME
45 minutes

HANDS-ON TIME
15 minutes

Pork and apples is such a classic combo that even Peter Brady sang its praises. Here it gets updated with sausages instead of chops and Indian-spiced apples for a take even a grown-up Brady would be psyched about.

TAKEAWAY: Roasting sausages.

You could use any sausage you want here although nothing too spiced—you don't want to compete with the flavors in the apples.

ROASTED SMOKED BRATWURST WITH CHUTNEY-STYLE APPLES

3 tbsp **canola, grapeseed, or peanut oil**

8 **mild smoked pork sausages (such as bratwurst;** 3 lb/1.4 kg**)**

3 **Fuji or Gala apples, cored and roughly chopped**

1 **yellow onion, roughly chopped**

4 **garlic cloves, halved**

¼ cup/60 ml **red wine vinegar**

1½ tsp **kosher salt**

⅓ cup/73 g **packed light brown sugar**

1 tsp **red pepper flakes**

1 tsp **mustard seeds**

One 2-in/5 cm piece **fresh ginger, sliced into coins**

Heat the oven to 400°F/200°C/gas 6 and arrange a rack in the middle. Heat 1 tablespoon of the oil in a large cast-iron or heavy-bottomed frying pan over medium-high heat and brown the sausages on all sides, about 10 minutes.

Meanwhile, toss the apples with the remaining 2 tablespoons of oil, onion, garlic, vinegar, salt, sugar, red pepper flakes, mustard seeds, and ginger until thoroughly coated. Spread the apple mixture on the bottom of a baking dish that measures 13 by 9 in/33 by 23 cm, top with sausages, and cover with aluminum foil. Roast for 10 minutes then baste with drippings.

Remove the foil then roast until the apples are fork-tender and the sausages are fully cooked, with an internal temperature of 160°F/70°C on an instant-read thermometer, 15 to 20 minutes more. Discard the ginger. Serve the bratwurst with the apple mixture spooned over the top.

DIFFICULTY
Easy

YIELD
8 to 10 servings

TOTAL TIME
2 hours

HANDS-ON TIME
20 minutes

After a roast chicken, a leg of lamb is one of the roasts everyone should know how to make. Flavored from the inside out with an herb-y, earthy pesto, this lamb is a shoo-in for dinner with the parents.

TAKEAWAY: How to roast a leg of lamb.
RECIPE WITHIN A RECIPE: The pesto can be mixed with plain Greek yogurt and used as a dip, tossed with pasta, or spooned over grilled fish for an instant sauce.
GOES WELL WITH: Roast the leg atop a bed of quartered potatoes, onions, or halved eggplant tossed with olive oil and your side will be taken care of.

ROASTING PAN
Roasting pans were made for big pieces of meat like this as they encourage even cooking. If you don't have one, a baking dish that measure 13 by 9 in/33 by 23 cm will work.

WALNUT PESTO—STUFFED LEG OF LAMB

WALNUT PESTO

½ cup/20 g **roughly chopped fresh Italian parsley**

¼ cup/10 g **roughly chopped fresh marjoram or thyme leaves**

4 tsp **kosher salt, plus more for rubbing**

8 **garlic cloves, smashed**

1 tsp **ground black pepper, plus more for rubbing**

1 tbsp **sherry or balsamic vinegar**

1 tbsp **honey or agave nectar**

3 tbsp **olive oil, plus more for rubbing**

¾ cup/75 g **toasted walnuts**

One 6-lb/2.7-kg **boneless leg of lamb**

This recipe calls for a boneless leg of lamb because it is widely available. You can also use a bone-in leg of lamb but it cooks at a different rate, so pay attention to the temperature.

FOR THE PESTO

Combine everything except the nuts in a food processor fitted with the metal blade and pulse until smooth. Add the nuts and pulse until finely chopped and just incorporated, about 10 pulses.

FOR THE LAMB

🕐 The lamb can marinate with the pesto for up to 1 day—just cover and refrigerate until ready to use.

As needed, remove the netting from the lamb and unroll the meat. Rub the meat with olive oil and generously season with salt and pepper. Rub half the pesto over the top side of the lamb, roll the meat back up, and tie it in several places with kitchen string.

Rub additional olive oil, salt, and pepper all over the outside of the meat roll, and place the lamb in a baking dish and let sit at room temperature for 20 to 30 minutes. Heat the oven to 450°F/230°C/gas 8 and arrange a rack in the middle.

Roast until the lamb is golden brown, about 20 minutes. Decrease the temperature to 375°F/190°C/gas 5 and roast until an instant-read digital thermometer registers 125°F/52°C to 130°F/54°C for medium-rare, 35 to 40 minutes.

Let the meat rest for 10 to 15 minutes before carving. While the roast is resting, add the remaining pesto to the pan and use a metal spatula to scrape up the drippings in the roasting pan and reserve. To carve, cut away the kitchen string and with a sharp carving knife, cut the meat against the grain into slices that are ½ in/12 mm thick. Serve with pan drippings spooned over the lamb.

RIFFS

- If you don't have walnuts, use almonds or pine nuts.
- Toss the pesto with grated cheese and pasta for a quick meal.
- Use the pesto rub on lamb chops and roast briefly.
- Add a handful of pitted, chopped olives to the pesto.
- Stir some crumbled feta or goat cheese into the pesto.

INSTANT-READ DIGITAL THERMOMETER
Use a good instant-read digital thermometer to keep track of the temperature.

Big pieces of meat like this continue to cook (a.k.a. carry-over cook) after they're removed from the oven, so keep that in mind when determining how done you want it.

Check out the meat and you'll notice that, similar to wood, it has a grain. Always slice at a 90-degree angle, perpendicular, to the grain.

Agrodolce means "sweet-sour" in Italian and refers to a sauce with those predominant flavors. Normally made simply with onions, vinegar, and sugar, this one adds pomegranate, pine nuts, and mint for a more colorful—in both looks and flavor—version (recipe pictured on pages 318–319).

TAKEAWAY: How to broil fish.

RECIPE WITHIN A RECIPE: The agrodolce sauce can be used as a condiment for grilled meats, sandwiches, or on toasts with goat cheese as an impromptu appetizer.

BROILED SWORDFISH WITH POMEGRANATE-MINT AGRODOLCE

POMEGRANATE-MINT AGRODOLCE

1 tbsp **olive oil, plus more for drizzling**

1 lb/455 g **shallots, halved and cut into 1-in/2.5-cm slices**

6 **garlic cloves, thinly sliced**

1 cup/240 ml **red wine vinegar**

½ cup/120 ml **apple juice**

¼ cup/50 g **packed light brown sugar**

1 tsp **kosher salt, plus more for seasoning**

½ tsp **freshly ground black pepper, plus more for seasoning**

1 **bay leaf**

½ cup/135 g **pomegranate seeds**

⅓ cup/70 g **toasted pine nuts**

¼ cup/55 g **thinly sliced fresh mint leaves**

Four **swordfish steaks** (about 2 lb/910 kg total)

FOR THE POMEGRANATE-MINT AGRODOLCE

Heat the oil in a medium saucepan over medium-high heat. When it shimmers, add the shallots and garlic, stirring occasionally, until they are golden brown and tender, 10 to 15 minutes.

Check out Seafood Watch online for current information about purchasing seafood.

The agrodolce can be made without the mint up to 2 days ahead and refrigerated in an airtight container. Heat over low heat before serving and stir in mint.

Stir in the vinegar, juice, brown sugar, the salt, the ½ teaspoon pepper, and bay leaf. Decrease the heat to low and simmer, stirring occasionally, until the shallots are very tender and the liquid is thick and syrupy, about 40 minutes. Stir in the pomegranate seeds, pine nuts, and mint. Season with salt and pepper.

FOR THE BROILED SWORDFISH

Heat the broiler to high and arrange a rack 6 to 8 inches from the heating element. Pat the fish dry, drizzle with oil, and sprinkle with salt and pepper. Place the fish on a baking sheet. Broil until the fish is flaky, opaque throughout, and has a 135°F/57°C internal temperature, 8 to 12 minutes. Serve topped with agrodolce sauce.

When you add the vinegar to the agrodolce, open a window or turn on a fan because the vinegar fumes released may sting your eyes or make you cough.

DIFFICULTY
Easy

YIELD
4 servings

TOTAL TIME
20 minutes, plus marinating time

HANDS-ON TIME
20 minutes

My father taught me to marinate fish in mayonnaise because it simultaneously flavors the fish while it creates a natural nonstick barrier, perfect for grilling. Here I use Dad's technique, but pair it with an apple-herb slaw with flavors from everywhere in Asia, yet nowhere in particular.

TAKEAWAY: How to grill fish.

RECIPE WITHIN A RECIPE: The marinade can be used for chicken or tofu or as a thick dressing. Use the dressing on other salads as desired. Use this slaw on its own or in place of more traditional slaw.

GRILLED TUNA STEAKS WITH VIETNAMESE-STYLE SLAW

TUNA

1 cup/240 ml **mayonnaise**

⅓ cup/80 ml **low-sodium soy sauce**

¼ cup/60 ml **fresh lime juice**

2 tbsp **brown-rice vinegar**

2 tbsp **honey or agave nectar**

2 tbsp **grated fresh ginger**

6 **garlic cloves, pressed or grated**

1 **serrano or Thai chile, halved and thinly sliced**

2 tsp **canola, grapeseed, or peanut oil**

4 **ahi tuna steaks** (each about 6 oz/170 g)

LIME-HONEY DRESSING

Grated zest of 1 lime

1 tbsp **freshly squeezed lime juice**

1 tbsp **Asian fish sauce**

2 tbsp **brown-rice vinegar**

1 tbsp **honey or agave nectar**

APPLE-HERB SLAW

2 **Gala or Fuji apples, peeled, cored, cut into matchsticks, and tossed with lime juice**

2 **carrots, coarsely grated**

3 **green onions (white and pale green parts), trimmed and thinly sliced**

¼ cup/10 g **finely chopped fresh mint leaves**

3 tbsp **finely chopped fresh cilantro leaves**

Canola oil, for brushing the grill

¼ cup/30 g **roasted, salted peanuts, roughly chopped, for garnish**

Check out Seafood Watch online for current information about purchasing seafood.

FOR THE TUNA

Whisk all ingredients except the fish together in small bowl to blend. Place the tuna in a nonreactive rimmed plate and pour the marinade over the top. Cover and marinate in the refrigerator for 1 hour or up to 4 hours. Meanwhile, make the slaw.

FOR THE DRESSING AND SLAW

About 30 minutes before serving, make the dressing. Whisk together the dressing ingredients in a nonreactive bowl until well combined. Toss with all the slaw ingredients except the peanuts, cover, and marinate in the refrigerator at least 15 minutes or up to 1 hour.

When ready to cook the fish, brush the grill with canola oil and heat to medium-high heat. Remove the tuna from marinade, brush off excess marinade, and pat with paper towels. Grill the tuna to desired doneness, about 4 minutes total for medium-rare.

To serve, top each piece of fish with slaw and sprinkle with peanuts.

RIFF: This would be equally tasty with halibut or swordfish.

The slaw dressing can be made up to 2 days ahead of time but don't marinate the salad for more than 1 hour before you plan to serve it or it will become limp.

Like meat, salmon and tuna are best cooked medium-rare, which is what the cooking time in this recipe will yield.

DIFFICULTY
Easy

YIELD
4 servings

TOTAL TIME
55 minutes, plus marinating time

HANDS-ON TIME
20 minutes

I was addicted to chickpeas as a child and have become equally addicted to North African flavors as an adult. So it was only a matter of time before I married the two by adding spicy harissa and nutty chickpeas to a braised cod.

TAKEAWAY: How to braise fish.
RECIPE WITHIN A RECIPE: Serve the chickpeas alone as a vegetarian dish or side dish.

HARISSA-MARINATED COD WITH BRAISED CHICKPEAS

MARINATED COD

3 tbsp **harissa paste**

1 tbsp **honey or agave nectar**

1 tbsp **olive oil**

Kosher salt and freshly ground black pepper

4 **Pacific cod fillets** (each about 6 oz/180 g)

BRAISED CHICKPEAS

¼ cup/60 ml **olive oil**

2 **shallots, thinly sliced**

1 head **garlic, peeled and thinly sliced** (about 10 cloves)

Kosher salt and freshly ground black pepper

1½ tsp **ground cumin**

4 **pickled peppers, trimmed, seeded and thinly sliced**

3 cups/490 g **cooked chickpeas, or two 15-oz/410-g cans, drained and rinsed**

2 tsp **capers**

1 tsp **red wine vinegar (optional)**

1¾ cups/420 ml **water**

¼ cup/10 g **finely chopped fresh Italian parsley**

2 **lemons, for serving**

Harissa is a spicy Tunisian chili paste that is becoming more popular and can be found in the ethnic aisle of many grocery stores. If you can't find it, chili garlic sauce makes an acceptable substitute.

Check out Seafood Watch online for current information about purchasing seafood.

Medium-hot pickled peppers, such as jalapeños, goathorn, or Peppadews, all work well here. Go ahead and use any pickled or fresh pepper you like, but use fewer if the peppers are particularly hot.

FOR THE FISH

Mix together the harissa, honey, oil, and a pinch of salt and pepper. Rub onto the fish, cover, and refrigerate for 30 minutes to 2 hours.

FOR THE CHICKPEAS

Heat the oil in a large frying pan over medium-high heat. When it shimmers, add the shallots and garlic, season with salt and pepper, and cook until golden brown, about 3 minutes. Add the cumin and chiles and cook until fragrant, about 1 minute. Stir in the chickpeas, capers, red wine vinegar (not needed if you used pickled peppers), and the water and bring to a boil.

The chickpeas can be made up to 1 day ahead and warmed and finished with the fish when ready to cook.

Decrease the heat to low, partially cover, and simmer until sauce is slightly reduced and the flavors are melded, about 20 minutes.

Meanwhile, halve one of the lemons and cut the other into ¼-in/ 6-mm slices; set aside.

Taste the chickpeas, add salt as desired, and stir in the parsley. Nestle the fish in the chickpea mixture, cover, and cook until the fish is just flaky but not falling apart, about 15 minutes.

Squeeze the lemon halves over all the fish, then lay the lemon slices over the fish and serve with chickpeas.

RIFFS

- Other lean, flaky flesh fish will work nicely in this recipe. Try halibut, hake, or tilapia.
- Stir spinach or chard into the chickpeas.
- Use the marinade on chicken or pork.

DIFFICULTY
Easy

YIELD
4 to 6 servings

TOTAL TIME
40 to 45 minutes

HANDS-ON TIME
10 minutes

Crisp and flaky, this breaded fish is a stellar contrast to the creamy, cool, yet spicy avocado-tomatillo sauce.

TAKEAWAY: How to broil fish.

RECIPE WITHIN A RECIPE: A nontraditional twist on tomatillo salsa, a.k.a. salsa verde, this sauce would work as well on chips as it would spooned on a tortilla.

PANKO-CRUSTED TILAPIA WITH TOMATILLO-AVOCADO SAUCE

TOMATILLO SAUCE

1 lb/455 g **fresh tomatillos, husked and halved**

½ **yellow onion, roughly chopped**

3 **garlic cloves, peeled**

½ **jalapeño chile, trimmed and seeded**

¼ cup/10 g **packed fresh cilantro leaves**

2 tsp **sugar**

1 tsp **freshly squeezed lime juice**

¼ cup/60 ml **water**

1 **firm-ripe avocado, peeled, pitted, and diced**

Kosher salt and freshly ground black pepper

PANKO-CRUSTED TILAPIA

2 **large eggs, beaten**

2 cups/120 g **panko bread crumbs**

2 tbsp **canola, grapeseed, or peanut oil**

4 **garlic cloves, minced**

2½ tsp **ground cumin**

1 tsp **grated lime zest**

4 tsp **kosher salt**

8 **tilapia fillets** (about 2 lb/910 kg)

Lime wedges, for serving

Tomatillos look like green tomatoes in husks. If you can't find them, use tomatoes instead, and add a few extra teaspoons of lime juice. Or, use store-bought salsa and mix in avocados.

Panko are Japanese bread crumbs that are particularly crunchy. If you can't find them, use crushed melba toasts or cornflakes.

Check out Seafood Watch online for current information about purchasing seafood.

FOR THE SAUCE

Heat the oven to 500°F/260°C/gas 10 and arrange a rack in the middle. Line a rimmed baking sheet with aluminum foil. Place the tomatillo halves, cut-side down, on the prepared pan along with the onion, garlic, and chile. Broil until browned and the tomatillos have collapsed, 10 to 15 minutes.

Transfer the tomatillo mixture, cilantro, sugar, and lime juice to a blender or food processor fitted with the metal blade. Add the water to the prepared baking sheet, scrape up any browned bits, and add the liquid to the food processor. Process the mixture until very smooth, about 30 seconds, then remove to a bowl and fold in the avocado. Season with salt and pepper. Cover and refrigerate until ready to serve.

FOR THE FISH

Decrease the oven temperature to 450°F/230°C/gas 8 and arrange a rack in the upper third. Place the eggs in a shallow bowl and set aside. In a second shallow bowl, combine the bread crumbs, oil, garlic, cumin, zest, and kosher salt and mix to coat the bread crumbs well in oil.

Dip each piece of fish in the egg mixture, letting any excess drip off, then place in the bread crumb mixture, pressing to adhere as necessary on both sides. Place the breaded fish on a baking sheet.

Bake until the bread crumbs are browned and the fish is opaque throughout and flaky, 10 to 15 minutes. Serve with a squeeze of lime and topped with sauce.

———

RIFF: If you can't find or don't like tilapia, use another lean, firm fish such as snapper or bass.

The sauce can be made up to 2 days ahead and refrigerated in an airtight container.

Be careful when mixing hot liquids in a blender as the heat can make them explode out of the carafe. To avoid this, only fill the blender halfway, remove the plastic plug in the blender cover, and start blending on low for a few seconds before you kick it up to full speed.

BLENDER OR FOOD PROCESSOR
If you don't have a blender, use a food processor; otherwise, just eat it chunky—the sauce is still tasty.

DIFFICULTY
Medium

YIELD
4 servings

TOTAL TIME
30 minutes

HANDS-ON TIME
15 minutes

The color and bright flavors in this citrus relish liven up even the drabbest of winter days.

TAKEAWAYS: How to pan-sear fish; how to segment citrus.
RECIPE WITHIN A RECIPE: This relish is also fabulous atop delicate greens for a simple salad, with seared shrimp or scallops, or on pan-roasted pork chops.

CAST-IRON SKILLET
A good-quality, heavy-bottomed pan (like a cast-iron skillet or stainless steel pan) is key for getting a good sear on the fish.

This is a dish to make in the heart of winter when citrus is at its best. I like the sour, sweet, earthy mix of these particular citrus but use whatever looks best at the store.

Check out Seafood Watch online for current information about purchasing seafood.

PAN-SEARED SALMON WITH THREE-CITRUS RELISH

THREE-CITRUS RELISH

1 **pink grapefruit**

2 **blood oranges**

2 **tangerines**

1 **shallot, halved lengthwise and sliced paper thin**

1 tbsp **extra-virgin olive oil**

1 tbsp **balsamic vinegar**

1 tsp **honey or agave nectar**

1 tbsp **thinly sliced fresh basil, chives, mint, or parsley**

Kosher salt and freshly ground black pepper

PAN-SEARED SALMON

4 **salmon fillets** (each 6 oz/170 g)

1 tbsp **canola, grapeseed, or peanut oil**

Kosher salt and freshly ground black pepper

CONTINUED

FOR THE RELISH

Slice off the tops and bottoms of the grapefruit, blood oranges, and tangerines. Segment the fruit as follows: slice downward, top to bottom, along the curve of the fruit, removing the peel and pith (the white stuff inside the peel) in strips; repeat all around each fruit.

For each citrus fruit, cut out the fruit segments with a sharp knife as follows: carefully slip the knife between the fruit membrane and the segment and gently cut until you reach the middle. Hook under the fruit to gently pop out the segment.

Combine the shallot, oil, vinegar, honey, herbs, and salt and pepper in a nonreactive bowl and toss to evenly coat. Let sit at room temperature for at least 15 minutes before serving.

FOR THE FISH

Heat a large heavy-bottomed pan over high heat. (The pan is heated when you place the fish in and it sizzles loudly.) Liberally season the salmon with oil, salt, and pepper.

Place the fish, skin-side down, in the hot pan and decrease the heat to medium. Do not move the fillets. Cook until well browned and cooked about three-fourths of the way through, about 3 minutes. Turn the fillets and cook until medium-rare (just barely pink in the center), about 3 minutes more. Serve immediately, topped with the relish.

The directions for cutting the citrus into segments (a.k.a. supremes) make for jewel-like pieces of fruit. If you don't have the patience or time, you can just carefully peel the fruit (be sure to remove all white pith).

The relish can be made up to 1 day ahead without the herbs and refrigerated in an airtight container until ready to use.

Like meat, salmon and tuna are best cooked medium-rare, which is what the cooking time in this recipe will yield.

SEAFOOD

Borrowing bright flavors from South India, this dish is an orchestra of textures and colors. The chutney infuses the fish with flavor as it roasts and the red tomatoes meld with the pan juices into a melt-y sauce.

TAKEAWAY: How to roast a fish.

RECIPE WITHIN A RECIPE: Cook the chutney briefly over low heat then use as a sauce to top a variety of meat and tofu dishes or use as a condiment.

DIFFICULTY
Easy

YIELD
4 to 6 servings

TOTAL TIME
1 hour

HANDS-ON TIME
25 minutes

ROASTED BASS WITH GREEN CHUTNEY AND MELTED TOMATOES

GREEN CHUTNEY

2 cups/80 g **packed fresh cilantro leaves**

½ cup/20 g **packed fresh mint**

⅓ cup/30 g **unsweetened flaked coconut**

One 2-in/5-cm piece **fresh ginger, peeled and cut into coins**

½ **red onion, roughly chopped**

2 tbsp **freshly squeezed lime juice**

1 tbsp **canola, grapeseed, or peanut oil**

1 tbsp **honey or agave nectar**

1 tsp **kosher salt**

Grated zest of 1 lime (about ½ tsp)

¼ tsp **ground cinnamon**

1 **Thai or serrano chile, trimmed and sliced**

1 tsp **kosher salt**

ROASTED BASS

4 **limes, 2 halved, 2 cut into wedges, for garnish**

1 **striped bass** (1½ to 2 lb/680 to 910 kg)**, cleaned and scaled**

Kosher salt and freshly ground black pepper

1 tsp **canola, grapeseed, or peanut oil**

2 **ripe plum tomatoes, thinly sliced**

1 **Thai or serrano chile, trimmed and sliced into rings**

½ **red onion, cut into ¼-in/ 6-mm slices**

Fresh cilantro, for garnish

Unsweetened flake coconut lends a deep coconut flavor without extra sweetness. If you can't find it, add some coconut milk to both the chutney mixture and the tomato mixture.

Check out Seafood Watch online for current information about purchasing seafood.

CONTINUED

CHUTNEY

Heat the oven to 400°F/200°C/gas 6 and arrange a rack in the middle. Combine all chutney ingredients in a food processor fitted with the metal blade and process until smooth. Taste and adjust seasoning as desired.

The chutney can be made up to 1 day ahead and refrigerated in an airtight container.

BASS

Squeeze the juice of 1 lime over the fish and sprinkle the fish all over with the salt. Spoon the chutney into the fish cavity.

Drizzle the oil in a roasting pan or large baking dish. In a bowl, squeeze the juice of the second lime, add the tomatoes, chile, and onion, season with a pinch of salt, and toss to coat. Scatter mixture along the bottom of the pan or baking dish and season with salt and pepper. Place the fish on top of the tomato mixture, cover with aluminum foil, and crimp the edges to enclose the fish.

Set the pan on a baking sheet and roast the fish until it is cooked through, has a 130°F/54°C internal temperature, and the flesh of the fish flakes easily when pushed with a fork, 30 to 35 minutes. Remove from the oven and let rest 5 minutes. Remove fillets from the fish (see page 107) and serve over the tomato mixture, topped with chutney and garnished with lime wedges and cilantro.

RIFF: Other white fish will also work well here such as snapper, hake, striped bass, black bass, or sea bream.

DIFFICULTY
Easy

YIELD
4 to 6 servings

TOTAL TIME
3 hours, 45 minutes

HANDS-ON TIME
15 minutes

In this pan-tropical slant on ceviche, the fish turns an innocuous opaque white color from the marinade. But one bite reveals it's bursting with citrus, fruit, chile, and herb flavors.

TAKEAWAY: How to make ceviche.

RECIPE WITHIN A RECIPE: Use the brine to marinate fish briefly (15 minutes) before broiling or grilling.

COCONUT MAHI MAHI CEVICHE WITH CHILES AND HERBS

Check out Seafood Watch online for current information about purchasing seafood.

This ceviche works with a variety of white, firm fish including swordfish, snapper, or sea bass. Tell your fishmonger that you're using the fish for ceviche, as you want the best-quality fish you can find.

1 lb/455 g **sushi-grade mahi mahi, cut into ¼-in/6-mm slices**

¾ cup/180 ml **freshly squeezed lime juice**

¼ cup/60 ml **freshly squeezed orange juice**

1 **serrano or Thai chile, thinly sliced**

½ **red onion, sliced paper thin**

One 14-oz/355-ml can **coconut milk**

½ cup/20 g **finely chopped fresh cilantro**

1 tsp **kosher salt, plus more for seasoning**

1 **mango, peeled, pitted, and cut into small dice**

½ cup/20 g **roughly chopped fresh basil**

1 **lime, cut into wedges, for garnish**

Make sure to keep the fish as cold as possible the whole time you're working.

Combine the fish, lime juice, orange juice, chile, and onion in a nonreactive bowl and toss until well coated. Cover and refrigerate for 1½ hours, or until the flesh is opaque.

Place a strainer over a bowl, strain the fish, and reserve ¼ cup/ 60 ml of the marinade. Return the fish to the nonreactive bowl along with the reserved marinade; discard the remaining marinade.

Eat ceviche within 2 days of making it and refrigerate until ready to eat.

To the fish and marinade, add the coconut milk, cilantro, and salt and marinate, refrigerated, another 2 hours (until well flavored). Season with salt as needed, and stir in the mango and basil. Serve with lime wedges.

A friend coined this "happy hour" food because it combines all his favorite flavors of happy hour—beer, mustard, honey, and spice—in one dish.

TAKEAWAY: How to simmer shrimp.

GOES WELL WITH: Perfect on their own, these shrimp are a shoo-in served over rice or other grains, potatoes, or pasta.

DIFFICULTY
Easy

YIELD
4 to 6 servings

TOTAL TIME
25 minutes

HANDS-ON TIME
20 minutes

SHRIMP SIMMERED IN GARLICKY BEER SAUCE

2 tbsp **unsalted butter**

1 lb/455 g **shrimp, peeled and deveined**

10 **garlic cloves, thinly sliced**

½ tsp **cayenne pepper**

¾ cup/180 ml **light lager beer**

2 tsp **Worcestershire sauce**

2 tsp **honey**

1 tbsp **Dijon mustard**

1 tbsp **freshly squeezed lemon juice**

2 tbsp **finely chopped fresh Italian parsley**

If you can't find cayenne or want to switch it up, use paprika or any chile powder you like.

Melt 1 tablespoon of the butter in large frying pan over medium-high heat. When it foams, add the shrimp and cook until pink on both sides, 2 to 3 minutes. Using a slotted spoon, transfer the shrimp to a large bowl.

Return the pan to the stove, add the 1 tablespoon of remaining butter, chopped garlic, and cayenne pepper. Cook until fragrant then stir in the beer, Worcestershire sauce, honey, mustard, and lemon juice and simmer until the sauce thinly coats the back of a spoon, about 10 minutes.

Return the shrimp to the sauce and simmer until the shrimp are just cooked through, 2 to 3 minutes. Season as desired, stir in parsley, and serve.

To make this ahead, add everything except the parsley; just stir that in come serving time.

DIFFICULTY
Easy

YIELD
2 to 4 servings

TOTAL TIME
20 minutes

HANDS-ON TIME
15 minutes

A simple scallop preparation that's packed with flavor, use this as an appetizer at your next dinner party or as a light dinner with a big green salad.

TAKEAWAY: How to sear scallops.
RECIPE WITHIN A RECIPE: Use the chile sauce to top anything from grilled chicken to shrimp, or slather it on your next sandwich for a twist.

SEARED SCALLOPS WITH SWEET-SPICY CHILE SAUCE

1 **roasted red, yellow, or orange bell pepper**

1 tbsp **tomato paste**

2 tsp **Dijon mustard**

2 tsp **red wine vinegar, sherry vinegar, or lemon juice, plus more for seasoning**

1 tsp **sugar, plus more for seasoning**

½ **serrano chile, trimmed and seeded**

2 **garlic cloves, smashed**

Grated zest of 1 lemon

½ tsp **kosher salt, plus more for seasoning**

Freshly ground black pepper

12 **large sea scallops**

1 tbsp **canola, grapeseed, or peanut oil**

Check out Seafood Watch online for current information about purchasing seafood.

🕐 The sauce can be made up to 2 days in advance and stored in the fridge, but know that the longer it sits, the spicier it gets.

Combine everything except the scallops and oil in a blender or small food processor and blend until smooth. Add water as needed to thin (it should be the consistency of tomato sauce). Season with additional salt and black pepper and set aside at least 15 minutes to let the flavor develop. Taste and add more sugar if it is sour or more vinegar if it is sweet.

Meanwhile, prepare the scallops. Pull off the lip, as needed (it looks like a piece of thick rubber band). Pat the scallops dry with a paper towel then season scallops well with salt and set aside.

Heat the oil in a large frying pan over medium-high heat until wisps of smoke come off the oil. Add the scallops (leaving 1 in/ 2.5 cm between each) and cook, undisturbed, until they release easily from the pan, a brown crust has formed, and the flesh is opaque two-thirds up the sides, about 3 minutes. Flip and cook until they are just heated through and beginning to brown, about 1 minute more. Remove the scallops to a plate and cover with aluminum foil.

Meanwhile, add the chile sauce to the pan and decrease the heat to medium-low. Stir to scrape up any browned bits on the bottom of the pan and let the sauce simmer until slightly thickened and broken down, 2 to 3 minutes. Spoon some sauce on each plate, top with scallops, and serve.

DIFFICULTY
Easy

YIELD
4 to 6 servings

TOTAL TIME
50 minutes

HANDS-ON TIME
20 minutes

Nowhere near traditional, this is an Italian take on the classic Southern succotash, with pancetta, cannellini beans, tomatoes, and basil replacing the standard ingredients.

TAKEAWAY: How to steam fish.

RECIPE WITHIN A RECIPE: The succotash can be used as an impromptu salad tossed with chopped-up greens or as a sauce to other grilled meats and fish.

STEAMED SNAPPER WITH ITALIAN "SUCCOTASH"

SUCCOTASH

2 lb/910 g **fresh cannellini or cranberry beans, shelled**

Kosher salt and freshly ground black pepper

1 lb/450 g **cherry or grape tomatoes, halved**

2 **garlic cloves, minced**

4 oz/115 g **pancetta, cut into small dice**

½ **red onion, finely chopped**

2 cups/200 g **fresh corn kernels**

1 tsp **balsamic or sherry vinegar**

⅓ cup/30 g **thinly sliced fresh basil**

RED SNAPPER

1 **red snapper** (3 lb/1.4 kg)**, cleaned and scaled**

Kosher salt

4 **garlic cloves, peeled**

1 tbsp **olive oil**

½ **red onion, thinly sliced**

Pinch of red pepper flakes (optional)

Fresh cannellini beans and cranberry beans (a.k.a. shelling beans) are available at farmers' markets from summer to early fall.

If you can't find fresh shelling beans, you can use dried. Just soak 1 cup beans in water overnight then proceed with the recipe (note that they will take almost twice as long to cook as the fresh beans).

Try to find a deli counter that will sell you a 4-oz/ 115-g chunk of pancetta as it'll be easier to cut than strips. Place it in the freezer about 5 to 10 minutes before cutting—it will be easier to dice. If sliced pancetta is all you can find, it will work but it may cook faster.

FOR THE SUCCOTASH

Bring a large pot of water to a boil over high heat. Add the beans, decrease the heat to medium, and cook until the beans are tender (not starchy nor mushy), 20 to 30 minutes. Remove from the heat, season with salt, and let cool in the cooking liquid.

Puree half of the tomatoes with the garlic in a blender; set aside.

Line a plate with paper towels and set aside. Put the pancetta in a large frying pan over medium heat and cook until crisp, about 6 minutes. With a slotted spoon, remove the pancetta to the prepared plate. Drain off all but 1 tablespoon of the drippings (if needed, add 1 tablespoon oil). Add the onion, season with salt, and cook until golden brown, about 5 minutes.

Add the corn, cooked beans, and tomato puree and season with salt and pepper. Simmer until heated and the sauce is slightly thickened, about 10 minutes.

When ready to serve, stir in the vinegar, remaining tomato halves, and the basil. Taste and adjust seasoning.

FOR THE FISH

Heat the oven to 425°F/220°C/gas 7 and arrange a rack in the middle. Lightly season the fish with salt and stuff garlic into the fish cavity. Rub the fish all over with oil.

Place a piece of heavy-duty aluminum foil that's 3 ft/92 cm long on a rimmed baking sheet. Scatter the onions on the foil and bend the sides of the foil so they are upright. Place the fish on the onions, sprinkle with a few tablespoons of water, and close up the foil to seal completely. Steam in the oven until the flesh is white and just flakes when pushed on with the back of a fork, 20 to 30 minutes.

Remove fillets from fish (see page 107) and serve topped with succotash and a pinch of red pepper.

Make the succotash without adding the herbs up to 2 days ahead. To serve, warm over low heat, adjust seasoning as needed, and stir in the herbs.

DIFFICULTY
Easy

YIELD
4 to 6 servings

TOTAL TIME
15 minutes

HANDS-ON TIME
15 minutes

An update on basic sautéed bell peppers, this recipe is just as simple to prepare but has a more intriguing mix of flavors and textures.

BELL PEPPER SAUTÉ WITH TOASTED WALNUTS

3 tbsp **olive oil, plus more for garnish**

1 tsp **ground cumin**

½ **yellow onion, halved and thinly sliced**

Kosher salt and freshly ground black pepper

3 **bell peppers (mixed colors), trimmed, halved, and sliced into ½-in/12-mm strips**

½ tsp **grated lemon zest**

2 tbsp **freshly squeezed lemon juice**

¼ cup/30 g **roughly chopped walnuts, toasted (page 119)**

Heat 2 tablespoons of the oil in a large, heavy frying pan over medium-low heat. When it shimmers, add the cumin and cook until fragrant, about 30 seconds. Stir in the onion, season with salt and black pepper, and cook, stirring occasionally, until golden brown, about 5 minutes.

Stir in the bell peppers and cook, stirring rarely, until golden brown, about 8 minutes. Stir in the lemon zest and juice and the remaining 1 tablespoon of the oil. Scrape up any browned bits in the pan, stir to coat, and season with additional salt and black pepper as needed. Serve with a drizzle of olive oil and walnuts scattered over the top.

This dish gets more flavorful as it sits so feel free to make it up to 2 days in advance. Warm and top with walnuts before serving.

RIFFS

- Use leftovers for impromptu steak and pepper sandwiches.
- Substitute a dash of ground paprika, coriander, or curry powder for the cumin.
- Nix the walnuts and mix into eggs for a scramble.
- Use as a pizza topping or appetizer.
- Stir with a few tablespoons of olive oil and a bit of pasta cooking water for an impromptu pasta sauce.
- Dice (without walnuts) and add to cooked beans or whole grains.

Brussels sprouts are usually weighed down with heavy ingredients like bacon and cream. But they're a whole other thing when paired with bright lemon and tangy horseradish.

TAKEAWAY: How to pan-braise vegetables.
RECIPE WITHIN A RECIPE: Use this method to cook asparagus, green beans, or broccoli.
GOES WELL WITH: A perfect pairing to lighten up a hearty braised or roasted meat meal.

DIFFICULTY
Easy

YIELD
4 servings

TOTAL TIME
25 minutes

HANDS-ON TIME
15 minutes

BRUSSELS SPROUTS WITH LEMONY HORSERADISH SAUCE

1 lb/455 g **small Brussels sprouts, trimmed and halved**

1 tbsp **olive oil**

2 **shallots, halved lengthwise and thinly sliced crosswise**

Kosher salt

¾ cup/180 ml **low-sodium vegetable or chicken broth, or water**

Grated zest and juice of ½ lemon

1 tbsp **prepared horseradish**

1 tbsp **unsalted butter**

Fill a large bowl halfway with ice water and set aside. Bring a large pot of heavily salted water to a boil over high heat. Add the Brussels sprouts and cook until bright green, 2 to 3 minutes. Drain and plunge into ice water until cool. Drain again and dry thoroughly.

Heat the oil in a large frying pan over medium-high heat. When it shimmers, add the shallots, season with salt, and cook until browned, about 5 minutes. Add the Brussels sprouts cut-side down and cook, undisturbed, until browned, 4 to 5 minutes.

Add the broth, partially cover, and decrease the heat until the liquid is simmering. Cook until the cores of the Brussels sprouts are knife-tender and the broth is slightly reduced, about 3 minutes.

Remove from the heat, add the zest, juice, horseradish, and butter and stir to coat the Brussels sprouts. Taste, adjust seasoning as needed, and serve.

Look for prepared horseradish in jars in the condiment aisle. Don't use horseradish cream as it has lots of added stabilizers and fat. If you can't find prepared horseradish, substitute prepared wasabi paste or spicy mustard.

If you're crunched for time, you don't need to parboil the Brussels sprouts though it does improve their texture.

The Brussels sprouts can be parboiled, cooled, and refrigerated in an airtight container up to 2 days in advance.

Subtly flavored, easy to prepare, and extremely versatile, this recipe plays the ultimate supporting role.

DIFFICULTY
Easy

YIELD
6 to 8 servings

TOTAL TIME
15 minutes

HANDS-ON TIME
15 minutes

BROILED ASPARAGUS WITH TOMATOES AND FRESH HERBS

8 oz/265 g **cherry or grape tomatoes, halved**

1 tbsp **sherry or balsamic vinegar**

Kosher salt

1½ lb/700 g **pencil-thin asparagus**

2 tbsp **olive oil**

4 **garlic cloves, thinly sliced**

Freshly ground black pepper

¼ cup/10 g **thinly sliced fresh herbs (such as chives, chervil, tarragon, basil, or mint)**

This could also be made with thick asparagus stalks but will take longer to cook.

Heat the oven to 475°F/245°C/gas 9 and arrange a rack in the middle. Toss together the tomatoes, vinegar, and a pinch of salt in a medium bowl to combine; set aside.

Place the asparagus on a rimmed baking sheet, add 1 tablespoon of the oil and the garlic, season with salt and pepper, and toss to combine.

Roast until the stalks are knife-tender, 7 to 10 minutes. Add the tomatoes, herbs, remaining 1 tablespoon of oil and season with salt and pepper and toss to combine. Serve hot or cold.

The asparagus cook quickly, so watch them carefully as they broil.

This dish is equally delicious hot or cold. If serving cold, do not add herbs until ready to serve.

RIFF: This same technique works well with green beans too.

YIELD
**6 to 8 servings
(about 6 cups/1.5L)**

TOTAL TIME
20 minutes

HANDS-ON TIME
5 minutes

This slaw has earned the nickname "chameleon slaw" as it's versatile enough to be served with a variety of foods from BBQ to Middle Eastern.

RECIPE WITHIN A RECIPE: Serve this dressing drizzled over an iceberg wedge with a few crumbles of feta or blue cheese.

CARROT AND CURRANT CABBAGE SLAW

DRESSING

²/₃ cup/145 ml **whole-milk plain yogurt**

2 tbsp **cider or brown rice vinegar**

2 tbsp **finely chopped fresh chives, dill, parsley, or cilantro**

1 tsp **Dijon mustard**

1 tsp **honey or agave nectar**

CABBAGE SLAW

One 1 lb/455 g **savoy cabbage**

4 **green onions (white and pale green parts), trimmed and thinly sliced**

1 **carrot, shredded on large holes of box grater**

4 oz/110 g **radish or clover sprouts, ends trimmed**

¼ cup/30 g **dried currants or raisins**

Savoy cabbage is a crinkly light green cabbage that is more mild than traditional green cabbage. If you can't find it, napa cabbage is a good substitute but be sure to remove the core and any tough ribs from the leaves before using.

Be sure to thoroughly wash and dry sprouts before using. If you can't find radish or clover sprouts, go ahead and leave them out.

FOR THE DRESSING

Combine all ingredients in a nonreactive bowl and whisk until smooth. Taste and adjust seasoning as desired.

FOR THE SLAW

Quarter and core the cabbage; thinly slice each quarter cross-wise into shreds that are ⅛ in/3 mm thick.

Place the shredded cabbage in a large bowl and add the green onions, carrot, sprouts, and currants or raisins. Pour the dressing over the top and toss to combine. Let marinate at least 15 minutes. Taste, adjust seasoning as desired, stir, and serve chilled or at room temperature.

RIFFS

- Stir in some peppery cress or arugula just before serving.
- Add some apple or pear cut into matchstick pieces.
- Add a pinch of curry powder or pure ground dried chiles, such as cayenne, to the dressing.

The slaw can be made up to 2 days ahead and refrigerated in an airtight container. A plus is that the dressing doesn't weigh down the slaw so it marinates without getting soggy.

The dressing may not seem like enough at first but it all works out—adding any more will result in a soggy, wilted slaw.

DIFFICULTY
Easy

YIELD
2 to 3 servings

TOTAL TIME
15 minutes

HANDS-ON TIME
15 minutes

It's hard to believe so much comes from such a simple recipe, but broccolini with just a few ingredients makes for a salty, savory side with bold flavor.

TAKEAWAY: How to pan-roast a vegetable.
GOES WELL WITH: A creamy main or a roasted meat.

CHARRED BROCCOLINI WITH GARLIC-CAPER SAUCE

1 tbsp **canola, grapeseed, or peanut oil**
2 **garlic cloves, sliced paper thin**
2 tsp **salt-packed capers, rinsed**
¼ tsp **red pepper flakes**
1 tbsp **unsalted butter**
1½ lb/550 g **broccolini, ends trimmed**
Pinch of kosher salt

After washing the broccolini, be sure to dry thoroughly so it can char well.

Heat the oil in a large frying pan over high heat until wisps come off the surface. Add the garlic, capers, and red pepper flakes and cook just until fragrant, about 30 seconds. Immediately add the butter and cook until melted and slightly browned.

Add the broccolini and a pinch of kosher salt and toss to coat. Cover the pan and cook, shaking the pan every 30 seconds so nothing sticks, until the broccolini is charred and knife-tender, 5 to 7 minutes.

Carefully remove the cover and add enough water to just coat the bottom of the pan. Shake the pan around to coat the broccolini and serve immediately.

RIFF: This same method would work well with broccoli, cauliflower, haricots verts, green beans, or asparagus.

DIFFICULTY
Easy

YIELD
2 servings

TOTAL TIME
25 minutes

HANDS-ON TIME
5 minutes

Creamy, with a lemony coriander note, this is a versatile side dish as suited to a classic roasted chicken as it is to a spicy grilled meat.

TAKEAWAY: How to braise a vegetable.
GOES WELL WITH: Spicy dishes that need a balancing accompaniment.

CREAMY CORIANDER LEEKS

1 tbsp **unsalted butter**

1 lb/455 g **leeks, white and light green parts halved and cut crosswise into 4-in/10-cm pieces**

Kosher salt and freshly ground black pepper

¾ cup/180 ml **low-sodium chicken or vegetable broth, or water**

¼ cup/60 ml **white wine or dry vermouth**

2 tbsp **crème fraîche or heavy cream**

1 tsp **ground coriander**

1 tbsp **finely chopped fresh Italian parsley**

½ **lemon, for garnish (optional)**

Clean leeks thoroughly before using. To do so, trim leeks and halve lengthwise. Hold leeks under running water and pull back each layer to remove any dirt. Dry thoroughly before using.

Melt the butter in a large frying pan over medium-high heat. When the foaming subsides and the butter starts to brown, add the leeks, cut-side down, season with salt and pepper, and cook until golden brown, about 5 minutes. Add the broth and simmer until the core of each leek just gives way when pierced with a knife, about 10 minutes.

Return the heat to medium-high, add the wine, and cook until almost all the liquid has evaporated and the leeks are golden brown, about 5 minutes more.

Add the crème fraîche, coriander, and parsley to the pan and simmer until thickened slightly, about 5 minutes. Season with salt and pepper and serve. If using heavy cream, squeeze some lemon juice over the dish before serving.

RIFF: This would work equally well with green beans, asparagus, or sweet potato.

Made from ingredients you probably already have on hand, this sweet-savory-salty side dish pairs with pretty much anything you can cook up.

TAKEAWAY: How to blanch green beans.

RECIPE WITHIN A RECIPE: You can just blanch the green beans and use them as an appetizer along with hummus or another dip. Or toss them with oil, lemon, salt, and pepper for a basic side.

DIFFICULTY
Easy

YIELD
4 to 6 servings

TOTAL TIME
20 minutes

HANDS-ON TIME
20 minutes

SAUTÉED GREEN BEANS WITH MUSTARD-SOY SHALLOTS

1 lb/455 g **green beans, ends trimmed**

1 tbsp **canola, grapeseed, or peanut oil**

2 **shallots, halved and sliced paper thin**

1 tbsp **hot sweet mustard**

1 tbsp **low-sodium soy sauce**

1 tbsp **sherry or balsamic vinegar**

Kosher salt and freshly ground black pepper

1 tbsp **toasted sesame seeds (optional)**

Hot sweet mustard brings a lot of depth to this dish. If you can't find it use honey mustard or Dijon mustard with a pinch of sugar added to the pan.

Bring a pot of heavily salted water to a boil over high heat. Fill a large bowl halfway with ice water and set aside.

Add the green beans to the boiling water and cook until bright and knife-tender, 2 to 3 minutes. Drain and place in the ice water bath until cool. Drain, pat dry, and set aside until ready to use.

Heat the oil in a medium pan over medium-high heat. When it shimmers, add the shallots and cook until golden brown, about 3 minutes. Add the green beans and cook until warmed through and golden brown, about 5 minutes.

Add the mustard, soy sauce, and vinegar and cook, stirring frequently, until the sauce just coats the bottom of the pan. Season with salt and pepper, scatter with sesame seeds, if using, and serve.

Only blanch the beans until they are bright green and crisp-tender. Any longer and they'll become overcooked and soft.

The green beans can be blanched up to 2 days ahead and refrigerated, wrapped in paper towels, in an airtight container.

RIFF: You could also use asparagus or broccolini here.

DIFFICULTY
Easy

YIELD
4 to 6 servings

TOTAL TIME
50 minutes

HANDS-ON TIME
10 minutes

Parsnips are like fake-out carrots as they look like they're related but their white color and vanilla flavor separates them from the rest of the root vegetable pack. Here they're glazed then topped with crunchy almonds in a comforting side dish for the colder months.

TAKEAWAY: How to oven-glaze root vegetables.

GINGERED PARSNIPS WITH TOASTED ALMONDS

2 lb/900 g **parsnips, trimmed and cut into 1-in/2.5-cm pieces**
¼ cup/60 ml **maple syrup**
2 tbsp **canola, grapeseed, or peanut oil**
6 **garlic cloves, smashed**
Kosher salt and freshly ground black pepper
1 tbsp **unsalted butter**
½ inch piece **fresh ginger, peeled and grated**
2 tbsp **toasted, sliced almonds (page 119)**

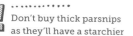

Don't buy thick parsnips as they'll have a starchier flavor.

Heat the oven to 450°F/230°C/gas 8 and arrange a rack in the upper third.

Combine the parsnips, syrup, oil, and garlic on a large rimmed baking sheet, season with salt and pepper, and toss to coat thoroughly.

Roast, turning occasionally, until fork-tender, about 40 minutes. Remove from the oven, season to taste with salt and pepper, add butter and ginger, and toss to coat. Sprinkle with the almonds and serve.

RIFFS

- Swap carrots or other root vegetables such as turnips or rutabaga for the parsnips.
- Add a few sprigs of rosemary, thyme, or sage for another layer of flavor.

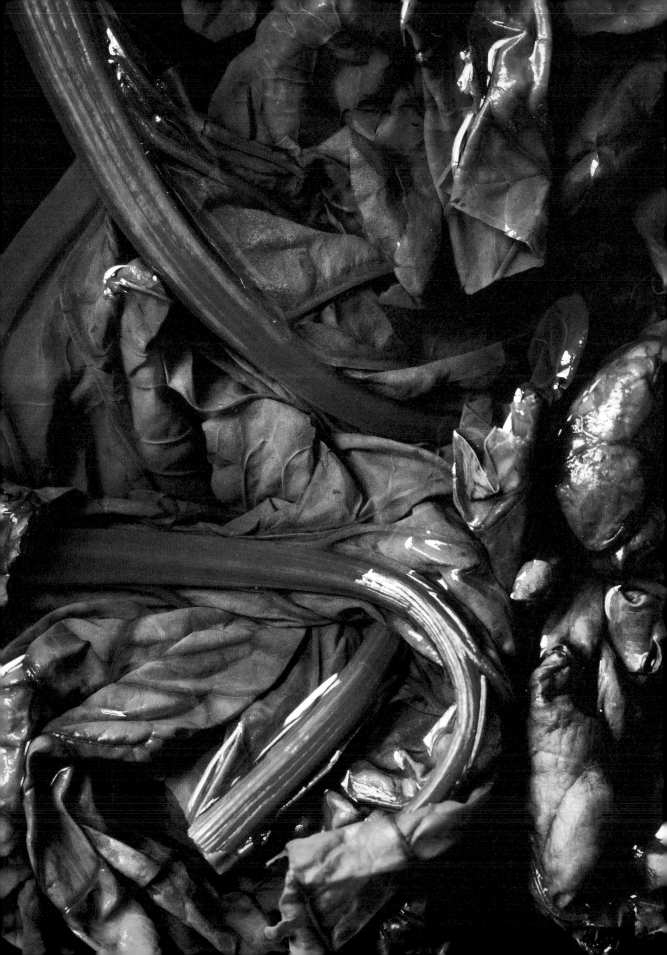

This side (pictured at bottom, page 349) is a mix of sweet and sour and smoky flavors that still allows the flavor of the greens to shine through.

TAKEAWAY: How to blanch greens.
GOES WELL WITH: Roasted meats, braises, or on top of toasted country bread for an easy first course.

DIFFICULTY
Easy

YIELD
4 servings

TOTAL TIME
25 minutes

HANDS-ON TIME
15 minutes

SWEET-SOUR WILTED GREENS WITH CRISP BACON

1 tbsp **red wine vinegar**

2 tsp **honey or agave nectar**

1 **garlic clove, minced**

Kosher salt and freshly ground black pepper

1 lb/455 g **Swiss chard, beet greens, turnip greens, or escarole, stemmed**

2 oz/60 g **bacon (about 2 strips), diced**

½ **yellow onion, halved lengthwise and thinly sliced**

If you buy beets or turnips with the tops on them, lop them off when you get home and save them for this recipe.

Whisk together the vinegar, honey, and garlic in a small non-reactive bowl, season with salt and pepper, and set aside at least 10 minutes.

Meanwhile, bring a large pot of heavily salted water to a boil over high heat; fill a bowl halfway with ice water. Wash the greens in 2 rinses of water. Add the greens to the boiling water and blanch until wilted and bright green, 1 to 2 minutes. Transfer immediately to ice water, then drain and squeeze the water out from the leaves; chop coarsely.

The greens can be blanched up to 1 day ahead. Just drain from the ice water and refrigerate in an airtight container.

Put the bacon in a large frying pan and cook over medium-high heat, stirring occasionally, until browned and the fat is rendered, about 4 minutes. Discard all but 1 tablespoon of the bacon drippings. Add the onion and cook until golden, about 5 minutes. Add the greens, stir in the vinegar mixture, and cook, stirring just to coat the greens and warm through, about 30 seconds. Taste, adjust seasoning as necessary, and serve.

Homemade apple turnovers are something I never tire of eating but I'm not always up to making them. This bread pudding—with layer upon layer of slow-cooked apple flavor—is how I satisfy my craving without all the extra work.

TAKEAWAY: How to make bread pudding.

APPLE TURNOVER BREAD PUDDING WITH MAPLE CREAM SAUCE

BREAD PUDDING

1 cup/3½ oz/100 g **dried apples, roughly chopped**

½ cup/4 oz/120 ml **apple cider**

2 tbsp/1 oz **unsalted butter, plus more for coating**

2 **Rome, Gala, or Fuji apples, peeled, cored, and cut into large dice**

2 cups/16 oz/480 ml **half-and-half**

5 **large egg yolks**

⅔ cup/4½ oz/130 g **packed dark brown sugar**

¼ cup/2 oz/60 ml **Grade B maple syrup**

1 tbsp **pure vanilla extract**

1 tsp **kosher salt**

1 lb/455 g **croissants or brioche (stale or toasted), cut into large dice**

MAPLE CREAM SAUCE

½ cup/4 oz/120 ml **Grade B maple syrup**

3 tbsp/1½ oz **unsalted butter**

½ cup/8 oz/120 ml **heavy cream**

¼ tsp **ground nutmeg**

Use the egg whites in the Oatmeal Breakfast Soufflé (page 126) or the Herbed Goat Cheese Soufflé (page 252).

Use a good-quality Grade B maple syrup here as it has an assertive flavor that is suited to baking.

FOR THE BREAD PUDDING

Heat the oven to 325°F/165°C/gas 3 and arrange a rack in the middle. Coat a 2-qt/2-L baking dish with butter and set aside. Combine the dried apples and apple cider in a bowl and set aside to soak for at least 45 minutes.

Meanwhile, heat butter in a large frying pan over medium-high heat. When the foaming subsides, add the fresh apples and cook, stirring frequently, until golden brown and just beginning to soften, about 5 minutes.

Whisk together the half-and-half, yolks, brown sugar, syrup, vanilla, and salt in a medium bowl until yolks are broken up and the mixture is smooth. Add the bread, apples, and dried apple mixture and mix in. Let soak for at least 15 minutes, mixing one more time in between to ensure all the bread is soaked. Transfer to the prepared baking dish. Meanwhile, make the sauce.

FOR THE MAPLE CREAM SAUCE

Heat the syrup and butter in a small saucepan and bring to a boil; cook until slightly thickened. Carefully add the cream and cook until it just comes to a boil, 2 to 3 minutes. Stir in the nutmeg.

Evenly distribute ¼ cup/60 ml of the sauce over bread pudding and reserve for garnish. Bake until the custard is set and the top is lightly browned, 40 to 55 minutes. Let sit at least 5 minutes before serving. Serve warm or at room temperature with remaining sauce.

RIFFS

- Pears would be a nice change of pace.
- Walnuts, pecans, or almonds would work, too.
- Use cinnamon-raisin or walnut bread for a twist.

Use an oven thermometer (see page 64) to make sure your oven is at the correct temperature. If your oven's too hot you risk overcooking and curdling the eggs.

The ultimate make-ahead dish, you can assemble it up to 1 day ahead and then bake it last minute. It also can be baked up to 2 days ahead and warmed in a low oven before serving. You can soak the apples overnight, too.

DIFFICULTY
Medium/Hard

YIELD
*6 to 8 servings
(about 4 cups/1 L)*

TOTAL TIME
*1 hour, plus
chilling time*

HANDS-ON TIME
30 minutes

Butterscotch seems to have fallen out of favor in recent years, overshadowed by caramel. What others have overlooked, I consider their loss, as the caramelized brown sugar flavor in this pudding makes it nothing short of addictive.

TAKEAWAY: How to make pudding.

CREAMY BUTTERSCOTCH PUDDING

5 **large egg yolks**

1 tbsp **cornstarch**

1 cup/7 oz/220 g **packed dark brown sugar**

½ cup/4 oz/235 ml **water**

1 tsp **kosher salt**

2 cups/16 oz/480 ml **half-and-half**

2 cups/16 oz/480 ml **heavy cream**

2 tbsp/1 oz **unsalted butter**

1 tbsp **whiskey**

1 tbsp **pure vanilla extract**

Crushed graham crackers, amaretti cookies, or biscotti, for garnish (optional)

Chocolate shavings, for garnish (optional)

Whipped cream, for garnish (optional)

Whisk the egg yolks and cornstarch in a bowl until thoroughly combined.

Put the brown sugar, water, and salt in a heavy medium saucepan over medium-low heat, stirring until the sugar dissolves and begins to bubble.

Increase the heat to high and boil, without stirring, until the mixture turns syrupy and a dark amber, occasionally swirling the pot and brushing down the sides with a wet pastry brush,

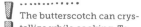
The butterscotch can crystallize while cooking. To avoid this, make sure all the utensils are clean; don't stir the caramel once the sugar dissolves (just swirl the pan to help it cook evenly). For extra insurance, you can brush the inside of the pan with a brush dipped in water.

about 5 minutes. Pull off the heat, add the half-and-half and the cream (the mixture will bubble vigorously), and whisk to dissolve any butterscotch bits that form on the bottom of the pan.

Return the pan to the stove over medium-high heat and bring the mixture to a boil, watching closely to prevent it from bubbling over. Immediately decrease the heat to medium and gradually whisk half of the hot butterscotch mixture into the reserved egg mixture. Return the custard to the pan, whisking to blend with the remaining butterscotch mixture.

Whisk over medium heat until the custard simmers and coats the back of a spoon, about 2 minutes. (When you draw your finger across the spoon, it should make a mark through the custard, which should not run back in on itself.) Immediately remove from the heat. Add the butter, whiskey, and vanilla and stir until the butter is melted and mixture is smooth; strain through a fine mesh sieve. Chill, uncovered, until cold and set, about 4 hours. Cover and store in the refrigerator until ready to use.

Serve topped with cookies, chocolate, and whipped cream, as desired.

FINE MESH SIEVE
Passing the cooked custard through a fine mesh sieve is not essential but it will ensure that the final pudding is smooth.

The pudding can be made up to 2 days ahead of time and refrigerated in an airtight container.

RIFFS

- Make with granulated sugar and sans whiskey and you'll have caramel pudding.
- Layer with pound cake and berries for an easy trifle.
- Make a pudding tart by filling baked tart shells with pudding, whipped cream, and toasted nuts.

DIFFICULTY	
Easy	

YIELD
6 to 8 servings

TOTAL TIME
1 hour, 15 minutes

HANDS-ON TIME
15 minutes

You've most likely never come across a plum crisp and certainly not one topped with cornmeal (recipe pictured on page 359). But these uncommon tweaks to a classic American dessert up the elegance without skimping on the comfort factor.

TAKEAWAY: How to make a crisp.

PLUM CRISP WITH TOASTED ALMOND–CORNMEAL TOPPING

CORNMEAL TOPPING

⅔ cup/3 oz/80 g **unbleached all-purpose flour**

½ cup/2½ oz/70 g **stone-ground cornmeal**

½ cup/3½ oz/100 g **packed dark brown sugar**

¼ tsp **kosher salt**

½ tsp **ground nutmeg**

½ cup/4 oz/115 g **unsalted butter, cut into small pieces**

⅔ cup/3½ oz/100 g **sliced almonds**

PLUM FILLING

2 lb/910 g **ripe plums, pitted, halved, and cut into ½-in/12-mm slices**

⅓ cup/2½ oz/80 ml **freshly squeezed orange juice**

½ cup/3½ oz/100 g **packed dark brown sugar**

2 tbsp **unbleached all-purpose flour**

1 tsp **grated orange zest**

2 tsp **pure vanilla extract**

Make sure you use cornmeal in this recipe. Using grits or polenta will result in a sandy texture.

Look for freestone (sometimes called cling-free) plums as they'll be easier to work with.

SWEETS

Heat the oven to 350°F/177°C/gas 4 and arrange a rack in the middle.

FOR THE TOPPING

Combine the flour, cornmeal, brown sugar, salt, and nutmeg in a bowl and mix until combined. Mix in the butter. (The topping is adequately mixed when it comes together in fist-sized clumps when squeezed.) Add the almonds and mix to evenly combine.

The topping can be made up to 2 days in advance and refrigerated in an airtight container.

FOR THE FILLING

Combine all ingredients in a medium nonreactive bowl and toss to combine. Transfer to a baking dish that measures 9 in/23 cm square and cover with the topping.

Bake until the fruit is tender, the filling is bubbly, and the topping is golden brown, 30 to 45 minutes. Let cool for at least 10 minutes before serving.

RIFFS
- Swap peaches or nectarines for the plums.
- Add in ½ cup/80 g dried cherries or fresh raspberries.
- Swap oats or more nuts for the cornmeal.

DIFFICULTY
Medium

YIELD
8 to 12 servings

TOTAL TIME
1 hour, 15 minutes

HANDS-ON TIME
15 minutes

The flavors of coffee cake—brown sugar and butter—marry with the spicy notes of a cup of chai for a modern, global take on this classic snack.

TAKEAWAY: How to make a basic cake.

COCONUT-CHAI COFFEE CAKE

STREUSEL

½ cup/4 oz/113 g **unsalted butter, melted, plus more for coating**

½ cup/2¼ oz/60 g **unbleached all-purpose flour, plus more for coating**

¾ cup/5¼ oz/102 g **packed light brown sugar**

1 cup/3 oz/5 g **unsweetened flaked coconut**

1 tsp **ground cardamom**

1 tsp **coarsely ground black pepper**

½ tsp **ground ginger**

¼ tsp **ground cloves**

½ tsp **kosher salt**

SOUR CREAM CAKE

2 cups/9 oz/255 g **unbleached all-purpose flour**

1½ tsp **baking powder**

½ tsp **baking soda**

½ tsp **kosher salt**

1½ cups/10½ oz/330 g **packed light brown sugar**

½ cup/4 oz/115 g **unsalted butter, at room temperature**

1 cup/240 ml **sour cream or whole-milk plain yogurt, at room temperature**

2 **large eggs, at room temperature**

1 tsp **pure vanilla extract**

Unsweetened flake coconut lends a deep coconut flavor without extra sweetness. If you can't find it, use sweetened coconut but start with half the sugar called for in the streusel and add more as needed.

There are a few uncommon spices in here and each helps to give it that chai flavor. If you hesitate to buy them, you can just use one of them, but know that I call for each spice multiple times in this book so you'll have plenty of other ways to use them.

 Room temperature is the key phrase here to ensure everything mixes together properly. To speed up the eggs, place them in a bowl of warm water for 10 minutes before using.

FOR THE STREUSEL

Heat the oven to 350°F/177°C/gas 4 and arrange a rack in the middle. Coat a 9-in/23-cm springform pan with butter and flour and set aside.

Combine the streusel ingredients in a small bowl and mix until well incorporated and clumped; refrigerate until ready to use.

FOR THE CAKE

Whisk together the flour, baking powder, baking soda, and salt in a medium bowl until aerated and lumps are broken up; set aside.

Put the brown sugar and butter in the bowl of a stand mixer fitted with the paddle attachment and beat over medium speed until light in color and airy. Add the sour cream or yogurt and mix well. Add the eggs and vanilla and mix until evenly combined. Remove the bowl from the mixer, and stir in the flour mixture until just moistened through.

Transfer the batter to the prepared pan and spread evenly. Sprinkle the streusel over the top and press in to adhere. Bake until a toothpick inserted in the center comes out clean with just a few crumbs remaining, 50 to 55 minutes.

Transfer to a rack and cool at least 20 minutes before unmolding and serving.

Nothing ruins a baked recipe faster than an oven that's off temperature. Use an oven thermometer to know if your oven skews hot or cold and adjust accordingly.

STAND MIXER
I used a stand mixer here but a handheld electric mixer and a bowl will also work fine.

The long baking time makes for a deep brown coffee cake. If you like your baked goods lighter, bake it at 325°F/165°C/gas 3); give yourself more time as it will take longer to finish baking.

 The coffee cake will last up to 1 week when stored at room temperature in an airtight container.

DIFFICULTY
Medium

YIELD
12 shortcakes

TOTAL TIME
1 hour, 15 minutes

HANDS-ON TIME
45 minutes

Not that I have anything against strawberries on shortcakes, but there are plenty of other fruits out there that make just as tasty a pairing. One of my favorites is this mix of citrus, underlined by whipped cream flavored with orange flower water for an edge of exotic sophistication.

TAKEAWAY: How to make shortcakes and whipped cream.
RECIPE WITHIN A RECIPE: The compote is delicious served over ice cream or slathered on biscuits or toast.

SHORTCAKES WITH CITRUS COMPOTE AND ORANGE FLOWER WHIPPED CREAM

CITRUS COMPOTE

2½ lb/1 kg **assorted citrus (such as kumquats, seedless tangerines, and oranges)**

¼ cup/2 oz/80 g **orange marmalade**

¼ tsp **kosher salt**

ORANGE FLOWER WHIPPED CREAM

1 cup/8 oz/240 ml **heavy cream**

1 tbsp **sugar**

½ tsp **orange flower water or almond extract**

Orange flower water, also known as orange blossom water, can be found in the spice aisle. If you can't find it, almond extract, rose water, or vanilla extract will work well.

The cream and butter for the shortcakes needs to be cold so they remain flaky.

SHORTCAKES

2 cups/9 oz/255 g **unbleached all-purpose flour**

⅓ cup/2¼ oz/65 g **sugar, plus more for topping**

2½ tsp **baking powder**

1 tsp **kosher salt**

6 tbsp/3 oz/85 g **unsalted butter, cut into small cubes and chilled**

1 cup/8 oz/240 ml **cold heavy cream, plus more for topping**

CONTINUED

The compote can be made up to 2 days ahead and refrigerated in an airtight container.

FOR THE FRUIT

Halve the kumquats and peel and segment tangerines and oranges. Cook three-fourths of the citrus with the marmalade in a medium pot over medium heat, stirring frequently, until the fruit is broken down and slightly thickened, about 10 minutes.

Remove from the heat and stir in the salt and remaining citrus. Transfer to a heatproof bowl and put into the refrigerator to chill and for flavors to develop, at least 30 minutes.

FOR THE WHIPPED CREAM

Combine the cream, sugar, and orange flower water in a chilled bowl and whisk with a chilled whisk until thick and fluffy and medium peaks have formed (see page 93), about 3 minutes.

 For success with whipped cream, make sure the cream is chilled and the bowl and beaters are clean, as fat will prevent the cream from holding air.

BISCUIT CUTTERS
Invest in sharp biscuit cutters and they'll reward you with a clean, uniform cut that allows for a taller biscuit.

FOR THE SHORTCAKES

Heat the oven to 400°F/200°C/gas 6 and arrange a rack in the middle. Whisk together the flour, sugar, baking powder, and salt until evenly combined and well aerated. Add the butter and rub between forefingers until the mixture resembles cornmeal.

Add the cream and stir until the dough is thoroughly moistened. Turn onto a floured surface and knead briefly until it just comes together. Pat into a circle that is 1 in/2.5 cm thick. Using a 2-in/ 5-cm) biscuit cutter, cut out as many shortcakes as possible. Reroll and cut out shortcakes until you have a total of 12 short-cakes. Brush the tops with additional cream and sprinkle with additional sugar.

Place on a baking sheet and bake until the bottoms are browned and tops are golden, 15 to 20 minutes. Remove from the oven and serve immediately or cool on a wire rack.

To serve, split the shortcakes horizontally, spoon on some of the compote, and top with a dollop of whipped cream.

 The shortcakes are best warm but can be made up to 1 day ahead and warmed before serving.

SWEETS

This brown sugar and pistachio twist on carrot cake has lots of fans in our house. Family feuds have broken out over who gets the last bite—don't say I didn't warn you.

TAKEAWAY: How to make cream cheese frosting.

DIFFICULTY
Medium

YIELD
8 to 10 servings

TOTAL TIME
1 hour, 20 minutes

HANDS-ON TIME
35 minutes

PISTACHIO CARROT CAKE WITH BROWN SUGAR—CREAM CHEESE FROSTING

BROWN SUGAR—CREAM CHEESE FROSTING

1 lb/455 g **cream cheese, at room temperature**

½ cup/4 oz/115 g **unsalted butter, cut into small pieces (at room temperature)**

1¼ cups/4¼ oz/160 g **powdered sugar**

1 cup/7 oz/220 g **packed dark brown sugar**

1 tsp **pure vanilla extract**

¼ tsp **kosher salt**

CARROT CAKE

Unsalted butter, for coating the pans

2¼ cups/10 oz/285 g **unbleached all-purpose flour, plus more for coating**

2 tsp **baking powder**

2 tsp **kosher salt**

1 tsp **ground allspice**

½ tsp **baking soda**

3 **large eggs, at room temperature**

1 cup/7 oz/200 g **granulated sugar**

1 cup/7 oz/220 g **packed dark brown sugar**

⅔ cup/5 oz/165 ml **canola, grapeseed, or peanut oil**

1 tbsp **pure vanilla extract**

1½ lb/700 g **carrots, peeled and grated**

2½ cups/11½ oz/325 g **finely chopped shelled roasted pistachios**

STAND MIXER
I used a stand mixer here but a handheld electric mixer and a bowl will also work fine.

"Room temperature" is the key phrase here to ensure everything mixes together properly. To speed up the eggs, place them in a bowl of warm water for 10 minutes before using.

Buy roasted pistachios as they have more flavor. If you can't find them, pecans or walnuts are a good substitute.

CONTINUED

FOR THE FROSTING

Put the cream cheese in the bowl of a stand mixer fitted with the paddle attachment. Beat on medium speed until very smooth. Add the butter, powdered sugar, brown sugar, vanilla, and salt and beat until airy and well combined. Refrigerate until ready to use.

FOR THE CAKE

Heat the oven to 350°F/177°C/gas 4 and arrange a rack in the middle. Coat two 8-in/20-cm round cake pans with butter and flour and tap out any excess flour; set aside. Combine the flour, baking powder, salt, allspice, and baking soda in a large bowl, and whisk to aerate and break up any lumps; set aside.

Combine the eggs, granulated and brown sugars, oil, and vanilla in another large bowl. Whisk until the eggs are broken up and the mixture is thoroughly combined. Using a rubber spatula, fold in the flour mixture until just combined. Fold in the carrots and pistachios until evenly mixed.

Divide the batter evenly between the prepared pans. Bake until a cake tester inserted in the centers comes out clean, 40 to 50 minutes. Remove cakes from the oven, run a knife around the perimeter of each, and turn the cakes out onto wire rack to cool completely.

To frost, place a cake layer on an inverted cake pan. Spread about one-third of the frosting over the top of the layer. Stack the second layer, and evenly spread another one-third of the frosting over the top and sides of the whole cake. (Don't fuss over looks at this point, as this is just a base coat.)

Place the coated cake in the refrigerator until the frosting is set up and slightly hard, 10 to 15 minutes. Remove from the refrigerator and spread the remaining frosting over the top and sides of the cake, ensuring it's as even as possible. Press pistachios into the sides of the cake and let the cake sit at room temperature 5 minutes before slicing with a knife dipped in hot water.

RIFF: This batter can be cooked in loaf pans like a quick bread or in muffin tins for cupcakes.

The frosting can be made up to 4 days in advance. Bring to room temperature before frosting and stir to evenly combine.

Nothing ruins a baked recipe faster than an oven that's off temperature. Use an oven thermometer to know if your oven skews hot or cold and adjust accordingly.

The cake can be baked up to 2 days ahead and stored, unfrosted, wrapped in plastic wrap at room temperature.

ROUND CAKE PAN
You'll need two 8-in/20-cm round cake pans.

If the top of the cake is domed, see trimming tips on page 94.

The assembled, frosted cake can be covered with a cake dome and refrigerated for up to 2 days. Serve at room temperature.

DIFFICULTY
Medium

YIELD
8 to 12 servings

TOTAL TIME
2 hours, 30 minutes, plus chilling time

HANDS-ON TIME
30 minutes

Use the egg whites in the Oatmeal Breakfast Soufflé (page 126) or the Herbed Goat Cheese Soufflé (page 252).

Dulce de leche is a slow-cooked milk caramel sauce that is popular in Latin America. It is becoming more readily available but, if you can't find it, go ahead and use a good-quality caramel sauce.

SPRINGFORM PAN
You'll need a 9-in/23-cm springform pan.

A light, lemon-sparked, creamy cheesecake with a caramel-y dulce de leche note, this dessert sets a new standard. This is a lengthy recipe but patience pays off with top-notch cheesecake, so don't rush it.

TAKEAWAY: How to make a cheesecake.

DULCE DE LECHE—FRESH LEMON CHEESECAKE

COOKIE CRUST

1½ cups/6 oz/170 g **finely ground vanilla wafers or graham crackers**

4 tbsp/2 oz/55 g **unsalted butter, melted**

2 tbsp **sugar**

DULCE DE LECHE FILLING

Four 8 oz/225 g **packages cream cheese, at room temperature**

½ cup/120 ml **sour cream or crème fraîche**

1¼ cups/8¾ oz/250 g **sugar**

2 tsp **pure vanilla extract**

Grated zest and juice of 1 lemon

2 **large egg yolks**

3 **large eggs**

¾ cup/8 oz/225 g **purchased or homemade dulce de leche sauce**

FOR THE CRUST

Heat the oven to 325°F/165°C/gas 3 and arrange a rack in the middle. Place crumbs, melted butter, and sugar in a medium bowl and mix until thoroughly combined. Pour the crumb mixture into a 9-in/23-cm springform pan and, using the bottom of a cup, press evenly into the bottom and slightly up the sides. Bake the crust until fragrant and golden, 8 to 10 minutes; set aside.

FOR THE FILLING

Put the cream cheese, sour cream, and sugar in the bowl of a food processor fitted with the metal blade and process until smooth. Stop the processor occasionally to scrape down the sides of the bowl and the blade as needed.

Add the vanilla, lemon zest and juice, and egg yolks and pulse to incorporate. Add the whole eggs and process until smooth.

Pour three-fourths of the batter into the prepared crust. Mix the remaining one-fourth of the batter with the dulce de leche sauce. Drop spoonfuls of dulce de leche mixture over the top of the cheesecake then drag a knife through the batter in a figure-eight to create a marbled pattern.

Bake until the edges of the cake are browned and the center is barely set, 45 minutes to 1 hour.

Turn off the oven and let the cake cool in the oven for 1 hour. Remove the cheesecake from the oven and place on a cooling rack. Run a knife around the inner edge then let cool to room temperature.

Tightly cover the cheesecake and refrigerate at least 2 hours before serving. To serve, run a knife around the inner edge of the pan, remove the sides, and slice.

FOOD PROCESSOR
I used a food processor here but a handheld electric mixer and a bowl will also work fine.

The cheesecake can be made up to 2 days ahead and stored covered and refrigerated until ready to use.

Dip a sharp knife in hot water to help slice the cake.

RIFF: Leave out the dulce de leche and you have a classic New York–style cheesecake.

DIFFICULTY
Medium

YIELD
**One 9½-in/24-cm
deep-dish pie**

TOTAL TIME
**1 hour, plus
chilling time**

HANDS-ON TIME
25 minutes

- - - - - - - - - - - - - -
Use the egg whites in
the Oatmeal Breakfast
Soufflé (page 126) or the
Herbed Goat Cheese
Soufflé (page 252).

ROLLING PIN
You'll need a rolling pin.
Look for a French rolling
pin (one with tapered edges
and no handle) as they're
more versatile for rolling
out doughs.

DEEP-DISH PIE PLATE
This dough will fit in a
9½-in/23-cm deep-dish pie
plate or smaller.

*My friend from Guam grew up eating custard pies and asked me
to re-create the flavor for her. Going off her pointers, I created this
spiced custard pie topped with sweet slices of tropical fruit.*

TAKEAWAY: How to make a piecrust.
RECIPE WITHIN A RECIPE: This piecrust can be used for sweet and
savory recipes alike from pies and quiches to tarts and pot pies.

MANGO CUSTARD PIE

CRUST

1⅓ cups/5½ oz/165 g **all-
purpose flour**

1 tbsp **sugar**

1 tsp **kosher salt**

½ cup/4 oz/115 g **cold
unsalted butter, cut into
small pieces**

¼ cup/2 oz/55 g **shortening**

1 tbsp **vodka**

2 to 4 tbsp **ice water**

MANGO CUSTARD FILLING

2 cups/16 oz/480 ml
half-and-half

⅔ cup/4½ oz/130 g **sugar**

8 **large egg yolks**

1 tbsp **cornstarch**

1 tbsp **pure vanilla extract**

1 tsp **pure almond extract**

1 tsp **ground nutmeg**

½ tsp **kosher salt**

1 **large ripe mango**

**Whipped cream or ice cream,
for serving**

FOR THE CRUST

Combine the flour, sugar, and salt in a large bowl and whisk to
aerate. Using clean hands, add half of the butter and toss until
just coated. Add the shortening, and rub the butter and shortening between thumb and forefingers until mixture resembles
cornmeal.

Add the remaining butter, toss to coat in the flour, then rub into
the flour mixture until pea-sized pieces are formed (some big
chunks should remain) and the mixture comes together in fist-
sized clumps when squeezed.

Drizzle in the vodka and 2 tablespoons of the ice water and rake
through the mixture with your fingers until just moistened. As
needed, drizzle in the remaining water, 1 tablespoon at a time,
and comb through the mixture with your fingers to moisten.

It will go from being a shaggy mess to coming together. Dough is moist enough when it is moistened through but is not sticky when pressed.

While rotating the bowl with 1 hand, push dough between other palm and the side of the bowl to gather into a ball. Turn dough onto a piece of plastic wrap, press it into a flat disk, and wrap securely. Refrigerate at least 1 hour before rolling out and forming into a crust.

Meanwhile, heat the oven to 400°F/200°C/gas 6, arrange a rack in the upper third, and place a baking sheet on the rack while the oven heats.

Roll out the dough on a lightly floured surface to a 11-in/28-cm circle that is approximately ⅛ in/3 mm thick. Transfer the dough to a 9½-in/24-cm deep-dish pie plate and trim edges so there is a ½-in/12-mm overhang. Use excess dough to press the crust into the pie plate. Fold the overhang back on itself and press, as desired, into a decorative crust.

Pierce the bottom of the crust all over with a fork. Line the crust with aluminum foil so it overhangs slightly and covers the edges of the crust and fill with dried beans or baking weights. Place the pie dish on a baking sheet and bake until the crust is set and the edges are slightly puffed up, 20 to 25 minutes. Remove the crust from the oven and decrease the temperature to 350°F/177°C/gas 4).

FOR THE FILLING

Combine the half-and-half, sugar, egg yolks, cornstarch, vanilla, almond extract, nutmeg, and salt in a medium bowl and whisk to evenly combine. Pour the custard in the partially baked piecrust. Peel and pit the mango. Cut the flesh into ½-in/13-mm dice and arrange the slices on the top of the custard.

Bake until the filling is set and a toothpick inserted in the center comes out clean, 40 to 45 minutes. Remove to a cooling rack and let cool to room temperature, about 1 hour. Drape with a paper towel then tightly cover with plastic wrap and refrigerate until thoroughly cooled, at least 2 hours. If condensation has formed on the pie, carefully blot with a paper towel. Serve topped with whipped cream or ice cream.

RIFF: The custard base is tasty without any fruit but you could also try it with other tropical fruit like kiwi, papaya, persimmons, or raspberries.

 The dough can be shaped, wrapped tightly in plastic wrap, and frozen up to 1 month before using.

Piecrusts are hard to make in hot kitchens so try to work in a cool space. Chilling the dough between the various steps helps the gluten in the dough relax and remain flaky so don't rush that step. If it is particularly hot outside, freeze the dough in the pie dish for 10 to 15 minutes before baking to help prevent it from shrinking.

 The dough can be made a few days ahead as desired. The dough can be rolled out and shaped in the pie dish up 2 days ahead and kept covered in refrigerator until ready to use.

BAKING WEIGHTS
Baking weights are ceramic balls that help prevent the crust from puffing up. You can use dried beans or rice instead; however their texture will be affected so don't use them for cooking.

DIFFICULTY
Easy

YIELD
40 cookies

TOTAL TIME
30 minutes

HANDS-ON TIME
15 minutes

Cream of tartar is a by-product of wine making and it helps give this cookie its distinct texture. If you can't find it, you can omit it although the cookie's crumb won't be as fine.

Sanding sugar is a large-crystal sugar that is used for decorating baked goods. If you can't find it, granulated or turbinado sugar will work.

"Room temperature" is the key phrase here to ensure that everything mixes together properly. To speed up the eggs, place them in a bowl of warm water for 10 minutes before using.

Superfine sugar (also known as baker's sugar) also helps give this cookie its fine crumb. If you can't find it, use regular granulated sugar and pulse in the food processor a few times to break up any larger crystals.

Nothing ruins a baked recipe faster than an oven that's off temperature. Use an oven thermometer to know if your oven skews hot or cold, and adjust accordingly.

The cookies will last up to 1 week when stored at room temperature in an airtight container.

Both tender and crispy, and just sweet enough, it's hard to eat just one of these cookies.

TAKEAWAY: How to make a sugar cookie.

CLASSIC SUGAR COOKIES

2¼ cups/10 oz/285 g **unbleached all-purpose flour**

½ tsp **baking soda**

½ tsp **cream of tartar**

1 tsp **kosher salt**

¼ cup/1¾ oz/60 g **sanding sugar**

½ cup/4 oz/113 g **unsalted butter, at room temperature**

¼ cup/2 oz/55 g **solid vegetable shortening**

1 cup/7 oz/200 g **superfine sugar**

3 **large egg yolks, at room temperature**

2 tsp **pure vanilla extract**

Heat the oven to 350°F/177°C/gas 4 and arrange a rack in the middle. Combine the flour, baking soda, cream of tartar, and salt in a bowl and whisk until aerated; set aside. Put the sanding sugar in a bowl and set aside.

Place the butter, shortening, and superfine sugar in the bowl of a stand mixer fitted with the paddle attachment and mix on medium speed until light and fluffy, about 3 minutes.

Scrape down the bowl sides and bottom. Add the yolks and vanilla, and mix on medium speed until smooth, about 1 minute. Add the flour mixture and stir until the dough just comes together. Scoop dough into rounded tablespoons and roll between your hands until smooth. (Dampen your hands as needed to help in rolling the cookies.)

Roll the dough in sanding sugar to coat and divide between 2 baking sheets. Bake the cookies (both baking sheets) until they are golden brown around the edges but still soft in the center, 10 to 13 minutes, rotating pans halfway through. Immediately transfer to a rack to cool completely.

A coffee lover's dream, this cookie has a mix of earthy coffee flavor and sweet chocolate bites. The ground, unbrewed coffee beans may seem like a strange addition but one bite and you'll be convinced.

TAKEAWAY: How to make a chocolate chip cookie.

DIFFICULTY
Easy

YIELD
32 cookies

TOTAL TIME
50 minutes

HANDS-ON TIME
20 minutes

CHOCOLATE CHIP—GROUND COFFEE BEAN COOKIES

2¼ cups/10 oz/285 g **all-purpose flour**

⅓ cup/¾ oz/20 g **finely ground coffee beans**

1 tsp **baking soda**

1 tsp **kosher salt**

1 cup/8 oz/225 g **unsalted butter, at room temperature**

¾ cup/5¼ oz/150 g **granulated sugar**

½ cup/3½ oz/110 g **packed light brown sugar**

2 **large eggs, at room temperature**

2 tsp **pure vanilla extract**

2 cups/12 oz/310 g **milk chocolate chips**

Heat the oven to 350°F/177°C/gas 4 and arrange a rack in the middle. Combine the flour, coffee, baking soda, and salt in a medium bowl and whisk to aerate; set aside.

Place the butter, granulated and brown sugars in the bowl of a stand mixer fitted with the paddle attachment. Beat on high speed until light in color and fluffy, about 3 minutes. Scrape down the sides and bottom of the bowl. Add the eggs and vanilla, mixing until completely incorporated.

Add the flour mixture and stir until just moistened through. Stir in the chocolate chips until just combined. Drop 2-tablespoon balls of dough on 2 rimmed baking sheets, leaving 2 in/5 cm between each cookie.

Bake, rotating sheets halfway through, until the bottoms are browned and tops are puffed and set, 12 to 15 minutes. Remove to cooling racks and repeat with remaining dough.

RIFFS

- Add 1 cup toasted walnuts.
- Add 1 cup dried tart cherries.

 "Room temperature" is the key phrase here to ensure everything mixes together properly. To speed up the eggs, place them in a bowl of warm water for 10 minutes before using.

I enjoy dark chocolate but this is not the place for it, as it would make the cookie too intense.

 Nothing ruins a baked recipe faster than an oven that's off temperature. Use an oven thermometer to know if your oven skews hot or cold and adjust accordingly.

ICE CREAM SCOOP
An ice cream scoop with a 2-tablespoon capacity will make quick work of portioning the dough.

The cookies will last up to 1 week stored at room temperature in an airtight container.

DIFFICULTY
Medium

YIELD
24 bars

TOTAL TIME
1 hour, 15 minutes, plus cooling time

HANDS-ON TIME
30 minutes

This tweak on classic lemon bars came about when I found myself at a friend's house whose citrus trees were particularly prolific. It's an update that is tart, sweet, and floral all at once making it more requested than the original.

TAKEAWAY: How to make shortbread.
RECIPE WITHIN A RECIPE: The base for the citrus bar is a coconut shortbread cookie so you could call it quits there for an easy cookie recipe.

TRIPLE CITRUS–COCONUT SHORTBREAD BARS

1½ cups/5 oz/140 g **unsweetened flaked coconut**

SHORTBREAD BASE

¾ cup/6 oz/170 g **cold unsalted butter, cut into small pieces, plus more for greasing the pan**

1¾ cups/215 g **unbleached all-purpose flour**

¾ cup/95 g **powdered sugar**

¾ tsp **kosher salt**

TRIPLE-CITRUS FILLING

2⅔ cups/340 g **powdered sugar, plus more for garnish**

6 **large eggs**

6 **large egg yolks**

6 tbsp/3 oz/85 g **unsalted butter, melted**

¾ cup/6 oz/180 ml **freshly squeezed lemon juice**

⅓ cup/2½ oz/75 ml **freshly squeezed lime juice**

⅓ cup/2½ oz/75 ml **freshly squeezed orange juice**

1½ tsp **grated lemon zest**

1½ tsp **grated lime zest**

1 tbsp **grated orange zest**

Look for unsweetened flaked coconut in the baking or health food aisle. If you can't find it, use the sweetened shredded coconut and know the final shortbread will be a bit sweeter.

Use the egg whites in the Oatmeal Breakfast Soufflé (page 126) or the Herbed Goat Cheese Soufflé (page 252).

Heat the oven to 350°F/177°C/gas 4 and arrange a rack in the middle. Spread the coconut on a baking sheet, and toast, tossing every few minutes to ensure even cooking, until golden brown, 5 to 8 minutes. Set aside to cool.

FOR THE BASE

Coat a baking dish that measures 13 by 9 in/33 by 23 cm with butter and line the pan with 2 pieces of parchment paper that overhang each side of the pan by 1 in/2.5 cm.

Combine 1 cup/95 g of the toasted coconut, flour, powdered sugar, and salt in a large bowl and whisk until evenly combined. Scatter butter pieces over the flour mixture, and, using a pastry cutter, two knives, or your fingers, blend until dough just begins to come together.

Crumble the dough into the prepared baking pan and, using the base of a measuring cup or a glass dipped in flour, evenly press the dough into the pan. Bake until the crust is fully set and just starting to brown on the edges, 25 to 30 minutes. Remove from the oven and let cool while you make the filling.

FOR THE FILLING

Combine all the ingredients in a large nonreactive bowl and whisk until the sugar is dissolved and the mixture is smooth, about 2 minutes.

Pour the filling over the baked crust, scatter with the remaining ½ cup/45 g coconut, return to the oven, and bake until just set in the middle, 25 to 35 minutes. Remove from the oven and let cool completely on a wire rack. Cover and place in the refrigerator to set up for 2 to 3 hours.

To serve, sift powdered sugar over the top, if desired, then, using a knife dipped in hot water, cut into squares.

BAKING DISH
You'll need a baking dish that measures 13 by 9 in/ 33 by 23 cm.

The base can be baked 1 day ahead. Just cool to room temperature, wrap airtight, and store at room temperature until ready to proceed.

If the dough gets too warm while you press it into the dish, place it in the freezer for 5 to 10 minutes before baking to improve the final texture.

The longer the finished bars set up in the fridge, the easier they will be to cut without breaking the crust.

Peach melba—a classic dessert of raspberries and peaches—is one of my favorite forgotten flavor combos. Here it combines with yogurt for a sweet, tangy, creamy, and healthy Popsicle that you can feel good about eating.

TAKEAWAY: How to make Popsicles.

DIFFICULTY
Easy

YIELD
8 Popsicles

TOTAL TIME
6 hours, 10 minutes

HANDS-ON TIME
10 minutes

PEACH MELBA CREAM POPSICLES

1 lb/455 g **frozen peaches, thawed**

1½ cups/5¼ oz/150 g **frozen raspberries, thawed**

1 cup/240 ml **plain or vanilla whole-milk yogurt**

¼ cup/2 oz/60 ml **agave nectar or honey**

¼ cup/2 oz/60 ml **freshly squeezed orange juice**

1 tbsp **freshly squeezed lemon juice**

¼ tsp **ground cloves**

Pinch of **salt**

POPSICLE MOLD

You'll need eight 4-oz/118-ml Popsicle molds.

Combine all ingredients in a food processor fitted with the metal blade and process until very smooth, at least 5 minutes.

Transfer to eight 4-oz/118-ml Popsicle molds (or paper cups with Popsicle sticks) and freeze at least 6 hours or overnight. Let rest a few minutes before unmolding and, as needed, run under warm water to help remove from the molds to serve.

FOOD PROCESSOR

I used a food processor here but a blender will also work.

⏱ The frozen, unmolded Popsicles last up to 2 weeks.

RIFF: You could also throw the blended mixture into an ice cream machine for a makeshift sorbet.

DIFFICULTY
Medium

YIELD
6 cups

TOTAL TIME
*1 hour, 30 minutes,
plus chilling time*

HANDS-ON TIME
35 minutes

As classic as it gets, this ice cream is rich, creamy, and take-no-prisoners decadent but worth every bite.

TAKEAWAY: How to make a custard-based ice cream.
RECIPE WITHIN A RECIPE: The chocolate-covered pretzels are a hit on their own.
GOES WELL WITH: I have faith you'll figure this out.

VANILLA BEAN ICE CREAM WITH CHOCOLATE-COVERED PRETZEL BITES

VANILLA ICE CREAM

4 cups/32 oz/960 ml **heavy cream or half-and-half**

¾ cup/5¼ oz/150g **granulated sugar**

½ tsp **kosher salt**

2 **vanilla beans, split lengthwise and scraped, seeds reserved, or** 1 tbsp **pure vanilla extract**

6 **large egg yolks**

CHOCOLATE-COVERED PRETZELS

6 oz/170 g **milk chocolate**

1½ cups/3 oz/80 g **bite-sized pretzel twists**

I like vanilla beans here because they add a floral aroma and fleck the ice cream with their seeds. If you can't find them or they're too expensive, use pure vanilla extract instead.

Use the egg whites in the Oatmeal Breakfast Soufflé (page 126) or the Herbed Goat Cheese Soufflé (page 252).

 Pouring the hot cream into the egg yolks helps temper the ice cream's custard base so the eggs don't get over-cooked by the mixture. So pay special attention here.

FOR THE ICE CREAM

Prepare an ice water bath by filling a large bowl halfway with ice and water; set aside. Combine the cream, sugar, salt, and vanilla beans and seeds in a medium saucepan. Bring to a simmer over medium heat, stirring occasionally, until the sugar is dissolved, about 10 minutes.

Meanwhile, whisk the egg yolks in a large heatproof bowl until smooth. Remove the cream mixture from the heat and slowly pour about 1 cup/240 ml of it into the egg yolks, whisking constantly until smooth. Pour the cream-egg mixture back into the pan and cook over low heat, stirring constantly, until the custard coats the spoon, about 5 minutes. (When you draw your finger across the spoon, it should make a mark through the custard, which should not run back in on itself.)

Remove the custard from heat and strain through a fine mesh strainer into another large heatproof bowl to remove any lumps, scraping as many vanilla seeds through the strainer as possible. Remove the vanilla bean pods from the strainer and add to the custard. Set the bowl of ice cream base over the ice bath to cool to room temperature, 20 to 25 minutes. Cover and place in the refrigerator to chill completely, at least 4 hours or overnight. Meanwhile, make the chocolate pretzels.

FOR THE PRETZELS

Line a baking sheet with parchment paper or a silicone baking mat. Make a water bath by nesting a heatproof bowl over a saucepan of simmering water. Add the chocolate to the bowl and cook, stirring frequently, until evenly melted. Remove from the heat, add the pretzels, and stir to coat. Transfer the pretzels to the prepared baking sheet and refrigerate until the chocolate is set. Roughly chop the coated pretzels and set aside until ready to use.

Once the ice cream base is chilled, process in an ice cream maker according to the manufacturer's instructions. When the ice cream is just finished, stir in the chocolate pretzels. Pack the ice cream into airtight containers, and then freeze for at least 4 hours before serving.

ICE CREAM MAKER
Use an ice cream maker and make sure the core piece is frozen according to manufacturer's directions before starting the recipe.

Once made, the ice cream will last up to 2 weeks in an airtight container in the freezer.

RIFFS

- This is a blank slate of an ice cream recipe that takes well to additions and alterations so let your creativity flow.
- Swap graham crackers, peanuts, or almonds for the pretzels.
- Stir caramel sauce, dulce de leche, or fudge sauce into the ice cream at the very end of mixing.
- For a lighter ice cream, use all half-and-half or half-and-half and whole milk.

PART 4

THE RIFF

Now that you've wrangled control of your kitchen, it's time to tap into some of your own culinary creativity. This section is like a crib sheet loaded with concepts that will convert you from a cook who relies on recipes to one who can deftly cook from the hip. It covers everything from entertaining and numerous menu ideas to suggestions for reinventing leftovers and the equally important cleanup.

Mastering the Meal

Cooking a single dish is one thing but being able to put together a whole meal in a timely manner is a totally different animal. Here are pointers to help you go from cooking for yourself to cooking for a crowd without breaking a sweat.

GENERAL MEAL-PLANNING TIPS

Even just a few minutes of planning goes a long way when it comes to a meal. Here are the main things to consider:

Determine Serving Style Match the serving style to the event. No one wants to sit down to a formally set table to watch Monday Night Football; likewise, having a potluck for a New Year's Eve party might take the wind out of the sails. The most common serving styles are (from most formal to least): seated, with multiple courses; seated, with platters of food passed family style (my favorite way to eat with friends and family); seated, single course; buffet (ideal for a potluck or sporting event); trays of tapas and passed hors d'oeuvres.

Be Realistic Be honest with yourself about how much time, money, and, most importantly, energy you have. There's nothing more frustrating than making an elaborate dinner to realize you're over it before the meal's even begun.

Practice Run First time meeting the parents? Or first time hosting the holidays? Do yourself a favor and test-run as many of your recipes as possible—perhaps even the whole meal— so you're comfortable with things before the day arrives.

Decide on Last-Minute Stuff First Consider the details that make the meal special (such as the garnishes, the tableware, etc.). Figure these details out well ahead of time so, even if you do get flustered, you can concentrate on the food and know that everything else is accounted for.

Sort Out the Serving Ware Along the same lines, decide on serving ware well before it's time to put out the food. For big events, use sticky notes to label everything you need, from the salad bowls to the linens. It's not only to ensure you have all the serving pieces you need, but also a system that comes in handy should a guest volunteer to help set the table.

Ask for Help Speaking of helpful guests, don't hesitate to ask for help. I know you may feel more accomplished if you try to pull it all off yourself, but sometimes a little help makes everything (including you) more enjoyable. Try to invite at least one person (significant other, sibling, or best friend) who you know you can pull away from the party and ask for help without hesitation.

Make It Ahead The theme here is to think ahead. For big meals, mentally rehearse the cooking and serving process from start to finish. That way you are sure you have everything you need, and also can identify what dishes or parts of a dish can be made ahead of time to help lighten the load later. When menu planning, it's wise to always choose a few things that can be prepared in advance.

Timing is the Linchpin To ensure you have control over the meal's timing, aim to have only one time-sensitive dish. Usually, that's going to be the centerpiece—be it a roast, a salmon steak, or a soufflé—so plan accordingly by choosing sides that can sit while you give your undivided attention to the main dish.

Work Backwards I'm referring to the timing here. To know when to start cooking, add up the estimated cook time for each dish, give yourself some buffer room for unaccounted odds and ends (to be social or for plating), and subtract it from your desired eating time. If you're serving food already on the plate (rather than family-style at the table), add extra time for portioning and garnishing each plate—anywhere from 5 to 20 minutes depending on how many people you're serving and if you have help.

MENU PLANNING

Here are general tips but for more related to mixing and matching flavors of foods, check out How to Riff, page 390.

Mind the Meal's Purpose That's to say keep in mind why this meal is even taking place. Is it a weeknight and you're just trying to feed hungry family members? Are you celebrating the first days of summer? Bottom line: let the purpose of the meal and the weather determine the food you're serving.

Decide Formality The setting of where you're hosting your meal should also come into play. After a long day of winter sports, you're not going to want formal fussiness. Go for something cozy and stick-to-the-ribs comforting.

Consider the Serving Timeline Plan a mix of dishes that can be made at different times (even up to a day ahead) so that you don't have to focus on too much at one time. Also, consider pacing a meal with distinct courses if you are doing something a bit more traditional.

Decide on a Flavor That's not to say you should decide on one sole ingredient, such as citrus, and then have every dish made with some sort of citrus—though that could be fun. This is a bit broader than that so you should find a theme in your menu—such as the season, type of cuisine, or a combination of flavors—and stick to it. For ideas on how to find the meal's food focus—what I call the flavor catalyst—check out Striking Balance, page 390.

Mix Up Temperatures Unless you're making a menu of foods that are second nature to you to cook, mix up the temperatures of the dishes you're serving. It not only adds another dimension to the meal but also gives you flexibility so that you aren't desperately trying to keep a tabletop full of food warm in a pint-sized oven.

And the Weight of Foods This one gets overlooked by home cooks, but can be just as important. A heavy braised dish with a heavy side can make for a leaden meal. Instead, balance out more substantial fare with lighter dishes for a meal that's both satiating and memorable.

And Colors In a perfect world, we'd have gorgeous colors on the plate all the time, but something that's highly attractive from a flavor standpoint doesn't always deliver on looks. When you're faced with a drab dish, pair it with something with color. When in doubt, serve a side salad.

Portion Planning Purchase about 8 oz/225 g of meat, fish, or chicken per serving in order to have about 4 to 6 oz/115 to 170 g of cooked food. If, however, it is a buffet and there are multiple food options, plan instead for about 4 oz/115 g of each type of protein. Account for about 1 fistful, about 1 oz/30 g of greens or ½ cup/85 g dry grains for one serving. Note that I'm talking in servings, which is an average estimate of what one person will eat. Some people will go for multiple servings, so take into account who you're feeding (bird-eating girlfriends or carnivorous men) and how you're feeding them (sit-down restrained serving meal or a graze-a-thon buffet or cocktail party style).

MENU IDEAS

Armed with the tips above and your own creativity, you can come up with a load of memorable menus for anything from a weeknight dinner to a winner of a potluck. Here are a few ideas to get things started:

AMERICANA

MENU 1

- Buttermilk Biscuits with Black Pepper—Brown Butter (page 170)
- Spinach Salad with Persimmons and Hazelnuts (page 201)
- Pan-Roasted Pork Tenderloin with Orange-Molasses Glaze (page 312)
- Creamy Butterscotch Pudding (page 354)

MENU 2

- Romaine Salad with Whiskey Onions, Corn Bread, and Buttermilk Dressing (page 209)
- Smoky Black Bean, Beef, and Green Pepper Chili (page 192)
- Apple Turnover Bread Pudding with Maple Cream Sauce (page 352)

MENU 3

- Grilled Huli Huli—Style Chicken (page 272)
- Purple Sweet Potato Salad with Green Beans and Peas (page 206)
- Mango Custard Pie (page 370)

MENU 4

- Pan-Roasted Pork Tenderloin with Orange-Molasses Glaze (page 312)
- Fall Salad with Crisp Apples and Pickled Fennel (page 214)

MENU 5

- Rosemary-Lemon Oven-Fried Chicken (page 282)
- Carrot and Currant Cabbage Slaw (page 342)
- Summer Vegetable—Farro Salad (page 215)
- Peach Melba Cream Popsicles (page 377)

BREAKFAST IN BED

- Arugula Pesto "Green Eggs and Ham" Sandwich (page 140)
- Asparagus, Tomato, and Feta Scramble (page 143)
- Masala-Spiced Spinach Omelet (page 152)
- Crisp Yeasted Waffles with Cocoa Whipped Cream (page 134)
- Hazelnut-Cocoa French Toast Sandwiches (page 129)
- Swiss Chard, Oyster Mushroom, and Ricotta Frittata (page 154)
- Crêpes with Meyer Lemon Curd and Fresh Berries (page 132)
- Toasted Walnut Pancakes with Red-Eye Maple Syrup (page 136)

BRUNCH

- Berry Muffins with Spiced Pistachio Streusel (page 168)
- Swiss Chard, Oyster Mushroom, and Ricotta Frittata (page 154)
- Chipotle—Sweet Potato Hash with Poached Eggs and Avocado (page 146)
- Cajun Strata with Mustard Sour Cream (page 144)
- Toasted Walnut Pancakes with Red-Eye Maple Syrup (page 136)
- Hazelnut-Cocoa French Toast Sandwiches (page 129)
- "Bacon" and Egg Breakfast Pizza (page 124)
- Buttermilk Biscuits with Black Pepper—Brown Butter (page 170)
- Oatmeal Breakfast Soufflé (page 126)
- Toasted Pecan and Date Scones (page 176)
- Crêpes with Meyer Lemon Curd and Fresh Berries (page 132)
- Crisp Yeasted Waffles with Cocoa Whipped Cream (page 134)
- Country-Style Spanish Tortilla (page 150)
- Creamy Baked Eggs with Hot-Smoked Salmon (page 149)
- Masala-Spiced Spinach Omelet (page 152)
- Toasted Pecan and Date Scones (page 176)

COCKTAIL PARTY

(ALSO CHECK OUT THE APPETIZER IDEAS IN
STRESS-FREE APPETIZERS, PAGE 398)

- Buttermilk Biscuits with Black Pepper—Brown Butter (page 170)
- Sage-Maple Skillet Corn Bread (page 174)
- Toasted Pecan and Date Scones (page 176)
- Roasted Carrot Soup with Toasted Coconut (page 188)
- "Bacon" and Egg Breakfast Pizza (page 124)
- Country-Style Spanish Tortilla (page 150)
- Swiss Chard, Oyster Mushroom, and Ricotta Frittata (page 154)
- Crêpes with Meyer Lemon Curd and Fresh Berries (page 132)
- Coconut Mahi Mahi Ceviche with Chiles and Herbs (page 332)
- Seared Scallops with Sweet-Spicy Chile Sauce (page 334)
- Miso-Marinated Beef and Charred Vegetable Skewers (page 302)
- Blood Orange—Braised Pork Shoulder (page 290)
- Lamb Chops with Fresh Cherry Salsa (page 300)

COMPANY'S COMING

MENU 1

- Harissa-Marinated Cod with Braised Chickpeas (page 322)
- Butter Lettuce Salad with Tahini-Honey Dressing (page 200)
- Broiled Asparagus with Tomatoes and Fresh Herbs (page 341)
- Plum Crisp with Toasted Almond—Cornmeal Topping (page 356)

MENU 2

- Herbed Goat Cheese Soufflé (page 252)
- Blood Orange—Braised Pork Shoulder (page 290)
- Arugula Salad with Roasted Squash, Currants, and Pine Nuts (page 198)
- Shortcakes with Citrus Compote and Orange Flower Whipped Cream (page 362)

MENU 3

- Fresh Heirloom Tomato Sauce with Burrata (page 234)
- Balsamic Caramel Chicken with Roasted Eggplant (page 264)
- Dulce de Leche—Fresh LemonCheesecake (page 368)

MENU 4

- Butter Lettuce Salad with Tahini-Honey Dressing (page 200)
- Brown Sugar Pork Chops with Mango-Horseradish Sauce (page 292)
- Sautéed Green Beans with Mustard-Soy Shallots (page 347)
- Creamy Butterscotch Pudding (page 354)

FARMERS' MARKET

- Roasted Carrot Soup with Toasted Coconut (page 188)
- Arugula Salad with Roasted Squash, Currants, and Pine Nuts (page 198)
- Fall Salad with Crisp Apples and Pickled Fennel (page 214)
- Raw Kale Salad with Heirloom Tomatoes and Roasted Cashews (page 202)
- Cold Cucumber Raita Soup (page 197)
- Fresh Pea and Fava Stew with Pistachio Gremolata (page 186)
- Caramelized Fennel Tarte Tatin (page 244)
- Plum Crisp with Toasted Almond—Cornmeal Topping (page 356)
- Pan-Seared Salmon with Three-Citrus Relish (page 326)
- Spinach Salad with Persimmons and Hazelnuts (page 201)
- Fresh Heirloom Tomato Sauce with Burrata (page 234)
- Steamed Snapper with Italian "Succotash" (page 336)
- Cranberry Bean Ragout with Olive-Citrus Butter (page 250)

DATE NIGHT

MENU 1

- Pistachio and Apricot Goat Cheese—Stuffed Chicken (page 276)
- Couscous (page 114)
- Sweet-Sour Wilted Greens with Crisp Bacon (page 351)
- Shortcakes with Citrus Compote and Orange Flower Whipped Cream (page 362)

MENU 2

- Spinach Salad with Persimmons and Hazelnuts (page 201)
- Prosciutto-Sage Chicken with Pan-Roasted Figs (page 278)
- Polenta (page 114)
- Creamy Butterscotch Pudding (page 354)

MENU 3

- Brown Sugar Pork Chops with Mango-Horseradish Sauce (page 292)
- Gingered Parsnips with Toasted Almonds (page 348)
- Raw Kale Salad with Heirloom Tomatoes and Roasted Cashews (page 202)
- Mango Custard Pie (page 370)

MENU 4

- Romaine Salad with Whisky Onions, Corn Bread, and Buttermilk Dressing (page 209)
- Lamb Chops with Fresh Cherry Salsa (page 300)
- Roasted Potatoes (page 111)
- Vanilla Bean Ice Cream with Chocolate-Covered Pretzel Bites (page 378)

FEED A CROWD

- Curried Chicken Soup with Roasted Peanuts (page 180)
- Smoky Black Bean, Beef, and Green Pepper Chili (page 192)
- Caribbean Jerk-Style Spareribs (page 295)
- Smoked Mozzarella, Zucchini, and Arugula Lasagna (page 232)
- Cajun Strata with Mustard Sour Cream (page 144)
- Apple Turnover Bread Pudding with Maple Cream Sauce (page 352)

HOSTESS GIFTS

- Peanut Butter—Banana Bread (page 173)
- Coconut-Chai Coffee Cake (page 360)
- Classic Sugar Cookies (page 372)

KID-FRIENDLY, NOT CHILDISH

- Tomato-Orange Soup with Grilled Cheese Croutons (page 194)
- Roasted Carrot Soup with Toasted Coconut (page 188)
- Sage-Maple Skillet Corn Bread (page 174)
- Oatmeal Breakfast Soufflé (page 126)
- Crêpes with Meyer Lemon Curd and Fresh Berries (page 132)
- Crisp Yeasted Waffles with Cocoa Whipped Cream (page 134)
- Hazelnut-Cocoa French Toast Sandwiches (page 129)
- Creamy Butterscotch Pudding (page 354)
- Vanilla Bean Ice Cream with Chocolate-Covered Pretzel Bites (page 378)
- Peach Melba Cream Popsicles (page 377)
- Itai-Style Meatballs (page 298)

MAKE-AHEAD

- Spiced Quinoa—Stuffed Bell Peppers (page 260)
- Roasted Carrot Soup with Toasted Coconut (page 188)
- Charred Chile and Hominy Corn Chowder (page 178)
- Curried Chicken Soup with Roasted Peanuts (page 180)
- Crisp Yeasted Waffles with Cocoa Whipped Cream (page 134)
- Cajun Strata with Mustard Sour Cream (page 144)
- Roasted Beet Salad with Creamy Caraway Dressing (page 212)
- Braised Chile Chicken with Raisins and Almonds (page 268)
- Cold Cucumber Raita Soup (page 197)
- Green Tea, Tofu, and Barley Soup (page 190)

MEATLESS MONDAY

- Spiced Quinoa—Stuffed Bell Peppers (page 260)
- Green Tea, Tofu, and Barley Soup (page 190)
- Roasted Carrot Soup with Toasted Coconut (page 188)
- Charred Chile and Hominy Corn Chowder (page 178)
- Oatmeal Breakfast Soufflé (page 126)
- Masala-Spiced Spinach Omelet (page 152)
- Swiss Chard, Oyster Mushroom, and Ricotta Frittata (page 154)
- Roasted Beet Salad with Creamy Caraway Dressing (page 212)
- Cold Cucumber Raita Soup (page 197)
- Fresh Pea and Fava Stew with Pistachio Gremolata (page 186)
- Triple-Mushroom Stroganoff (page 238)

STICK TO YOUR RIBS

- Cajun Strata with Mustard Sour Cream (page 144)
- Caribbean Jerk-Style Spareribs (page 295)
- Smoky Black Bean, Beef, and Green Pepper Chili (page 192)
- Braised Chile Chicken with Raisins and Almonds (page 268)
- Blood Orange—Braised Pork Shoulder (page 290)

ONE-DISH WONDER

- Curried Chicken Soup with Roasted Peanuts (page 180)
- Swiss Chard, Oyster Mushroom, and Ricotta Frittata (page 154)
- "Bacon" and Egg Breakfast Pizza (page 124)
- Country-Style Spanish Tortilla (page 150)
- Fresh Pea and Fava Stew with Pistachio Gremolata (page 186)
- Smoked Mozzarella, Zucchini, and Arugula Lasagna (page 232)
- Braised Chile Chicken with Raisins and Almond (page 268)

PICNICS AND OTHER OUTINGS

- Raw Kale Salad with Heirloom Tomatoes and Roasted Cashews (page 202)
- Roasted Beet Salad with Creamy Caraway Dressing (page 212)
- Summer Vegetable—Farro Salad (page 215)
- Purple Sweet Potato Salad with Green Beans and Peas (page 206)
- Caribbean Jerk-Style Spareribs (page 295)
- Country-Style Spanish Tortilla (page 150)
- Rosemary-Lemon Oven-Fried Chicken (page 282)

POTLUCK WINNER

- Buttermilk Biscuits with Black Pepper—Brown Butter (page 170)
- Crêpes with Meyer Lemon Curd and Fresh Berries (page 132)
- Cajun Strata with Mustard Sour Cream (page 144)
- Country-Style Spanish Tortilla (page 150)
- Purple Sweet Potato Salad with Green Beans and Peas (page 206)
- Caribbean Jerk-Style Spareribs (page 295)

SUMMER COOKOUT

MENU 1

- Purple Sweet Potato Salad with Green Beans and Peas (page 206)
- Grilled Huli Huli—Style Chicken (page 272)
- Summer Vegetable—Farro Salad (page 215)
- Mango Custard Pie (page 370)

MENU 2

- Coconut Mahi Mahi Ceviche with Chiles and Herbs (page 332)
- Cold Cucumber Raita Soup (page 197)
- Miso-Marinated Beef and Charred Vegetable Skewers (page 302)
- Grilled Tuna Steaks with Vietnamese-Style Slaw (page 320)
- Triple Citrus—Coconut Shortbread Bars (page 374)

MENU 3

- Summer Vegetable—Farro Salad (page 215)
- Broiled Asparagus with Tomatoes and Fresh Herbs (page 341)
- Bell Pepper Sauté with Toasted Walnuts (page 338)
- Steamed Snapper with Italian "Succotash" (page 336)
- Plum Crisp with Toasted Almond—Cornmeal Topping (page 356)

MENU 4

- Rosemary-Lemon Oven-Fried Chicken (page 282)
- Caribbean Jerk-Style Spareribs (page 295)
- Carrot and Currant Cabbage Slaw (page 342)
- Butter Lettuce Salad with Tahini-Honey Dressing (page 200)
- Peach Melba Cream Popsicles (page 377)

VEGETARIAN FAVORITE

- Charred Chile and Hominy Corn Chowder (page 178)
- Chipotle—Sweet Potato Hash with Poached Eggs and Avocado (page 146)
- Swiss Chard, Oyster Mushroom, and Ricotta Frittata (page 154)
- Fattoush Salad with Pita Crips (page 208)
- Summer Vegetable—Farro Salad (page 215)
- Cold Cucumber Raita Soup (page 197)
- Fresh Pea and Fava Stew with Pistachio Gremolata (page 186)
- Roasted Carrot Soup with Toasted Coconut (page 188)
- Mushroom "Patty" Melt (page 257)
- Indian "Burritos" with Curried Cauliflower (page 254)
- Caramelized Fennel Tarte Tatin (page 244)
- Charred Chile, Corn, and Zucchini Tacos (page 248)

WEEKEND PROJECT

- Almond Brioche Sticky Buns (page 156)
- Basic Yeasted White Bread (page 166)
- Crisp Yeasted Waffles with Cocoa Whipped Cream (page 134)
- Vanilla Bean Ice Cream with Chocolate-Covered Pretzel Bites (page 378)

WEEKNIGHT FAVORITE

- Peruvian Skirt Steak Stir-Fry (page 306)
- "Bacon" and Egg Breakfast Pizza (page 124)
- Cheat Sheet Beef Pho (Faux Pho Bo) (page 183)
- Pan-Roasted Pork Tenderloin with Orange-Molasses Glaze (page 312)
- Roasted Carrot Soup with Toasted Coconut (page 188)
- Mushroom "Patty" Melt (page 257)
- Mustard Greens and Lemongrass Beef Stir-Fry (page 304)
- Indian "Burritos" with Curried Cauliflower (page 254)
- Charred Chile, Corn, and Zucchini Tacos (page 248)
- Papaya Chicken Stir-Fry (page 285)
- Harissa-Marinated Cod with Braised Chickpeas (page 322)
- Roasted Squash Pasta with Sage Brown Butter (page 223)
- Panko-Crusted Tilapia with Tomatillo-Avocado Sauce (page 324)
- Shrimp Simmered in Garlicky Beer Sauce (page 333)

TO EAT NOW

- Creamy Baked Eggs with Hot-Smoked Salmon (page 149)
- Prosciutto-Sage Chicken with Pan-Roasted Figs (page 278)
- Shrimp Simmered in Garlicky Beer Sauce (page 333)
- Mushroom and Edamame Fried "Rice" (page 258)
- Indian "Burritos" with Curried Cauliflower (page 254)
- Peruvian Skirt Steak Stir-Fry (page 306)

Cooking from the Hip

Now it's time to riff on what you've learned. The following pages are dedicated to improving your kitchen skills and providing tips and techniques to help you become a more instinctive cook.

HOW TO RIFF

Keep Your Eyes (and Your Mouth) Open

The best way to become a better cook is to become a better eater. I don't mean to eat more, but to eat more mindfully. That's not to say you need to be spiritual about it but rather that you should commit intriguing food and meals to memory.

Confession: I always carry a journal and camera with me so that I can snap photos and jot down notes about my food experiences. Over time, this collection works like a culinary mood board. Many times a photo of a place or notes about a dish meld together to become one of my recipes, such as the swordfish that uses Persian flavors in a traditionally Italian technique (see Broiled Swordfish with Pomegranate-Mint Agrodolce, page 316).

Striking Balance
Once you're in the kitchen and cooking, the main thing to consider is striking balance in the dish. Here are the factors that I weigh in order to achieve a well-rounded dish.

FIVE TASTES

There are five general tastes and it's helpful to know them so you can identify the role each ingredient plays in your cooking. (Also, when a recipe is off in flavor or taste, it's usually because one of these elements is out of whack.)

Salty: salt, soy sauce, fish sauce, olives, capers, cheese, miso, anchovies

Sweet: sugar, honey, agave, maple syrup, sweet wine, fresh fruit, dried fruit, coconut milk, caramelized vegetables

Sour: vinegar, lemon juice, plum sauce, tamarind, kaffir lime, lime, mustard

Bitter: bitter greens, herbs, olives, mustard, cocktail bitters, tea, chocolate, walnuts, artichokes

Umami (a.k.a. savory): soy sauce, mushrooms, Parmigiano-Reggiano cheese, seaweed, miso, tomato, Worcestershire sauce

Balance isn't just about taste though, so also consider the following:

Weight: balance fat in the dish with acidity or bitterness or both

Temperature: balance hot and cold

Texture: balance crunchy and creamy

This may seem complicated but you don't need to incorporate every element in every dish. Just tuck this away in your memory, and, with time, it will become second nature to balance these elements in your food.

FIND YOUR CATALYST

Figure out what will be the central element of your dish. Here are the most common focal points:

Season: Cook what's in prime shape at the farmers' market.

Cuisine: Do you want to cook a specific cuisine? See Common Ingredients of Ethnic Cuisine (page 392) for more information about which flavors are paramount to different cuisines.

Ingredient: Is there an ingredient you've encountered but don't know how to use in the kitchen? This might be a perfect time to try it.

Cooking Equipment: Consider what equipment is available. If you're headed to a grilling party you shouldn't make something that requires a stove.

Experiential and Experimental: Do you have a dish that you want to re-create? Is there some travel, event, or memory that you want to translate into food? This is the most abstract of the ways to do food but it can be really rewarding when you realize that curry truly does taste amazing with chocolate.

The best way to achieve balance is to use complementary or contrasting flavors, much like an artist uses color.
Note: Umami works more as a background element to everything else rather than being complementary or contrasting.

	SALTY	SWEET	SOUR	BITTER
SALTY	N/A	COMPLEMENT	CONTRAST	COMPLEMENT
SWEET	COMPLEMENT	N/A	COMPLEMENT	CONTRAST
SOUR	CONTRAST	COMPLEMENT	N/A	COMPLEMENT
BITTER	COMPLEMENT	CONTRAST	COMPLEMENT	N/A

COMMON INGREDIENTS OF ETHNIC CUISINES

Each ethnic cuisine has a few primary ingredients that define its flavor. Being able to look at food through this perspective will help you better understand the basics of each cuisine. Just as knowledge of music theory gives you the confidence to do freestyle, learning these flavor profiles will help you to more easily mix, match, and manipulate them. These are also the ingredients you should to have on hand to cook these cuisines.

	COMMON INGREDIENTS	HERBS AND SPICES
CARRIBEAN	brown sugar/molasses, white vinegar/lime juice, coconut milk, chiles, garlic	ginger, nutmeg, allspice, cloves, cilantro
CHINESE	hoisin sauce, mushrooms, soy sauce, sesame, chiles, garlic, ginger, green onions	star anise, peppercorns, cloves, cinnamon
FRENCH	radishes, olives, red wine vinegar, mushrooms, Dijon mustard, garlic, wine	parsley, tarragon, chervil, bay leaf, thyme, peppercorns
GREEK	honey, dried fruit, tomatoes, lemon/vinegar, olives, feta, garlic	oregano, mint, cinnamon, anise
INDIAN	jaggery sugar, lemon/lime, tomatoes, yogurt, garlic, ginger, chiles, mustard	mint, cilantro, mustard seed, cloves, cardamom, coriander, cumin
ITALIAN	sugar, caramelized vegetables, tomatoes, Parmesan cheese, capers, balsamic vinegar/lemon, garlic, pine nuts	rosemary, oregano, basil, black pepper, fennel seeds, red pepper flakes, peppercorns
JAPANESE	mirin, sake, rice vinegar, soy, miso, seaweed, mushrooms, ginger, chiles, garlic	shiso, mitsuba, chives, Japanese chives
LATIN	sugar, lime, tomatoes, olives, chiles, beer, chocolate, almonds, ginger	cilantro, mint, cumin, cinnamon, oregano
MIDDLE EASTERN	honey, dried fruit, tomatoes, lemon/lime/vinegar, olives, yogurt, garlic, walnuts/almonds/sesame, pomegranate, red peppers	cilantro, mint, cinnamon, cloves, sumac, anise, cardamom
NORTH AFRICAN	honey, preserved lemons, tomatoes, ginger, red wine vinegar/lemon, garlic, ginger, dried fruit, almonds/sesame, yogurt	mint, peppercorns, paprika, cumin, coriander, cinnamon, saffron
SOUTHEAST ASIAN	coconut, tamarind, lime, fish sauce, chiles, lemongrass	cilantro, mint, galangal
SPANISH	anchovies, lemon, garlic, sherry, red bell peppers, tomatoes, orange, almond	saffron, paprika, parsley, thyme

COOKING FROM THE PANTRY

Keeping a well-stocked pantry (see page 56) isn't just for looks—it'll allow you to feed yourself even if you've arrived home late at night after a long day. In Part 3: The Recipes (page 122) there are quite a few recipes that can be tailored to accommodate what's available. A few to turn to are Swiss Chard, Oyster Mushroom, and Ricotta Frittata (page 154), Country-Style Spanish Tortilla (page 150), Masala-Spiced Spinach Omelet (page 152), and Mushroom and Edamame Fried "Rice" (page 258); swap the veggies for whatever you have on hand. Here are some other pantry-based recipe ideas:

SIMPLE TUNA–WHITE BEAN SALAD

Mix together a can or two of **oil-packed tuna** with a few handfuls of **pot beans** (page 112) (canned work here too), a few glugs of **oil**, a dash of **vinegar or citrus juice**, and any raw diced **veggies** you have on hand (such as celery, bell peppers, fennel, or scallions). Season with a handful of minced **fresh herbs** or 1 pinch dried **ground spice** (paprika, cayenne, coriander). Taste and season with **salt** or **pepper**, as desired. Serve on toast or over greens.

EGGS IN PURGATORY

Take **Basic Tomato Sauce** (page 116), add **some flavoring** (a spoonful of prepared harissa, chile-garlic sauce, or chopped olives), and a few chopped **roasted red peppers**. Simmer this mixture until just thickened, then crack **eggs** into the tomato sauce, cover, and simmer until the eggs are set. Taste and season with **salt or pepper**, as desired. If available, garnish with fresh herbs and serve with pita or bread for dipping.

SUPER-QUICK HUEVOS RANCHEROS

Heat the oven to 350°F/177°C/gas 4, grate **cheese** (Cheddar, Jack, or Parmesan work well) over **tortillas or flatbread**. Toast until the cheese is melted and the tortilla is golden and crisp. Meanwhile, make some poached (page 117) or fried (page 116) **eggs**. Layer the tortillas with the eggs, a drizzle of **salsa**, a handful of chopped **fresh herbs** (cilantro, parsley, or chives), and, as available, a few slices of **avocado or sour cream** or both.

LATE-NIGHT EGG SANDWICH

Cook up a fried **egg** (page 116) then place **bread** in the pan and toast, using the fat used to cook the egg. Slather the toast with your **favorite sandwich condiment** (like mustard, mayo, or pesto), some sliced **cured meat** (try prosciutto or Canadian bacon), and a slice of good **cheese**.

EGG-DROP SOUP

Heat **low-sodium vegetable, mushroom, or chicken broth** in a saucepan over medium heat until simmering. Stir in **any flavorings** you may have (such as a few slices of fresh ginger, a few garlic cloves, or some green onions). Whisk 1 or 2 **eggs** with a drizzle of **soy sauce or a pinch of salt** until smooth. Remove the soup from the heat, drizzle eggs into the pan in a circular motion, then stir to break the egg into strands. Taste and add any **condiments** you desire (like soy, chili garlic sauce, or herbs).

MISHMASH MINESTRONE

Add enough **oil** to coat the bottom of a saucepan then set over medium heat until shimmering. Stir in a handful each of finely chopped **carrots, celery**, and a few **cloves of garlic** and cook until golden. Add one 15-oz/430-g can **tomatoes** in their juices, 1 can of **water**, and a few cups of **pot beans** (page 112) or one 15-oz/430-g **can of beans or homemade beans** and simmer until flavors are melded and the soup is slightly thickened. Stir in a handful of shelled **peas**, a handful of chopped **green beans** or any **greens** you have on hand (like roughly chopped chard, kale, or spinach), along with a handful of chopped **fresh herbs** (such as parsley, basil, or a sprig of chopped rosemary), and simmer briefly. Taste and season with **salt or pepper**, as desired. Top with a grating of **hard cheese**, and a drizzle of **olive oil**.

TOMATO-BREAD SOUP

Add enough **oil** to coat the bottom of a saucepan and set over medium heat until shimmering. Add a few finely chopped **garlic cloves** and cook until golden brown. Add one 15-oz/430-g can **tomatoes** and their juices, 1 can **water**, and a pinch of **dried herbs** (such as oregano, basil, or even a clove or bay leaf). Bring to a simmer, tear up a few handfuls of crustless stale or toasted **French or ciabatta bread** and stir into the pan, and simmer until the mixture is porridge-like; remove the bay leaf. Taste and season with **salt or pepper**, as desired Garnish with a handful of chopped **fresh herbs** or a few gratings of a **hard aged cheese** or both. Drizzle with **olive oil** and **balsamic vinegar**.

TOMATO-MASALA SOUP

Add enough **oil** to coat a saucepan and set over medium heat until shimmering. Add half a roughly chopped **onion**, a few cloves of crushed **garlic**, and a pinch of **salt** and **black pepper**. Cook, stirring occasionally, until the onion is browned. Add a pinch of **garam masala** (or curry powder, paprika, or ras el hanout) and cook until fragrant. Add one 15-oz/430-g can diced **tomatoes** with their juices and a cup/240 ml of water or broth. Bring to a simmer and cook until tomatoes are very soft. Puree in batches in a blender until smooth. Taste and add more **salt or pepper**, as desired. Serve topped with a dollop of yogurt or toasted pappadum or pita, if available.

PASTA E BRODO

Add enough **oil** to coat the bottom of a saucepan and set over medium heat until shimmering. Add a few smashed **garlic cloves** and cook until fragrant. Add as much broth as you'd like and bring to a simmer. Add any **small pasta or grain** you have around (such as orzo, stars, couscous, or quinoa) and cook until al dente. Stir in a handful of sliced **green onions or chopped fresh herbs** or both, top with a grating of **hard cheese**, and season with **salt** and **pepper**. Taste and add more salt or pepper, as desired. Top with a drizzle of **olive oil** and serve.

ULTIMATE QUESADILLA

Heat a cast-iron skillet or frying pan over medium heat. Add 1 **flour tortilla**, top with a handful of grated **cheese** (such as Cheddar, Jack, or Swiss), **any of the following condiments** you may have on hand (diced roasted red peppers, a handful of chopped fresh herbs, wilted spinach, pickled jalapeños, sautéed onions and garlic), and another flour tortilla. Cook, flipping once, until the cheese is melted and the tortilla is golden.

BEAN AND GRAIN BURRITOS

Warm 4 **whole-wheat tortillas, pitas, or flatbread** then fill each with **quinoa** and **wilted greens** (see page 115), warmed **beans**, shredded **cheese**, sliced **avocado**, and some pickled **jalapeños, onions, or chile peppers**. Serve with sour cream or Greek yogurt.

SOUPED-UP GRILLED CHEESE

Heat a cast-iron skillet or frying pan over medium heat. Add 1 piece of **buttered bread**, a slather of **your favorite condiment** (such as mustard, horseradish, onion jam, red pepper spread, pesto, or mayo), and a handful of grated **cheese** (do a few different kinds). As desired, add **a few**

veggies or fruit (like sliced tomato, pickled jalapeños, kimchi, roasted peppers, apples, peaches, or pear). Top with another piece of buttered bread, and cook, flipping once, until the cheese is melted and bread is golden.

QUICK BREAD SALAD

Cut **tomatoes** and **cucumbers** in large dice and toss with **salt**; let sit for 20 minutes. Drain and add a few handfuls of **spinach or arugula**, a handful of torn **fresh herbs**, a glug of good **oil**, and a drizzle of **lemon juice** or any **wine vinegar**. Add day-old or toasted **bread** torn into bite-sized pieces, **salt**, and **pepper**, and toss to combine. Add more oil and vinegar as needed to amp up the flavor. Taste, add more salt or pepper, as desired, and serve.

POLENTA WITH DRIED MUSHROOMS AND CHEESE

Cook **polenta** (page 114). Meanwhile reconstitute some **dried mushrooms** by topping with heated **broth or alcohol** (such as vermouth, sherry, or marsala) or a combo thereof. When the polenta is done, stir in the mushrooms and a few spoons of **capers, roasted red peppers, or oil-packed sun-dried tomatoes** and cook until just warmed through. Top with a **creamy cheese** like Gorgonzola, Brie, or Crescenza and heat through. Serve with a handful of chopped fresh herbs and a grating of a good aged cheese or with a poached egg (page 117).

SIMPLE BREAKFAST FLATBREAD

Warm **flatbread or baked pizza dough** according to directions (see page 162). Slather with **crème fraîche, horseradish-spiked sour cream, or ricotta**. Top with **cured meat or smoked fish**, a handful of chopped **fresh herbs**, a handful of thinly sliced **red onion or green onions**, and a few grinds of **black pepper**.

TUNA SALAD

Combine some **oil-packed tuna or salmon** with a handful of diced **fennel, celery, or radish**; a handful of diced **red onion or scallion**; a handful of chopped **fresh herbs**; and a big spoonful of **mustard, horseradish, or miso**. Stir in a drizzle of **rice or wine vinegar**. Taste, season with **salt or pepper**, as desired, and serve.

SMOKED FISH PASTA

Cook 1 lb/455 g **dried pasta** according to package directions then drain, saving 1 cup/240 ml of cooking water. Meanwhile, add enough **oil** to a saucepan to coat the bottom, and heat over medium heat until shimmering. Add a handful of diced **onion**, a pinch of **red pepper flakes**, and a few **garlic cloves**, and cook until golden brown. Stir in **flaked smoked fish**, the drained pasta, and enough cooking water to make the sauce cling to the pasta. Season with **salt** and freshly ground **black pepper**, a handful of chopped **fresh herbs** (such as parsley, cilantro, chives), and a dollop of **crème fraîche or a drizzle of heavy cream**.

BLACK BEAN AND CORN PASTA

Cook 1 lb/455 g of **dried pasta** according to package directions then drain, saving 1 cup/240 ml of cooking water. Meanwhile, add enough **oil** to a saucepan to coat the bottom, and heat over medium heat until shimmering. Add a handful of diced **onion** and a few **garlic cloves** and cook until golden. Stir in some **pot beans** (page 112) or one 15-oz/430-g can drained and rinsed **black beans** and equal parts fresh or frozen **corn kernels**. Add enough **broth** to cover and bring to a simmer. When everything is tender, add a handful of chopped **fresh herbs** (such as parsley, cilantro, or chives), and, if desired, a few chopped **jalapeños**. Simmer until the flavors are melded and sauce is thickened. Add pasta and enough cooking water to coat the pasta. Taste and season with **salt** and **pepper**, as desired. Crumble a soft goat cheese or grate a hard cheese over the top and serve.

HERBED BROWN BUTTER PASTA

Cook 1 lb/455 g of **dried pasta** according to package directions then drain, saving 1 cup/240 ml of cooking water. Meanwhile, make **brown butter** (page 93) and add 2 sprigs of **any woody herbs** (thyme, rosemary, marjoram, sage) so it perfumes the butter. Discard the herbs. Add the pasta to the brown butter then add just enough pasta water to make it cling to the pasta. Taste and season with **salt and pepper**, as desired. Shave any **hard aged cheese** over the top and serve immediately.

SLOW-ROASTED GARLIC CREAM PASTA

Make slow-roasted **garlic** (page 115). When it's 10 minutes from being done, cook 1 lb/455 g of **dried pasta** according to package directions then drain, saving 1 cup/240 ml of the cooking water. Return the pasta pot over medium-low heat, add enough **half-and-half** to make a sauce, stir in the roasted garlic, and simmer until slightly thickened. Add the drained pasta and enough pasta water and **olive oil** to coat the pasta. Taste and season with **salt** and **pepper**, as desired. Grate in some **good aged cheese** (like a Pecorino, Parmesan, Manchego, or Cheddar), and serve immediately.

BAKED CREAMY CHEESE PASTA

Cook 1 lb/455 g of **dried pasta** according to package directions then drain, saving 1 cup/240 ml of the cooking water. Make Baked Brie (page 398) with any **soft-rind cheese** you have on hand (such as Brie, Camembert, triple-cream) then dump into the pot along with the drained pasta and enough cooking water to make it creamy. Taste and add more **salt** and **pepper**, as desired. Serve immediately.

VEGETABLE TAJINE

Heat **olive oil** in a large, heavy pot over medium-high heat. Add **onion** and **garlic** and cook until golden. Add a pinch of **any North African spice** you may have (like paprika, cumin, ginger, ras el hanout), garlic, and **tomato paste**; stir 1 minute. Add some cut-up **root vegetables** (such as carrots, sweet potatoes, turnips, or rutabaga) and if you have it, some **olives or sun-dried tomatoes** or both. Cover with **broth or water** and simmer, partially covered, until vegetables are tender. If available, stir in roughly chopped **fresh parsley, cilantro**, and **mint**. Season to taste with **salt** and **pepper** and serve.

VEGETARIAN POSOLE

Add enough **oil** to a heavy-bottomed large pot to coat the bottom. Heat over medium-high heat. When the oil shimmers, add ½ finely chopped **onion** and a few cloves of minced **garlic** and cook until golden. Add one 15-oz/430-g can **hominy**, 1 can diced **tomatoes**, about 1 can **water or low-sodium vegetable broth**, and a few chopped **chipotles en adobo**. Simmer until the flavors are melded and liquid slightly thickened. Serve topped with **any Mexican condiments** you have on hand (baked tortilla chips, radishes, sour cream, avocado, lime wedges, shredded cabbage).

PANTRY PIZZA

Heat the oven to 425°F/220°C/gas 7. Defrost frozen homemade (page 163) or storebought **pizza dough** and roll it to a 12-inch/30.5-cm round. Top it with **tomato sauce** (page 116) **or pesto** (pages 140 and 218), and crumbled or **grated cheese**. Top with **any of the following of items** you have on hand: marinated artichoke hearts, olives, and roasted red peppers. Cook until heated through then serve topped with **greens**, additional cheese, and a drizzle of **olive oil**.

SIMPLE PEANUT NOODLES

Blend together 1 part each **honey** and **soy**, 2 parts **rice vinegar**, and 4 to 6 parts **peanut butter**. Add water to thin it to the consistency of melted ice cream then stir in minced **garlic** and grated **ginger**, as desired. Toss with cooked **soba noodles or whole-wheat spaghetti**, some sliced **bell pepper**, some thinly sliced **English cucumber**, a few sliced **green onions**, and chopped toasted **peanuts**.

VEGETARIAN TURNOVERS

Heat the oven to 400°F/200°C/gas 6. Defrost **pie or puff pastry dough** and cut into individual serving-sized squares (4 in/10cm). Top half of each square with **whatever you have on hand** (sautéed mushrooms, grated cheese, frozen peas or edamame, roasted red peppers, green onions). Fold in half to form a triangle, press edge of seam with fork tines to seal, brush with egg wash (1 **egg yolk** mixed with a few tablespoons **water** until smooth), and bake until the pastry is golden brown throughout and dry. Serve immediately.

STRESS-FREE APPETIZERS

Oh, appetizers—they're so often overly fussy or overlooked. But a well-executed appetizer makes for a memorable start to a meal. Some of the recipes you've already come across can also work as appetizers like Broiled Asparagus with Tomatoes and Fresh Herbs (page 341) or Sautéed Green Beans with Mustard-Soy Shallots (page 347), or by turning Fresh Cherry Salsa (page 301) into a dip, or adding Pickled Fennel (page 214) to a cheese board.

Here are a few more ideas that are low-maintenance. (For dips and salsas, check out the section that follows, beginning on page 406.)

BAKED BRIE

Heat the oven to 350°F/177°C/gas 4. Top a piece of **semisoft cheese** (like Camembert, Brie, or Taleggio) with a handful of **pine nuts or walnuts**, a few sprigs of **thyme, oregano, marjoram, or rosemary**, and a drizzle of both **oil** and **honey**. Bake until bubbly then top with freshly cracked ground **pepper** and serve immediately.

SERVE WITH: dried fruit, crackers, and cured meats

BAKED RICOTTA

Heat the oven to 325°F/165°C/gas 3 and arrange a rack in the upper third. Coat a small (about 1 qt/ 960 ml) baking dish with some **olive oil** and set aside. Mix together 3 lb/1.4 kg **ricotta**, ¼ cup/30 g grated **hard cheese** (such as Parmigiano-Reggiano, Manchego, or Pecorino), 2 tablespoons of **olive oil**, and grated zest of 1 **orange**. Taste and add **salt** and **pepper**, as desired. Evenly spread the ricotta mixture in the baking dish, sprinkle another ¼ cup/30 g grated hard cheese on top, and drizzle with olive oil. Bake until bubbly and the Parmesan on top is melted, 20 to 25 minutes.

SERVE WITH: crackers, fresh sliced figs, and onion jam

SPICED KETTLE CORN

Heat a large, heavy-bottomed pot over medium heat. When it's hot, add enough **vegetable oil** to coat the bottom of the pan, add a few handfuls of **popcorn**, cover, and shake continuously until the majority of the corn is popped. When popping slows down, remove from the heat, and immediately season with a pinch of **salt**, a pinch of **sugar**, and a **spice mixture** such as chili powder, Japanese furikake, curry powder, ras el hanout, or Chinese five-spice, and toss to coat. Serve immediately.

BROILED MUSSELS

Heat the broiler. Clean **mussels** (page 81) and place on a rimmed baking sheet. Broil until mussels open then serve topped with **pesto** (pages 140 and 218) **or green chutney** (page 329).

OYSTERS ROCKEFELLER-ESQUE

Heat a few tablespoons of **butter** in a medium pan over medium heat until it is nut brown and smells toasted. Immediately remove from the heat and swirl in a few minced **shallots**, a shot of **anise-flavored liqueur** (such as Pernod, absinthe, or ouzo), and a few handfuls of chopped fresh **Italian parsley**. Heat the broiler, arrange rack in upper third, shuck **oysters** (page 106), and place the oyster halves (filled with liquid and meat) on a bed of **rock salt** on a rimmed baking sheet. Drizzle each oyster with butter sauce and broil until the oysters are cooked through. Serve immediately.

BLISTERED PEPPERS WITH SALT

Find some **mild peppers** such as shishito, banana, or Padrón peppers. Heat about ½ in/ 12 mm **vegetable oil** in a large frying pan over medium-high heat until it's good and hot but not smoking. (The oil is ready when you dip peppers in and tiny bubbles form around the pepper.) Add clean, very dry peppers and cook over high heat, turning occasionally, until they blister. Remove to a paper towel to drain then sprinkle with **sea salt** and serve.

SPICED CRISP CHICKPEAS

Gather some cooked **chickpeas** (this appetizer goes fast so you'll need a few handfuls per guest). Whisk together a handful of **flour** and a pinch of **salt, pepper**, and **spices** (try smoked paprika, ground cumin, ground coriander, or a spice mix like curry powder). Toss chickpeas in the flour mixture then place in a sieve and tap to remove any excess flour. Meanwhile, heat about ½ in/12 mm of **oil** in a large frying pan over medium-high heat until it's good and hot but not smoking. (The oil is ready when you dip chickpeas in and tiny bubbles form around them.) Add the chickpeas and cook over high heat, turning occasionally, until they "sing," puff up, and are golden. Remove to a paper towel to drain. Taste and add more salt, as desired. Serve.

ROASTED RAW ALMONDS

Heat the oven to 400°F/200°C/gas 6. Toss **raw almonds** with a glug of **olive oil**, a pinch of **salt**, a few smashed **garlic cloves**, and a few **thyme, oregano, or rosemary sprigs**. Spread the nuts on a rimmed baking sheet in one layer and roast, turning occasionally, until the nuts are golden and toasted. Remove from the oven and toss with some grated **orange zest**. Taste and add more salt, as desired, and serve.

SPICED NUTS

Heat the oven to 375°F/190°C/gas 5. Whisk together 1 or 2 **egg whites**, a pinch each of **salt**, freshly ground **black pepper, brown sugar**, and **spices** (such as mustard powder, celery seed, or ground fennel seed). Toss with enough **raw, unsalted nuts** to coat well. Spread the nuts on a rimmed baking sheet in one layer and roast, turning occasionally, until the nuts are golden and toasted. Remove from the oven, taste, and toss with additional salt as needed, and serve.

CITRUS TOASTS

Make **Three-Citrus Relish** (page 326) and serve it on toasted **bread** slathered with a good **soft cheese** (Cotija, feta, goat cheese, or ricotta). Top with a pinch of **salt**, some freshly ground **black pepper**, a drizzle of **olive oil**, and serve.

BRESAOLA STUFFED WITH PESTO

Make a **pesto** recipe such as the arugula pesto (page 140) or the creamy pesto (page 218). Lay out some **bresaola** (about ½ lb/230 g works for 10 to 15 people as an appetizer) or other cured meat (try prosciutto or Serrano ham) on a clean work surface and put a dollop of pesto in the middle of each piece of meat. Roll meat up to enclose filling and set on a serving platter. Repeat until all the bresaola is used up. (Can be made up to 4 hours ahead and refrigerated in an airtight container.)

SALT-ROASTED BABY BEETS

Heat the oven to 350°F/177°C/gas 4. Cut off the ends of **beets**, wash, and trim. Bury in a mound of **salt**, and roast until the beets are knife-tender, about 1 hour. Let cool slightly, then peel with a paper towel under running water. Halve the beets, toss with **oil**, and season with **lemon juice or vinegar**, as desired. Serve scattered with feta, Cotija, or shaved ricotta salata **cheese**; place on a skewer with cubed feta cheese; or serve with one of the dips in the following section (see page 406).

RICOTTA SALATA, FIG, AND HONEY CROSTINI

Simple enough to always remember and easily riff on. Top toasted **bread** with **ricotta salata or farmer's cheese**, a few sliced figs, and a drizzle of **olive oil**, and **honey or balsamic vinegar** or both. Add a pinch of **salt** and some freshly ground **black pepper** and serve.

TOMATO-OLIVE TART

Heat the oven to 400°F/200°C/gas 6. Thaw and unroll a piece of store-bought **puff pastry**. Meanwhile, toss a handful of halved **olives**, a few handfuls of halved **cherry, grape, or Sweet 100 tomatoes**, and a handful of **bocconcini mozzarella (little mozzarella balls) or large-dice mozzarella** with a drizzle of **olive oil** and pinch of **fresh thyme, oregano, or marjoram leaves**. Cut the puff pastry into individual-serving-sized squares. Divide the tomato mixture evenly among the puff pastry squares. Bake until the pastry is puffed, golden, and cooked through, the tomatoes soften, and the cheese begins to melt. Drizzle with olive oil, sprinkle with **salt** and **pepper**, and serve immediately.

VARIATION: Toss the tomatoes with pomegranate molasses, red pepper flakes, fresh thyme leaves, fresh rosemary leaves, capers, or minced garlic.

BACON-WRAPPED DATES

Such a classic, it's essential you know how to make them. Heat the oven to 350°F/177°C/gas 4. Wrap pitted **dates** (preferably Medjool variety) with enough **bacon** to fit around with a ½-in/12-mm overhang. Secure with a toothpick and bake until the bacon is crisp.

VARIATION: You can stuff the dates with blue cheese or mascarpone before baking. It also works well with bacon wrapped around scallops, shrimp, fresh figs, and dried apricots.

PROSCIUTTO-WRAPPED ASPARAGUS

Another classic that fails to get old. Heat the oven to 400°F/200°C/gas 6. Toss **asparagus** spears with **olive oil** and freshly ground **black pepper.** Wrap with a thin slice of **prosciutto** (can also add a thin slice of provolone as desired) and roast until the prosciutto is crisp.

ROASTED GRAPES WITH BLUE CHEESE

Heat the oven to 350°F/177°C/gas 4. Toss **grapes** with **olive oil, salt**, and freshly ground **black pepper**. Spread on a rimmed baking sheet and roast until fork-tender. Drizzle with **balsamic vinegar** and toss to combine. Serve with **crackers** and mild **blue cheese or a spreadable cheese** such as fresh goat cheese.

APPLE OR PEAR CHIPS

Heat the oven to 200°F/95°C. Combine **sugar** and a pinch of **spices** (ground cloves, ground cinnamon, ground cayenne all work well) in a small bowl and mix until evenly combined. Stem the **fruit** and, using a mandoline (page 67) or a very sharp knife, carefully slice lengthwise into paper-thin slices, about ⅟₁₆ in/2 mm thick. Line rimmed baking sheets with parchment paper or silicone baking mats and evenly space the fruit on the sheets. Sprinkle sugar mixture over the fruit and bake until lightly brown, dry, and crisp around the edges, about 2 hours. Let cool on the baking sheets. Can be stored at room temperature in an airtight container for up to 10 days.

HAWAIIAN POKE

Get some high-quality **sushi-grade fish** (ahi tuna is a classic) and cut it into large dice. Drizzle with **soy sauce** and **sesame oil** then add grated fresh **ginger**, some thinly sliced **sweet onions**, and thinly sliced **chiles**, and toss to coat. Cover and refrigerate at least 2 hours before serving. Top with toasted **sesame seeds** and thinly sliced **green onions** and serve with chopsticks or chips.

FRITTATA BITES

Make the **Country-Style Spanish Tortilla** (page 150) **or the frittata** (page 117) and let cool. Cut into squares and serve topped with a dollop of **sour cream** or a scattering of chopped fresh **cilantro, parsley, or chives**. Alternatively, bake them in greased mini muffin tins and serve like individual crustless quiches.

WATERMELON SKEWERS

Toss cubes of **watermelon** with **olive oil, salt**, and **pepper** and alternately thread on a skewer with cubes of **feta** and **mint or basil**. Drizzle with reduced **balsamic vinegar** (page 57) and serve.

GRILLED CHEESE BITES

Heat the oven to 425°F/220°C/gas 7. Obviously, the combinations are almost endless here. At its most simple, grate your **favorite melting cheese** (or cut if soft like Brie), load it on a slice of **bread** cut ½ in/12 mm thick, close it with another bread slice, and brush the outside of the sandwich with melted **butter**. Any one of those elements can vary and you can add condiments like hot-spicy mustard or marmalade. I also like to melt a compound butter (page 410) and brush that on the outside for extra flavor. Bake until golden, crisp, and the cheese is melted. Skewer with a toothpick every inch or so, cut into small bites, and serve.

VARIATION: Brie, fresh cherries, and balsamic vinegar; mozzarella and orange marmalade with rosemary butter; mascarpone, bananas, and Nutella; avocado, Cheddar, and pickled jalapeños.

ROASTED OVEN FRIES

Heat the oven to 450°F/230°C/gas 8. Cut any assortment of **potatoes** (russets, sweet potatoes, or purple potatoes) into wedges and throw into water mixed with a dash of **vinegar** to soak a few minutes. Drain, pat very dry, and toss with **olive oil, salt**, and **pepper** (or other spices such as za'atar, curry powder, paprika, or cayenne). Spread on a baking sheet in a single layer and roast until golden brown and fork-tender. Serve with sour cream or yogurt dip (see page 406 for ideas) or with other traditional fry condiments.

ROASTED CHICKEN SKEWERS

Cut the **chicken** into small dice and marinate in one of the **various marinades** such as Mojo, Balsamic Cherry, Beer Lemon, or Apple Cider Mustard (or one of the marinades on page 412). Heat the oven to 450°F/230°C/gas 8 and spread the chicken on a rimmed baking sheet. Roast until the juices run clear and the chicken is cooked through, basting with excess marinade occasionally. Serve with toothpicks and a dip (page 406).

CUBAN SANDWICH BITES

Heat the oven to 425°F/220°C/gas 7. Cut a loaf of crusty **French bread or baguette** in half lengthwise. Layer **mustard** on one half of the bread then top with **pickles, roast pork, ham**, and **provolone or Swiss cheese**. Drizzle with **Mojo** (see page 412), close, and press to flatten. Place the sandwich on a baking sheet. Weight the sandwich down with a heavy object (a filled teapot, a brick wrapped in foil, or a frying pan works well) for a few minutes until flattened slightly. Bake until the bread is toasted and the cheese is melted, turning over halfway through. Let rest a few minutes. Skewer with a toothpick every inch or so, cut into small bites, and serve.

PRESSED SANDWICH

Halve a **baguette** lengthwise and pull out most of the interior bread. Slather the bread with **olive paste** (a.k.a. Tapenade, page 405), mustard, or pesto (pages 140 and 218) then layer on **roasted red peppers, mozzarella**, some **salami** (as desired), and **sun-dried tomatoes**. Wrap the sandwich in parchment or waxed paper then aluminum foil. Place the sandwich on a baking sheet. Weight the sandwich down with a heavy object (a filled teapot, a brick wrapped in foil, or a frying pan works well) for a few minutes until flattened slightly. Skewer with a toothpick every inch or so, cut into small bites, and serve. (Great for picnics too, if left whole.)

TOFU BANH MI BITES

Cut **tofu** into rectangles then marinate in a mixture of **soy, sugar, garlic, ginger**, and **green onions** while the oven heats up. Heat the oven to 400°F/200°C/gas 6. Remove the tofu from the marinade, place on a baking sheet, and bake until golden brown. Meanwhile, halve a **baguette** lengthwise and pull out most of the interior bread. Spread with **mayonnaise**, and layer roasted tofu, **pickled cucumber**, shaved **radishes** and **carrots**, and a few slices of **jalapeños**. Wrap the sandwich in parchment or waxed paper then aluminum foil. Place the sandwich on a baking sheet. Weight the sandwich down with a heavy object (a filled teapot, a brick wrapped in foil, or a frying pan works well) for a few minutes until flattened slightly. Skewer with a toothpick every inch or so, cut into small bites and serve. (Great for picnics too, if left whole.)

KALE CHIPS

Heat the oven to 300°F/150°C/gas 2. Remove the ribs from 2 bunches of **kale** (preferably curly), tear into bite-sized pieces, and place on a rimmed baking sheet. Drizzle with toasted **sesame oil**, add a dollop of **white miso**, and rub between fingers until thoroughly coated. Arrange leaves in single layers on a few (you may need 2 or 3) baking sheets (lined with parchment paper for easier cleanup). Bake until crisp and golden brown but not burnt, about 20 minutes. Best when eaten within a few hours.

SPICED MUSHROOM POPCORN

Heat the oven to 450°F/230°C/gas 8 or a grill to medium-high. Toss some cleaned, halved **wild mushrooms** (you'll need ¼ lb/225 g raw mushrooms per person as an appetizer because they cook down significantly) with some **olive oil, salt, pepper**, and a **spice mixture** such as ras el hanout, garam masala, or curry powder. Roast the mushrooms, turning occasionally, until crisp and browned. Remove from the oven, toss with a drizzle of **balsamic vinegar**, and serve. Best when eaten within a few hours.

WARMED OLIVES

Place 8 oz/225 g of mixed **oil-cured and brine-cured olives** (such as niçoise, kalamata, picholine, Cerignola, or Moroccan) in a large frying pan and place over medium heat. Add a drizzle of **olive oil** and some combination of **herbs and spice** such as orange peel, rosemary, and garlic; bay leaves and peppercorns; dried chiles, fennel seed, and lemon peel.

ROASTED EDAMAME

Heat the oven to 375°F/190°C/gas 5. Rinse 1 pound shelled **edamame** (soy beans) and drain well. Place the edamame in a bowl and toss with a few glugs of **olive oil, salt**, and **pepper** (or **other seasonings** such as dry mustard, curry, Chinese five-spice, cayenne). Taste and add more seasonings if desired. Spread in a single layer on a rimmed baking sheet and roast, stirring occasionally, until the edamame are puffed and golden brown. Best when eaten within a few hours.

FLAVOR BOOSTERS

It happens to the best cooks out there: you taste test a dish and it's good, but not amazing. First, check out Striking Balance (see page 390) for inspiration as to what you can do with the ingredients in the recipe you already have. If that's not doing it, or you just want extra oomph, look here. I call these garnishes and condiments flavor boosters, which are like flair for your food. I've already used a few in recipes like Pistachio Gremolata (page 186) for the fava stew, or Mango-Horseradish Sauce (page 292) for the pork chops, but here are a few more ideas.

NEEDS: MORE RICHNESS

Infused Oil

Add the grated zest of a few **lemons or oranges** or both to a few cups of **mild peanut, olive, or grapeseed oil**. Cover and store in a cold, dark place until the oil is flavorful, about 3 to 4 days. Use within 2 weeks.

VARIATION: Infuse the oil with cinnamon sticks, smashed cardamom, rosemary sprigs, thyme sprigs, garlic, or dried chiles.

USE: As a finishing oil to drizzle over ready-to-serve dishes or in vinaigrettes.

Brown Butter

Make **brown butter** (page 93) and add **something aromatic** such as capers, herbs, or red pepper flakes and cook until fragrant (careful, as the butter may sputter when the ingredients are added). Immediately remove from the heat and use.

USE: As a quick pasta sauce, atop sautéed fish, to finish a dip, folded into cookie batter in place of regular butter.

NEEDS: MORE SPICE

Pineapple Sambal

Combine a few cups diced fresh **pineapple** with ½ grated **red onion**, a minced fresh **chile**, a few minced **garlic cloves**, a spoonful of grated fresh **ginger**, and equal parts **lime juice** and Asian **fish sauce**. Stir in some fresh **mint or cilantro** and some **brown sugar**, as desired. Refrigerate until ready to use. Will last 4 to 6 days.

VARIATION: Make with mango, cucumber, or papaya.

Piccalilli

Mix together a few chopped **cucumbers** with some roughly chopped **bell peppers**, some minced **red onions**, a pinch of **sugar**, and some **red wine vinegar**. When the onion flavor is mellowed out, stir in a combination of **red pepper flakes, celery seed**, and **mustard seed**.

USE: As a garnish for grilled fish or chicken.

Harissa-Spiked Cheese Spread

In a food processor fitted with the metal blade, combine **harissa paste** (or chili garlic sauce) with **feta, ricotta, or goat cheese** and pulse with **olive oil** until evenly combined. Serve topped with a drizzle of olive oil and some freshly ground black pepper.

USE: As a garnish or a dip.

NEEDS: CRUNCH

Croutons

Heat the oven to 350°F/177°C/gas 4. Dice **day-old bread**, drizzle with **oil or melted butter**, toss until well coated, and season with **salt**, and freshly ground **black pepper**. Spread on a rimmed baking sheet and bake until golden brown and crisp.

VARIATION: Toss with brown butter before roasting, toss with grated Parmesan when just removed from the oven, or add minced garlic, minced parsley, celery salt, or caraway seed to bread before tossing.

Crisp Shallots

Heat ½ in/12 mm of **neutral oil** (like canola or peanut) in a frying pan over medium heat. Toss thinly sliced **shallots** with seasoned flour (**flour** mixed with **salt, pepper**, and any other ground **spices** desired) to coat, and knock off excess flour. Oil is ready when you place a shallot in the pan and small bubbles of oil form around it. Add the shallots to oil, stir briefly so they can cook evenly, and cook until golden brown. Transfer the shallots to a paper towel–lined plate.

USE: As a garnish or a snack.

NEEDS: A HIGH NOTE OF FLAVOR

Meyer Lemon Crème Fraîche

Mix together **Meyer lemon juice**, fresh **chives**, and **crème fraîche** with a dash of **salt**.

USE: As a garnish or a dip.

Pickle

Use the method for quick pickling radish (page 211) and swap thinly sliced **carrots, fennel, or cucumbers** for the radishes. When ready to serve, spread **toasts** with **ricotta, hummus, or another bean spread**, and top with pickle. Sprinkle good salt on top and serve.

USE: As an appetizer or garnish.

NEEDS: MORE SAVORY FLAVOR

Pan-Roasted Tomatoes

Halve **plum, cherry, or grape tomatoes** and toss with **olive oil, salt**, and **pepper**. Heat a pan over medium-high heat and add the tomatoes, cut-side down, and cook until browned and starting to soften, 3 to 5 minutes. Top with a squeeze of **citrus juice or drizzle of vinegar**. Taste and season with salt and pepper, as desired.

USE: As a garnish.

Tapenade

In a food processor fitted with the metal blade, pulse pitted **olives** with a few **anchovies**, a few **capers**, some **red wine vinegar** and a few **garlic cloves** until evenly combined but still a tad chunky. Stir in minced fresh **parsley or basil**, as desired.

USE: As a garnish or a dip.

Muhammara Dip

In a food processor fitted with the metal blade, pulse together a few **roasted peppers**, 1 fresh **chile**, a squeeze of **lemon juice,** a handful of toasted **bread crumbs or walnuts**, a drizzle of **pomegranate molasses**, a few smashed **garlic cloves**, and a pinch of **cumin** until evenly combined but still a tad chunky. Stir in minced fresh **cilantro or parsley**, as desired.

USE: As a garnish or a dip.

Roasted Nut and Date Spread

Heat the oven to 400°F/200°C/gas 6. Combine a few handfuls of **shelled nuts** (walnuts, almonds, pistachios, or pecans) on a rimmed baking sheet and toss with **olive oil**, a pinch of ground **cinnamon or cloves**, and some **salt** and freshly ground **black pepper**. Roast until the nuts are toasted. Place in a food processor fitted with the metal blade and pulse until evenly ground up. Add a few handfuls of roughly chopped **Medjool dates or dried figs**, the grated **zest of 1 orange**, a few drizzles of a **sweet wine** such as Marsala or sherry. Pulse to create a smooth paste. Season with salt and freshly ground black pepper. Serve with cheeses, crackers, and dried fruit.

USE: As a garnish or a spread.

GARNISHES AND DIPS

Creamy mixes can be used as garnishes, as dips, or even as marinades (for example, the tuna, page 320). An easy way to mix one up is to mix mayonnaise, sour cream, or yogurt with a sauce you've already made like tapenade (page 405) or an herb garnish (page 414).

The basic make-up of these sauces is as follows:

MAYONNAISE (OR)
SOUR CREAM (OR)
PLAIN YOGURT (OR)
OIL + SEASONINGS + SALT

HORSERADISH CREAM

Fold a few tablespoons each grated **lemon zest** and prepared **horseradish** into some **sour cream** along with a few small diced tart **green apples** (optional). Season with **sugar, salt**, and freshly ground **black pepper**, as desired. Let sit at least 30 minutes before serving.

AIOLI

Stir some **mayo** with a few cloves of roasted garlic (page 115) and a dollop of **Dijon mustard**. Season with **salt** and freshly ground **black pepper**, as desired.

TARTAR

Stir together 1 part **mayo or sour cream** and 1 part **mustard** with a few spoonfuls chopped **capers, pickles** (preferably cornichons), and fresh **chives**. Season with **salt** and freshly ground **black pepper**, as needed.

BUTTERMILK DIP

Stir together 1 part **mayo** or plain **whole-milk Greek yogurt** and 1 part **buttermilk** with a few spoonfuls of snipped fresh **chives** and chopped fresh **dill**. Season with **salt** and freshly ground **black pepper**, as needed.

SUN-DRIED TOMATO-BASIL

Blend together 1 part **mayo or plain whole-milk Greek yogurt** with 1 part chopped **sun-dried tomatoes**. Stir in a few dashes **red wine vinegar**, a pinch of **sugar**, and a few handfuls of fresh **basil leaves**. Season with salt and freshly ground **black pepper**, as needed.

CARAMELIZED ONION

Blend together 1 part **sour cream or plain whole-milk Greek yogurt** with 1 part **Onion Jam or caramelized onions** (page 116) with a few spoonfuls of **soy sauce, sugar, rice vinegar**, and toasted **sesame seeds**. Stir in thinly sliced **green onions or fresh chives** before serving.

CURRIED

Stir together 1 part **sour cream or plain whole-milk Greek yogurt** with a few pinches of **curry powder**, some grated **lemon zest**, a few spoonfuls minced **pickles**, and a spoonful of strong **mustard**. Season with **salt** and freshly ground **black pepper**, as needed.

CHILI-GARLIC

Blend together 1 part **red wine vinegar** with 4 parts **mayo**, a dollop of **chili garlic paste**, and a few spoonfuls **tomato paste**. Garnish with toasted **sesame seeds**.

VINAIGRETTES

Useful for a salad, as a garnish, to easily flavor cooked vegetables, or to spoon over as an instant sauce, vinaigrettes are something you must master.

VINAIGRETTE FORMULA: 1 part acid (vinegar or citrus) plus 3 to 4 parts oil.

For a refresher on how to make a vinaigrette check out page 198.

HONEY-POPPY SEED

Blend together 1 part **red wine vinegar** with 1 part **honey**, 3 to 4 parts **olive oil**, and a few spoonfuls of **poppy seeds**. Stir in minced fresh **chives**, as desired, and season with **salt** and freshly ground **black pepper**.

CILANTRO-LIME

Blend together 1 part **lime juice** with 3 to 4 parts **oil**, a dash of **agave nectar or honey**, and some minced fresh **cilantro**. Season with **salt** and freshly ground **black pepper**.

SHERRY-BALSAMIC

Whisk together 1 part **sherry vinegar**, 1 part **balsamic vinegar**, and 1 minced **shallot** and set aside for 10 to 15 minutes. Whisk in 4 parts **olive oil**, and a spoonful of roasted **garlic** (page 115). Season with **salt** and freshly ground **black pepper**.

SICHUAN PEPPERCORN

Whisk together 1 part **balsamic vinegar** with a dash of **soy sauce** and toasted **sesame oil**, a drizzle of **honey**, and 3 parts **canola or peanut oil**. Stir in cracked **Sichuan peppercorns** (can substitute black peppercorns), and season with **salt** and freshly ground **black pepper**.

DATE VINAIGRETTE

Blend together 1 part **red wine vinegar** with 1 part **cider vinegar** and 3 parts **olive oil**, 1 minced **shallot**, and a few handfuls pitted chopped **dates**. Stir in a small pinch of ground **cinnamon**, as desired, and season with **salt** and freshly ground **black pepper**.

MARMALADE VINAIGRETTE

Blend together 1 part **marmalade** with 2 parts **red wine vinegar** and 2 to 4 parts **olive oil**. Stir in minced **garlic** and minced fresh **thyme**, as desired. Season with **salt** and freshly ground **black pepper**.

ROASTED RED PEPPER

Blend a few spoonfuls minced **roasted red pepper** with a spoonful of **mustard**, 1 minced **garlic clove**, 1 part **sherry vinegar**, and 3 parts **olive oil**. Season with **salt** and freshly ground **black pepper**.

MANGO-CHILE VINAIGRETTE

Blend ripe **mango** with **red wine vinegar**, fresh **chiles, olive oil**, and grated fresh **ginger**. Season with **salt** and freshly ground **black pepper**.

APPLE CIDER-MUSTARD

Whisk together 1 part **hard apple cider** with 1 part **cider vinegar,** 1 part **maple syrup**, a spoon of **mustard**, and 3 parts **oil**. Add a pinch of **cayenne**, as desired, and season with **salt** and freshly ground **black pepper**.

SALSAS

Technically, these aren't all true salsas (a.k.a. Latin-origin fresh or cooked sauces), but they are fruit or vegtable condiments that are served room temperature or cold. They work as dips, as sauces, for finishing dishes, or as a condiment. You could also use the Heirloom Tomato Sauce (page 234), tomatillo sauce (page 324), or Italian "Succotash" (page 336).

NOTE: Be sure to use a nonreactive container, such as glass, ceramic, or stainless steel as other materials (such as aluminum, copper, or cast iron) will react with any acidic ingredients and discolor or impart a metallic flavor on the salsas.

MIDDLE EASTERN TOMATO CRUDO

Combine thinly sliced roasted **bell peppers**; halved **grape, cherry, or Sweet 100 tomatoes**; and some finely chopped fresh **cilantro or mint** or both with a pinch of ground **cinnamon or cloves**; a drizzle of **pomegranate molasses**; and a good deal of **olive oil**; and stir well. Season with **salt**, freshly ground **black pepper**, and some **red wine vinegar** then let the mixture marinate at least 10 minutes and up to 2 hours. Stir, taste, and add a drizzle of **honey** and **salt** or freshly ground **black pepper**, as desired. Stir in a few **pomegranate arils** (optional) and adjust seasoning before serving.

ITALIAN TOMATO CRUDO

Make the **Heirloom Tomato Sauce** (page 234) and add **additional flavors**, such as capers, chopped anchovies, olives, dried chiles, chili-garlic sauce, or roasted bell peppers. Let sit until the flavors have melded, at least 20 minutes, season with **salt** and **pepper**. Serve on toasted bread as a simple bruschetta topping.

CAPONATA DIP

Heat the oven to 400°F/200°C/gas 6. Toss diced **eggplant** with **oil** and **salt** and spread on a rimmed baking sheet. Bake until golden brown and fork-tender. Toss with toasted **pine nuts**, chopped fresh **parsley**, chopped **red bell peppers**, chopped **black olives**, a few dashes of **red wine vinegar**, and a pinch of **sugar**. Add **salt** and freshly ground **black pepper** and stir to combine. Let sit at least 15 to 30 minutes before serving.

PICO DE GALLO

Dice and seed a few handfuls of **plum or grape tomatoes**, and stir together with minced **red onion**, minced **serrano chile**, a few squeezes of fresh **lime juice**, minced fresh **cilantro**, and a drizzle of **oil.**

JICAMA MANGO

Stir together diced ripe **mango**, diced **jicama**, a pinch of **cayenne pepper**, a squeeze of **lime juice**, a drizzle of **agave nectar**, and lots of minced fresh **cilantro, parsley, or basil**.

PEACH SALSA

Stir together diced ripe **peaches**, chopped **lemongrass**, chopped fresh **basil**, chopped fresh **chiles**, a squeeze of **lime juice**, and a dash of **coconut milk** or a bit of **toasted coconut**.

SUMMER SQUASH SALSA

Dice **summer squash** (a.k.a. zucchini), toss in **salt**, and let sit in a sieve until it lets off some water, about 15 minutes. Fold together with fresh **oregano**, grated **lemon zest**, minced **shallots, red wine vinegar**, and **olive oil**.

CUCUMBER

Dice **cucumber**, toss in **salt**, and let sit in a sieve until it lets off some water, about 15 minutes. Toss with **lemon juice**, toasted **sesame oil**, toasted **sesame seeds**, and sliced **green onions**.

BEET SALSA

Toss diced roasted **beets** (see page 111) with **salt**, diced **apples, apple juice**, diced **red onions, red wine vinegar**, and **olive oil**. Let sit at least 15 minutes before using.

CORN SALSA

Stir together pan-toasted **corn**, minced fresh **chiles**, cooked **black beans, cider vinegar**, minced **red bell peppers**, and a pinch of **brown sugar**. Add a drizzle of **oil** and some minced **parsley or cilantro**.

COMPOUND BUTTERS

Compound butters are simply flavored butters, but their usefulness goes well beyond toast. Use them to top a meat as an instant sauce or as a garnish for a variety of foods.

The method used to make them is the same as that used for Olive-Citrus Butter (page 250). With a spatula, work ½ cup (4 oz/115 g) of room-temperature unsalted butter in a bowl until it is very spreadable. Add a pinch of salt and mix in the following ingredients, then form into a cylinder. Wrap in waxed paper or place in a crock, cover, and refrigerate until solid. (Can be stored in the freezer for up to 1 month.)

CHIPOTLE-CILANTRO

Chop up 1 or 2 **chipotles en adobo** and mix in with a drizzle of **honey** and some minced fresh **cilantro**.

USE: On bean ragout, grilled vegetables, and grilled fish, chicken, or steaks.

BLUE CHEESE-COGNAC

Mix in a few tablespoons of crumbled **blue cheese** and 1 tablespoon **cognac**.

USE: On bean ragout, grilled fish, chicken, or steaks.

TARRAGON-MUSTARD

Finely chop some fresh **tarragon leaves** and mix in 1 or 2 tablespoons of **Dijon mustard**.

USE: On grilled fish, chicken, or steaks.

DATE-MINT

Stir in some finely chopped pitted **dates** and some finely chopped fresh **mint leaves**.

USE: On bean ragout, grilled fish, chicken, or steaks.

ROASTED RED PEPPER-PAPRIKA

Mince 1 or 2 **roasted red peppers** and mix in with some ground **smoked paprika**.

USE: On bean ragout, grilled fish, chicken, or steaks.

CAPER-PARSLEY-LEMON

Chop up some **capers**, fresh **parsley**, and grated **lemon zest**, and mix in with some freshly ground **black pepper**.

USE: On bean ragout, grilled fish, chicken, or steaks.

GARAM MASALA—PECAN

Stir in toasted **pecans** and **garam masala** spice mix.

USE: On bean ragout, baked potatoes, sautéed asparagus.

ROSEMARY-BALSAMIC

Simmer ¼ cup **balsamic vinegar** until it is very thick and syrupy. Mix in with some chopped fresh **rosemary leaves**.

USE: On bean ragout, grilled fish, chicken, or steaks.

MISO-SHERRY

Mix in **white miso**, 1 tablespoon at a time, until the mixture is salty but not overpowering, and add in a drizzle (about 1 tablespoon) of **sherry or Marsala wine**.

USE: On bean ragout, grilled fish, chicken, or steaks.

RUBS

As the name suggests, rubs are spice mixtures that are rubbed into meat to add flavor. Think of them as a drier version of a marinade and use them anywhere you need flavor, from tofu to fish to chicken. A rub can be made by combining spices and adding a pinch of sugar or salt for some extra flavor. You've already come across a rub for pork chops (page 292), lamb chops (page 300), and jerk seasoning (page 295) but here are a few more ideas.

USE: Rubs can be applied right before cooking or can be rubbed in up to 24 hours in advance and left to soak into the meat or vegetable. In general, you'll want to use about 1½ teaspoons rub for every 1 lb/455 g of meat. These rubs are very versatile but avoid using the stronger ones with delicate fish or vegetables as they will overwhelm the food.

RAS EL HANOUT

Mix together 1 part ground **clove** with 2 parts each ground **cinnamon, nutmeg,** and **allspice** and 3 parts each ground **ginger** and **coriander.**

STAR ANISE–CLOVE

Grind together (see page 90) 1 part **star anise,** 1 part **whole cloves,** 2 parts **fennel seed,** and 3 parts freshly ground **black pepper.**

ANISE–BLACK PEPPER

Grind together (see page 90) equal parts **anise seed,** freshly ground **black pepper,** and **garlic.** Stir in enough **brown sugar** to make it sweet.

CITRUS-PEPPER-ROSEMARY

Stir together 1 part each grated **lemon zest,** grated **orange zest,** minced **garlic,** and **rosemary.** Stir in freshly ground **black pepper** and salt to taste.

NOLA

Stir together equal parts ground **cayenne,** minced fresh **thyme,** and minced **garlic,** with 3 parts **paprika.** Add **salt** and **brown sugar** to taste.

CURRY

Stir together equal parts **curry powder,** ground **cumin, chili powder,** and **brown sugar.**

CHILI-OREGANO

Stir together equal parts **chili powder,** minced **garlic,** and minced fresh **oregano.** Add enough **sugar, agave nectar, or brown sugar** to make it just sweet.

MISO RUB

Blend together 1 large diced **onion,** a few spoonfuls of **miso paste,** a few minced **garlic cloves,** and a drizzle of **sesame oil.** (The mixture should be a very thick paste. If needed, add more miso.) Stir in enough **honey** to make it just sweet and enough grated fresh **ginger** to make it spicy.

HARISSA

Soak 10 to 12 dried **New Mexico or guajillo chiles** in hot water until soft then drain. In a blender, puree together with a few **garlic cloves, salt, olive oil,** and equal parts ground **coriander,** ground **cumin,** and **caraway seed.**

MARINADES

Contrary to common belief, marinades do relatively little in the way of tenderizing meat, but they make up for it by imparting lots of flavor. Use marinades on anything from vegetables to meats and for any cooking application from braising to grilling to roasting. You've come across a few marinades already. Huli huli chicken (page 272) and red curry roast (page 308) are a couple marinade ideas, but this is a perfect place to riff once you get the basic formula down.

ACID (OR) TENDERIZER + OIL + SEASONINGS + SWEETNESS (OPTIONAL) + SALT (OPTIONAL)

NOTE: Just be sure to put only enough salt (or salty ingredient like soy sauce) and sweetness to bring it in balance. Any excess and you may affect the final texture of the dish or may cause the marinade to scorch.

How to marinate: Use a nonreactive container, such as glass, ceramic, or stainless steel as other materials will react with the acid and impart a metallic flavor to the marinade.

How long to marinate: Over-marinating can cause the meat to become spongy so use the following times as guidelines:

VEGETABLES AND TOFU: 15 minutes to 1 hour

FISH: 30 minutes to 4 hours (only go over 1 hour for large cuts such as whole fish or shrimp)

POULTRY: 30 minutes to overnight (only go over 6 hours with large, skin-on pieces like a whole bird)

BEEF, LAMB, AND PORK: 1 hour to overnight (marinate small, lean cuts of meat for less time and tough, larger cuts of meat longer)

When to marinate: Choose to marinate not only to boost your food with flavor, but also as a means to cut down on prep time for a big meal or for a cookout.

MOJO

Blend together 1 part each freshly squeezed **orange juice** and **grapefruit juice** with 2 parts **olive oil**, a handful of smashed **garlic cloves**, and a few pinches each of ground **cumin** and **salt**.

USE: Marinating vegetables, tofu, seafood, pork, beef, lamb, and chicken.

WHISKEY-MOLASSES-CITRUS

Whisk together equal parts **whiskey** and **orange juice** with 2 parts neutral **oil**, a few dashes **Worcestershire sauce, molasses** to taste, a pinch of **salt**, and a handful of **thyme sprigs.**

USE: Marinating seafood, pork, beef, lamb, and chicken.

BALSAMIC-CHERRY

Whisk equal parts **balsamic vinegar, soy sauce,** and **cherry juice** (or cranberry juice and sugar), plus a few glugs of **olive oil**, a few tablespoons each grated fresh **ginger** and **garlic**, and a dash of **maple syrup or honey**.

USE: Marinating salmon, pork, beef, lamb, and chicken.

POMEGRANATE JUICE—PORT

Whisk together equal parts **pomegranate juice** and **port** (or Marsala wine). Add a few glugs of **olive oil**, a handful of **peppercorns**, a pinch of **salt**, 1 **bay leaf**, and a handful of **sprigs of a woody herb** (thyme, marjoram, rosemary).

USE: Marinating salmon, pork, beef, lamb, and chicken.

BEER-LEMON

Whisk together 1 part **citrus marmalade** with 3 parts **wheat beer**, a few cloves minced **garlic**, a handful of **peppercorns** and enough **salt** and **honey** to make it balanced in flavor.

USE: Marinating seafood, pork, beef, lamb, and chicken.

HERB-VERMOUTH

Whisk together 1 part **vermouth** with a few glugs of **olive oil**, grated zest and juice of 1 **lemon**, a drizzle of **agave nectar or honey**, and a handful of **sprigs of a woody herb** (sage, thyme, oregano, rosemary, or marjoram).

USE: Marinating vegetables, tofu, seafood, pork, beef, lamb, and chicken.

COCONUT-LEMONGRASS

Whisk together a few cans of **coconut milk**; a stalk of **lemongrass**; a few handfuls of fresh **basil**; some grated fresh **ginger, honey, or brown sugar**; and **salt or soy sauce** to taste.

USE: Marinating vegetables, tofu, seafood, pork, beef, lamb, and chicken.

PINEAPPLE-GINGER

Whisk together 3 parts **pineapple juice** with 1 part each **soy sauce** and a **neutral oil**, a few spoonfuls of **molasses**, and a few pinches of any of the following **ground spices** (or a combination): ginger, nutmeg, cloves, allspice, or cinnamon.

USE: Marinating vegetables, tofu, seafood, pork, beef, lamb, and chicken.

COFFEE-MOLASSES

Whisk together 1 part each **soy sauce** and **balsamic vinegar** with 1½ parts each **coffee** and **molasses**, 2 parts **olive oil**, a dried **chile**, a few **garlic cloves**, a few dashes of **Worcestershire sauce**, and 1 grated **onion**.

USE: Marinating salmon, pork, beef, lamb, and chicken.

APPLE CIDER-MUSTARD

Whisk together 1 part **hard cider** (or apple cider) with 1 part **neutral oil**, a few glugs **cider vinegar**, a spoonful of **Dijon mustard**, a few diced **tart apples**, a few pinches of **red pepper flakes**, and a few spoonfuls of **dark brown sugar**.

USE: Marinating salmon, pork, beef, lamb, and chicken.

CHILE GARLIC–GREEN ONION

Whisk together equal parts **soy sauce** and **sake** with a few dashes of toasted **sesame oil**, a few spoonfuls **chile garlic sauce**, a bunch of chopped **green onions**, and some **sugar**.

USE: Marinating salmon, pork, beef, lamb, and chicken.

CILANTRO-JALAPEÑO

Whisk together 1 part **lime juice** with 3 parts **olive oil**, a few smashed **garlic cloves**, a bunch of fresh **cilantro**, a few sliced **jalapeños**, and a dash of **sugar**.

USE: Marinating salmon, pork, beef, lamb, and chicken.

HERB GARNISHES

Finishing a dish with a garnish of herbs really helps it sing. Try one stirred into soup or stew like Pistachio Gremolata (page 186), used as a stuffing like Green Chutney (page 329), as a garnish, as a sandwich spread, or tossed with pasta for a quick sauce.

CLASSIC GREMOLATA

Combine equal parts **lemon zest**, minced **garlic**, and minced fresh **Italian parsley**. Store, refrigerated, up to 2 days.

PUMPKIN SEED—MINT

Combine a handful of toasted **pumpkin seeds** with a handful of chopped fresh **mint**. Stir in enough **olive oil** to moisten it through. Store, refrigerated, up to 4 days.

PECAN-PARSLEY

Combine equal parts roughly chopped toasted **pecans**, roughly chopped fresh **parsley leaves**, and a **squash or nut oil**. Store, refrigerated, up to 4 days.

GARLIC AND HAZELNUT SAUCE

In a food processor fitted with the metal blade or in a blender, combine a few handfuls of toasted **hazelnuts** with a few minced **garlic cloves** and blend until combined but still a bit chunky. Stir in a few tablespoons minced fresh **parsley**, a few drizzles of **lemon juice**, and a few pinches of **red pepper flakes**, as desired. Store, refrigerated, up to 4 days.

CHIMICHURRI

Whisk together 1 part **red wine vinegar** and 2 parts **olive oil**. Stir in 1 minced **shallot or red onion**, a few minced **garlic cloves**, a few handfuls minced fresh **parsley, cilantro, or mint**, and a few pinches of **red pepper flakes**. Let sit a few hours then stir, taste, and adjust seasoning before serving. Store, refrigerated, up to 2 days.

SALSA VERDE

Stir together 1 part **olive oil** with 1 part chopped fresh **parsley leaves**, a spoonful of minced **capers**, a few minced **garlic cloves**, a few spoonfuls of **mustard**, and a spoonful of **lemon juice**. Season with **salt** and freshly ground **black pepper**. Store, refrigerated, up to 4 days.

CHARMOULA

Stir together equal parts chopped fresh **cilantro** and **parsley** with enough **lemon juice** and **oil** (equal parts) to make a paste. Stir in a few minced **garlic cloves**, a grated **yellow onion**, and a pinch of any or all of the following **spices:** sweet paprika, freshly ground black pepper, cumin, or coriander. Store, refrigerated, up to 4 days.

OLIVE-BASIL-PARSLEY

Dice **olives** and mix together with equal parts fresh **basil** and fresh **parsley leaves**. Store, refrigerated, up to 1 day.

TARRAGON-FENNEL

Cut **fennel** into small dice and toss in **lemon juice**. Combine with roughly chopped fresh **tarragon leaves** and the grated zest of **1 lemon**. Store, refrigerated, up to 2 days.

STRESS-FREE DESSERTS

The ultimate easy dessert would be to serve sundaes, a fruit salad, some chocolate-covered pretzels (page 378) or nuts, a cheese plate, or not go for dessert at all. But, if you want to make something without killing yourself, turn to one of these simple desserts.

CRISP

Heat the oven to 350°F/177°C/gas 4. Combine **oats, flour, sugar**, and **salt**, and toss to combine. Drizzle with enough melted **butter** to just moisten the mixture (it should hold together when squeezed) then refrigerate until ready to use. Toss **pears or apples** with juice from ½ **lemon**, enough **sugar** to keep things sweet, a pinch of some **spice** (ground cinnamon, cloves, allspice, black pepper), and, as desired, some **dried fruit** (raisins, cherries, or cranberries all work well). Turn the fruit filling into a baking dish that measures 8 by 8 in/20 by 20 cm (the fruit should be a little bit drippy and juicy; add a bit more sugar and lemon juice, as needed) then scatter the oat mixture on top. Bake until the oats are golden brown, the filling is bubbling, and the fruit is knife-tender, about 30 to 45 minutes. Let sit 5 to 10 minutes before serving with whipped cream, ice cream, or a drizzle of cream.

TRIFLE

A trifle is the perfect way to use up **leftover cake or custard**. Simply layer the leftovers in a glass dish with **whipped cream** and anything else that tempts you (chocolate shavings, toasted nuts, fresh fruit). Let it set up in the refrigerator at least 2 hours before serving.

FOOL

The formula for a fool is simply **whipped cream** (page 93) folded with a fruit puree (berries, kiwis, mango, and papaya are especially good). For the puree, place 12 oz/340 g of clean, peeled **fruit** in a blender and add ½ cup/100 g **sugar** and puree until it is mostly smooth but with a few chunks remaining. Fold the puree together with the whipped cream, divide it into serving glasses, and refrigerate until ready to use.

FREE-FORM GALETTE

Heat the oven to 425°F/220°C/gas 7. Make the **plum filling** from the plum crisp (page 356) and use storebought **pie dough** (or homemade, page 164). Roll the dough to a round that is ⅛ in/3 mm thick. Pile the fruit in the middle, leaving a border of dough that is 2 to 3 in/5 to 7.5 cm. Carefully fold the dough over the filling and pleat and press it to close it over the filling (some of the filling will still peek out). Dot **butter** over the filling, brush the crust with 1 beaten **egg yolk**, and sprinkle the crust with **sugar** and **spice**. Bake until the filling is bubbly and knife-tender and the crust is golden brown, about 45 minutes. Serve as is, or drizzle with a very small amount of brandy or sweet dessert wine before serving.

PINEAPPLE FOSTER

In a large skillet, cook 4 tbsp/50 g **butter** over medium-high heat until lightly browned, 1 to 2 minutes. Stir in ½ cup/100 g packed **light brown sugar** and a pinch of **cinnamon**. Add 1 fresh **pineapple**, peeled, cored, and cut into 8 spears, and cook, shaking the skillet, until the sugar is melted and the pineapple is slightly tender, about 2 minutes. Flip the pineapple spears. Remove from the heat, add a shot of **rum**, carefully ignite, and cook until the flames subside. Transfer to plates and serve with ice cream.

VARIATIONS: Do the classic bananas or try with mango, plum, or pear.

CHOCOLATE-BANANA ICEBOX CAKE

Follow the directions for **whipping cream** (page 93). As desired, spike the whipped cream with **sugar, cocoa powder, or a fruit or honey liqueur** (no more than 1 to 2 tablespoons). Have ready old-fashioned **Nestlé chocolate wafers or chocolate graham crackers**. "Ice" the cookies with the whipped cream and form about one-fifth of them into a ring cake (put it on a platter, cake stand, or in a springform pan that can fit in your fridge) and top with one-fifth of the whipped cream and thin slices of **banana**. Repeat until all the cookies and whipped cream are used up. Refrigerate at least 4 hours and up to 24 hours before serving.

VARIATION: Fold together the whipped cream with Meyer Lemon Curd (page 132) and stack it with graham crackers.

ICE CREAM CAKE

Coat the inside of a loaf pan or springform pan with **butter** then line the pan with plastic wrap (to help release the cake). As desired, toast a few handfuls of your favorite **nuts** or grind up some of your favorite **cookies** (graham crackers, gingersnaps, or chocolate cookies) into crumbs or use a mix of both. Let 3 pints/1.4 L of your favorite **ice cream** soften at room temperature. Alternatively layer the nuts (or cookies or nut-cookie mixture) with the ice cream, spreading about 1 pint/473 ml at a time in the pan. (It helps to do 1 layer, then freeze it for 5 to 15 minutes, and proceed). Let it freeze at least 4 hours before unmolding (dip the pan in warm water until the cake is loose) and serving.

VARIATIONS: Graham crackers, chocolate, peanut butter ice cream, and banana ice cream (or bananas mixed into vanilla ice cream); chocolate cookie crumbs layered with mocha ice cream, salted caramel ice cream, and vanilla ice cream; gingersnaps layered with lemon ice cream, strawberry ice cream, and pistachio ice cream.

BREAD PUDDING

Heat the oven to 325°F/165°C/gas 3. Cut day-old **stale bread** into large dice (you want about 5 cups). Whisk together 2 cups/480 ml **half-and-half**, ½ cup/120 ml **packed brown sugar**, 3 **egg yolks**, 2 **whole eggs**, a pinch of **salt**, and a dash of **vanilla extract** (or rum or coffee liqueur). Pour over the bread and let soak at least 15 minutes and up to 12 hours (cover and place in the fridge). Before baking, fold in **any toppings you'd like** (toasted nuts, chocolate chips, toasted coconut, dried fruit) and bake until the custard is set in the center, about 45 minutes to 1 hour.

VIETNAMESE BAKED BANANAS

Place 1 can **coconut milk** in a saucepan and bring to a simmer over medium heat. Stir in a pinch of **salt** and enough **dark brown sugar** to make it just sweet (about ½ cup/100 g should do). Meanwhile, peel 6 to 10 medium firm-ripe **bananas** and halve them crosswise then lengthwise. Place the bananas in the saucepan and simmer until coconut milk is bubbling, and bananas are very soft and tender but not mushy, about 10 to 15 minutes. Let cool slightly in cooking liquid before serving. Serve topped with toasted coconut, peanuts, or whipped cream.

FROZEN BANANA "ICE CREAM"

Dice a few ripe bananas and place in the freezer until just frozen. Place in a food processor fitted with the metal blade and process until smooth. Add a spoonful of **cocoa powder**, some **sugar**, and a dash of **vanilla or coconut extract**, and pulse until combined. Serve topped with sundae toppings, such as toasted coconut, chopped nuts, or chocolate sauce.

POACHED FRUIT

Bring 4 cups/1 L of **port** and 1 cup/240 ml of **water** to a boil in a medium saucepan. Add some **aromatic spices** such as a piece of fresh ginger, some orange zest, a few peppercorns, or a cinnamon stick or star anise piece, or use them all. Bring to a simmer, add peeled, cored **apples or pears** and cook until the fruit is knife-tender, at least 10 minutes. Let the fruit cool in the poaching liquid, drain, and serve cold or room temperature with some whipped cream, ice cream, or custard.

NO-BAKE GOAT-CHEESE CHEESECAKE

Mix together a few cups of **cookie crumbs** (chocolate wafers or gingersnaps are perfect) with a few tablespoons of melted **butter** until the mixture is moist throughout and holds together when pressed together. Press into a tart pan with a removable bottom or a springform pan and place in the fridge until set up, at least 30 minutes. Meanwhile, combine equal parts softened **cream cheese** and **goat cheese** in a food processor fitted with the metal blade and add a pinch of **salt**, a dash of **vanilla extract**, and enough **sugar** to make it sweet but not cloying. Pour into the crust and chill at least 30 minutes. Serve as is or top with fresh sliced berries, toasted nuts, a drizzle of caramel sauce or dulce de leche, or some whipped cream and cocoa nibs.

CHOCOLATE COCONUT ICE CREAM

Combine two 14 oz/400 g cans **unsweetened coconut milk** with ½ cup/50 g Dutch process **unsweetened cocoa powder**, ⅓ cup/75 ml **honey or agave nectar**, and 1 teaspoon **vanilla extract**. Chill for 30 minutes then process according to your ice cream machine's directions. Serve topped with toasted coconuts or toasted sesame seeds or both.

VARIATION: Make with a shot or two of espresso for a Thai coffee flavor. Stir in cocoa nibs, toasted coconut, or toasted cashews before freezing.

The Aftermath

The party's over and you've got loads of dishes and leftovers to deal with. Here are ways to lower the hassle of the cleanup and up the usefulness of the leftovers.

CLEANING SOLUTIONS

Oh, joy, cleaning up! No matter how you spin it, cleaning is definitely the least fun part of hosting a dinner party. While I don't have any ideas for making cleaning more exciting, here are a few ways to make it easier.

Before I dive into cleaning tips, it must be said that the most immediate way you can make your kitchen more eco-friendly is to use eco-friendly cleaning products. There are many companies out there who make very effective products such as Method, Seventh Generation, Mrs. Meyers, and Dr. Bronner's. Or, if you're so inclined, you can also whip up your own cleaners. I go for a combination of the two since so many of the ingredients needed for DIY cleaners are ones I already have on hand.

THE INGREDIENTS

Baking Soda

Best known for absorbing odors, baking soda is also an effective surface cleaner.

Use as an abrasive scouring cleaner (less abrasive than kosher salt), deodorizer, and drain cleaner.

Castile Soap

A plant-based soap that's more eco-friendly than the commercial ones that are petroleum-based, it can be used anywhere you'd normally use soap.

Chlorine-Free Bleach

A highly effective disinfectant and mildew remover. Most of the chores you would use bleach for can be done with white vinegar so use bleach as a back-up or extreme cleaner. Make sure you buy chlorine-free bleach as it's better for you and the environment.

Club Soda

A very effective stain-lifter for fabrics.

Olive Oil

Olive oil and other plant-based cooking oils do a great job at polishing surfaces so use it to give your stainless steel surfaces an extra shine.

Lemon Juice

This is a sleeper of a cleaning agent because you probably think of it solely as a cooking ingredient. But lemon juice has a high acid level and pleasant scent that makes for a disinfectant, deodorizer, rust remover, scouring agent, and water scale remover.

CAUTION: Lemon juice will have a bleaching effect on fabrics so be careful not to use it on fabrics with colors that might bleed.

Kosher Salt

Not just a seasoning, kosher salt also works as a scouring agent (see cleaning cast iron, page 420) and as a rust remover (see cleaning copper, page 420).

Distilled White Vinegar

Easily the most all-purpose of the natural cleaning agents, white vinegar is a highly acidic cleaner that is especially good at removing tarnish, deodorizing, and disinfecting. There's a good chance that you already have white vinegar on hand.

CAUTION: While you can use straight vinegar on tougher materials, it is best to use it diluted as it can eat away at grout over time. Don't ever use it on marble as it will "scratch" it.

CLEANING RECIPES

Abrasive Scrub

Combine equal parts **olive oil** and **kosher salt** and use to scrub burnt-on bits of foods on pans, baking dishes, and cast iron.

CAUTION: Do not use on nonstick pans.

All-Purpose Cleaner #1

Mix equal parts **lemon juice or distilled vinegar** and **water**. Shake before using.

All-Purpose Cleaner #2

Mix two 2 tablespoons **lemon juice**, 2 teaspoons **liquid castile soap**, and ½ teaspoon **baking soda** into 2 cups/240 ml hot **water**. Mix until dissolved.

Nonabrasive Scrub

Mix together equal parts **lemon juice** and **vinegar** with enough **baking soda** to make a paste.

Drain Opener

Pour equal parts **baking soda** and **vinegar** down the drain. Let stand at least 30 minutes to overnight then run very hot water through the drain.

Tarnish Scrub

Halve a **lemon** and sprinkle **baking soda** on the cut section. Use the lemon to scrub dishes, surfaces, and stains.

Sanitizing Solution

Use 1 tablespoon chlorine-free **bleach** for 1 gl/ 3.8 L **water**.

CLEANING TIPS AND TRICKS

Linens

I use a very gentle cleaner or even lemon juice to get rid of anything from tomato sauce to red wine.

Glasses

WINEGLASSES: Don't use soap for cleaning your wineglasses as it will leave a residue. Instead rinse in very hot water and then rinse with the all-purpose cleaner (see page 419). (Do this anytime you want spotless glasses.) To air dry, turn glasses upside-down on a clean dish towel.

STAINED GLASSWARE: Fill with 1 part baking soda and 2 parts water and soak a few hours or overnight.

Hands

Garlic and fish are the two main offenders here. You can get rid of the smell by rubbing your hands with lemon juice or rubbing your hands on a stainless steel surface (yes those stainless steel bars do work) or both.

Cast-Iron Pans

Make a scrubbing paste with canola oil and a teaspoon of coarse salt to combat cooked-on debris then rinse with hot water.

Starchy Film or Burnt-On Bits from Pots

Place a few drops of vinegar and a bit of water in the pot and bring it to a boil. Remove from the heat and let sit a few minutes before scrubbing clean.

Other Tough Stains

Moisten the stained area with water, sprinkle with baking soda, and leave for 15 to 20 minutes before scrubbing away.

Stainless Steel and Copper

Polish with a paste of equal parts lemon juice and baking soda or equal parts vinegar and cream of tartar. Alternatively, sprinkle salt on a lemon half and scrub away.

Cutting Boards

CLEANING: Wash with warm soapy water and clean with a rinse of 1 part vinegar and 1 part water. Dry well.

STAIN REMOVAL: To remove stains from cutting boards, squeeze lemon juice onto the surface, rub in, and let soak for 30 minutes before cleaning.

SANITIZING: For true sanitation (especially important if they were used to prep raw meat), clean your boards with Sanitizing Solution (page 419) or chlorine-free bleach.

OILING: If you have a wood board, it needs to be oiled with a neutral, foodsafe oil about once a month.

Blender or Food Processor

Fill the blender jar or processor work bowl halfway with warm water and a few drops of liquid castile soap and blend away. It will foam up and help clean all the surfaces.

Spice or Coffee Grinder (not for a grinder with a burr blade)

No need for anything except bread for this one. Break up crustless bread and grind to the size of bread crumbs. Repeat until residual spices or coffee is pulled out of the carafe and off the blade.

Cleaning Counters

MARBLE: Use a solution of equal parts warm water and liquid castile soap.

TILE: Create a homemade soft scrubber by combining 1 part liquid castile soap to 5 parts baking soda.

Deodorizing Refrigerators and Freezers

A box of baking soda does wonders, but just don't use that same baking soda for cooking or it will give off flavors to your food.

Faucets

Rub lemon on your stainless steel and porcelain faucets to remove soap residue.

Floors

You can mop almost any type of floor with a solution of 1 part liquid castile soap to 10 parts warm water. If the floors are greasy, add some vinegar instead of the soap to a bucket of warm water.

CAUTION: Do not use the vinegar solution on marble or wood.

Stove and Hood

Add a few squeezes of liquid castile soap to a few cups/1 L of hot water—it will cut through the accumulated grease.

Dishwasher

To disinfect the interior of the machine, pour some vinegar into the reservoir and run an empty cycle.

Add half a lemon to the dishwasher load for sparkling, spot-free, clean-smelling dishes.

Garbage Disposal

Throw some used citrus into the garbage disposal to get rid of odors and deodorize the drain.

Drains

Clean drains—and the pipes they're attached to—by flushing them with vinegar. After 30 minutes, flush with cold water.

Rust

Cover the rust with lemon juice and let soak for 30 minutes before cleaning. If it doesn't work the first time, you can keep repeating it until the rust is gone.

TIPS FOR STORING LEFTOVERS

Storing leftovers properly has two advantages: it not only protects you from food-borne illness but it also helps the food retain its good texture and taste.

Dodge the Danger Zone Keep your food out of the danger zone, the temperature range where bacteria thrives—40°F to 140°F/5°C to 60°C—whenever possible. It will usually be in this range while you're serving it, but aim to get it hotter or colder than that range within 2 hours of serving.

Two-Hour Time Limit Get the food in the refrigerator within 2 hours of serving. Large amounts of food (like a pot of soup) should be divided into small containers in order to cool down as quickly as possible. Alternatively, place food in a bowl then nest in an ice water bath until cool.

Four-Day Life Limit The USDA recommends that we only keep leftovers for 4 days but some things (baked goods, acidic dressings, and pickles) will last longer. I have indicated the shelf life of most of the recipes in their notes. If you need help working through your leftovers in that time period, check out FreshedOvers (page 423) for ideas.

Don't Always Blindly Follow the Sell-By Date

Keep in mind it's the sell-by date, not the expiration date, so it is safe beyond that date. However, if the package instead has an expiration date, be sure to follow that closely. Of course, if in doubt (or it smells off, has mold, or anything else odd), throw it out.

Don't Overload Whenever practical divide food into small (single or 2- to 3-serving) portions. This not only will allow the food to cool more quickly but will also make it more manageable to defrost, if you decide to freeze it.

Label It How are you going to know what it is and when it went into the refrigerator or freezer if you don't label it?

Defrosting Frozen Foods The best way to defrost is to plan ahead and let it do its thing in the fridge, but sometimes we don't have the time for that, do we? The next best thing is to place the food (if it is not already) in an airtight container, immerse it in lukewarm water, and check it every 15 minutes. The last option is to microwave the food to defrost it, but this is the least desirable method because it often ruins the texture of food. Also, to avoid any foodborne illness it is imperative that you cook and eat it immediately.

To Refreeze or Not If you have defrosted food in the refrigerator and it has been left in there (not reheated for eating), you can refreeze it. However, do not refreeze food that you have reheated or anything that has sat at room temperature for more than 2 hours.

Reheat to 165°F/75°C The best way to heat your food is to put it in the oven at 350°F/177°C/gas 4 or to microwave it in 1-minute intervals, stirring the food often. Food is properly reheated when it has an internal temperature of 165°F/75°C. Another way to test this is to put a knife in the middle of the food for 10 seconds and then place the knife against your lower lip. If it is warm, the food is ready.

Mystery Meat If in doubt, you know the drill, throw it out.

FRESHEDOVERS

Leftovers are underappreciated and often forgotten until they make their way to the trash. I ask you to change that and take my leftover challenge. Part of the challenge is in our perception: think about them not as yesterday's castaways but as today's food adventure. While some leftovers are great the next day (sometimes even better), others need reinvention, a process I've nicknamed "FreshedOvers." Here are some ideas for common leftovers.

ROAST CHICKEN

Jerk Chicken Salad

Shred the **meat**, toss with **orange juice**; a seeded, chopped **chile; olive oil**; and a pinch of **ground cinnamon, ground cloves, or ground allspice**. Let it sit until the flavors have melded, at least 15 minutes. To serve, top **salad greens** with the chicken mixture, grated **carrots**, grated **beets**, sliced **green onions**, toasted **almonds**, and chopped fresh **cilantro**.

Korean Tacos

Toss shredded **meat** with **sesame oil** and some **lime juice** then place in a **taco** with shredded **cabbage, cucumber or radish pickle** or both, a drizzle of **chile garlic sauce**, and **mayonnaise**, and serve.

Quesadillas

Shred **chicken** and toss with **tomatillo salsa** (page 324). Layer on **flour tortillas** with shredded **Jack cheese**, chopped fresh **cilantro**, and close. Toast in a cast-iron skillet over medium heat until golden brown and the cheese is melted.

PORK TENDERLOIN

NOLA-Inspired Sandwiches

Toast a **French bread roll** then spread with **tapenade**; layer with **arugula or other salad greens; salami;** sliced **provolone, mozzarella, or Fontina cheese;** thinly sliced **pork tenderloin;** and a few **sun-dried tomatoes**.

Makeshift Ramen

Heat **sesame oil** in a large saucepan and sauté a few minced **garlic cloves** and grated **ginger** until aromatic. Add **chicken broth** (page 270) and a halved fresh **chile**, and bring to a boil. Add **sake, soy sauce**, and **sugar** to taste. Spoon into individual bowls and add **bok choy**, thinly sliced **pork, ramen** noodles (cooked according to package directions), and some additional sliced chiles, as desired.

Fried Rice

Heat **oil** in a large, nonstick frying pan over medium heat. When it shimmers, add chopped **pork** and cook until just browned, about 5 minutes. Add **garlic** and cook until fragrant. Add day-old cooked **rice** (or another grain) and stir-fry until it's heated through. Drizzle in beaten **eggs** and cook, stirring frequently, until the rice is coated in egg. Add **any vegetables you'd like** such as peas, or chopped carrots, broccoli, bell pepper, or sprouts, and cook until warm. Add sliced **green onions**, a few dashes of **soy sauce** and **sesame oil**, stir to coat, and serve.

BRAISED PORK

Quick Carnitas

Heat the oven to 450°F/230°C/gas 8. As needed, use a couple of forks to shred the **meat** into bite-sized pieces about 2 in/5 cm. Place in an oven-proof pan or roasting pan and cook until crispy and caramelized, about 15 minutes. Remove from the oven and serve with warmed **tortillas** and **taco fixings** such as salsa, sour cream, and guacamole.

Hash

Heat the broiler. As needed, use a couple of forks to shred the **meat** into bite-sized pieces about 1 in/2.5 cm. Heat **oil** in large ovenproof skillet over medium heat. Add the shredded pork and cook until slightly brown. Stir in parboiled **potatoes** (or any other parboiled root vegetable), a pinch of fresh **thyme leaves or other chopped fresh herb**, some diced **onion, garlic, bell pepper**, and enough **broth or water** to cover. Cook until vegetables are cooked through. Place under the broiler and broil until the surface of the hash is crisp and golden brown, about 2 minutes. Sprinkle with additional herbs.

Makeshift Ragù

Make **basic tomato sauce** (page 116) and stir in shredded **pork** and a dash of **whole milk**. Simmer until slightly thickened then toss with cooked **pappardelle pasta** and some chopped fresh **parsley**. Serve with grated **cheese**.

Sliders

Shred **pork** and toss in **braising liquid or a good barbecue sauce or marinade** (page 412). Pile onto toasted slider **buns** with a mess of **carrot slaw** (page 342), some fresh **herbs**, and even a **pickle** or two.

LAMB SHOULDER

All the above options for pork shoulder will work for lamb shoulder and vice versa.

Sandwich

Layer **lamb** on country-style **bread** with any of the **flavor boosters** (page 404) **or some pesto** (pages 140 and 218). Pile on some peppery **greens** (like watercress or arugula), some thinly sliced **red onion**, and a good deal of **mustard**.

Cheater Steak Sandwich

Heat the broiler. Thinly slice the **lamb**. Heat **oil** and **garlic** in a medium frying pan over medium heat. Add some thinly sliced **onions** and cook until browned. Add thinly sliced **bell peppers** and cook until browned. Add a pinch of **red pepper flakes or a pinch of chopped fresh parsley** (or both) and a splash of **water**. Cover and cook until the peppers are soft. Pile the lamb into a **French roll**, top with **peppers** and **provolone or Swiss cheese**, and broil until bubbly.

Whole-Grain Pilaf

Heat **oil** in a frying pan over medium heat. Add chopped **onion** and cook until browned. Add some **ground spices** (cumin, coriander, mustard, ginger) and cook until fragrant. Stir in the **grain** and add the amount of liquid needed to cook that grain (it's a 2:1 ratio for most grains). Cover and simmer until the liquid is aborbed. Meanwhile, heat oil in another pan and fry chopped **lamb** with additional spices. Stir in **peas** and some chopped fresh **parsley, cilantro, or mint**. Stir the lamb into the rice, cover and let sit for 5 to 10 minutes before serving. Serve with a squeeze of **lemon juice, yogurt**, and **chutney**, as desired.

BEANS

Bean Dip

Blend **beans** together with a few **garlic cloves**, a few glugs of **olive oil**, some bean cooking **water or broth**, a few pinches of **cumin**, and a squeeze of **lemon juice**. Season with **salt** and **pepper** and fold in **minced herbs**, as desired.

Bean Dal

Heat **oil** in a large pan over medium heat. When it shimmers, add grated fresh **ginger**, sliced **garlic cloves**, a sliced **jalapeño chile**, and a pinch of ground **cumin**. Cook until fragrant. Add a spoonful of **tomato paste** and a diced **tomato** and cook until the tomato is broken down. Add a drizzle of **cream** (enough cream to just lighten up the sauce) and a knob of **butter** and bring to a simmer. Stir in the **beans** and simmer over low heat until thickened.

Chopped Bean Salad

Toss cooked **beans** with any of the following: diced **red onions**, diced **tomatoes**, chopped **olives**, chopped **greens** (spinach, arugula, or chard), chopped fresh **parsley or mint**, or some crumbled **feta cheese**. Add a squeeze of **lemon juice**, a drizzle of **red wine vinegar**, and a good amount of **olive oil**. Toss and season with **salt** and freshly ground **black pepper**, as desired.

SHRIMP

Kimchi Quesadillas

Fill a **flour tortilla** with grated **Jack cheese**, scatter with **kimchi** and cooked **shrimp**, and toast in a pan until cheese is melted.

Spicy Pasta

Heat **oil** in a large frying pan over medium heat. Add **garlic** and **onion** and cook until soft. Add thinly sliced **bell peppers** and cook until soft and golden brown. Remove from heat and deglaze with rum. Return to the heat, add **1 can diced tomatoes** and a pinch of **red pepper flakes** and simmer until slightly thickened. Season with **salt** and **pepper** and add **shrimp** and some chopped fresh **parsley**. Cook until heated through then toss with **linguine** and a bit of pasta water. Serve topped with crumbled goat cheese and additional herbs.

Shrimp Roll

Brush inside of **rolls** with butter and toast until golden. Stir **shrimp** together with some **mayonnaise, lemon juice**, a pinch of **cayenne pepper**, and thinly sliced **celery** to make a salad. Season with **salt** and **pepper**. Load roll with shredded **lettuce**, top with shrimp salad and diced **tomatoes**, and serve.

PESTO

There are countless ways to reuse pesto such as in a dollop as a soup garnish, slathered on chicken or fish before roasting, on pizzas instead of tomato sauce, on sandwiches, or as an omelet filling, but here are a few other ones too.

Salmon in Foil

Heat the oven to 350°F/177°C/gas 4. Tear off a piece of aluminum foil large enough for one **salmon fillet**. Oil the inside of the foil and add some **asparagus, thinly sliced fennel, or haricots verts**. Place the salmon on top, dollop some **pesto** on the salmon, and close up the foil over salmon into a packet by crimping the edges. Bake until the fish flakes easily and is light pink, about 10 minutes.

Spread

Blend pesto with **goat cheese, ricotta, or mascarpone cheeses** for an easy spread. Amp it up even more by adding chopped **sun-dried tomatoes** or **olives** to the mix.

POACHED CHICKEN

Chicken Chilaquiles

Heat the oven to 350°F/177°C/gas 4. Cut up **tortillas**, toss with **oil**, season with **salt**, and toast in the oven until golden brown. Add some oil to a frying pan over medium heat. Add pureed (smooth) **red or green salsa** and let the salsa cook until it's heated through and sputtering. Stir in the tortilla pieces and shredded **chicken** and turn until they are all well coated with salsa. Let cook for a few minutes more. Remove from the heat. Serve chilaquiles with an assortment of garnishes such as fried eggs and beans, sour cream, onion, cilantro, avocado, pickled jalapeños, or radishes.

Tortilla Soup

Add enough **oil** to a large pot to coat the bottom, then heat over medium-high heat. Add a sliced **onion** and cook until soft. Stir in a clove of minced **garlic**, a diced **jalapeño chile**, and a **can of diced tomatoes**. Cook until the mixture thickens a bit. Remove from the heat, add 2 qt/2 L of **low-sodium chicken broth**. Add 3 cups of water and bring the soup to a simmer. Add shredded **chicken** meat and cook until heated through. Serve topped with garnishes such as tortilla chips, cilantro leaves, lime wedges, avocado, or all of them.

RICE

The "FreshedOver" potential of rice is nearly endless. Add it to soup instead of potatoes or pasta (or along with them), make fried rice (page 423), make pilaf (page 424), replace the bulgur as the filling for the eggplant casserole (page 240), or do one of the following.

Chai Rice Pudding

Combine equal parts **rice, milk** and **coconut milk** in a 3-qt/2.8 L heavy saucepan over medium-low heat. Stir in a pinch of **salt**, a **cinnamon stick**, and a spoonful of **sugar**, stirring frequently, until thickened, about 40 minutes. Stir in a dash of **vanilla extract**, a pinch of ground **cardamom**, and additional sugar, as desired. Serve warm.

Rice Salad

Use it in your favorite rice salad recipe or in place of farro in Summer Vegetable—Farro Salad (page 215).

MASHED POTATO

Potato Cakes

Mix **potato** with **onion**, diced **green onions**, and a lightly beaten **egg**. Shape into 3- to 4-inch cakes and lightly dust with **flour**. Heat a spoonful of **oil** in a frying pan over medium heat and fry until golden brown, about 4 minutes per side.

Samosas

Heat the oven to 400°F/200°C/gas 6. Make or defrost **pie dough** (page 164). Cut the dough into diamond shapes. Meanwhile, sauté **onions, garlic**, and fresh **ginger**, and stir into **mashed potatoes** along with fresh **cilantro** and **peas**. Place a dollop of potato mixture in the center of the pastry diamond, fold into a triangle to close, brush with **egg** wash, and repeat with remaining samosas. Bake until golden brown, about 20 to 30 minutes, and serve with **chutney** (page 329) and **Greek yogurt**.

Shepherd's Pie

Top **your favorite stew** (page 83) with mashers. Spoon the **mashed potatoes** onto the stew, run a fork over the mashers to create texture on the surface, brush with melted **butter**, and broil until the top is browned but not burnt.

SWEET POTATOES AND ROASTED ROOT VEGETABLES

Soup

In a food processor fitted with the metal blade, combine **cooked vegetables** with equal parts **low-sodium broth** and **coconut milk**. Stir in a pinch of **ground spice** (such as ground nutmeg, ginger, paprika, or curry). Transfer to a saucepan and simmer over medium-low heat until warmed through. Serve with chopped fresh herbs, spiced croutons, toasted nuts, or toasted coconut.

Indian "Burritos"

Mash it up and use it in place of the filling in Indian "Burritos" (page 254).

Make a Grain Salad

Make some **whole-wheat couscous, quinoa, or bulgur** then mix in extra vegetables along with a **Flavor Booster** (page 404).

TURKEY

You can use leftover turkey in any of the chicken "FreshedOvers" ideas (on preceding pages) and vice versa.

Salad

Shred **turkey** and place over **salad greens** with **corn, tomatoes, green onions**, and **croutons** (see pages 194 and 209). Top with a **creamy dressing** (page 212) and serve.

Turnovers

Heat the oven to 400°F/200°C/gas 6 and place a rimmed baking sheet on a middle rack while the oven heats. Meanwhile, make **pie dough** (page 164) or defrost storebought puff pastry according to package directions. Cut dough into serving-sized squares. Shred turkey and place in the middle of pastry squares along with grated **Swiss, Cheddar, or Brie cheese**; top with minced **shallots**, frozen **peas**, sautéed **mushrooms**, or diced **ham**; or use all. Enclose the pastry around the filling, crimp edge with the tines of a fork to seal, and brush with an egg wash made from 1 **egg yolk** mixed with 1 tablespoon of **water**. Bake turnovers until dough is crisp and golden, 15 to 20 minutes.

Turkey Chili

Add enough **oil** to a large pot to coat the bottom and place over medium heat. When it shimmers, add a handful each of diced **onions, carrots**, and **celery** and cook for a few minutes to soften.

Add a few minced **garlic cloves**, some **pot beans** (page 112), or a few drained cans of beans, minced fresh **oregano**, and **spices** of your choice (cumin, paprika, cayenne, curry). Add **turkey** and cook until browned. Add a **can of tomatoes** with juices, a can of **water**, and some chopped fresh **cilantro**. Decrease the heat to low and simmer until slightly thickened, about 30 minutes. Season with **salt** and **pepper**. Transfer to a large serving bowl and serve with avocado, sour cream, and cheese.

WASTE NOT

Take a look at what you have on hand and do your best to use it.

EXCESS TOMATOES

- Fresh Heirloom Tomato Sauce with Burrata (page 234)
- Tomato-Orange Soup with Grilled Cheese Croutons (page 194)
- Curried Chicken Soup with Roasted Peanuts (page 180)
- Roasted Bass with Green Chutney and Melted Tomatoes (page 329)
- Broiled Asparagus with Tomatoes and Fresh Herbs (page 341)

EXCESS HERBS

- Coriander Chicken, Cilantro, and Chard Stew (page 270)
- Arugula Pesto "Green Eggs and Ham" Sandwich (page 140)
- Roasted Bass with Green Chutney and Melted Tomatoes (page 329)

TONS OF COOKING GREENS

- Sweet-Sour Wilted Greens with Crisp Bacon (page 351)
- Mustard Greens and Lemongrass Beef Stir-Fry (page 304)
- Coriander Chicken, Cilantro, and Chard Stew (page 270)
- Raw Kale Salad with Heirloom Tomatoes and Roasted Cashews (page 202)
- Swiss Chard, Oyster Mushroom, and Ricotta Frittata (page 154)
- Kale Chips (page 402)

AN OVERABUNDANCE OF CITRUS

- Shortcakes with Citrus Compote and Orange Flower Whipped Cream (page 362)
- Pan-Seared Salmon with Three-Citrus Relish (page 326)
- Triple Citrus—Coconut Shortbread Bars (page 374)

STALE BREAD

- Make Bread Salad (page 395)
- Make Croutons (page 194)
- Make Bread Crumbs (page 91)
- Make Bread Pudding (page 416)
- Make Tomato-Bread Soup (page 394)
- Make Muhamarra Dip (page 405)

PAST-PRIME PRODUCE

- Swiss Chard, Oyster Mushroom, and Ricotta Frittata (page 154)
- Roasted Carrot Soup with Toasted Coconut (page 188)
- Tomato-Orange Soup with Grilled Cheese Croutons (page 194)
- Roasted Beet Salad with Creamy Caraway Dressing (page 212)
- Mushroom "Patty" Melt (page 257)

VANILLA BEANS

- Halve and scrape the seeds out of the pods. Pulse in a food processor with sugar or salt to make vanilla sugar or vanilla salt.
- Add to a bottle of oil or alcohol for infusion.

BEEF OR CHICKEN BONES

- Gather them in a freezer bag and use them to make stock (see page 110).

CHEESE RIND

- Save it to add more flavor to broths and soups like the pea and fava stew (page 186).

FREQUENTLY USED KITCHEN TERMS

If you learn a bit of kitchen lingo, we both benefit, because you can then understand pretty much any recipe and I get to stop explaining the same technique over and over. Here are the most common terms I use in this book:

AL DENTE Translated from Italian as "to the tooth" this term is used to describe the doneness of a food. Pasta is *al dente* when it is no longer chalky tasting but cooked enough that it retains a bit of texture.

BAIN MARIE see *Water Bath*

BRINE A salt-water mixture that is used for pickling or infusing foods (especially poultry) with moisture. It can have spices, herbs, and sweeteners to flavor the food. It is known as a *dry brine* if no water is used (as in the case of the Balsamic Caramel Chicken with Roasted Eggplant , page 264).

COAT A SPOON An indicator used to check if a cooked cream, custard, or other egg-based sauce (such as the Crêpes with Meyer Lemon Curd and Fresh Berries, p 132) is done. To check, dip a spoon in the mixture, remove it, and drag your finger horizontally across the sauce on the back of the spoon to create a line. If the sauce doesn't run and the line remains, it is done; if not, it still needs to be cooked.

CURDLE This is when a dairy product separates into curds and whey. While spoiled milk curdles naturally, you can also cause it to occur by overheating or adding an acid to an egg- or dairy-based sauce.

DEGLAZE Most commonly done when a meat has been seared or browned. Once the food is removed from the pan there are flavorful browned bits (a.k.a. the *fond*) so you deglaze in order to incorporate the *fond* into the final sauce. Deglazing is done by using a liquid (typically wine or juice though it can be stock, juice, water, or vinegar) to cook and scrape up the browned bits off the bottom of the pan. This is usually then used as the base of a sauce for the finished recipe.

DEGREASE To remove the fat from a soup or broth. There are three ways to do this: 1) Bring the mixture to a boil and skim the fat off the surface (it will collect at the edges mostly); 2) Pour the mixture into a defatter and pour off and discard the fat; 3) Let the mixture cool down or refriegerate it for a few hours then remove the fat in one piece from the surface.

DOCK To pierce a pie or cracker dough in order to prevent it from puffing up during baking.

FOLD A method used to combine a lighter, airier substance into a denser one. The most common use of folding is for baking, especially with soufflés (see Herbed Goat Cheese Soufflé, page 252). To fold: stir one-third of the lighter mixture into the denser mixture until no streaks remain. Then add the remaining light mixture and, while rotating the bowl with one hand, use a rubber spatula in your other hand to drag the lighter mixture down through the middle of the bowl then up and over in a circular motion as if you're "folding" the light into the heavy.

REDUCE To boil a sauce until it evaporates to a desired level.

RENDER To cook a meat (such as bacon) until the fat melts and separates from the meat.

ROLL OUT To use a rolling pin to roll a dough (such as the pie dough, p 164) into a shape.

SCORE To make shallow cuts in the surface of a food (usually meat or bread) for decorative purposes or, in the case of breads, to help promote even cooking and help to render the fat, in the case of meats.

SHIMMERS This is a common indicator written in recipes to indicate when an oil is hot enough for cooking. The oil's surface will start to move slightly and have a rippling or slight shimmering effect to it when it is properly heated.

TEMPER In the kitchen, this word has two different meanings. One refers to a process where you stabilize the crystals in chocolate so that it doesn't melt at room temperature. While good to know, it is not something I address in this book. The other is to heat a dairy- or egg-base by adding a bit of a cooked sauce (think custard or ice cream base) so as to prevent curdling.

WATER BATH Also known by the French term, *bain marie*, a water bath is another method used to prevent egg- or dairy-based recipes from overcooking or curdling. To make a water bath, you place a dish of food (such as a baked custard) in a large, shallow pan of water so that the dish cooks with gentle heat. This technique can also be used to keep cooked foods (such as sauces, soups, or mashed potatoes) warm.

PAN SIZE EQUIVALENTS

It happens: you get everything ready for a recipe only to find you don't have the proper size pan. Fortunately, it's possible to swap in another pan, so long as you keep a few things in mind:

1 / Measure the volume of your batter by pouring it into a liquid measuring cup (the kind that looks like a carafe with a spout).

2 / Find a pan that will fit the batter and will best approximate the dimensions of the pan you are replacing. To properly measure a pan's dimensions, measure from one inside edge to the other inside edge. For pan depth, measure from the inside bottom of the pan straight up to the top edge. A pan's volume can be measured by pouring premeasured cups of water into the pan until you reach the top edge.

3 / Account for baking time differences. If the substitute pan causes the batter to sit lower than it would in the original pan, decrease the baking time and increase the oven temperature a few degrees. Or, if the substitute pan causes the batter to sit higher than in the original pan, increase the baking time and decrease the oven temperature a few degrees. Also, if the shape of the pans are different (for example, you're using a square pan instead of a round one) be aware that the edges may cook at a different rate.

VOLUME (CUPS/ML)	PAN SIZE (INCHES)	PAN SIZE (CM)
4 C/960 ML LOAF	8-BY-4-BY-2.5 IN	20-BY-10-BY-6 CM
4 C/960 ML ROUND	6-BY-2 IN	15-BY-5 CM
4 C/960 ML ROUND	8-BY-1½ IN	20-BY-4 CM
6 C/1.4 L LOAF	8½-BY-4½-BY-2½ IN	21-BY-11-BY-6 CM
6 C/1.4 L RECTANGLE	11-BY-7-BY-2 IN	28-BY-18-BY-5 CM
6 C/1.4 L ROUND	8-BY-2 IN	20-BY-5 CM
6 C/1.4 L ROUND	9-BY-1½ IN	23-BY-4 CM
6 C/1.4 L SQUARE	8-BY-8-BY-1½ IN	20-BY-20-BY-4 CM
8 C/2 L LOAF	9-BY-5-BY-3 IN	23-BY-13-BY-8 CM
8 C/2 L ROUND	9-BY-2 IN	23-BY-5 CM
8 C/2 L SQUARE	8-BY-8-BY-2 IN	20-BY-20-BY-5 CM
8 C/2 L SQUARE	9-BY-9-BY-1½ IN	23-BY-23-BY-4 CM
10 C/2.4 L SPRINGFORM	9-BY-2½ IN	23-BY-6 CM
10 C/2.4 L SQUARE	9-BY-9-BY-2 IN	23-BY-23-BY-5 CM
11 C/2.6 L ROUND	10-BY-2 IN	25-BY-5 CM
12 C/2.8 L SPRINGFORM	9-BY-3 IN	23-BY-8 CM
12 C/2.8 L SPRINGFROM	10-BY-2½ IN	25-BY-6 CM
12 C/2.8 L SQUARE	10-BY-10-BY-2 IN	25-BY-25-BY-5 CM
14 C/3.3 L RECTANGLE	13-BY-9-BY-2 IN	33-BY-23-BY-5 CM

RESOURCES

Here are some of the places I frequent online when I'm on the lookout for good food and specialty ingredients.

Broadway Panhandler A cook's shop in New York City's SoHo neighborhood that sells any and everything for the kitchen.
www.broadwaypanhandler.com

Citarella The New York City grocer sells a variety of fresh and pantry foods online and ships them almost anywhere.
www.citarella.com

Cook's Thesaurus An online resource that provides information about everything from cheeses to spices, including varieties and substitutes.
www.foodsubs.com

Dean & Deluca The online arm of the gourmet retailer that sells everything from wine and specialty food to high-end kitchenware.
www.deananddeluca.com

Earthy Delights A website devoted to shipping hard-to-find seasonal products around the nation from mushrooms to tart cherries.
www.earthy.com

Foodzie An artisanal marketplace where you can buy hard-to-find ingredients and explore some of the best food products from around the nation.
www.foodzie.com

Gilt Taste Part online magazine and part online marketplace, Gilt sells hard-to-find artisanal products and gourmet goods.
www.gilttaste.com

Gourmet Sleuth A multifaceted resource, Gourmet Sleuth offers an extensive food dictionary, how-to articles and recipes, and an online marketplace selling an assortment of (largely ethnic) ingredients and cookware.
www.gourmetsleuth.com

Heritage Foods Heritage helps increase awareness of heritage and humanely raised foods and offers many of those products for purchase on their website.
www.heritagefoodsusa.com

igourmet.com Though this site sells an assortment of fine foods, it's become my go-to for online cheese buying because it has hundreds and hundreds of varieties.
www.igourmet.com

Kalustyan's This New York City food shop has a great selection of ethnic ingredients and spices.
www.kalustyans.com

Le Sanctuaire This West Coast food shop sells avant-garde ingredients used in molecular gastronomy and also offers a stellar assortment of tableware and spices.
www.le-sanctuaire.com

Local Harvest If you're based in the United States, Local Harvest is a great resource for buying and eating local.
www.localharvest.org

Penzys An excellent resource for spices, with a large selection and high turnover (in other words fresh) of spices.
www.penzys.com

Rancho Gordo The place to learn about all things legumes, Rancho Gordo has recipes, tips, and a large selection of heirloom beans for purchase.
www.ranchogordo.com

Seafood Watch The Seafood Watch program is an excellent, well-maintained resource that helps consumers make informed purchasing decisions about seafood.
www.montereybayaquarium.org

Straub's This St. Louis–based group of markets has an impressive online store with foods from across the globe as well as across the midwest.
www.straubs.com

Surfas The online arm of the Culver City–based restaurant supply store, Surfas offers great deals on an assortment of kitchen equipment.
www.culinarydistrict.com

Zabar's The original New York City store is nearly 22,000 square feet in size, which converts to an extensive online catalog of foods.
www.zabars.com

Zingerman's This Ann Arbor–based food store is like Mecca for food lovers. Their mail order catalog and website are carefully curated and it's the place I go whenever I'm looking to explore new flavors and ingredients.
www.zingermans.com

BOOKS WORTH READING

By now you've probably caught the cooking bug, and, if you're inquisitive enough to get to this point, then you're probably going to read up on things. Here are a few of my favorite reference books to get you started.

BakeWise, by Shirley Corriher

Chef's Secrets, by Francine Maroukian

CookWise, by Shirley Corriher

The Flavor Bible, by Karen Page and Andrew Dornenburg

Food Rules, by Michael Pollan

The King Arthur Flour Baker's Companion

The New Food Lover's Companion, 4th ed., by Sharon Tyler Herbst

The New Food Lover's Tiptionary, by Sharon Tyler Herbst

On Food and Cooking, by Harold McGee

Ratio, by Michael Ruhlman

What's a Cook to Do?, by James Peterson

What to Drink with What You Eat, by Andrew Dornenburg and Karen Page

INDEX

D

ACKNOWLEDGMENTS

If this were an awards show, I'd definitely have music played over my acknowledgments—not so much because I'm verbose but because I have that many people to thank. I come from an enormous family and over the years have only added more people into the fold. They have become my greatest confidantes and, in the case of this book, my most honest taste testers and critics. I'm extremely thankful for all the feedback each of them has provided to make this book a reality.

To Lorena, Sarah, Alice, and the gems that make up the rest of the team at Chronicle Books: Thank you. From day one, you have been my dream publisher and have proven to be an even better team than I could have hoped for. You helped refine my voice, have given me a visual language, and allowed me to create a book that I only partially understood when I began the journey.

To Alex Farnum, Christine Wolheim, and Lillian Kang: I've spent a lot of hours at photo shoots but have never before had them be as invigorating and inspiring. You helped capture the essence of this book down to every last frame, prop, and crumb. Thank you, Alex, for always searching out the best light, Christine, for knowing my style better than I could ever describe it, and to Lillian for plating with panache.

To Ken Slotnick, Andy McNicol, Jeffrey Googel, Justin Ongert, Suzanne Lyons, and the whole crew at WME Entertainment: Thanks for taking care of the heavy lifting, the legalese, for playing bad cop, and, most of all, for letting me forge my own path.

To Ryan Revel: Thanks for always picking up the phone and putting out fires no matter the time, temperature, or occasion. But, even more so, thanks for sticking with me through the roller coaster ride that has gotten us here.

To Heidi Swanson and Bryant Terry: Thanks for setting me on the right path from the start and giving me hope that writing my own cookbook was truly a goal worth pursuing.

To Lillian Kang: Lady, your talent is evident in every page of this book. From your thorough tasting notes to your tireless recipe testing, you do the work of a thousand test kitchens. And, for your fearless food styling, I am grateful. You are always willing to push the envelope just enough so as to make things intriguing without being unrealistic. Thanks for helping me find that balance.

To the crew at Fort McKinley: Thanks for providing me with a place to lay my head, for your laughs, and for drinks from your well-stocked liquor cabinet.

To Chris Kalima: You are a rock and you rock.

To Yoko Hirabayashi: From day one, you've always been there for me, be it at soccer camp in second grade or during late night recipe testing sessions. You truly are the best friend a girl could ask for.

To Melissa Gibson, Elizabeth Bing, Julia Pinover, Melissa Riggs, Helen Struck, and the other ladies of Paraquet Palace: Thanks for being my sounding boards and my informal focus group. Your apprehensive curiosity about cooking is why I wrote this book. I can only hope you find it a fraction as helpful as you've been to me.

To the Homcys, the Kalimas, the Chidiacs, Yoko, and everyone else who lent me some counter space and a stove: Your generosity with your houses, your kitchens, and your hearts has not gone unnoticed.

To The Mollenkamps, The Lindstroms, The Brulands, and The Chidiacs: The advantage of coming from such an enormous family is all the unerring love and support you provide. Thank you for always being there for me, and with this book, for your opinions and palates.

To Noni: Thanks for teaching me how to put the perfect dent in each and every gnocchi.

To Marianne Lindstrom: Thanks for always making me your "number one taster" and for encouraging me from the very first moment I ever stepped foot in the kitchen. And, for your elbow grease. I owe you a lifetime of thanks for having patiently helped clean each and every one of my sometimes disastrous early cooking experiments.

To James Mollenkamp: Thanks for supporting me on my journey in the food world despite your hopes for me becoming a doctor, a dentist, a lawyer, or any other more practical, stable career path I could have chosen.

Finally, I want to thank you, the reader, for picking up this book. It's the adventurous, inquisitive souls such as yourselves who have made the concept of this book a success. There's a generation of people who know how to eat but not how to cook; I hope this book helps you bridge that gap.